Dictionary for Readers of Modern Chinese Prose

Your Guide to the 250 Key Grammatical Markers in Chinese

Stanley L. Mickel
Wittenberg University

Far Eastern Publications, Yale University
1999

This is an **FEP** book.

Library of Congress Cataloging in Publications data:
Dictionary for Readers of Modern Chinese Prose:
Your Guide to the 250 Key Grammatical Markers in Chinese
Stanley L. Mickel
1. Chinese Language: reading
2. Chinese language: dictionary, post-basic, for foreign speakers, English
3. High School and College I. Title
1999

ISBN 088710-193-3

Publisher: Far Eastern Publications, Yale University, New Haven, CT
Managing Editor: John S. Montanaro
Printed in the United States of America by McNaughton and Gunn Company, Saline, MI

10 9 8 7 6 5 4 3 2 1

First Printing, January, 1999

In appreciation to Karen for her unending confidence and support,

and to Wittenberg University for creating an environment that made this work possible

Table of Contents

FOREWORD

This dictionary makes it easy for you to find explanations and examples of the 250 grammatical markers most frequently found in modern Chinese expository prose. The book is organized to allow you to find individual markers quickly, even when you are unclear about pronunciation, meaning or grammatical function. If you know the pīnyīn spelling of a marker, all you need to do is turn to its alphabetical place in the book; if you do not know how to spell it, there is an index which has both traditional and simplified versions of the characters. Nuances of meaning between synonyms are also explained, and attention is given to identifying which markers have formal prose (i.e., shūmiànyǔ) qualities and which are more oral in nature.

This approach is distinctly different from traditional grammatical reference works. Those works focus on analyzing, discussing and understanding categories of markers with only occasional attention given to the discrete "building block" members of the categories. This means, for example, that to find 尽管 jǐnguǎn in a traditional style reference grammar, you have to know that it is a 'forward linking conjunction,' find that category in the book, and then look through it hoping to find 尽管; most individual markers are not listed in the index. Chinese-English dictionaries are also of little help in understanding the usages and nuances markers have. These dictionaries usually simply give an English equivalent of the marker--though occasionally not even this is provided--along with example sentences. Dictionaries seldom comment on the subtleties of how a grammatical marker is used or how it differs from its synonyms. There are some Chinese reference works which are organized on a word-by-word basis, but you have to be able to read Chinese fluently to use them. The result is that it can be quite difficult for second year, third year or even quite advanced students of Chinese to look up the meaning and usage patterns of individual grammatical markers. In this book, you simply look up the markers alphabetically. This makes it much easier for you to review those semi-forgotten markers studied earlier, and it provides a convenient place to look up those markers you do not know.

In this book markers are arranged alphabetically, so if you know the pīnyīn spelling, you can easily find any marker by looking it up alphabetically. For example, 般 bān comes between 把 bǎ and 被 bèi. Strict alphabeticization sometimes means that a marker represented by two characters may come later than you would expect from the spelling of its first character; for example, 但是 dànshì comes after 当 dāng rather before it. Words with the same spelling are listed in order of their tones; e.g., 于 yú comes before 与 yǔ. If you do not recognize the character representing a grammatical marker, the index in the back of the book that has both simplified and full form characters makes it easy to find out how a marker is spelled in pīnyīn. From there it is easy to turn to the marker in its alphabetical place in the work and determine its meanings and grammatical functions. Another index gives the English language equivalents of the markers. This will further help you come to grips with nuanced differences among sets of markers which are often translated into the same English values. For example, under the listing "according to, based on" you will find eight Chinese equivalents: 按 àn, 按照 ànzhào, 照 zhào, 根据 gēnjù, 据 jù, 本着 běnzhe, 随着 suízhe, and 凭 píng. Comparative examination of them will give you an understanding of the actual differences between these words.

Each entry in this dictionary follows the same format. On the first line are the simplified character(s), pīnyīn pronunciation, full form character(s) when different from the simplified, a tag definition for each distinct usage, and the grammatical category to which scholars have assigned the marker. The body of each entry first shows an outline of its usage pattern and an English equivalent of the pattern. The remainder discusses how the marker is used. Example sentences which demonstrate how the markers are used are given at the end of each section of each entry. When possible, the first example sentence is given in 1st or 2nd year level vocabulary and the rest in 3rd or 4th year vocabulary. A feature of the work which may help you more fully understand some of the nuances of modern Chinese prose is articulation of the similarities and differences between members of a set of markers which can be translated with the same English meaning; for example, 往 wàng, 对 duì, 朝 cháo, and 向 xiàng can all be translated as "to, towards," but they represent slightly different concepts; 但是 dànshì, 可是 kěshì and 不过 bùguò are all contrastive conjunctions translated as 'but,' but they have somewhat different connotative values. There are many other sets of markers which this book introduces and analyses.

A further feature of this dictionary which you will find useful is the attention given to distinctions between oral (口语 kǒuyǔ) and formal prose (书面语 shūmiànyǔ) synonyms. For example, while both 不但 bùdàn and 不仅 bùjǐn are translated as 'not only,' 不但 is used both orally and in writing while 不仅 is more formal and is more often used in expository prose. Distinctions of this type are little treated upon in English language grammatical studies of Chinese or in Chinese language textbooks, but it is important that you be aware that words which may be used in the same way and translated into the same English equivalent can carry significantly different connotative values. If you wish to develop a nuanced understanding of modern Chinese prose, it is important that you are aware of what is erudite language and what is not and how the one differs from the other.

Compilation of this book has benefitted form the work of many scholars. The single most influential book was "现代汉语八百词" by 吕叔相 et al, but "现代汉语常用虚词辞典" by 许乃征 et al, Y. R. Chao's "A Grammar of Spoken Chinese" and Li & Thompson's "Modern Chinese: A Functional Reference Grammar" were very helpful. In addition to information garnered from these and other grammatical studies, scattered comments given in Chinese language textbooks have helped me in my thinking about various markers; the one that most immediately comes to mind is the comment about the meaning of 再 zài to be found in Chou & Link's "Chinese Primer."

Many people have seen elements of this book and generously made suggestions which have improved it significantly. Among them are Professors Robert Eno of Indiana University, John Montanaro of Yale University, and Zheng Yide of the Beijing Languages and Culture Institute. Dr. Peter Cheng and many classes of students at Wittenberg University and EASLI at Indiana University have helped improve the format. In addition, Professors Zheng Yide (郑懿德) plus Ma Jingheng (马敬恒) and Bai Di (柏棣) of Wellesley University have been extremely helpful in making sure that the example sentences are in accurate Chinese. I thank all of these people for their help and offer my apologies for the errors which have slipped through. Very importantly, thanks to the Wittenberg University Faculty Research Fund and the Faculty Development Organization for their financial support of all the Xerox copies, ink jet cartridges and all the other logistical necessities for writing this book.

CONVENTIONS

1. All entries are alphabetically arranged. Homophones are arranged according to tone category. Alphabetization sometimes results in a monosyllabic word coming before a disyllabic one; e.g., jiào is placed before jiărú. The fifth or "no tone" is marked only when the grammatical functions of the marker are discussed, not when they occur in example sentences. Note that in discussions and example sentences 不 bù is always marked in the fourth tone and 一 yī is marked in the first tone.

2. The grammatical function of all markers are indicated by tag identifiers such as Conjunction, Verb, Adverb, etc. This will give you an initial feel for where a marker fits in a sentence. A list of all the abbreviations used for these tags is given below. "Markers" refers to items which are used for a grammatical function whether or not the marker also has a semantic value in other usages; e.g.,得 de is a marker which can also be the verb dé 'get, obtain' while 佛 fú is only used as a marker. Markers are always underlined, vocabulary items are not underlined. This will help you more easily recognize what is or is not a grammatical marker.

3. "Sets" refers to groups of grammatical markers which overlap in areas of meaning and function but which differ from each other in distinct ways. For example, while 不过、然而、但是、可是、而 and 但 can all be translated as "but, however," they each carry their own tone of voice and connotative distinctions.

4. "Shūmiànyŭ" (书面语), also refered to as "formal prose" or "literary language," refers to the words and grammatical structures derived from Neo-Classical prose (文言文) that are found in modern Chinese expository prose. The situation is a little bit like the use of Latin phrases such as 'ad hoc,' 'vis a vis,' and 'etc.' in modern English, but there are many, many more shūmiànyŭ structures in Chinese than there are Latin structures in English. There are no firm rules that demarcate whether any one word or structural marker has shūmiànyŭ values or not, and as more people have higher levels of education and use educated language in daily life, more and more words which had traditionally been considered to be shūmiànyŭ now seem less formal. In addition, there are also some differences among dialects of Chinese about what is or is not shūmiànyŭ. This leads to occasional disagreement about whether something may or may not be shūmiànyŭ. This dictionary gives the preponderant scholarly view of the degree to which an entry has a shūmiànyŭ quality.

When this dictionary says that a marker has shūmiànyŭ qualities, it means that while the marker could conceivably be used in conversation, it is primarily used in writing to impart an erudite tone of voice. The reverse is the case for kŏuyŭ markers. Predominant use of shūmiàn or kŏuyŭ elements in a text gives different stylistic qualities to the Chinese. A text which has kŏuyŭ vocabulary and markers has a feeling of spontaneity, naturalness, informality and the everyday. The same text written with shūmiànyŭ elements has a tone of formality, solemnity, and erudition. These differences can be hard for you to recognize and control because synonymous shūmiànyŭ and kŏuyŭ words can often be translated accurately with the same English equivalents; e.g., translating 因为 and 由于 as 'because,' 要是 and 假若 as 'if,' or 虽然 and 尽管 as 'although' is accurate but does not reflect the shūmiànyŭ values involved. If you wish to understand some of the subtleties at work in modern prose, you need to be aware of which words are considered to have shūmiànyŭ qualities and which do not.

One further erudition factor to be remembered is the use of some older and more complex variant forms of characters, especially in ROC writings; e.g., 著 for 着 and 龢 for 和.

5. As a general rule, the first example sentence uses vocabulary appropriate to the first or second year level; further examples use vocabulary from the third year and later. Exceptions are examples for markers which have only a strong shūmiànyǔ value and thus tend to be found in the company of more sophisticated concepts. It is infrequent to find clear examples in printed texts which use only the marker under examination and/or which are not too long to be useful, so the majority of the example sentences were composed for this dictionary rather than quoting from published texts. The vast majority of the example sentences were very thoroughly scrutinized by Professor Zheng Yide of the Beijing Language and Cultures Institute. Professor Ma Jingheng and Bai Di of Wellesley most graciously offered to review the last entries when Professor Zheng could not continue.

TABLE OF ABBREVIATIONS

<u>Am</u> Auxiliary markers are called Structural markers (Sm) in this work. This is to avoid confusion with the next item, Auxiliary verbs.

<u>Ax</u> Auxiliary verbs are quasi-verbs which have some but not all features of full verbs. Examples are 可以、要、会.

<u>Av</u> Adverbs are words which modify verbs. Chinese adverbs always go before the verb. Some "moveable adverbs" may also go before the subject of the sentences rather than directly before the Vb. Examples are 都、也、还.

<u>Aj</u> Adjective. This work identifies as Stative verbs what some linguists call Adjectives or Predicate adjectives. See the comments under Sv.

<u>Cv</u> Coverbs are words that function partly like verbs and partly like prepositions. They are most often translated into English prepositions. Formed with a Coverb and a noun, Coverb structures modify the verb of the sentence. Examples are 给、按照、除了 and many, many others.

<u>Ms</u> Measures are words which must be placed between a number and/or specifier and a noun. They often suggest a general conceptual category of nouns. Examples are the generic 个 and 本、枝、条, etc.

<u>Np</u> Noun phrases consist of at least one noun or pronoun representing a person, a thing or class of things, an activity or an abstract quality or concept. A Noun phrase may be a single word, or it be a lengthy structure. If at the head of a sentence, the Noun phrase will probably be the Subject, though sometimes it will be the Object or the Topic which is being discussed.

<u>Nu</u> Numbers are nouns which represent a numerical concept. For example, 万、亿 and 万万.

<u>O</u> Object is the person or thing which is the recipient of a verb action. It will usually be a sentence end, but the Object is sometimes placed at the head of a sentence for emphasis or comment. In this book, <u>O</u> always refers to the Direct Object of the sentence.

<u>Pl</u> Place refers words which mark the location of a verb action or condition. 在、于、当 are examples.

<u>S</u> Subject is the person or thing doing a Verb action or being in a Stative verb condition. It is usually found towards the head of a sentence.

<u>Sm</u> Structural markers are words which mark grammatical functions such as 'aspect' (过、着、了), 'structure' (所、的、得), or 'mood' (吗、吧、呢). They are often called Auxiliary markers in other studies.

<u>Sv</u> Stative verbs represents the idea of "being in a state or condition." Many scholars identify these words as Adjectives or Predicate adjectives, but the term Stative verb makes a clear statement that they function to represent "being in a state or condition of." Remember that since a Stative verb already contains the idea of "<u>to be</u> in a state or condition," 是 is used with a Stative verb only to mark strong emphasis. Examples of Stative verbs in this work are 般、一般 and 一样.

<u>Tm</u> Time markers are words used to identify the time of the verb action or condition.

<u>Vb</u> Verbs are words which represent an action.

<u>Vc</u> Verb complements are words added to the end of a verb to add a degree of specificity to the verb action. Examples are 到、过、起.

Vp Verb phrases are the nucleus of a sentence. A Verb phrase includes everything in a sentence except the Subject or Topic of Comment. Thus a Vp could include the Time, Place, Verb and Object of a sentence. Keep in mind that the Verb is one part of the Vp, sometimes the only part.

X X and Y are used when different grammatical structures can be used with the marker under consideration. When you see X and Y, be prepared to be flexible in identifying what can be used with the marker.

Y See the comments under X.

A Dictionary for Readers of Modern Chinese Prose: Your Guide to the 250 Grammatical Markers in Chinese

按 àn (一) 'according to' Coverb

1.**按 X Vp = Y happens according to X** (Cv) 按 is a member of the set of words that mark the basis on which a verb phrase is done. 按 specifically marks that the verb action is done in light of the standards (expl a) or criteria (expl b) listed in X. X may be either a noun phrase or a verb phrase of any length. Y will be either a clause or a verb phrase. When the 按 structure comes before the subject, it must be end marked with a comma. When X is multi syllabic, 着 zhe 1 may be placed after按 to mark the ongoing standards for an action; e.g., 按着原定的计划继续干吧！Ànzhe yúandìng de jìhuà jìxù gàn ba! 'Continue to work based on the original plans!' When the verb following 按 X is 说shuō 'speak,' the structure marks the logic, conditions or rules of the following verb situation (expl c).

按照 ànzhào 1 is a synonym often used with goals, rules and principles. 照 zhào 1 is a synonym which marks the model to be used in the verb action. See 根据 gēnjù 1 for overall comments on this set of markers. Note that 按 is also used as a verb meaning 'press down on; control; grip.'

a. 已被录取的学生，应按学校规定的日期报到。
Yǐ bèi lùqǔ de xuésheng, yīng àn xuéxiào guīdìng de rìqī bàodào.
Students who have been accepted should report on the date set by the school.

b. 按个地区、个部门的实际情况落实党的经济开放政策。
Àn gè dìqū、gè bùmén de shíjì qíngkuàng luòshí dǎng de jīngji kāifàng zhèngcè.
Carry out the Party's economic development policy in light of the true conditions in each area and each department.

c. 按气节来说，现在该是春暖花开的时候了。
Àn qìjié lái shuō, xiànzài gāi shì chūn nuǎn huā kāi de shíhou le.
According to the season, this should be the time when the spring is warm and flowers bloom.

按照 ànzhào (一一) 'according to' Coverb

1. 按照X, Y = Y is based on X (Cv) 按照is a member of the set of words which mark the basis on which a verb action is done. 按照 specifically marks X as the starting point (expl a), rules (expl b), or guiding principles (expl c) of a verb situation. X may be a noun phrase or a verb phrase, but it may not be monosyllabic. Y will be either a clause or a verb phrase. The synonym 按 àn 1 marks X as the criterion for a verb act but has no restrictions about the size of X. 照 zhào 1 is a synonym used to mark the model to be followed in doing a verb act. See 按 àn 1 and 照 zhào 1 for further comments and examples. See 根据 gēnjù 1 for further synonyms and overall comments on this set of words.

a. 小白按照自己的学习计划，每天都抽出一定的时间学习英语。
Xiǎo Bái ànzhào zìjǐ de xuéxí jìhuà, měi tiān dōu chōuchū yīdìng de shíjiān xuéxí Yīngyǔ.
Based on his personal study plan, Little Bai sets aside a definite time to study English everyday.

b. 党是按照民主集中制组织起来的。
Dǎng shì ànzhào mínzhǔ jízhōngzhì zǔzhī qilai de.
The (Communist) Party is organized according to the principle of democratic centralism.

c. 希望他们按照毛主席的教导，实践自己的声明，认真改正错误。
Xīwang tāmen ànzhào Máo zhǔxí de jiàodǎo, shíjiàn zìjǐ de shēngmíng, rènzhēn gǎizhèng cuòwù.
We hope that based on Chairman Mao's teachings they will put their proclamations into practice and conscientiously correct their errors.

把 bǎ (—) "marker of action on the object" Coverb

B

1. (Np) 把 O Vp = (Subject) VERBS the OBJECT (Cv) 把 marks that the direct object is placed before the verb and thus draws attention to the object and how the verb action affects it. 把 is only used with verbs involving a disposal, handling or processing action, thus 把 is not used with verbs such as 有 yǒu 'have,' 想 xiǎng 'think,' 喜欢 xǐhuan 'like,' 知道 zhīdao 'know,' etc. The object will be a noun known through the context in which it is found and should be translated as 'the noun' (expls a & c), though it can sometimes be a verb phrase (expl b). Be alert for the possibility that the object might be heavily modified and thus many characters away from the 把 marker (expl c); in lengthy 把 Object structures look for the 的 de 1 noun description marker, this will help you find the distant noun that is the object (expl c).

The verb used in 把 structures must be followed by other elements. This may be as simple as a 了 le 1, though more often it is a complement such as 作 zuò 'be,' 成 chéng 'become,' 为 wéi 2, 到 dào 1, 在 zài 2 (expl a) etc. and a second object in a S 把 O1 V 为 O2 structure (expl b). Remembering this requirement will help you find the verb no matter how distant it might be from the 把. 将 jiāng 1 is a shumianyu synonym of 把. Note that although 把 is sometimes used as part of words centering on the idea of 'take; control,' the 把 O Vp structure has no direct English equivalent and can be difficult to translate. Be careful to avoid translating it as 'take the object and verb,' to do so obscures the meaning. 把 is also used as a noun and as a measure centered on the concept of 'a handle.' When used as an measure, 把 will almost always be preceded by a number or a specifier, which makes it easily distinguished from the 把 Object pattern.

a. 小朱把第十四课的生词都写在本子上。
Xiǎo Zhū bǎ dì-shísì kè de shēngcí dōu xiě zài běnzi shàng.
Little Zhu wrote the vocabulary from the fourteenth lesson in the notebook.

b. 毛主席强调指出，无产阶级要把解放全人类做为自己的历史使堰。
Máo zhǔxí qiángdiào zhǐchū, wúchǎn jièjí yào bǎ jiěfàng quán rénlèi zuòwéi zìjǐ de lìshǐ shǐmìng.
Chairman Mao emphatically pointed out that the proletariat makes liberating mankind their historical mission.

c. 戴蒙德夫人在会上把斯诺夫人在斯诺逝世后整理出版的遗作《漫长的革命》赠给中国客人做为纪念。
Dàiméngdé fūren zài huì shàng bǎ Sīnuò fūren zài Sīnuò shìshì hòu zhěnglǐ chūbǎn de yízuò "Màncháng de Gémìng" zènggěi Zhōngguó kèrén zuòwéi jìniàn.
As a souvenir, Madame Diamond gave the Chinese guests at the meeting a copy of the posthumous book "Everlasting Revolution" which Madame Snow had prepared and published after (Edgar) Snow passed away.

B

般 bān (—) "similarity" Stative verb

1. X 般的 Np/Vp = X resembles the Np/Vp (Sv) A less used member of the set of similarity markers, 般 is used in description structures to mark that the noun or verb phrase has X-like qualities. X will be a noun phrase. When it modifies a noun, 般 will be followed by 的 de 1 (expl a); when describing a verb it will be followed by the adverbial marker 地 de 1 (expl b). 般 is also used in the structure X 象 Y 般的~地 (expl b). 般 may replace its synonym 一般 yībān 1 when the preceding descriptive structure is two or more syllables long. See 一般 yībān 1 for further comments.

a. 总理讲到这里，台下响起了暴风雨般的掌声。
Zǒnglǐ jiǎngdào zhèli, táixià xiǎngqǐle bàofēngyǔ bān de zhǎngshēng.
When the Prime Minister reached this point in his talk, thunderstorm-like applause resounded.

b. 我们两国人民要象兄弟般地团结在一起。
Wǒmen liǎng guó rénmín yào xiàng xiōngdì bān de tuánjié zài yīqǐ.
Our two peoples should unite like brothers.

被 bèi (—) "passive marker" Coverb

1. Np1 被 Np2 (所) Vp = Np1 verbed by Np2 (Cv) 被 has traditionally focused attention on Np1 as the sufferer of what was at best a neutral but more often an unfavorable verb action (expl a). The undesirable aspect may be as direct as 杀 shā 'kill' or as indirect as 看见 kànjiàn 'see.' However, while undesirable verb actions are still more common, current written usage of 被 seems more and more to allow verb situations which may be neutral or even positive in their effect on Np1 (expl b). Whether unpleasant or not, the 被 marked verb action must be one that represents a handling, manipulating or processing of Np1; e.g., 打 dǎ 'hit,' 批评 pīpíng 'criticize,' 偷 tōu 'steal,' 证 zhèng 'prove,' etc. 被 is not used with verb actions, whether undesirable or not, that do not involve handling: e.g., 被 does not occur with verbs such as 恨 hèn 'hate' or 气 qì 'anger.' 所 may be added directly before disyllabic verbs for greater emphasis and a shumianyu flavor; 所 must appear before monosyllabic verbs where it marks an even greater shumianyu connotation; see 所 suǒ 1. Also see 叫 jiào 2, 让 ràng 2 and 给 gěi 3 & 4 usages as oral synonyms for 被 used in less formal situations. 为 wéi 3 is a synonymous shumianyu passive structure. See also the neutral to positive passive structure Np1 是 Np2 V 的 shì...de 3 where the focus is on Np2.

Keep in mind that Chinese uses marked passive structures less frequently than English does. Rather, Chinese often uses other structures which translate into English passives. For example, see Np1 由 Np2 V where 由 yóu 1 focuses attention on a verb action done by N2. Consider also structures such as Np Vp which form the equivalent of English passive structures. Such structures are especially common when the noun phrase represents an inanimate noun; e.g., 书买了 Shū mǎi le 'The book was bought.' Topic-Comment structures such as 他写的汉字大家都看得懂 Tā xiě de Hànzì dàjiā dōu kàn de dǒng 'The Chinese characters he writes can be understood by everybody' are also translatable into the English passive voice. See also 于 yú 1.d and 与 yǔ 1.

B

a. 叛徒已被省委枪毙了。
Pàntú yǐ bèi Shěngwěi qiāngbì le.
The traitor has been executed by the Provincial Committee.

b. 老刘被工人选为小组长。
Lǎo Liú bèi gōngrén xuǎnwéi xiǎozǔzhǎng.
Mr. Liu has been elected group head by the workers.

2. Np1被 V = Np1 is verbed (Av) In this structure 被 marks that Np1 suffers an unfavorable or neutral verb action but does not tell who did the act. 所 is not used in this pattern. The 叫, 让 or 给 passive structures mentioned above do not appear without Np2.

a. 日本男排被打败了。
Rìběn nánpái bèi dǎbài le.
The Japanese men's volleyball team was defeated.

b. 敌人的司令部已被炸毁了。
Dírén de sīlìngbù yǐ bèi zhàhuǐ le.
The enemy's headquarters has been blown to pieces.

本 běn (一) 'this, one's own' Pronoun; 'in accordance with, based on' Coverb

1. 本 Noun = This noun (Pn) 本 is placed before a noun phrase to mark specificity about the noun. A noun headed by 本 is often related to the speaker, creator or manager of the noun (expls a & b), though not always (expl c). 本 is also often used with time nouns (expl c) and measures to mark which one is under discussion. 这 zhè is a synonym which differs in never connoting a relationship. 本 is also used in many words which evolve out of its basic meaning of 'roots; bottom.' 本 is also the commonly seen measure for bound printed materials.

a. 本校定于八月二十八日开学。
Běn xiào dìng yú bā yuè èrshibā rì kāixué.
This school (of ours) will start classes on August 28.

b. 他本人已经同意做手术，再问问家属的意见。
Tā běn rén yǐjīng tóngyì zuò shǒushù, zài wènwen jiāshǔ de yìjian.
He himself has agreed to the operation and will get his family's opinion.

B

c. 我们一定能够在本世纪末把我国建成一个社会主义的现代化强国。
Wǒmen yīdìng nénggòu zài běn shìjì mò bǎ wǒ guó jiànchéng yī ge shèhuì zhǔyì de xiàndài huà qiángguó.
We will definitely be able to establish our country as a socialistic modernized power by the end of this century.

2. 本 Np Vp = Verb in accordance with the noun (Cv) 本 is a shumianyu member of the group of words which mark the basis for a verb condition. As a shumianyu synonym of 本着 běnzhė 1, 本 also marks the spirit, attitude, guidelines or policies behind a verb action (expl a).

a. 本此进行，必能成功。
Běn cǐ jìnxíng, bì néng chénggōng.
If we go on in accordance with this (point), we must succeed.

本着 běnzhė (——) 'in accordance with' Coverb

1. 本着 Np Vp = Verb in accordance with the noun (Cv) One of the set of words which mark the basis on which a verb action is done, 本着 specifically marks that the verb is done in line with abstract principles such as policies (expl a), guidelines, spirit, attitude (expl b), etc. When a 本着 structure starts the sentence, it is end marked with a comma, which makes it easier to determine the exact length of the noun phrase (expl a). The synonymous 本 běn 1 is a more shumianyu synonym of 本着. See 根据 gēnjù 1 for comparative comments on the other members of this set of words; e.g., 按照 ànzhào 1, 照 zhào 1, and 随着 suízhe 1. See also the discussion at 以 yǐ 1.

a. 本着现行的一胎化政策，生育一个以上子女的要罚款。
Běnzhe xiànxíng de yītāihuà zhèngcè, shēngyù yī ge yǐshàng zǐnǚ de yào fákuǎn.
In accordance with the current one child policy, those having more than one child will be fined.

b. 两国政府本着增进友好关系的愿望，签订了一项交流学生的协议。
Liǎng guó zhèngfǔ běnzhe zēngjìn yǒuhǎo guānxì de yuànwàng, qiāndìngle yī xiàng jiāoliú xuésheng de xiéyì.
The two governments signed an agreement on student exchanges in light of their desire to further friendly relationships.

比 bǐ (—) "comparison > superiority" Coverb

1. X 比 Y Sv/Vp = X is superior to Y in terms of a Stative verb or verb phrase

B

situation (Cv) 比 is a member of one of the three sets of words which mark comparative structures. 比 specifically marks that X is superior to Y in either terms of a Stative verb condition (expls a & c) or in doing a verb action (expls b & d). There will often be a complement of degree after the verb structure to show the amount of superiority (expl c). X and Y will be structurally and conceptually similar noun (expl a) or verb phrases (expl b). When the same noun is compared in different time frames, the noun will be given as X, and Y will be the time referent (expl c). You will usually see a Stative verb in this structure, but verbs involving abilities, desires, loves, or increases also occur (expl d); all other 比 verb comparisons must be structured as discussed in 比 2 below. The adverbs 不 hái 1 and 也 yě 1 go before 比, while the adverb of degree 很 must go after the Stative verb; e.g., 他比我忙得很 Tā bǐ wǒ máng de hěn 'He is much busier than I,' 更 gèng 1 and 还 hái 1 go before it; e.g.,他比我更忙. 要 yào 3 before 比 marks an estimate about probability. 较 jiāo can be used as a shumianyu synonym; see also 于 yú 1.d.

The second set of comparative markers focuses on similarity and uses 一样 yīyàng 1 and its synonyms. If you keep in mind that 比 marks superiority and 一样 marks similarity, you will avoid the mistake of writing the incorrect pattern *X 比 Y 一样 Sv; 比 and 一样 go together like rice and potatoes! The third set of comparative markers involve inferiority and is structured with 没有 méiyǒu 3 and its synonyms. It is instructive to consider the differences in meaning between negative 比 superiority and 没有 méiyǒu 3 inferiority; e.g., 他不比我大 'He is not superior to me in age' = 'He is not older than I am' (could be the same age) and 他没有我大 'He is inferior to me in age' = 'He is younger than I.' 比 is also used in words for values revolving around the concept of 'compare.'

a. 她比西施漂亮！
Tā bǐ Xīshī piàoliang!
She is prettier than Xishi!

b. 写汉字比写英文有意思。
Xiě Hànzì bǐ xiě Yīngwén yǒu yìsi.
Writing Chinese characters is more interesting than writing English.

c. 今年的气候比去年热得多。
Jīnnián de qìhòu bǐ qùnián rè de duō.
The weather this year is much hotter than last year.

d. 第三油井的产量比第二的增加百分之十七・八。
Dì-sān yóujǐng de chǎnliàng bǐ dì-èr de zēngjiā bái fēn zhī shí qī diǎn bā.
Production at Well #3 increased 17.8% more than Well #2.

2. X (V) (O) V 得 比 Y Sv = X verbs (an object) in a more Stative verb manner than Y (Cv) 比 marks that X does a verb action (to an object) in a manner superior to the way Y does it. The placement of 比 Y is flexible; it may go right after X (expl b), directly before the Sv (expl c), or even between the (V) O and V 得 (expl a). There may be a complement after the verb to show the degree of difference (expl a). 不 bù 1, 也 yě 1 and other adverbs go before 比. The meaning and usages of the three sets of comparison markers described in 1 above also apply when comparing verb actions. See 没有 méiyǒu 3 and 一样 yīyàng 1 for comments and examples on their use with verbs.

a. 小华英语比我说得快一点儿。
Xiǎo Huá Yīngyǔ bǐ wǒ shuō de kuài yīdiǎnr.
Hua speaks English a bit more quickly than I do.

b. 那位翻译员比谁都翻译得通顺。
Nèi wèi fānyì yuán bǐ shéi dōu fānyì de tōngshùn.
That translator translates more smoothly than anyone else.

c. 胡适的现代散文比诗写得好。
Hú Shì de xiàndài sǎnwén bǐ shī xiě de hǎo.
Hu Shi's modern prose is better written than his poetry.

边 biān (邊) "simultaneous verb actions" Adverb

1. S边Vp1边 Vp2 (边 Vp3) = Subject does verb 1 and verb 2 (and verb 3) at the same time (Av) This pattern marks a tight inter-relationship between two (or more) verb actions done by the same subject at the same time. If more than two verb phrases are involved, each will be marked with 边. The synonymous structure 一边 yībiān 1 marks a looser inter-relationship between verb actions, which may or may not have different subjects. See also the synonymous 一方面 yīfāngmiàn 1 which marks either two aspects of one action or the sequential occurrence of two activities. 边 is also widely used in many location words.

a. 我们边走边谈，不知不觉地就到了研究所。
Wǒmen biān zǒu biān tán, bùzhī bùjué de jiù dàole yánjiūsuǒ.
We walked and talked, and before we knew it we had arrived at the research institute.

b. 在雨季里，工程师边排水边施工，保证了修铁路的进度。
Zài yǔjì li, gōngchéngshī biān páishuǐ biān shīgōng, bǎozhèngle xiū tiělù de jìndù.
In the rainy season the engineers drained away the water while doing construction and guaranteed the rate of railroad construction.

便 biàn (—) 'then' Adverb; "affirmation" Adverb; 'even if (hypothesis)' Conjunction

1. X, 便Y = X, then Y (Av) The shumianyu便 marks a close sequence of events between X and Y in this usage. X may be a verb phrase (expl a), a clause (expl b), or the first part of the "as soon as" 一Verb 1, 便 Verb 2 structure (expl c). Y will be a verb

B

phrase (expl b) or a clause (expls a & c). The more oral 就 jiù 1 is a near synonym with a wider range of usages. 便 may be translated as 'then' in usages 1, 2 and 3, but they are somewhat different. Therefore you need to carefully analyze the context to determine whether "then 便," "inter-related 便" or "time 便" is before you. 便 is also used in words having to do with 'convenience; informality; relieve oneself.' Also, note the pronunciation of 便 in the commonly found word 便宜 piányi 'cheap.'

Be careful not to confuse the three frequently seen grammatical markers: 便 biàn 1, 更 gèng 1, and 使 shǐ 1. While their written shapes are confusingly similar, they have different pronunciations, and more importantly, they have distinctly different grammatical functions.

a. 听了这消息，小刘便出去告诉同学们。
Tīngle zhè xiāoxi, Xiǎo Liú biàn chūqù gàosu tóngxuémen.
Hearing this news, Little Liu (then) went out to tell his classmates.

b. 袁世凯掌握政权以后，便背叛了孙中山的主张。
Yuán Shìkǎi zhǎngwò zhèngquán yǐhòu, biàn bèipànle Sūn Zhōngshān de zhǔzhāng.
After Yuan Shikai took political control, he (then) betrayed Dr. Sun Yatsen's ideas.

c. 会议一结束，他便把下一段的工作盘算好了。
Huìyì yī jiéshù, tā biàn bǎ xià yī duàn gōngzuò pánsuan hǎo le.
As soon as the meeting concluded, he (then) planned the work for the next stage.

2. 一 Verb / 只要 / 由于 / 既然 / 为了 etc. X, 便 Y = As soon as/if only/because/ since/in order to, etc. X, then Y (Av) In this usage, 便 marks a connection between X and Y situations. The exact meaning of X of course depends on which marker is used in it, but 便 clearly marks that the two structures are inter-related. In addition to the examples given here, see those entries for further examples. 就 jiù 2 is a more oral synonym.

a. 如果身体健康，便不易生病。
Rúguǒ shēntǐ jiànkāng, biàn bùyì shēngbìng.
If your health is good, (then) it is not easy to get sick.

b. 因为临时有事，便在香港逗留了两天。
Yīnwei línshí yǒushì, biàn zài Xiānggǎng dòuliúle liǎng tiān.
Because I had something to do at that moment, I (then) stopped in Hongkong for two days.

3. Time 便 Verb phrase = A situation occurred long before at the time frame (Av) In this usage, 便 functions to mark that a past verb act occurred in the past at either a specific point in time (expl a) or within a particular time frame (expl b). 就 jiù 3 is a synonym which is also used with Stative verbs.

a. 我的美国朋友张森十五岁便上了大学。
Wǒ de Měiguó péngyou Zhāngsēn shíwǔ suì biàn shàngle dàxué.
My American friend Johnson (then) went to college when she was 15 years old.

b 这个数学问题四、五年以前便研究好了。
Zhèige shùxué wèntí sì-wǔ nián yǐqián biàn yánjiū hǎo le.
This mathematical problem was (then) solved four or five years ago.

B

4. 便(是) X = It is indeed X (Av) 便 is often used in conjunction with 是 to mark confirmation of the following X. X may be a noun (expl a) or a verb phrase. 就(是) jiù(shì) 6 is a less shumianyu synonym. You can differentiate this use from its use as a conjunction in 5 below by where you find 便 in the sentence. Also consider 即 jí 1.

a. 这儿便是我们学校。
Zhèr biànshì wǒmen xuéxiào.
This is our school.

5. 便 X, 也 Y = Even if X, Y (Cj) 便 is also an infrequently used shumianyu synonym of 即便 jíbiàn 1 and 即使 jíshǐ 1. It marks that X is a hypothetical situation which does not affect whatever the situation is in Y (expl a). See 即便 jíbiàn 1 for further discussion of this set of concessive markers.

a. 便是再多的困难，也能克服。
Biànshì zài duō de kùnnan, yě néng kèfú
Even if many difficulties remain, we can overcome them.

并 bìng (並) 'and, moreover' Conjunction; 'definitely (negative)' Adverb

1. X 并 Y = X and Y as well (Cj) The shumianyu conjunction 并 marks that Y is a further development of the X situation. X and Y may be disyllabic verbs (expl a), but 并 more often appears at the head of a subjectless Y structure to mark that Y is a furthering of the X situation (expl b). 并且 bìngqiě 1 is a close oral synonym. 而且 érqiě 1 and the shumianyu 而 ér 1 are also synonyms. See the comment in 2 below on the adverbial use of 并 to mark the equal verbing of two or more matters. 并 is also used for the verb representing the idea of 'combine, merge.'

a. 我上次访问日本，看到并学到很多有意思的东西。
Wǒ shàng cì fǎngwèn Rìběn, kàndào bìng xuédào hěn duō yǒuyìsi de dōngxi.
When I visited Japan last time, I saw and learned many interesting things.

b. 教育部门应该规定“中小学生严禁吸烟”，并认真落实。
Jiàoyù bùmén yīnggāi guīdìng "zhōng xiǎo xuésheng yánjìn xīyān", bìng rènzhēn luòshí.
Educational sectors should rule that "Middle and Elementary Students Are Strictly Forbidden to Smoke"; moreover, they should conscientiously carry it out.

2. 并 Negative Vp = Definitely negative verb (Av) 并 emphasizes the negative condition of the verb phrase and imparts a sense that previously expressed information is wrong or irrelevant and that the record is being set straight. 并 negative sometimes connotes an air of explanation, sometimes an air of reproach. Compare this with the neutral 决 negative Vp jué 1 which simply intensifies the negative with no further connotation conveyed.

It is easy to distinguish the two main uses of 并: if there is a negative adverb such as 不 bù 1, 没 méi 1, 没有 méiyǒu 1, 未 wèi 1, etc., after 并, it is certainly being used to refute and set the record straight; if there is no negative, 并 is being used as a connector in the ways described in 1 above

Note that the adverb 并 is also occasionally used with a limited range of monosyllabic verbs to mark that two or more matters either occur simultaneously or are verbed equally; e.g., 学习外语应当听、说、读、写并重 Xuéxí wàiyǔ yīngdāng tīng, shuō, dú, xiě bìng zhòng 'When studying a foreign language, it should be that listening, speaking, reading and writing are equally important.'

a. 这个句子虽然有一点儿长，但并不难懂。
Zhèige jùzi suīrán yǒu yīdiǎnr cháng, dàn bìng bù nán dǒng.
Although this sentence is a bit long, it is actually not at all hard to understand.

b. 试验证明，南京药学院研制出的新药并没有什麽副作用。
Shìyàn zhèngmíng, Nánjīng Yàoxuéyuàn yánzhì chū de xīn yào bìng méiyòu shénme fù zuòyòng.
Tests prove that the new medicine designed by the Nanjing Pharmaceutical College definitely has no side effects.

并且 bìngqiě (並一) 'and, moreover' Conjunction

1. X, 并且 Y = X moreover Y (Cj) 并且 marks that Y is a further development of the X situation. Whether composed of clauses (expl a), verb phrases (expl b), or Stative verbs (expl c), X and Y will be grammatically and conceptually parallel structures. If there are three or more verb phrases in a sentence, 并且 goes directly before the last one. In lengthy sentences, 并且 will often be immediately preceded by a comma to mark a pause. When 不但 bùdàn 1, 不仅 bùjǐn 1 or a synonym heads X, a 并且 marked Y imparts an even stronger sense of developing the X situation; 也 yě 1, 还 hái 2 or a synonym often precedes the verb in Y in this type sentence (expl a). 并 bìng 1 is a shumianyu synonym which has the same values and usage patterns. 而且 érqiě 1 is a very close synonym; 况且 kuàngqiě 1 is a synonym which links two or more reasons for a situation. See also 且 qiě 1.

a. 我父亲不但喜欢西方古典音乐，并且也喜欢中国的古典音乐。
Wǒ fùqīn bùdàn xǐhuan xīfāng gǔdiǎn yīnyuè, bìngqiě yě xǐhuan Zhōngguó de gǔdiǎn yīnyuè.
My father not only likes classical Western music, he also likes China's classical music.

b. 去年行政院讨论并且通过了关于环境保护的若干决定。

B

Qùnián Xíngzhèngyuàn tǎolùn bìngqiě tōngguòle guānyú huánjìng bǎohù de ruògān juédìng.
Last year the Legislative Yuan debated and passed a number of decisions about environmental protection.

c. 那些新宿舍的房间宽敞并且明亮。
Nèixiē xīn sùshè de fángjiān kuānchǎng bìngqiě míngliàng.
The rooms in those new dorms are spacious and bright.

不 bù (一) "verb condition non-existent" Adverb; "question marker" Adverb; "unable to verb" Adverb

1. 不 Verb phrase = Verb/Stative verb condition non-existent (Av) One of the set of adverbs that mark negation of verbs and Stative verbs, 不 marks the non-existence of a verb action or Stative verb condition; e.g., 不买 bù mǎi marks that there is no action of 'buying' in the discourse (see expls a, b & c), and 不高 bù gāo marks that there is no condition of 'tallness' present (see expl d). 不 is most frequently used with present (expl a) or future (expl c) verb events or Stative verb conditions, but it may also be used with past situations (expl b). Since 不 is not of itself indicative of any particular time frame, you need to examine the context for the point in time involved in order to determine the correct tense of the English equivalent.

Activity verbs negated with 不 tend to be ones which customarily happen; e.g., 吃 chī 'eat,' 问 wèn 'ask (for information),' 说 shuō speak,' etc.(expl a). When used with Auxiliary verbs such as 会 huì 1, 可以 kěyǐ 1 & 2, etc., 不 marks a subjective statement that the Auxiliary-verb situation does not exist; e.g., 不可以去 bù kěyǐ qù 'may not go' conveys a subjective opinion about the 'inability to go' in addition to marking the absence of the verb action (see expl e).

Understanding the differences between 不 and 没 méi 1, the commonly seen marker for "verb non-occurrence," is very important. See 没 méi 1 for a comparative discussion of the two. Note that 不 is NEVER EVER used with the verb 有 yǒu 'have.' 未 wèi 1 is a less frequently used, very shumianyu synonym.

a. 我不吃面，就吃白饭。
Wǒ bù chī miàn, jiù chī báifàn.
I do not eat noodles. I just eat rice.

b. 我上高中的时候，竺先生不是校长。
Wǒ shàng gāozhōng de shíhou, Zhú xiānsheng bù shì xiàozhǎng.
When I was in high school, Mr. Zhu was not the principal.

c. 咱们学生俱乐部明天不去香山看红叶，要去颐和园划船。
Zámen xuésheng jùlèbù míngtiān bù qù Xiāngshān kàn hóngyè, yào qù Yìhéyuán huáchuán.

Our student club is not going to Fragrant Hills to see the autumn leaves tomorrow, we are going rowing at the Summer Palace.

d. 路不远，我们走着回宿舍吧！
Lù bù yuǎn, wǒmen zǒuzhe huí sùshè ba.
It's not far, let's walk back to the dorm.

e. 没有先进设备的工厂当然不能生产在市场上受欢迎的产品。
Méiyou xiānjìn shèbèi de gōngchǎng dāngrán bù néng shēngchǎn zài shìchǎng shang shōu huānyíng de chǎnpǐn.
Factories which do not have up to date equipment cannot produce products which succeed in the market place.

2. Vp 不 Vp = Does the verb phrase happen? (Av) 不 is placed between repeated syllables of a verb to form a neutral question structure; that is, a question which does not presuppose any particular answer. The verb phrase may be either a verb (expl a & c) or a Stative verb (expl b). When the verb structure is disyllabic, often just the first syllable of the verb phrase is given at the head of the question structure; e.g., 知不知道 zhī bu zhīdào, 可不可以 kě bu kěyǐ, 吃不吃饭 chī bu chīfàn, etc. When there is an object to the verb, the 不 Verb phrase structure may come after it, though this structure is less used in contemporary China (expl d). Be careful here, a Vp 不 Vp marked question is neutral, so do not translate it as a tag question: e.g., to translate expl d below as 'Do you eat Chinese food or not?' is wrong and misrepresents the tone of the text. See the other major question marker 吗 ma 1 which pre-supposes either a positive or negative answer.

a. 你买不买？
Nǐ mǎi bu mai?
Are you going to buy it?

b. 你早上洗的衣服干净不干净？
Nǐ zǎoshang xǐ de yīfu gānjìng bu ganjing?
Is the clothing you washed this morning dry?

c. 俄国走不走资本主义道路是一个关系到世界和平的问题。
Èguó zǒu bu zou zīběn zhǔyì dàolù shì yī ge liánxì dào shìjiè hépíng de wèntí.
Whether Russia goes the capitalist route is a question which affects world peace.

d. 你吃中国菜不吃？
Nǐ chī Zhōngguó cài bu chi?
Do you eat Chinese food?

3. (Action) verb 不 (result) verb = Unable to verb (Av) In this usage 不 marks the negative version of a verb-potential (sometimes called "resultative verb") structure. Verb-potentials are usually composed of three syllables 看不懂 kàn bù dǒng 'unable to understand,' sometimes four 代表不了 dàibiǎo bù liǎo 'can't represent,' or occasionally five syllables 研究不出来 yánjiū bù chūlái 'unable to research.'

Verb-potentials are always marked by 不 (or its positive counterpart 得 de 2) as the middle element. Be careful to translate these verb forms with 'can't' or 'unable to' to reflect their potential aspect.

B

a. 糟糕，我听不懂纠正发音的老师说的问题。
Zāogāo, wǒ tīng bù dǒng jiūzhèng fāyīn de lǎoshī shuō de wèntí.
Uh-oh, I can't understand the questions the pronunciation instructor asks.

b. 一年级学生当然比不上三年级学生的汉语水平。
Yīniánjí xuésheng dāngrán bǐ bù shàng sān niánjí xuésheng de Hànyǔ shuǐpíng.
Of course first year students' Chinese can't compare to that of third year students.

不单 **bùdān** (一單) 'not only' Conjunction

1. 不单 X, Y = Not just X, Y (Cj) The oral 不单 marks that there is further information about X in Y (expl a). It is used in the same way as its close synonym 不但 bùdàn 1 except that it is not used with 反而 fǎn'ér 1. 不光 bùguāng 1 is a very close synonym.

a. 人民解放军不单是战斗队，也是工作队和生产队。
Rénmín Jiěfàngjūn bùdān shì zhàndòuduì, yě shì gōngzuòduì hé shēngchǎnduì.
The People's Liberation Army is not merely a fighting force. It is a working force and a production corps as well.

不但 **bùdàn** (——) 'not only' Conjunction

1. 不但 X, Y = Not only is there the X situation, there is also Y (Cj) 不但 marks that there is further development in Y of the X situation. X may be either a verb phrase (expl a), a noun phrase (expl b), or depending on placement of the subject, a clause; Y will be a verb phrase or a clause. As is the case with most of the conjunctions used in X, when X and Y have the same subject, 不但 usually comes after the subject (expl a); when they have different subjects the first subject will generally be after 不但 (expl b).

不但 is generally followed a Y structure which has markers that focus attention on specific aspects of the inter-relationship of Y to X: e.g., 而且 érqiě 1 and its synonyms simply draw attention to further development of the X situation in Y with no further connotation; when Y has 还 hái 1 or 又 yòu 1, it more strongly marks that Y supplements the X situation (expl c); when the Y marker is 更 gèng 1, Y is more prominent than X (expl d); 也 yě 1 marks that X and Y belong to similar categories and also points to further development of the X situation in Y (expl e); when X contains a negative verb phrase, 反而 fǎn'ér 1 is used to mark that Y is different from X or is unexpected (expl f). Note that 不但 is sometimes omitted, but the presence of 而且 or 并 bìng 1, etc. in Y still marks the sentence as a not only X, Y structure. 不仅 bùjǐn 1 is a shumianyu synonym. 不单 bùdān 1, 不光 bùguāng 1, and 不只 bùzhǐ 1 are close oral synonyms with various usage restrictions. (The oral 不独 bùdú X, 就是 Y was mainly used in fiction earlier in this century.)

a. 古波不但要学习中国语文，而且要学习中国现代历史。
Gŭbō bùdàn yào xuéxí Zhōngguó yŭwén, érqiě yào xuéxí Zhōngguó xiàndài lìshǐ.
Not only does Gubo want to study the Chinese language, he also wants to learn about modern Chinese history.

b. 不但纺织工厂的所有工人，并且几乎所有的家属都参加了那次义务劳动。
Bùdàn fāngzhī gōngchăng de suŏyŏu gōngrén, bìngqiě jīhū suŏyŏu de jiāshŭ dōu cānjiāle nèi cì yìwù láodòng.
Not only did all of the textile workers take part in the voluntary labor, most all of the family members did as well.

c. 他不但自己读中国的小说名著，还鼓励同学们读。
Tā bùdàn zìjĭ dú Zhōngguó de xiăoshuō míngzhù, hái gŭlì tóngxuémen dú.
He not only read the famous Chinese novels, he additionally encouraged his classmates to read them.

d. 我们工厂企业不但要出上等产品，更要出优秀的技术人才。
Wŏmen gōngchăng qĭyè bùdàn yào chū shàngděng chănpĭn, gèng yào chū yōuxiù de jìshù réncái.
Not only should our factories produce first class products, we must pay even greater attention to producing excellent talented technical personnel.

e. 她不但是个好工程师，将来肯定也是个好局长。
Tā bùdàn shì ge hăo gōngchéngshī, jiānglái kěndìng yě shì ge hăo júzhăng.
Not only is she a good engineer, she will definitely make a fine section chief.

f. 暴风雪不但没停，反而越来越利害。
Bàofēngxuě bùdàn méi tíng, făn'ér yuèlái yuè lìhai.
The blizzard has not only not stopped, it's actually getting worse and worse.

不到 bùdào (——) "not that much" Verb phrase

1. 不到 Amount = Less than the amount stated (Vp) 不到 marks that a verb action occurred for less than the quantity given after it. 不到 is mostly used with time references (expls a & b), but you will also find it used with other quantities to mark that less than that amount was involved in a verb situation (expl c). Keep in mind that when 不到 is followed by a place name, it means 'not arrive at (the place).'

Compare this "quantity of time" marker with the discussion at 以来 yĭlái 1 for comments on the three sets of structures which mark the time frame prior to a verb action; see also 直到 zhídào 1 which marks X as the time frame for a Y situation.

a. 那个传道电视台成立了不到一年。
Nèige chuándào diànshìtái chénglìle bùdào yī nián.
That Christian television station has been established for less than a year.

B

b. 叶教授教了<u>不到</u>半年就知道外语系有许多问题了。
Yè jiàoshòu jiāole <u>bùdào</u> bànnián jiù zhīdao Wàiyǔxì yǒu xǔduō wèntí le.
Professor Ye had taught <u>for less than</u> half a year when she realized that there were some problems in the Foreign Languages Department.

c. 昨天来参观的人<u>不到</u>十位。
Zuótiān lái cānguān de rén <u>bùdào</u> shí wèi.
<u>Less than</u> ten people came to visit yesterday.

不断 **<u>bùduàn</u> (—斷) 'continue, go on' Adverb**

1. <u>不断 Vp</u> = <u>Continue doing a verb action</u> (Av) <u>不断</u> is placed before verbs to mark that one particular verb action continues without interruption over a period of time. You will sometimes see this written as <u>不断地</u>. <u>继续 jìxù</u> 1 is a synonym with wider usage patterns. The near synonyms 连续 liánxù and 陆续 lùxù mark that similar events are continuing on one after the other.

a. 我們还<u>不断</u>加强能源、交通、港口等基础设施建设，并努力改善外商投资的软环境。
Wǒmen hái <u>bùduàn</u> jiāqiáng néngyuán, jiāotōng, gǎngkǒu děng jīchǔ shèshī jiànshè, bìng nǔlì gǎishàn wàishāng tóuzī de ruǎn huánjìng.
We are also <u>continuing</u> to strengthen the construction of fundamental power, transportation, harbors and other facilities. Moreover, we are working hard to improve the soft environment for foreign investments.

不管 **<u>bùguǎn</u> (——) 'regardless (of possibilities)' Conjunction**

1. <u>不管 X, Y</u> = <u>No matter what X might be, Y takes place</u> (Cj) <u>不管</u> is a more oral member of one of the three sets of conjunctions which mark that no matter what the situation in <u>X</u> might be, <u>Y</u> is unaffected. <u>不管</u> specifically marks that no matter whether the situation in <u>X</u> is phrased as a <u>Sv 不 Sv</u> or <u>X 还是 Y</u> alternative question structure (expl a), or as an indefinite structure question structure formed with 什么...都，谁...也，etc. (expl b), <u>X</u> has no impact at all on the situation articulated in <u>Y</u>. <u>X</u> will be structured as either a clause, a noun phrase, or a verb phrase. <u>Y</u> will be a verb phrase. The adverbs <u>都 dōu</u> 1, <u>也 yě</u> 2, or <u>还 hái</u> 1 will usually head the <u>Y</u> structure. The oral synonym <u>管 guǎn</u> 1 conveys the same meaning through rhetorical force without the use of a negative adverb; it also gives a more emotional feeling and stronger tone of voice. <u>不论 bùlùn</u> 1 and <u>无论 wúlùn</u> 1 are close synonyms used both orally and in written texts. <u>凭 píng</u> 2 is a less frequently used oral synonym. See <u>虽然 suīrán</u> 1 for comparative comments and examples of the other members of these three sets of markers.

a. 不管是老师还是学生，上课的时候都不能说英语。
Bùguǎn shì lǎoshī háishì xuésheng, shàngkè de shíhou dōu bù néng shuō Yīngyǔ.
No matter whether it is teachers or students, no one is allowed to speak English during class.

b. 美国总统强调指出，不管采矿工业多么重要，必须先治理环境污染。
Měiguó zǒngtǒng qiángdiào zhǐchū, bùguǎn cǎikuàng gōngyè duōme zhòngyào, bìxū xiān zhìlǐ huánjìng wūrán.
The American President emphatically pointed out that no matter how important the mining industry is, we must first take care of environmental pollution.

不光 **bùguāng** (——) **'not only' Conjunction**

1. 不光 X, Y = Not only X, Y (Cj) 不光 marks that the Y situation is a further development of the situation in X. 不光 is used in the same way and for the same values as its synonym 不但 bùdàn 1. 不单 bùdān 1 is a very close synonym. See 不但 for a comparative discussion of this set of conjunctions.

a. 这里不光生产毛线，而且生产毛毯。
Zhèli bùguāng shēngchǎn máoxiàn, érqiě shēngchǎn máotǎn.
This area not only produces knitting wool, it also produces woolen blankets.

不过 **bùguò** (—過) **'though, but, yet' Conjunction; 'merely, simply' Adverb**

1. X, 不过 Y = X, but Y (Cj) 不过 is an oral member of the set of conjunctions which mark Y as a change from the direction of events found in X. 不过 gives a light toned, tactful suggestion that Y is either a concession (expl a) or a condition (expl b) related to the X event. In this second usage it is closest to its more shumianyu synonym 但是 dànshì 1. 只是 zhǐshì 1 is an oral synonym which gives an even lighter tone to Y. See 但是 dànshì 1 for a further discussion of this set of corrective conjunctions.

a. 这个人好像很面熟，不过我一时想不起来她是谁。
Zhèige rén hǎoxiàng hěn miànshú, bùguò wǒ yīshí xiǎngbùqǐlái tā shì shéi.
This person seems quite familiar, though I can't quite remember who she is.

b. 心脏移植手术做得很好，不过病人四天以后就过世了。
Xīnzàng yízhí shǒushù zuò de hěn hǎo, bùguò bìngrén sì tiān yǐhòu jiù guòshì le.
The heart transplant went pretty well, but the patient died four days later.

2. 不过 Verb = Simply verb (Av) When used as an adverb 不过 brings a value of 'simply, just' to the verb phrase structure. A reinforcing 只 zhǐ 1 is often placed before

不过. Since Conjunction 不过 comes at the head of a second or later clause in a sentence and Adverb 不过 must come directly before the core verb of a structure, it is easy to distinguish between the two usages.

a. 这不过是我个人的意见，不一定正确。
Zhè bùguò shì wǒ gèrén de yìjiàn, bù yīdìng zhèngquè.
This is just my opinion; it isn't necessarily correct.

不仅 bùjǐn (—僅) 'not only' Conjunction

1. 不仅 X, Y = Not only is there the X situation, there is also Y (Cj) The shumianyu 不仅 marks that there is further development of the X situation in Y. X may be either a noun phrase, a verb phrase, or a clause; Y will be a verb phrase or a clause. As tends to be the case with conjunctions which appear in X, when there is one subject for the whole sentence, 不仅 appears after it (expl b); when X and Y have different subjects, 不仅 comes before the first subject (expl a). 不仅 is always used in connection with conjunction markers in Y such as 并且 bìngqiě 2 and 而且 érqiě 2, etc. which focus attention on specific aspects of the inter-relationship of X and Y. Note that when the more shumianyu 而 ér 1 is used in Y, stronger emphasis is conveyed and a change from the X situation is marked. See 不但 bùdàn 1 for further comments on the oral synonyms of 不仅 and the values conveyed by various adverbial markers in Y. 不仅 is sometimes seen as 不仅仅 with no change in meaning or usage.

a. 老舍小说中的一些北京方言，不仅我们不懂，就是生长在北京的许多青年人也不太懂。
Lǎoshè xiǎoshuō zhōng de yīxiē Běijīng fāngyán, bùjǐn wǒmen bù dǒng, jiùshì shēngzhǎng zài Běijīng de xǔduō qīngniánrén yě bù tài dǒng.
Not only do we not understand some of the Beijing dialect in Lao She's stories, even many young people born in Beijing don't fully understand them.

b. 为了实现四个现代化，我们不仅要学会管理科学，而且要精通管理科学。
Wèile shíxiàn Sìge Xiàndàihuà, wǒmen bùjǐn yào xuéhuì guǎnlǐ kēxué, érqiě yào jīngtōng guǎnlǐ kēxué.
In order to achieve the Four Modernizations, we must not only learn managerial science, we must become masters at it.

不论 bùlùn (—論) 'regardless (of alternative possibilities)' Conjunction

1. 不论 X, Y = No matter what X says, Y is unchanged (Cj) 不论 is a member of one of the three sets of conjunctions which mark that no matter what the situation in X may be, Y is unaffected. 不论 is used in both oral and written passages to specifically mark that whether X is structured as an indefinite interrogative with a 什么....都，哪儿....也, etc. structure (expl a), or as a X 还是 Y or Sv 不 Sv (expl b) choice structure, the Y situation is unchanged. The Y verb structure will usually be headed by 都 dōu 1, 总 zǒng, or 也 yě 1. 无论 wúlùn 1 is a very close synonym used in both written and oral communications. 不管 bùguǎn 1 is a very close oral synonym. See 虽然 suīrán 1 for further comparative comments on the three sets of alternative, factual and hypothetical concessive conjunctions. Consider also the discussion at 尽管 jǐnguǎn 1.

a. 不论是什么课，那个留学生都非常认真地学习。
Wúlùn shi shénme kè, nèi ge liúxuéshāng dōu fēicháng rènzhēn de xuéxí.
Regardless of whatever class it is, that foreign student is extraordinarily conscientious.

b. 别人的意见，不论正确还是不正确，都要耐心听取。
Biéren de yìjiàn, bùlùn zhèngquè háishi bù zhèngquè, dōu yào nàixīn tīngqǔ.
No matter whether they are correct or not, other people's opinions must be take note of.

2. X, 不论Y = X is unchanged regardless of Y (Cj) 不论 may be placed in Y to mark greater emphasis on the idea that what follows it has no impact on the X situation. In this case, Y has the same structural features listed for X above.

a. 它的进攻是能够打败的，不论是在什么地方和在什么战线上。
Tā de jìngōng shi nénggòu dǎbài de, wúlùn shi zài shénme dìfang hé zài shénme zhànxiàn shang.
The enemy's attack can be defeated regardless of the place or battlefield.

b. 意见总是要提的，不论你愿意听还是不愿意听。
Yìjiàn zǒngshì yào tí de, bùlùn nǐ yuànyi tīng háishi bù yuànyi tīng.
Opinions must be brought forth whether or not you want to hear them.

不然 bùrán (——) 'otherwise, or else' Conjunction

1. X, 不然 Y = X, otherwise Y (Cj) 不然 either introduces the hypothetical Y conclusion of an X situation (expl a), or it marks alternatives to an X condition (expl b). When 的话 dèhuà 1 is added after 不然, the hypothetical tone of voice is increased (expl c). 要不然 yàoburán 1 and 要不 yàobù 1 are oral synonyms which give a stronger hypothetical tone. 否则 fǒuzé 1 is a somewhat shumianyu synonym. Note that as a Stative verb 不然 means 'is not that way.'

a. 去中国留学的时候应该常写信回家，不然家里会不放心的。
Qù Zhōngguó liúxué de shíhou yīnggāi cháng xiěxìn huíjiā, bùrán jiālǐ huì bù fàngxīn de.
When you go to China to study you should often write home, otherwise your

family will really worry.

B

b. 礼拜天他总是去看英语电影，不然就去看朋友，再不然就去动物园看熊猫。
Lĭbàitiān tā zŏngshì qù kàn Yīngyŭ diànyĭng, bùrán jiù qù kàn péngyou, zài bùrán jiù qù dòngwùyuàn kàn xióngmāo.
On Sundays he always goes to English language movies, or he goes to see friends, or else he goes to the zoo to see the pandas.

c. 二十五号以前，必须把大型车床送来，不然的话，就要耽误生产。
Èrshíwŭ hào yĭqián, bìxū bă dà xíng chēchuáng sòng lái, bùrán dehuà, jiù yào dānwù shēngchăn.
They have to send the large model lathe before the 25th. Otherwise, it will delay production.

不如 bùrú (——) "comparison > inequality" Verb

1. X 不如 Y (Sv) = X is not equal to Y (in terms of the stative verb) (Vb) 不如 is a member of one of the three sets of words which mark comparative situations. 不如 specifically marks that X is inferior to Y. The exact way X is inferior to Y can either be unstated (expls a & b) or it can be specified by a final Stative verb (expl c), but in all cases the comparison is to the disadvantage of X. When 还 hái 2 (no tone) comes before 不如, it marks that X is worse than an already unsatisfactory Y. X and Y will normally be structurally and conceptually similar noun phrases (expls a & c) or verb phrases (expl b). X没有Y(这/那么) Sv méiyŏu 3 is a synonymous oral structure. See 比 bĭ 1 for an overview of the three different sets of comparison markers.

a. 谁说四年级的女学生不如二年级的？
Shéi shuō sìniànjí de nǚ xuésheng bùrú èr niánjí de?
Who says senior women students are not equal to sophomore women?

b. 学习日语不如学习汉语。
Xuéxí Rìyŭ bùrú xuéxí Hànyŭ.
Studying Japanese is not as good as studying Chinese.

c. 我们学校的图书馆不如国立的那么舒服。
Wŏmen xuéxiào de túshūguăn bùrú guólì de nàme shūfu.
Our school library is not as as comfortable as the one at the state school.

2. X (V) (O) V 得 不如 Y Sv = X verbs (an object) in a Stative verb manner inferior to the manner Y verbs (it) (Vb) In this structure 不如 marks that X is inferior to Y in doing a verb action (to an object). The (V) (O) V 得 structure can be placed either between X and 不如 (expl b) or immediately after Y (expl a) with the same meaning. X and Y will be grammatically and conceptually similar noun or verb phrases. The same comparative concept can be structured with the more oral X(V)(O)V得没有Y这/那么 Sv; see 没有 méiyǒu 3. See 比 bǐ 2 for discussion of the three sets of words which mark how verb actions are compared.

a. 三友摄影室不如大众摄影室照得好。
Sānyǒu Shèyǐngshì bùrú Dàzhōng Shèyǐngshì zhào de hǎo.
The Three Friends Studio does not do photography as well as The Masses Studio does.

b. 那本文学史写得不如施老师的这本好。
Nèi běn wénxuéshǐ xiě de bùrú Shī lǎoshī de zhèi běn hǎo.
That literary history is not as well written as Professor Shi's.

不是 bùshì (——) 'if not' Adverb; "rhetorical question" Adverb

1. 不是 X, 就是 Y = If not X, then definitely Y (Av) This is a negatively structured member of the set of patterns which mark 'if' situations. It may mark that X and Y are the two possibilities in a situation (expl a), or it may present X and Y as two aspects of one situation (expls b & c). Whether composed of verb phrases (expls a & b) or noun phrases (expl c), X and Y will be similar in concept and structure. 便 biàn 1 may replace 就 jiù 1 in Y for a more shumianyu flavor.

When the shumianyu conjunction 而 ér 1 is used in Y, it marks that X is not a possibility and that Y is the only possibility (expl c). 非X即Y fēi...jí is a synonymous shumianyu structure. See 如果 rúguǒ 1 for a more detailed discussion of conditional structures. Note carefully that it is always possible for 不是 simply to be a negation of a X是Y 'X is Y' structure; be careful to examine the context in which you see 不是.

a. 从中国到美国去不是坐船，就是坐飞机。
Cóng Zhōngguó dào Měiguó qù bùshì zuòchuán, jiùshì zuò fēijī.
When going from China to the US, if you don't go by boat, (then) you go by plane.

b. 抗战时期，中国不是受日本的打击，就是受自然灾难的危害。
Kàngzhàn shíqī, Zhōngguó bùshì shòu Rìběn de dǎjī, jiùshì shòu zìrán zāinán de wēihài.
During the War of Resistance, if China wasn't being attacked by Japan, (then) it was suffering natural disasters.

c. 孙中山先生考虑的不是自己，而是国家和人民的利益。
Sūn Zhōngshān xiānsheng kǎolǜ de búshì zìjǐ, érshì guójiā hé rénmín de lìyì.
That which Dr. Sun Yat-sen thought about was not himself but rather the interests of the country and the people.

2. (X) 不是 Y 吗 = Isn't it (that X is) Y (Av) This structure creates a rhetorical question which bears an air of reproach and/or disbelief and negatively suggests that the answer is in the affirmative. X will be a noun phrase and Y will be a verb phrase. The answer is in the affirmative. X will be a noun phrase and Y will be a verb phrase. The adverb 难道 nándào 'Do you mean to say?' can be added to give a stronger tone of voice. See 没有 méiyǒu 2 for additional discussion of negative rhetorical question structures.

B

a. 天气预报不是说今天晚上要下雪吗？
Tiānqi yùbào bùshì shuō jīntiān wǎnshang yào xiàxuě ma?
Didn't the weather forecast say that it would snow tonight?

b. 帝国主义国家的连续攻击不是实实在在地被我们粉碎了吗？
Dìguó zhǔyì guójiā de liánxù gōngjī bùshì shíshí-zàizài de bèi wǒmen fěncuì le ma?
Weren't the continuous attacks by the imperialist nations in fact crushed by us?

不只 bùzhǐ (——) 'not only' Conjunction

1. 不只 X, Y = Not only X, Y (Cj) 不只 is used in X to mark that Y is a continuation and further development of the situation found in X. Y will usually be marked with 而且 érqiě 1, 还 hái 1, etc. 不但 bùdàn 1 is a close synonym, though it has a wider flexibility of structural usages; see 不但 for further comments.

a. 厦门不只有现代化的大工厂，并且有许多中小型工厂。
Xiàmén bùzhǐ yǒu xiàndàihuà de dà gōngchǎng, bìngqiě yǒu xǔduō zhōng xiǎo xíng gōngchǎng.
Xiamen not only has large, modernized factories, it also has many medium and small scale factories.

才 <u>cái</u> (纔) 'then (and only then)' Adverb; 'just (then)' Adverb; "emphasis" Adverb; 'only (amount)' Adverb

C

1. <u>才 Vp</u> = <u>Verb action then done</u> (Av) In this first usage, <u>才</u> marks that the verb action which follows it happens relatively later than anticipated. When used with the only verb in a structure, <u>才</u> marks that the verb finally occurred (a). When used with the second verb in a two clause sequence, <u>才</u> marks that the second verb happened only after the first (expls b, first ½ of c & d). There will usually be a time structure given along with this usage (expls a, b & c). <u>才</u> most often refers to past events (expls a, b & c), but it can also refer to future events (expl d). You will occasionally see the more complex character form <u>纔</u> used in ROC texts for all four functions discussed in this entry.

a. 我昨天晚上三点半<u>才</u>睡觉。
Wǒ zuótiān wǎnshang sān diǎn bàn <u>cái</u> shuìjiào.
I <u>finally</u> got to sleep last night at 3:30.

b. 篮球赛七点开始，八点差一刻小马<u>才</u>来。
Lánqiúsài qīdiǎn kāishǐ, bā diǎn chà yī kè Xiǎo Mǎ <u>cái</u> lái.
The basketball game started at 7:00. Ma <u>finally</u> arrived at a quarter of eight.

c. 她住校一个月<u>才</u>能回家一次，常常想家，有时还哭鼻子。
Tā zhù xiào yī ge yuè <u>cái</u> néng huíjiā yīcì, chángcháng xiǎngjiā, yǒushí hái kū bízi.
She stayed at school for a month, and <u>only</u> then was she able to go back home. She was always homesick, and sometimes she cried to herself.

d. 受刑人假释规定原本是必须服满刑期三分之一<u>才</u>能申请假释，……
Shòuxíngrén jiǎshì guīdìng yuánběn shì bìxū fúmǎn xíngqī sān fēnzhī yī <u>cái</u> néng shēnqǐng jiǎshì,...
The regulation for parole of prisoners was originally that they had to serve a full 1/3 of the sentence and could <u>only then</u> apply for parole...

2. <u>只有/由于/为了 Vp1, 才 Vp2</u> = <u>Second verb then happened because of the conditions, reasons, goals, etc. given in the first clause</u> (Av) This <u>才</u> usage is closely related to 1 above, but it is treated separately here to bring attention to the use of <u>才</u> in complex sentences. <u>才</u> retains the value of 'then (and only then)' in these texts, but it is also colored by the meaning of the conjunctions at the head of the first verb phrase. See <u>只有 zhǐyǒu</u> 1, <u>只要 zhǐyào</u> 1, <u>由于 yóuyú</u> 1, <u>为了 wèile</u> 1, etc. for comments and examples of their functions.

a. 我们只有认真研究，<u>才</u>能进一步明确教育发展与改革的方向，使教育更好地适应经济和社会发展的需要。
Wǒmen zhǐyǒu rènzhēn yánjiū, <u>cái</u> néng jìnyībù míngquè jiàoyù fāzhǎn yǔ gǎigé de fāngxiàng, shǐ jiàoyù gèng hǎo de shìyìng jīngji hé shèhuì fāzhǎn de xūyào.
Only if we conscientiously do research can we <u>then</u> be more explicit about the direction of educational expansion and reforms and cause education to further

meet the needs of economic and social growth.

b. 疫苗虽已陆续抵达并立刻对猪只等偶蹄类动物进行注射，但由于在注射一星期之后，才会产生抗体，因此养猪户仍应该……

C

Yìmiáo suī yǐ lùxù dǐdá bìng lìkè duì zhūzhī děng ǒutí lèi dòngwù jìnxíng zhùshè, dàn yóuyú zài zhùshè yī xīngqī zhīhòu, cái huì chǎnshēng kàngtǐ, yīncǐ yǎngzhūhù réng yīnggāi...

Although the vaccine has arrived and hogs and other similarly hoofed animals were immediately inoculated, because it takes a week for antibodies to (then and only then) develop, hog farmers still should...

3. 才 Vp = Verb just happened (Av) In this usage 才 marks that a verb action happened very recently (expls a & b). You may also find this 才 before the first verb in a two verb sequence with the second verb marked by 就 jiù 1; this structure marks that the second verb happened very soon after the first (expl c). 刚才 gāngcái, 刚刚 gānggāng and 方才 fāngcái are synonyms, though they are not used in a sequence of two verb phrases. 才 is also used to mark that a number or a level of something is low; e.g., 才三号，还早呢 Cái sān hào, hái zǎo ne 'It's just the 3rd, it's still early.'

a. 史老师才从哈尔滨回来不久。

Shǐ lǎoshī cái cóng Háěrbīn huí lái bùjiǔ.

Professor Shi just got back from Harbin.

b. 第三阶段的历史意识是以平民百姓为主题的历史，是最近才有的观念。

Dì sān jiēduàn de lìshǐ yìshí shi yǐ píngmín bǎixìng wéi zhǔtí de lìshǐ, shi zuìjìn cái yǒu de guānniàn.

The third period of historiography is history which has common man as its theme. This is a concept which has existed only recently.

c. 天才亮爸爸就到河边钓鱼去了。

Tiān cái liàng bàba jiù dào hébiān diàoyú qù le.

It had just gotten light out and dad went off to the river to fish.

4. 才 Sv/(negative) Vp 呢 = Truly Stative condition/(NOT) verb action (Av) 才 Sv 呢 emphasizes that a Stative verb condition exists, usually to a high degree (expl a). 才是 X suggests that X is the real article and that nothing else comes close (expl b). When used with other verbs, "emphasis" 才 is generally followed by a negative adverb and 呢 ne at sentence end (expl c). Use the negative and the 呢 to distinguish this 才 from the other values of 才.

a. 一到过年中国家庭才热闹呢！

Yīdào guònián Zhōngguó jiātíng cái rènao ne!

Come New Year's and Chinese homes are just bustling with noise and excitement!

b. 这才是名副其实的英雄！

Zhè cái shi míng fù qí shí de yīngxióng!

This, this is a true hero!

c. 我<u>才</u>不上这个当呢！
Wǒ <u>cái</u> bù shàng zhèi ge dāng ne!
I'm <u>certainly</u> not falling for this trick!

5.<u>才 (verb) amount</u> = <u>Only that amount</u> (Av) When you see <u>才</u> before an amount (expl a) or before a verb directly followed by an amount, <u>才</u> is being used to mark that an amount or level is considered to be low. The presence of a number and/or a measure distinguishes this use of <u>才</u> from those discussed above.

C

a. 这个孩子<u>才</u>六岁，已经认得不少字了。
Zhèige háizi <u>cái</u> liù suì, yǐjing rèndé bù shǎo zì le.
This child is <u>just</u> six years old, and she already knows quite a few characters.

b. 那个书店的服务员每年<u>才</u>赚一万多块钱。
Nèige shūdiàn de fúwùyuán měi nián <u>cái</u> zhuàn yī wàn duō kuài qián.
The clerks in that bookstore <u>only</u> earn $10,000 some dollars a year.

纔 <u>cái</u> (才) 'then (and only then)' Adverb; 'just (then)' Adverb; "emphasis" Adverb

1. <u>纔 Vp</u> = <u>才 verb</u> You will occasionally see <u>纔</u>, a traditional character variant of <u>才</u>, used in texts from the ROC for the values that <u>才</u> <u>cái</u> 1, 2, 3 and 4 have. See <u>才</u> for comments and examples.

曾 <u>céng</u> (一) "did occur" Adverb

1. <u>曾 Vp/Sv</u> = <u>Verb situation/condition did occur</u> (Av) The shumianyu <u>曾</u> marks affirmation that a verb situation or condition did occur at some time relatively long ago, but that it is no longer happening. Since <u>曾</u> marks that a verb action did occur, it logically would not be negated; however, you may occasionally see the adverbs 不曾 bùcéng or even 未曾 wèicéng 'never did (the following verb action).' They are independent words not related to the function of <u>曾</u> described here. <u>曾</u> itself is not used with negatives. <u>曾经</u> <u>céngjīng</u> 1 is a more commonly used synonym.

a. 台湾人民<u>曾</u>长期遭受过日本帝国主义的压迫。
Táiwān rénmín <u>céng</u> chángqī zāoshòuguo Rìběn dìguó zhǔyì de yāpò.
The Taiwanese people <u>did indeed</u> suffer Japanese imperialistic repression for a long period of time.

曾经 céngjīng (—經) "did occur" Adverb

C

1. 曾经 Vp/Sv = Verb situation did indeed exist (Av) 曾经 marks that a verb situation definitely occurred at some point in the past, most often far from the present, and is now completely over. The situation may be structured as either as a full verb (expl a) or as a Stative verb (expl b). 曾经 Verb is often followed by a reinforcing 过 guo 1 or 了 lè 1 (expl a); 曾经 Stative verb must be followed by 过 or 了 (expl b). 曾 céng 1 is a more shumianyu synonym of 曾经.

Compare this 'verb action over and done with' marker 曾经 with 已经 yǐjīng 1 which marks a verb situation as one done in the relatively recent past, but one which might continue. For example, compare 我曾经在这里住过几天 Wǒ céngjīng zài zhèlǐ zhùguo jǐ tiān 'I lived here for a few days (but do not live here now)' with 我已经在这里住了几天 'I have already lived here for a few days (and may continue living here).'

a. 那个高中学生曾经在南开大学学习过一个月汉语。

Nèige gāozhōng xuésheng céngjīng zài Nánkāi Dàxué xuéxíguo yī ge yuè Hànyǔ.

That high school student studied Chinese at Nankai University for one month.

b. 刚患癌症的时候，我也曾经悲观过，是同学们的鼓励使我变得坚强了。

Gāng huàn áizhèng de shíhou, wǒ yě céngjīng bēiguānguo, shì tóngxuémen de gǔlì shǐ wǒ biàn de jiānqiáng le.

When I first got cancer, I was pessimistic; but my classmates' encouragement made me strong.

朝 cháo (—) 'towards' Coverb

1. 朝 Np Vp = Verb towards the noun phrase (Cv) 朝 is a member of one of the two sets of words which mark the location involved in a verb action. In an extension of its basic meaning of 'face towards,' the direction marker 朝 is used when the verb action involves a stationary facing towards a location rather than physical movement to it (expls a & c). However, you may find 朝 also used in sentences which have actual movement towards a place as long as there is also a sense of facing towards that direction (expl b). The noun which 朝 marks may range from the name of a place or person (expl a), to a point on the compass (expl b), to an abstract concept (expl c). 着 zhe 1 may be used after 朝 for a more shumianyu tone except with monosyllabic direction names. 朝 is also used as the verb 'face towards' and the noun 'dynasty'; when it is read zhāo 朝 represents the concept of 'early morning.'

向 xiàng 1 is a close synonym which can be used for all instances of 朝, though the reverse is not true: 朝 is not used with abstract verbs in reference to human activities, and 朝 never comes after the verb; see 向 for further comments. 照 zhào 1 is a close synonym which is less frequently used. 对 duì 2 is a synonym which marks the noun phrase as the target of the verb action.

Be careful to distinguish between this set of "to" words which marks stationary facing and the 往 wàng 1 set which marks actual physical movement towards a noun. The two sets can be used interchangeably in situations where there is both a sense of facing and actual movement towards the noun phrase (expl b). However, there are times when one or the other does not fit; e.g., in the sentence 太和殿正门朝南开 Tàihédiàn zhèngmén cháo nán kāi 'The main door of the Hall of Great Harmony opens to the south' 往 could not be used since there is no sense of actual physical movement involved (对 could not be used since a compass point cannot be used with 对). See 向 xiàng 1 and 往 wàng 1 for further comparative comments.

a. 小黄朝我打了个招呼，我朝她点了点头。
Xiǎo Huáng cháo wǒ dǎle ge zhāohu, wǒ cháo tā diǎnle diǎntóu.
Little Huang waved to me and I nodded to her.

b. 你一直朝南走，银行前边儿就是三友书店。
Nǐ yīzhí cháo nán zǒu, yínháng qiánbiānr jiùshì Sānyǒu Shūdiàn.
Head directly (to the) south. The Three Friends Bookstore is in front of the bank.

c. 副主任提议研究小组应该开始朝新领域作更深的研究。
Fùzhǔrén tíyì yánjiū xiǎozǔ yīnggāi kāishǐ cháo xīn lǐngyù zuò gèng shēn de yánjiū.
The Vice-director suggested that the research team should begin doing more intensive research in a new direction

重 chóng (一) 'completely do again' Adverb

1. 重 Vp = Completely re-do the Verb phrase (Av) 重 is member of the set of words which mark 'again.' 重 is used with monosyllabic verbs to mark that the verb action is re-done from beginning to end. 重新 chóngxīn is a close synonym used with both monosyllabic and disyllabic verbs. See 又 yòu 1 and 再 zài 1 for further discussion of synonyms in this set of words. Note that 重 is pronounced chóng when it means 'again' and zhòng when it represents concepts having to do with 'heavy.'

a. 我这篇报告上写错了好几个字，索性重抄一遍。
Wǒ zhèi piān bàogào shang xiěcuòle hǎo jǐ ge zì, suǒxìng chóng chāo yī biàn.
I have written quite a few characters incorrectly on this paper. I had best re-copy the whole thing.

C

重新 chóngxīn (— —) 'completely do again' Adverb

1. **重新 Vp = Re-do the verb from start to finish** (Av) 重新 is a member of the set of words which mark 'again.' 重新 differs from its synonyms by marking specifically that the verb action is to be completely re-done, from beginning to end. 重 chóng 1 is a synonym which differs in being only used with monosyllabic verbs. See 又 yòu 1 and 再 zài 1 for further discussion of this set of 'again' markers.

a. 试验如果失败了，我们重新整顿力量再干，绝不垂头丧气。

Shìyàn rúguǒ shībàile, wǒmen chóngxīn zhěngdùn lìliàng zài gàn, jué bù chuí tóu sāng qì.

If the experiments fail, we will completely reorganize our efforts and carry on, we won't be crestfallen about it.

除 chú (—) 'besides' Coverb; 'except for' Coverb

1. **除 X(以)外, Y = Besides/Except for X, Y** (Cv) An X headed by the more shumianyu 除 will usually be end marked with 外 wài 1 or a synonym. Use of 都 dōu 1 in Y marks that the X structure has a meaning of 'except X.' When Y has a 还 hái 1 or a synonym, X should be translated as 'besides, in addition to X.' See 除了 chúle 1 for further discussion and examples.

a. 中国是一个多民族国家，除汉族外，还有五十多个少数民族！

Zhōngguó shì yī ge duō mínzú guójiā, chú Hànzú wài, hái yǒu wǔshi duō ge shǎoshù mínzú!

China is a country of many ethnic groups. Besides the Han people, there are over fifty minority nationalities.

除非 chúfēi (— —) 'only if' Conjunction; 'unless' Conjunction

1. **除非 X, Y = When X does take place, (then) Y happens** (Cj) 除非 is one of the set of three words which mark X as a condition required for Y to happen. 除非 specifically marks that Y cannot happen without X (literally 除 'get rid of' the 非 'not' X). X can be a noun phrase (expl a) or a verb phrase (expl b); Y will be a verb phrase or a clause. Y will often be marked with 才 cái 1. 除非 has a heavier tone to it than the synonymous 只有 zhǐyǒu 1, which approaches the situation from the positive side; see that entry for a comparative discussion of this set of markers. Consider also the somewhat synonymous 非 féi 2.

a. 除非老王，才能把这件事办好。

Chúfēi Lǎo Wáng, cái néng bǎ zhèi jiàn shì bàn hǎo.

Only if is it Old Wang can this matter (then and only then) be taken care of.

b. 除非击败上海队，广东排球队才有可能参加今年的锦标赛。
Chúfēi jībài Shànghǎiduì, Guǎngdōng páiqiúduì cái yǒu kěnéng cānjiā jīnnián de jǐnbiāosài.
Only if they defeat the Shanghai team can the Canton volleyball team be in this year's championship.

C

2. 除非 X, Y = Unless X, Y (Cj) In this usage, 除非 marks that X is an exceptional condition that will affect the events that occur in Y. Y will usually contain 否则 fǒuzé 'otherwise, or else' or 不然 bùrán 1 (expl a). The order may be reversed with 除非 appearing in Y without change in meaning (expl b).

a. 藤森曾一再表示，除非有人质受到伤害，否则他不会下令攻击占地广大的日本大使馆官邸。
Téngsēn céng yīzài biǎoshì, chúfēi yǒu rénzhì shòu dào shānghài, fǒuzé tā bù huì xiàlìng gōngjī zhàndì guǎngdà de Rìběn dàshǐguǎn guāndǐ.
Fujimori repeatedly said that unless the hostages were harmed, (otherwise) he would not order an attack on the huge Japanese embassy mansion.

b. 下午他们一定去打棒球，除非下大雨。
Xiàwǔ tāmen yīdìng dǎ bāngqiú, chúfēi xià dà yǔ.
They will definitely play baseball this afternoon, unless there is a big rain.

除了 chúlė (——) 'besides' Coverb; 'except for' Coverb

1.除了X 以外, 还/也/又 Y = In addition to X, also Y (Cj) 除了 marks that X has either an inclusive or exclusive relationship to Y. The clearest clue to knowing which relationship X has actually lies in Y. When Y includes an adverb such as 还 hái 1 (expl a), 也 yě 1 (expl b), and sometimes 就 jiù 1, 除了 marks that X is to be translated as the inclusive 'besides/ in addition to X, also Y' (expls a & b). When there is a 都 dōu 1 in Y, X is to be excluded from the situation given in Y, and the 除了X structure means 'except for X'; see the discussions in 2 and 3 below.

X can be a noun phrase, a verb phrase or a clause; Y will be a verb phrase or a clause. 除了 may appear alone at the head of X, but it is most frequently used in connection with 以外 yǐwài 1 or a synonym to form a 除了X 以外 structure. 除 chú 1 is a more shumianyu synonym; 除开chúkāi and 除去 chúqù are infrequently seen synonyms. 以外 may be written with the more shumianyu synonyms 外 wài 1 or 之外 zhīwài 1 with no overt change in meaning. Either 除了 or 以外 may be omitted with no change in meaning, especially when X is brief, but one or the other must be present.

a. 除了第四课以外，我们还要考第五课。
Chúle dì-sì kè yǐwài, wǒmen hái yào kǎo dì-wǔ kè.
Besides the fourth lesson, we will also have a test on the fifth lesson.

b. 除了生产者以外，消费者也要负担起保护自然资源的责任。
Chúle shēngchǎnzhě yǐwài, xiāofèizhě yě yào fùdān qǐ bǎohù zìrán zīyuán de zérèn.
In addition to the producers, consumers also must take up the responsibility for protecting natural resources.

C

2. 除了 X 以外, 都 Y = Except for X, Y (Cv) Here too 除了 is generally seen in connection with 以外. When Y contains 都 dōu 1 or 全 quán 'entire,' the structure 除了...以外 marks that X is definitely not part of Y, and X should be translated as 'except for' (expls a & b). X can be a noun phrase, a verb phrase or a clause; Y will be a verb phrase or a clause. 除 chú 1 is a more frequently found shumianyu synonym, while 除开 chúkāi and 除去 chúqu are less frequently seen synonyms. 以外 may be written with the more shumianyu 外 wài 1 or 之外 zhīwài 1. Either 除了 or 以外 may be omitted from X, but at least one or the other must be present to mark X as 'excluded (from Y).'

a. 除了章学修以外，我们都去过洛阳。
Chúle Zhāng Xuéxiū yǐwài, wǒmen dōu qùguo Luòyáng.
Except for Zhang Xuexiu, we have all been to Luoyang.

b. 除了极少数人以外，大多数人都认识到我国妇女付出的代价。
Chúle jí shǎoshù rén yǐwài, dà duōshù rén dōu rènshi dào wǒguó fùnǚ fùchū de dàijià.
Except for a minuscule handful of people, everybody recognizes the price the women of our country have paid for us.

3. 除了 X 以外, Y = Besides/Except for X, Y (Cv) The difference between this structure and 1 and 2 above is in the absence of 都/还 adverbs in Y. Translation of X as the inclusive 'besides' or exclusive 'except for' depends on the informational content of Y plus the overall content of the sentence (expl a). However, if the Y verb is negated by a negative adverb such as 不 bù 1 or 没 méi 1, the 除了 X 以外 structure then clearly marks that X is the thing or action not included in the situation and should be translated as 'except for X' (expl b).

a. 进城除了买几件衣服以外，我想顺便看朋友去。
Jìnchéng chúle mǎi jǐjiàn yīfu yǐwài, wǒ xiǎng shùnbiàn kàn péngyou qù.
Besides going into the city to buy some clothing, I thought I'd also take the opportunity to visit some friends.

b. 我下午除了看两三个小时的电视剧以外，没有别的事。
Wǒ xiàwǔ chúle kàn liǎng sān ge xiǎoshí de diànshìjù yǐwài, méiyǒu biéde shì.
Except for watching soap operas for two or three hours in the afternoon, I don't do nothing.

C

从 cóng (從) 'from' Coverb; 'never' Adverb

1. 从 X Vp = Verb from place (Cv) 从 marks X as the point of origin for a verb action. X may be a noun phrase (expls a & b) or a verb phrase (expl c). The X noun phrase may represent a time (expl a), a place (expl b), or occasionally other things. The X verb phrase will be the scope or basis (expl c) for the main verb in the sentence. 从 X is often followed by 到 Y (expls a & c); see 到 dào 2. 由 yóu 1 and the more shumianyu 自 zì 1 are synonyms. For use of 从 in other patterns also see 自从 zìcóng 1, 以来 yǐlái 1, 往 wàng 1 and 起 qǐ 1.

a. 那些工程师从早到晚，忙着修南京长江大桥。
Nèixiē gōngchéngshī cóng zǎo dào wǎn, mángzhe xiū Nánjīng Chángjiāng Dàqiáo.
Those engineers are busy from morning to night working on the Nanjing Bridge.

b. 从这儿往东过三条街就是中央图书馆。
Cóng zhèr wàng dōng guò sān tiáo jiē jiùshì Zhōngyāng Túshūguǎn.
Go east three blocks from here, and that will be The Central Library.

c. 从不明白到比较了解到完全理解是学习的自然过程。
Cóng bù míngbai dào bǐjiào liǎojiě dào wánquán lǐjiě shì xuéxí de zìrán guòchéng.
Going from not being clear, to somewhat understanding, to completely comprehending are natural stages in learning.

2. 从 Negative verb = Never verbed (Av) 从 is a shumianyu word used with negative adverbs to mark that beginning with a point in the past and continuing right up to the present, the verb situation has never occurred. Which negative adverb occurs makes a difference; when used with 不 bù 1, 从 marks that the verb action did not exist in the past, that the non-existence has continued right up to the present, and suggests that the non-existence of the verb action may continue (expl a). Compare this to use with 没 méi 1 or 未 wèi 1 which mark that the verb never ever occurred (expl b). The verb phrase used with 从 is always disyllabic in structure. 从来 cónglái 1 is an oral synonym used with both negative and positive verb structures.

a. 梅副部长很慎重，从不轻易发表意见。
Méi fùbùzhǎng hěn shènzhòng, cóng bù qīngyì fābiǎo yìjiàn.
Vice Minister Mei is very discrete. He never casually expresses his opinions.

b. 陆大夫工作认真负责，动手术从未出过事故。
Lù dàifu gōngzuò rènzhēn fùzé, dòng shǒushù cóng wèi chūguo shìgù.
Dr. Lu's work is conscientious and responsible. She has never made an error during an operation.

从而 cóngér (從 —) 'thus, thereby' Conjunction

1. X,从而 Y = X, thus Y (Cj) The shumianyu 从而 is a member of the set of words placed at the head of Y to show it is a result of an X cause. Specifically, 从而 marks both that Y is a further development of the X situation and that Y is the result of the X cause or condition (expl a). 进而 jìn'ér 1 is a close synonym which marks only that Y is development of X. See 所以 suǒyǐ 1 for further discussion of this set of cause and result markers.

C

a. 经过多年的摸索，终于找到了麻风病的病因，从而为彻底战胜这种疾病创造了条件。
   Jīngguò duōnián de mōsuo, zhōngyú zhǎodàole máfēngbìng de bìngyīn, cóngér wèi chèdǐ zhànshèng zhèi zhǒng jíbìng chuàngzàole tiáojiàn.
   After many years of trial and error, they finally found the cause of leprosy and thereby created the conditions for thoroughly defeating this illness.

从来 cónglái (從來) 'never/always' Adverb

1. 从来 Negative Vp = Never verb (Av) 从来 is mostly used before negative verb phrases to mark the past non-occurrence of a verb situation. When used with 没 méi 1 or 没有 méiyǒu 1, 从来 marks that starting from a point in the past and going right up to the present a verb phrase situation never happened; 过 guo 1 usually appears with 从来没 Verb, especially when the verb is monosyllabic (expl a). When used with 不 bù 1, 从来 marks a condition which started in the past, has continued to the present, and suggests that it may continue into the future (expl b).

While usually associated with negative sentences, 从来 can also be used with affirmative verb structures to mark that the verb condition has always been thus, and remains so right up to the present (expl c). In affirmative sentences, there is often a reinforcing 都 dōu 1 heading the core verb phrase (expl c). 从 cóng 2 is a more shumianyu synonym used only with 不 bù 1, 没 méi 1 or 未 wèi 1 in multi-syllabic negative verb phrases. 向来 xiànglái 1 is a milder toned synonym of 从来 used mainly in positive verb situations. 历来 lìlái 1 is a lighter toned shumianyu synonym used only in positive sentences. See 以来 yǐlái 1 for a set of structures which mark the length of time prior to the occurrence of a verb situation.

a. 她说他从来没吸过烟。
   Tā shuō tā cónglái méi xīguo yān.
   She said he has never smoked.

b. 岳教练尽管得到过一些奖品，但从来不骄傲。
   Yuè jiàoliàn jǐnguǎn dédàoguo yīxiē jiǎngpǐn, dàn cónglái bù jiāo'ào.
   Even though Coach Yue has received some awards, he has never been conceited.

c. 我跟小施赛跑从来都要输的。
   Wǒ gēn Xiǎo Shī sàipǎo cónglái dōu yào shū de.
   I have always lost to Little Shi when we race!

D

但 <u>dàn</u> (—) 'however, but, still' Conjunction

1. <u>X, 但 Y</u> = <u>X, however Y</u> (Cj) <u>但</u> is a shumianyu member of the set of conjunctions which mark <u>Y</u> as a turn in the course of events which either limits (expl a) or supplements (expls b & c) the information stated in <u>X</u>. <u>Y</u> will be either a verb phrase or a clause, and it is the focal point of the sentence. <u>X</u> will often contain a marker such as <u>虽 suī</u> 1, <u>既 jì</u> 1, etc. which makes clearer the inter-relationship of information in <u>X</u> and <u>Y</u>. <u>Y</u> will often have <u>也 yě</u> 1, <u>还 hái</u> 1, etc. <u>但</u> tends to be used instead of its synonym <u>但是 dànshì</u> 1 when the sentence is short (expl a) or when <u>Y</u> already has a <u>是 shì</u> in it (expl b). <u>但</u> can also join two parallel words or phrases in a descriptive structure (expl c). See <u>但是</u> for discussion of the various synonyms in this set of "turn of events" markers. Note that as an adverb, 但 is used as the equivalent of 'only, barely.'

a. 汪教授喜欢看字画，<u>但</u>不想藏字画。
Wāng jiàoshòu xǐhuan kàn zìhuà, <u>dàn</u> bù xiǎng cáng zìhuà.
Professor Wang likes to look at scrolls, <u>but</u> he doesn't plan to collect them.

b. 虽然他家有个游泳池，<u>但</u>他还是愿意到河里去游泳。
Suīrán tā jiā yǒu ge yóuyǒngchí, <u>dàn</u> tā háishi yuànyi dào hé li qù yóuyǒng.
Although he has a swimming pool at home, (<u>but</u>) he is still willing to swim in the river.

c. 小冯是一个只有书本知识<u>但</u>还没有接触实际的人。
Xiǎo Féng shì yī ge zhǐyǒu shūběn zhīshì <u>dàn</u> hái méiyǒu jiēchù shíjì de rén.
Little Feng is a person who has book knowledge <u>but</u> who has never come in contact with reality.

当 <u>dāng</u> (當) "time and location marker" Coverb

1. <u>当 X Verb</u> = <u>Verb precisely at X</u> (Cv) <u>当</u> is a shumianyu member of the small set of words that mark the particular time or place that a verb action takes place. When <u>X</u> represents a time, <u>当</u> must be used either in combination with <u>的时候 de shíhou</u> 1, <u>之前 zhīqián</u> 1, <u>之后 zhīhòu</u> 1, etc. to form a relative time clause (expl a), or it must be used with a time phrase (expl b). <u>当</u> is never used with an unmodified time word; e.g., *<u>当</u>1990年 *<u>dāng</u> yī jiǔ jiǔ líng nián is wrong. <u>当</u> is also used with a limited number of monosyllabic names of locations, primarily 面 miàn but also 头 tóu, 场 chǎng, etc., to mark that the subject does the verb act in face to face contact with someone, not behind the back (expl c). When marking place, <u>当</u> is not used with place end-markers such as 上 shàng, 前 qián, 后 hòu, etc., so *<u>当</u>我的面前说 <u>dāng</u> wǒ de miànqián shuō is incorrect (see expl c). The ongoing verb action markers <u>着 zhe</u> 1 and <u>正 zhèng</u> 1 are often part of a <u>当</u> structure (expl c).

<u>在 zài</u> 1 is a more widely used synonym whose usage restrictions for marking

place and time are the reverse of those for 当. Consider also the shumianyu location marker 于 yú 1. 当 dāng also appears in words centered on the idea of 'ought to, must; equal; serve as; manage,' etc. Distinguish this from 当 dàng which is used in words for meanings such as 'proper; regard as; to pawn.'

a. 当小邢看到榜上有他名字的时候，他心里是多么高兴，多么激动啊！
Dāng Xiǎo Xíng kàndào bāngshang yǒu tā de míngzì de shíhou, tā xīnli shì duōme gāoxìng, duōme jīdòng a!
When Little Xing saw his name on the list, he was so happy, so pumped up!

b. 当他考上研究所的那一年，他姐姐从瑞典回来了。
Dāng tā kǎoshàng yánjiūsuǒ de nà yī nián, tā jiějie cóng Ruìdiǎn huílái le.
That year he got into graduate school his older sister returned from Sweden.

c. 请你当着大家的面把昨天发生的那件事情解释清楚。
Qǐng nǐ dāng dàjiā de miàn bǎ zuótiān fāsheng de nèi jiàn shìqing jiěshì qīngchu.
Please explain in front of everybody exactly what happened yesterday.

D

但是 dànshì (——) 'however, but, still' Conjunction

1. X, 但是 Y = X, nevertheless Y (Cj) 但是 is a member of the set of conjunctions which mark that the information in Y is a change of direction from the flow of information given in X. 但是 specifically marks that Y either sharply contradicts (expl a & c) or qualifies (expl b) the situation articulated in X. Y is the focal point of the sentence. X and Y can both be either a verb phrase or a clause. X will frequently be headed with markers such as 虽然 suīrán 1 or 尽管 jǐnguǎn 1, so when you see one of them expect 但是 or a synonymous member of this set of contrastive conjunctions to head Y. Y will also often have a reinforcing adverb such as 却 què 1, 也 yě 1, 仍然 réngrán 1, etc. which bring their particular values to the sentence. 但是 is also occasionally used at the head of a sentence to mark that it limits or supplements information given earlier in the discourse. Note that 但是 can be also used to link two words or phrases in a descriptive structure (expl c).

Other members of this set of contrastive conjunctions are 不过 bùguò 1 which gives a more tactful and lighter tone of voice to the change which Y represents; 只是 zhǐshì 1 which gives an even lighter tone to Y; and the oral synonym 可是 kěshì 1 which suggests Y is in contrast to X. 但 dàn 1, 然 rán 1, 然而 rán'ér 1, 而 ér 1, and 可 kě 1 are more strongly shumianyu members of the set. See also 却 què 1 and the weaker 则 zé 2 for shumianyu adverbs which mark specific types of change from X to Y.

a. 他虽然已经八十多岁了，但是身体还很硬朗。
Tā suīrán yǐjing bāshi duō suì le, dànshì shēntǐ hái hěn yìnglǎng.

Although he is already over 80, he is <u>nevertheless</u> still hale and hearty.

b. 八十年代以来，我们已经培养了不少科技人员，<u>但是</u>还不能满足四个现代化的实际需要。

Bāshi niándài yǐlái, wǒmen yǐjing péiyǎngle bùshǎo kējì rényuán, <u>dànshì</u> hái bù néng mǎnzú Sì ge Xiàndàihuà de shíjì xūyào.

Since the 80's we have trained quite a few science and technology personnel, <u>but</u> we are still unable to fulfill the real needs of the Four Modernizations.

D

c. 在昨天的座谈会上，他作了一个简短的<u>但是</u>很有说服力的发言。

Zài zuótiān de zuòtánhuì shang, tā zuòle yī ge jiǎnduǎn de <u>dànshì</u> hěn yǒu shuōfúlì de fāyán.

At yesterday's symposium he made a brief <u>but</u> persuasive talk.

到 <u>dào</u>(一) 'arrive at, get to' Verb; 'towards, to' Coverb; 'achieve, complete (a verb action)' Complement

1. <u>到 X</u> = <u>Arrive at X</u> (Vb) When representing the concept 'go to, arrive at,' <u>到</u> can take the adverbs <u>没</u> <u>méi</u> 1 (expl a), <u>也</u> <u>yě</u> 1, <u>都</u> dōu 1, etc., and suffixes such as <u>了</u> <u>le</u> 1, <u>过</u> <u>guo</u> 1, etc. that other verbs do; this can help you distinguish this usage from the others described below. <u>X</u> may be a place (expl a), a point in time (expl b) or, rarely, a numerical amount.

a. 我没<u>到</u>过延安，你呢？

Wǒ méi <u>dào</u>guo Yán'ān, nǐ ne?

I have never gone to Yan'an. How about you?

b. 我们休息吧，<u>到</u>八点再开会。

Wǒmen xiūxi ba, <u>dào</u> bā diǎn zài kāihuì.

Let's take a break. We will meet again at 8:00.

2. <u>到 X</u> = <u>Towards X</u> (Cv) When <u>到</u> is followed by a place name and the verb 来 lái 'come' or 去 qù 'go,' it marks actual physical movement towards a place (expls a & b). In this it is partially synonymous with <u>往</u> <u>wàng</u> 1, though <u>到</u> is not used with the names of directions. Distinguish this usage from the other set of "towards" markers that mark stationary facing towards rather than actual movement; see the discussion at <u>朝</u> <u>cháo</u> 1. <u>到</u> can also be used with time expressions (expl c). <u>到</u> is very often used in the structure <u>从 (X) 到 (Y) (来/去)</u> in which <u>X</u> and <u>Y</u> will usually both be places (expl b) or times (expl c), but they may be any kind of parallel concepts (expl d); see <u>从</u> <u>cóng</u> 1 for further examples. <u>至</u> <u>zhì</u> 1 is a relatively infrequently seen shumianyu synonym of <u>到</u>.

a. 他们几点钟<u>到</u>国父纪念馆来？

Tāmen jǐ diǎn zhōng <u>dào</u> Guófù Jìniànguǎn lái?

When will they come <u>to</u> the Sun Yatsen Memorial?

b. 吴老师是上星期五从台北<u>到</u>香港去的。

Wú lǎoshī shì shàng xīngqīwǔ cóng Táiběi dào Xiānggǎng qù de.
Professor Wu went from Taipei to Hong Kong last Friday.

c. 我们班每天从十点二十分到十一点二十分上中文课。
Wǒmen bān měitiān cóng shídiǎn èrshi fēn dào shíyī diǎn èrshi fēn shàng Zhōngwén kè.
We have Chinese class everyday from 10:20 to 11:20.

D

d. 从无到有。
Cóng wú dào yǒu.
Grow from nothing to something.

3. Verb 到 = Verb to the point of (Cp) In this usage, 到 marks that the verb action has reached a goal (expl a), a conclusion (expl b), or a magnitude (expl c). When the object is a place, 来 or 去 may follow it. When the object is a time phrase, it marks that the verb action continues until that time; see 止 zhǐ 1 for further comments and examples of this usage. When 到 follows a Stative verb, it marks that the Sv reaches a certain degree (expl c). As a verb complement, 到 is helpful in locating the main verb, even in very complex sentences, since 到 comes right after the verb.

a. 春季的成绩单已经寄到学生家里去了。
Chūnjì de chéngjīdān yǐjīng jìdào xuésheng jiāli qù le.
The spring semester grades have already been mailed to the students' homes.

b. 你昨天要的那本中国经济史稿，我已经买到了。
Nǐ zuótiān yào de nèi běn Zhōngguó Jīngji Shǐgǎo, wǒ yǐjīng mǎidào le.
I have already bought that book on China's economic history you were looking for yesterday.

c. 冬天黑龙江可以冷到零下三十度。
Dōngtiān Hēilóngjiāng kěyǐ lěngdào língxià sānshi dù.
In the winter Heilongjiang can get as cold as 30 degrees below zero.

倒 dào (一) 'but, however' Adverb

1. 倒 Verb phrase = However, verb phrase (Av) Extending from its basic verbal meaning of 'upside down,' the oral adverb 倒 marks a condition which is contrary to what might be normally expected (expl a). When marking a sharp change of perceptions, 倒 is always followed by a positive comment (expl b). 倒 is also used to mark concessions or a softening of tone in both positive and negative statements (expl c). 倒 can also mark an urging tone. Be careful to distinguish these usages from the verb 倒 dǎo 'topple, fall.'

倒是 dàoshì 1 is an oral synonym used in the same ways that 倒 is. 并 bìng 2 is a shumianyu synonym which differs from 倒 by marking that Y is a correction of the expectations aroused by the immediately preceding text in X, whether or not they would normally be expected. See 却 què 1 for a discussion of this set of markers.

a. 多年的老朋友，他倒跟我客气起来了。
Duō nián de lǎo péngyou, tā dào gēn wǒ kèqi qǐlái le.
We are really old friends, but he has gotten formal with me.

b. 剧场虽小，布置得倒很雅致。
Jùchǎng suī xiǎo, bùzhì de dào hěn yǎzhì.
Although the theater is smallish, it is arranged quite tastefully.

c. 我倒不反对这么办，只是说要考虑周到一点。
Wǒ dào bù fǎnduì zhème bàn, zhǐshì shuō yào kǎolǜ zhōudào yīdiǎn.
But I don't actually oppose doing it this way, I just mean that it should be a bit more carefully thought out.

倒是 dàoshì (— —) 'but, yet' Adverb

1. 倒是 Verb phrase = Actually verb (Av) 倒是 is an oral adverb which marks a condition that is contrary to what might be normally expected from earlier information; this condition may involve a change of perception, concession or a softening of tone (expl a). 倒 dào 1 is an oral synonym with the same usage features. 并 bìng 2 is a shumianyu synonym which differs from 倒是 by negatively correcting the expectations aroused by immediately preceding information. See 却 què 1 for further comment and examples about this set of "however" markers.

a. 芝加哥市图书馆的中文书不多，倒是有很多法语书。
Zhījiāgē Shì Túshūguǎn de Zhōngwén shū bù duō, dàoshì yǒu hěn duō Fǎyǔ shū.
The Chicago Public Library does not have many Chinese books; however, it has many French books.

地 dė (—) "adverbial usage marker" Structural marker

1. X 地 Verb phrase = adverbially verb (Sm) 地 marks that X is being used as an adverb that modifies the following verb. The focus in an X 地 Vp pattern is on describing the subject's outward behavior in doing a verb action, and there is often a subjective element to the description. Compare this with V/Sv 得 X where the focus is on the manner of doing the verb as expressed in X.

X will usually be something that is not itself an adverb. It will most often be constructed with a disyllabic Stative verb (expl a & b), though it can also be formed with a verb (expl c) or a verb phrase (expls d & f). Occasionally X may be structured with one of a handful of abstract nouns (expl e) or with a four character structure such as 自言自语 zì yán zì yǔ 'think aloud' or 一步一步 yī bù yī bù 'step by step.' Rarely, 地 marks

D

modification of a following Stative verb (expl f). Note that X 地 does not always translate directly into an English adverb (expls a & d).

Awareness that 地 is used to mark adverbial structures is very helpful for finding the core verb in a sentence; the core verb will always come immediately after the 地. Do however keep in mind that the character 地 is also used in a great many words having to do with 'earth; land; floor; place,' etc. Be careful, even though 地 is pronounced dì in these words, 地 is always pronounced de when used as an adverbial marker.

To be clear about what may or may not be an adverb, it is important to be aware that the adverb usage marker 地 is not usually used with words which are inherently adverbs; e.g., 已经 yǐjīng 1, 都 dōu 1, 刚 gāng 'just now,' etc. Also, 地 is not generally used to mark adverbial structures formed with monosyllabic Stative verbs; e.g., 快 kuài 'fast,' 少 shǎo 'few,' etc., or those made with demonstrative pronouns such as 这样 zhèiyàng 'thus,' 那么 nàme 'so,' etc. 地 usage is optional with reduplicated Stative verb adverbial structures such as 慢慢 mànmān 'slowly' or 高高兴兴 gāogāo-xingxìng 'happily.' 地 is also optional with onomatopoeic words and some conceptually close knit disyllabic Sv-Vp structures such as 详细查问 xiángxì cháwèn 'carefully interrogate.'

It is over the last 50-75 years that the practice of using 的 de 1, 得 de 1 and 地 to distinguish between the various values represented by the sound de has become established in Chinese prose. See 的 de 1 for a comparative discussion of the usage parameters of each of these three structural markers.

a. 二弟疲倦地闭上了眼睛，靠在土炕上。
Èrdì píjuàn de bìshàngle yǎnjīng, kào zài tǔkàng shang.
Younger brother closed his eyes in exhaustion and leaned on the kang.

b. 俄罗斯联邦委员会主席愉快地接受了访问中国的邀请。
Éluósī Liánbāng Wěiyuánhuì zhǔxí yúkuài de jiēshòule fǎngwèn Zhōngguó de yāoqǐng.
The Chair of the Russian Federation Council happily accepted the invitation to visit China.

c. 昨天雨不停地下，不能去放风筝。
Zuótiān yǔ bù tíng de xià, bù néng qù fàng fēngzheng.
It rained incessantly yesterday, and we couldn't fly kites.

d. 贵州从"七五"期间就开始……在全省范围内有组织、有领导、有计划地开展大规模农村使用技术培训工作。
Guìzhōu cóng "Qī Wǔ" qījiān jiù kāishī...zài quánshěng fànwéi nèi yǒu zǔzhī, yǒu lǐngdǎo, yǒu jìhuà de kāizhǎn dà guīmó nóngcūn shǐyòng jìshù péixùn gōngzuò.
Starting with the "7th 5 Year Plan" Guizhou began...to develop on a large scale rural training in the use of technology throughout the whole province in a way that had organization, leadership and planning.

e. 我们得创造性地解决校长上星期提出的那些问题。
Wǒmen děi chuàngzàoxìng de jiějué xiàozhǎng shàngxīngqī tíchū de nèixiē wèntí.

We must creatively solve the problems the President posed last week.

f. 我今天说不出地高兴，我中了爱国奖。
Wǒ jīntiān shuō bu chū de gāoxing, wǒ zhòngle Àiguójiǎng.
I am so happy that I can't even talk today. I hit the national lottery.

D

的 dė (一) "noun modification" Structural marker; "affirmation" Structural marker; "emphasis" Structural marker; "passive" Structural marker

1. X 的 Noun = X describes the following noun (Sm) The primary grammatical function of 的 is to mark that the noun following the 的 is described by the information before the 的. This modification can literally have any kind of grammatical structure ranging from something as simple as a single noun (expls a & second 的 in c) or Stative verb (expl b), to the very complex (expls c, d, e, & f). The modified noun will most often be the subject (expl a, c, e f, & g) or object (expl b, c, d, f & g) of a structure, but you will also find modified place structures (expls e & f).

Because 的 noun modification structures can be impressively complex, because 的 is used in four other common patterns, and because 的 is the single most frequently used Chinese character, understanding 的 is very important to your ability to read Chinese. The following analyses of the complex noun description structures to be found in the examples given on pages 40-41 may be helpful models of the processing you will sometimes have to do to read modern Chinese prose; e.g., modification before the first 的 in expl c has the structure Av V T Cj Av V O 的 Subject and expl d has Av Cv V O 的 Object. Some sentences will have two or more complex modification structures; e.g., expl e has both P Cv S V 的 Subject and Av V 的 T 的 Place structures, and expl f has Cv V O Av V O Cv S V O 的 Subject followed immediately by 在 P V T O 的 Place. Always focus on the 的 in a Chinese text.

Although scholars often regard 的 in certain contexts as marking a possessive relationship between the descriptor and the described; e.g., 我的哥哥 wǒ de gēge 'my (older) brother,' you may find it simpler and cleaner to understand this 的 as also marking description.

Note that the hyper-busy 的 is also used as part of some vocabulary items; e.g., 有的 yǒude 'some,' 要饭的 yàofànde 'beggar,' 的确 díquè 'really,' 目的 mùdì 'goal, purpose,' etc.

There are some noun description structures in which 的 is not used. Some of the more common and important instances are 1) 的 is not used in specialized terms; e.g., 工业城市 gōngyè chéngshì rather than *工业的城市 for 'industrial city,' 急救车 jíjiùchē rather than *急救的车 for 'emergency vehicle,' etc.; 2) 的 is optional when the modifying element is one syllable long. When it is used with one syllable of description, the 的 suggests emphasis on the descriptive element; e.g. 这是个新问题：旧的问题解决了，又会出现新的问题 Zhè shì ge xīn wèntí: jiù de wèntí jiějuéle, yòu huì chūxiàn xīn de wèntí 'This is a new problem; as the old problems are solved, there appear new problems'; 3) when the descriptive structure is two or more syllables in length, 的 is generally used, except when the description and the described are frequently used together; e.g., 我们学校 wǒmen xuéxiào 'our school,' 先进单位 xiānjìn dānwèi 'advanced unit,' etc. 4) when several 的 could appear in a modification string, one or more is often deleted for metrical reasons; e.g., 被捕的侦探的方案的主要的内容 becomes 被捕侦探方案的主要内容 bèi bǔ zhēntàn fāng'àn de zhǔyào nèiróng 'the essentials in the case of the arrested spies.' 5) 的 is never used after a number-measure structure, the logic being that this speaks of an amount, not of description; e.g.,*一条的裙子 would not occur.

D

之 zhī 1 is a very shumianyu synonym of 的 used in modern prose mostly to mark noun modification. However, as markers of noun modification, 之 and 的 do have some usage differences: see 之 zhī 1 for further comments and examples. The variant form 底 de 1 found in texts written soon after the May 4th Movement (1919) started is no longer used.

Prior to this century there were no written distinctions that showed the separate functions of the oral de to mark noun, adverbs, or verb manner modification. Since the May 4th Movement, there has grown an acceptance that the character 的 should be used to mark noun description along with the other uses described below in this entry, 得 de should mark manner and potential in verb actions, and 地 de should mark adverbial usages. See 得 de 1, 2 & 3 and 地 de 1 for discussion and examples of their specific features. However, keep in mind that some Republican writers do not make these distinctions but rather use 的 for all three values. For example, the second 的 in expl g comes between the adverb 顯著 and the verb 展示 that it modifies; 地 de would be used by many other writers.

a. 早晨的空气很新鲜。
Zǎochén de kōngqì hěn xīnxiān.
The morning air is quite fresh.

b. 那是一本很好的汉英词典。
Nà shì yī běn hěn hǎo de Hàn-Yīng cídiǎn.
That is a very good Chinese-English dictionary.

c. 已经实施10年并已取得丰硕成果的中国高技术研究发展计划(即 "863计划")吹响了决战的号角。
Yǐjīng shíshī 10 nián bìng yǐ qǔdé fēngshuò chéngguǒ de Zhōngguó Gāojìshù Yánjiū Fāzhǎn Jìhuà (jí "863 Jìhuà") chuīxiǎngle juézhàn de hàojiǎo.
China's High Technology Research Development Plan (i.e., Plan #863) that has been in effect for 10 years and achieved brilliant results sounded the bugle for the decisive battle.

d. 歌仔剧是最能代表台湾文化<u>的</u>民间歌曲。
Gēzǎijù shi zuì néng dàibiǎo Táiwān wénhuà <u>de</u> mínjiān gēqǔ.
The Gezai Theater are the folks songs <u>which</u> are best able to represent Taiwanese culture.

e. 此间由「华盛顿时报」发行<u>的</u>「政治内幕」杂志，在其最新出版<u>的</u>五月号一期<u>的</u>封面故事中，披露中共……
Cǐjiān yóu "Huáshèngdùn Shíbào" fāxíng <u>de</u> "Zhèngzhì Nèimù" zázhì, zài qí zuìxīn chūbǎn <u>de</u> wǔyuèhào yīqī <u>de</u> fēngmiàn gùshi zhōng, pīlù Zhōnggòng...
In the cover story <u>of</u> the recently published May issue #1 of "Insights" magazine that is published by "The Washington Times," it is revealed that the Chinese communists...

f. 观察家指出，自事发后即一再敦促藤森以和平手段解决危机<u>的</u>日本当局在这场持续长达十八周<u>的</u>危机中一直落居次要角色。。。
Guānchájiā zhǐchū, zì shì fā hòu jí yīzài dūncù Téngsēn yǐ hépíng shǒuduàn jiějué wēijī <u>de</u> Rìběn dāngjú zài zhèi chǎng chíxù chángdá shíbā zhōu <u>de</u> wēijī zhōng yīzhí luòjū cìyào juésè...
Observers point out that the Japanese authorities <u>who</u> had repeatedly pressed Fujimori to settle the crisis through peaceful means ever since it had occurred had steadily fallen to a secondary role in this crisis <u>that</u> had reached 18 weeks...

g. 美國國防部長柯恩說，美國在亞太地區的駐軍顯著<u>的</u>展示了美國對這個地區所作的承諾，嚇阻潛在敵對國家的侵略，並……
Měiguó Guófáng bùzhǎng Kē'ēn shuō, Měiguó zài Yàtài dìqū de zhùjūn xiǎnzhù <u>de</u> zhǎnshìle Měiguó duì zhèi ge dìqū suǒ zuò de chéngnuò, hèzǔ qiánzài díduì guójiā de qīnlüè, bìng..
The US Secretary of Defense Cohen said, "The American military forces stationed in the Asian-Pacific area clear<u>ly</u> demonstrated that the promises America made to this area have deterred aggression by possibly hostile nations. Moreover,..."

2. <u>X 的 (Noun)</u> = <u>X describes an omitted noun</u> (Sm) In this usage <u>的</u> also marks noun description; however, the noun itself is not overtly given in the text. The noun that is left out may be either the subject (expls a & b) or object (expl c) of the sentence. When the omitted noun is the subject of the sentence, it is easier to recognize the deleted noun structure since the <u>的</u> will be towards the head or middle of the sentence and will be directly followed by the Verb phrase. Note that you will sometimes find a comma separating the <u>X 的 (subject)</u> from the verb (expl b).

When the deleted noun is the object and at the end of the sentence, it can be hard to be sure whether you are looking at this <u>X 的 (noun)</u> usage or the end <u>的</u> from the patterns <u>S (是) T P V O 的</u>, <u>O 是 S V 的</u>, and <u>S 是 V 的</u> mentioned in #4, 5 and 6 below; however, careful examination of what comes between the <u>是</u> and the <u>的</u> will usually clarify the situation. See <u>是...的</u> 1, 2 & 3 for further comments and examples on how to tell the different patterns apart. Consider also the comments made in the discussion of the "end of the sentence 的" discussed in 3 below. Note that when there is no 是 in the S (是) T P V O 的, recognition can be more difficult. The modification of the omitted noun can run the gamut of structural patterns: it may be simple (expl b) or complex (expl a).

D

Sub-categories of "deleted noun 的" are found in 1) the words formed by this process; e.g., 要饭的 yàofànde 'beggar,' 当家的 dāngjiāde 'head of a family.' 卖报的 màibàode 'newspaper seller,' and 2) V的 V structures such as 拉的拉 lā de lā 'those who pull pull' or 粗的粗 cū de cū 'the coarse ones are coarse.' Slightly differently, when used at the end of a list of nouns or actions, 的 means 'etc.' (expl d).

a. 今天在游泳池游泳的都是我们学院的学生。
   Jīntiān zài yóuyǒngchí yóuyǒng de dōu shi wǒmen xuéyuàn de xuésheng.
   Those swimming in the pool today are all students from our school.

b. 令我印象深刻的，是公司非常強調員工發揮個人的技能。
   Lìng wǒ yìnxiàng shēnkè de, shi gōngsī fēicháng qiángdiào yuángōng fāhuī gèrén de jìnéng.
   What impressed me the most was(,) that the company highly emphasized that the workers bring into play their individual skills.

c. 美国人多半不喜欢吃酸的，喜欢吃甜的。
   Měiguórén duōbàn bù xǐhuan chī suān de, xǐhuan chī tián de.
   For the most part Americans do not like to eat sour things, they like to eat sweets.

d. 这屋子象个仓库，桌椅板凳的，什么都有。
   Zhèi wūzi xiàng ge cāngkù, zhuō yǐ bǎndēng de, shénme dōu yǒu.
   This room is like a warehouse. It has tables, chairs, benches, whatever.

3. Declarative sentence 的 = Definitely declarative sentence (Sm) When placed at the end of a declarative sentence, 的 marks strong affirmation of it. The declarative sentence may be either positive (expl a) or negative (expl b). This usage may be distinguished from the 的 which marks emphasis, passive, and past action summarized in #4, 5 and 6 below by the absence of 是 along with the overall declarative tone to the sentence. 的 also appears after the Sv in some (V) (O) V 得 Sv structures to mark vividness (expl c).

a. 大夫一会儿会来的，你不要着急。
   Dàifu yīhuìr huì lái de, nǐ bù yào zháojí.
   The doctor will be here in a bit. Don't be impatient.

b. 我永远不会忘记你的。
   Wǒ yǒngyuǎn bù huì wàngjì nǐ de.
   I will never ever forget you.

c. 有些美国人喜欢晒得黑黝黝的。
   Yǒuxiē Měiguórén xǐhuan shài de hēiyōuyōu de.
   Some Americans like to get deep, dark tans.

4. S (是) T P Vp 的 = The subject verbed (an object) at a particular time/ place/ circumstance (Sm) This usage focuses attention on the time, place and/or circumstances

of a past verb action. See 是...的 shì...de 1 for discussion and examples.
5. Object 是 Subject Verb 的 = The object was verbed by the subject (Sm) This pattern conveys the idea that the verb act is in the past, the voice passive, and the object definite. See 是...的 shì...de 3 for discussion and examples.
6. Subject 是 Verb 的 = stresses that the subject does the verb (Sm) This pattern marks emphasis on the subject as the one who does the verb action. See 是...的 shì...de 4 for comments and example sentences.

D

底 dė "description marker" Structural marker

1. Noun 1 底 Noun 2 = Noun **1 modifies noun 2** (Sm) 底 was used in the early May Fourth period to mark a possessive or hierarchical relationship between noun one and noun two. It is no longer used, 的 dė 1 has replaced it.

a. 作家底感情
zuòjiā de gǎnqíng
a writer's emotions

得 dė (—) "manner of verb action" Structural marker; "verb potential" Structural marker

1. Vp/Sv 得 X = Verb act/Stative verb condition in an X way (Sm) 得 is placed between the core verb and X to mark the manner (expls a, d & e) or result (expls b, c & f) of the core verb action or Stative verb condition. The purpose of the Verb/Sv 得 X pattern is to place focus on the X manner or result of the core verb action; compare this with X 地 Vp which marks (subjective) description of the behavior of the subject in doing the core verb action. Both are most often translated into English with an adverb, but their focal points differ. 得 is generally used with past events (expls a, c, d, and f) or frequently occuring verb actions (expls b & e). X may be as simple as a Stative verb (expls a & e) or just 很 hěn 'very' (expl b). X can be a disyllabic or longer verb phrase (expls c & d), or X can be a S Vp structure (expl f). When the core verb phrase includes an object, the structure is usually V O V 得 Sv/Vp (expl d), though O V 得 Sv/Vp is also used to place emphasis on the object (expl a). Note that the negative form is created by placing the negative adverb after the 得, not before the core verb (expl e).

Recognizing how 得 is used can be very helpful in finding the core verb of a sentence. However, since 得 can be read either de, dé or děi and have very different values with each reading, precise and reliable understanding of a text relies upon your being able to analyze context and determine which 得 is before you. When 得 is used in the Vp/Sv 得 X structure to focus attention on the condition or result of the verb and when it occurs in the Verb 得 result potential structure described in #2 as well as in the

Verb 得 potential structure described below in #3 to mark that a verb act can be done, it is the de described in this entry. When a verb follows it, 得 is read děi and means 'must verb.' When it is used in 不得不 Verb 'have no choice but to verb' 得 is read dé; when a noun follows 得, it is a verb to be read dé and means 'obtain the noun.' (Notice that when a noun follows 得到, 得到 Noun is read dédào 'get the noun'; when a place name follows 得到, 得到 Place is děi dao 'must go to the place.') 得 is also used for all three readings in various vocabulary items: e.g., 获得 huòdé 'obtain,' 记得 jìde 'remember,' and 必得 bìděi 'must.' The values 得 represents are exceptionally context sensitive, but if you keep this discussion in mind, 得 can be a very useful tool when reading modern Chinese prose.

D

Over the last 50-75 years the practice of using 的 de, 地 de, and this 得 to distinguish between the various values represented by the sound de has become established in Chinese prose. However, keep in mind that there are still some writers who simply use 的 rather than 得 in all of the usages described in this entry. See 的 de 1 for a comparative discussion of the usage parameters of each of these structural markers.

Examples of "manner" 得 are:

a. 爸爸中国民歌唱得非常好。
Bàba Zhōngguó míngē chàng de fēicháng hǎo.
Dad sings Chinese folk songs super well.

b. 梅老师的书多得很！
Méi lǎoshī de shū duō de hěn!
Professor Mei has a ton of books.

c. 是的，时下的电话购物可以说是方便得令主妇们笑逐颜开。
Shìde, shíxià de diànhuà gòuwù kěyǐ shuō shì fāngbiàn de lìng zhǔfùmen xiào zhú yán kāi.
Right, you can say that buying things over the telephone is so convenient that it makes housewives beam with joy.

d. 小黄看史记看得入了迷。
Xiào Huáng kàn **Shǐjì** kàn de rù le mí.
Huang read the "Historical Records" and was enchanted.

e. 大姐每天起得不早。
Dàjiě měitiān qǐ de bù zǎo.
My older sister gets up late everyday.

f. 今天中午热得我直出汗。
Jīntiān zhōngwǔ rè de wǒ zhí chūhàn.
At noon it was so hot I kept on sweating.

2. V 得 complement of result = Able to verb (Sm) When 得 is placed between a verb and a complement of result such as 见 jiàn 'see,' 懂 dǒng 'understand,' 出 chū 'out,' etc., 得 marks that the subject is able to do the verb act. The verb may be either one or two syllables long and the complement may also have either one or two syllables, so a potential verb structure may be from three (expl a) to five syllables in length (expl c). The object in the verb phrase, if any, comes after the complement (expls b & d). The negative is formed by placing 不 bù 3 between the verb and the complement (expl d and end of expl a). Remember to translate this structure as "can/able to verb" or "can't/ unable to verb."

D

Note: there are a few idiomatic vocabulary items which have been generated by this structure. With some of these words, either 得 or 不 bù 3 and not the other must be used; e.g., 跟他过不去 gēn tā guò bu qù 'be hard on him,' there is no *跟他过得去. With other items, when 得 is used instead of 不, or vice versa, the meaning changes; e.g., 对不起 duìbuqǐ 'be sorry' v.v. 对得起 duìdeqǐ 'treat somebody fairly.' Learn these words as you encounter them.

a. 我说个谜语给你听，看你猜得着猜不着。
Wǒ shuō ge míyǔ gěi nǐ tīng, kàn nǐ cāi de zháo cāi bu zháo.
I will tell you a riddle and see if you can or can't guess it.

b. 你看得见白老师在黑板上写的字吗？
Nǐ kàn de jiàn Bái lǎoshī zài hēibǎn shàng xiě de zì ma?
Can you see the characters that Professor White wrote on the blackboard?

c. 那个检察官一定调查得清楚那些涉嫌人想利用什么关系网。
Nèi ge jiǎncháguān yīdìng diàochá de qīngchu nèixiè shèxiánrén xiǎng lìyòng shénme guānxiwǎng.
That investigator will certainly be able to pinpoint what old boy network those suspects plan to use.

d. 愚公一个人搬不动他房子前边儿的那座大山。
Yúgōng yī ge rén bàn bu dǒng tā fángzi qiánbiār de nèi zuò dà shān.
The Foolish Old Man was unable to move the mountain that was in front of his house by himself.

3. V 得 = Able/allowed to verb (Sm) This less frequently seen use of 得 marks that a verb action is doable or is permissible. The verb will be monosyllabic and generally have a passive connotation. Note that except for a few words such as 顾不得 gùbudé 'unable to take care of' or 舍得 shěde 'be willing to part with,' the verb in this structure does not have an object. When in the negative, the negative adverb is placed between the verb and 得 (end of expl a). In texts from earlier in this century, Verb 得 marks completion of the verb action; e.g., 老婆出得门来 Lǎopo chū de mén lái 'The missus came out the door.'

a. 这种蘑菇吃得；那种有毒，吃不得。
Zhèi zhǒng mógū chī de; nèi zhǒng yǒu dú, chī bù de.
This kind of mushroom may be eaten; that type is poisonous, it may not be eaten.

D

的话 <u>dėhuà</u> (—話) 'if' Auxiliary

1. <u>(如果) X 的话, Y</u> = <u>If X, Y</u> (Ax) The oral marker <u>的话</u> is added to the end of conditional structures to intensify their "if" value. The conditional structure will usually be headed with <u>如果</u> <u>rúguǒ</u> 1, <u>要是</u> <u>yàoshi</u> 1 or a synonym (expls a & c). <u>X</u> will usually be a verb phrase though it can be a noun phrase. Sometimes <u>的话</u> occurs without an initial 'if' marker (expl b), and it sometimes occurs as part of <u>Y</u> (expl c), but in all cases it enhances the conditional nature of the sentence. See <u>如果</u> <u>rúguǒ</u> 1 for discussion of conditional structures and another example of a <u>的话</u> sentence.

a. 如果这种中药能稳定病情<u>的话</u>，就不必动手术。
Rúguǒ zhèi zhǒng Zhōngyào néng wěndìng bìngqíng <u>dehuà</u>, jiù bùbì dòng shǒushù.
<u>If it happens</u> that this type of Chinese medicine can stabilize the illness, there will be no need for an operation.

b. 明天没事<u>的话</u>，请替我去办那件事。
Míngtiān méishì <u>dehuà</u>, qǐng tì wǒ qù bàn nèi jiàn shì.
<u>If it appears that</u> you not have anything to do tomorrow, please go take care of that matter for me.

c. 再让我看看，如果可以<u>的话</u>。
Zài ràng wǒ kànkan, rúguǒ kéyi <u>dehuà</u>.
Let me take another look; if that's <u>at all</u> possible.

等 <u>děng</u> (—) 'etc., and so forth' Structural marker; 'this number of nouns' Structural marker

1. <u>List of nouns 等</u> = <u>The nouns given in the list along with unstated others.</u> (Sm) When the shumianyu <u>等</u> is found at the end of a list of nouns without a number directly following it, it marks that an unspecified amount of additional nouns could be included in the list. The listed nouns may be either the subject (expl a) or the object of a structure (expl b). <u>等</u> is often found in the company of a preceding listing comma 、; see 、 in Punctuation. <u>等等</u> <u>děngděng</u> 1 is a synonym of this usage, but it differs in 1) not usually being used with proper nouns and 2) generally occurring only at the very end of a sentence. See also <u>的</u> <u>de</u> 2 expl d.

Be careful, when a number follows it, <u>等</u> marks that the list of nouns is "finished off," not that there are further nouns that could be added; see the discussion at 2 below. 等于 děngyú 'equivalent to' is a vocabulary item not related to this usage of <u>等</u>. Note that 等 also represents the verb action 'wait, await' as well as the noun 'class, rank.'

a. ……原本以为会是一个只有蚊虫陪伴的夜晚，结果，猫啦、狗啊、甚至是草蛇<u>等</u>，都进屋来陪伴他们。
...yuánběn yǐwéi huì shì yī ge zhǐ yǒu wénchóng péibàn de yèwǎn, jiéguǒ, māo la,

gǒu ā, shènzhì shì cǎoshé <u>děng</u>, dōu jìn wū lái péibàn tāmen.
...they originally had thought that the evening would just be one of some mosquitos accompanying them, but in the end cats, dogs, and even grass snakes, <u>etc.</u> came into the room with them.

b. 唐代著名诗人有李白，杜甫，白居易<u>等</u>。
Táng dài zhùmíng shīrén yǒu Lǐ Bái, Dù Fǔ, Bái Jūyì <u>děng.</u>
Among the famous poets of the Tang Dynasty are Li Bo, Du Fu, Bai Juyi, <u>etc.</u>

D

2. <u>List of nouns 等 Number</u> = <u>Just that list of nouns</u> (Sm) When immediately followed by a number, the shumianyu <u>等</u> marks that the list is complete and contains that exact number of items. This value of <u>等</u> is quite distinct from that discussed above in section 1.

a. 这学期我选修了现代汉语，报刊阅读，写作，翻译<u>等</u>四门课程。
Zhèi xuéqī wǒ xuǎnxiūle xiàndài Hànyǔ, bàokān yuèdú, xiězuò, fānyi <u>děng</u> sì mén kèchéng.
This semester I have chosen to take Modern Chinese, Newspaper Readings, Composition, and Translation(, <u>these</u> four classes).

b. 中国有长江、黄河、黑龙江、朱江<u>等</u>四大河流。
Zhōngguó yǒu Chángjiāng, Huáng Hé, Hēilóngjiāng, Zhū Jiāng <u>děng</u> sì dà héliú.
Chang has <u>four</u> major rivers: the Yangtze River, the Yellow River, the Heilong River, and the Pearl River.

等等 <u>děngděng</u> (——) 'and so on, etc.' Structural marker

1. <u>List 等等</u> = <u>The items given in the list plus unstated others</u> (Sm) <u>等等</u> is placed at the end of a list to mark that additional items could be included. The list will almost always be composed of common nouns (expl a), but <u>等等</u> is also occasionally used with lists of verbs phrases (expl b). <u>等等</u> has two usage restrictions: 1) it is rarely used with proper nouns, and 2) <u>等等</u> most often comes at the very end of sentences or comma end-marked structures. <u>等等</u> may be used twice in a row (expl a). <u>等 děng</u> 1 is a shumianyu synonym which has slightly wider usage patterns. Also note that 等等 děngdeng is a verb meaning 'wait a moment.'

a. 这批货物品种不少，包括布匹、呢绒、手表、收音机、电视机，<u>(等等，)等等</u>。
Zhèi pī huòwù pǐnzhǒng bù shǎo, bāokuò bùpǐ, níróng, shǒubiǎo, shōuyīnjī, diànshìjī, <u>(děngděng,)</u> <u>děngděng</u>.
There are quite a few kinds of merchandise in this shipment. It includes piece goods, woolen goods, wrist watches, radios, tv sets, <u>(etc.,)</u> <u>etc.</u>

b. 青年有青年的特点，比如说，他们积极，热情，有朝气，求知欲强，接受新事物快，<u>等等</u>。

Qīngnián yǒu qīngnián de tèdiǎn, bǐrúshuō, tāmen jījí, rèqíng, yǒu zhāoqì, qiúzhīyù qiáng, jiēshòu xīn shìwù kuài, děngděng.
Young people have their own special characteristics. For example, they are positive, enthusiastic, are full of vigor, thirst for knowledge, are quick to accept new things, etc.

D

的时候 dė shíhou (—時—) 'when, while, during' Time marker

1. X的时候, Y = While X, Y (Tm) A primary member of one of the four sets of words used to mark the time frame involved in a Y situation, 的时候 marks that X occurs at the same time that Y does. X will be either a verb phrase (expl a) or a clause (expl b), never a noun phrase. 的时候 will occur directly at the end of X and will generally be end-marked with a comma (expls a & b). 之时 zhīshí 1 and 时 shí 1 are shumianyu synonyms; *的时 and *的候 do not occur. 以后 yǐhòu 1, 以前 yǐqián 1 and 以来 yǐlái 1 are the other major members of this set of markers. See 以来 for a comparative discussion of these four sets of time frame markers. Note that as a noun 时候 can refer to either a specific point in time or to a period of time.

a. 休息的时候，我们经常打太极拳。
Xiūxi de shíhou, wǒmen jīngcháng dǎ tàijíquán.
While on break, we usually do Taichi exercises.

b. 等我们到了体育场的时候，篮球赛已经开始了。
Děng wǒmen dàole tǐyùchǎng de shíhou, lánqiúsài yǐjīng kāishǐ le.
When we got to the gymnasium, the basketball game had already started.

点儿 diǎnr (點兒) 'a little bit, somewhat' Measure; 'not the least little bit' Adverb

1. Verb/Stative verb 点(儿) = Verb a bit (Ms + Av) 点儿 is an oral abbreviation of 一点儿 yīdiǎnr 1 and 2. It is used in the same manner for the same values. See 一点儿 yīdiǎr 1 and 2 for a discussion and examples of its usages.

都 dōu (—) 'all' Adverb; 'even' Adverb; 'already' Adverb; "reason for" Adverb

1.都 Verb = All verb (Av) 都 marks that all members of a particular set of nouns are included in a verb action or a Stative verb condition. The nouns may represent humans (expls a & e), times (expl b), organizations (expl c), events (expl d), etc. The nouns to which 都 refers must be placed before 都. The only exception to this placement is with question structures; e.g., 你都去哪儿 Nǐ dōu qù nǎr 'Where (all) are you going?' You will often see a reinforcing 每 měi 'each' directly before the noun. 都 may also be phrased as 全都 quándōu to give a stronger sense of inclusiveness (expl e). 都 also frequently occurs in the second half of compound sentences; this is discussed in 2 below. Pronounced as dū the character 都 is also used to represent the concept of 'capital (city); metropolis.' 均 jūn 1 is a shumianyu synonym.

Whether the negative adverb 不 bù 1 is placed directly before or immediately after 都 is very important because its position affects the inclusiveness 都 represents. When 不 comes before 都 only a part of the set of nouns is included in the verb situation; e.g., 我们不都是美国人 Wǒmen bù dōu shi Měiguórén 'Not all of us are Americans' (some are, some are not). Compare this with 我们都不是美国人 'We are all not Americans (not one of us is from the States)' where 不 comes after 都 and all of the nouns are included in the negative situation.

Be sure to remember that while they may both be translated into English as 'all,' 所有(的) suǒyǒu(de) and 都 have distinctly different usage patterns. 所有(的) only occurs directly before nouns while 都 must be used at the head of verb phrases. See 所有(的) suǒyǒu(de) 1 for further discussion and examples.

a. 他们俩都是南京人。
Tāmen liǎ dōu shì Nánjīngrén.
They are both from Nanjing.

b. 达赖喇嘛说，中国过去三年几乎都是采行集体领导体制，对西藏政策方面并没有任何改变。
Dálài Lǎma shuō, Zhōngguó guòqù sān nián jīhū dōu shì cǎixíng jítǐ lǐngdǎo tǐzhì, duì Xīzàng zhèngcè fāngmian bìng méiyou rènhé gǎibiàn.
The Dalai Lama said that for the last three years China has almost only had a system of collective leadership. Its policy towards Tibet actually hasn't had any changes.

c. 世界各地的马祖宫庙都是福建莆田湄州马祖庙的分灵，其中台湾的分灵约为800多座。
Shìjie gèdì de Mǎzǔ Gōngmiào dōu shì Fújiàn Fǔtián Méizhōu Mǎzǔ Miào de fēnlíng, qízhōng Táiwān de fēnlíng yuē wéi bā bǎi duō zuò.
All of the Matzu Temples in the world branched off from the Meizhou Mazu Temple in Futian, Fukien (Province). Among them are the 800 plus in Taiwan.

d. 李总统很清楚，任何改革，都不免遭遇一些困难或障碍，也不免会带给团体或个人相当程度的冲击。
Lǐ zǒngtǒng hěn qīngchu, rènhé gǎigé, dōu bù miǎn zāoyù yīxiē kùnnan huò zhàng'ài, yě bù miǎn dài gěi tuántǐ huò gèrén xiāngdāng chéngdù de chōngjī.
President Li was clear that all reforms cannot avoid encountering some difficulties and obstacles, and they cannot avoid troubling groups or individuals to a fair

degree.

e. 这些新来的德国同学，全都会说汉语。
Zhèi xiē xīn lái de Déguó tóngxué, quándōu huì shuō Hànyǔ.
Each and everyone of the newly arrived German students can speak Chinese.

2. 无论 X, 都 Y = Regardless of X, all Y (Av) You will often find 都 in the second half of a compound sentence headed with 无论 wúlùn 1 or a synonym. In these sentences 都 marks that regardless of the situation in X, all of Y is done (expls a & b). 也 yě 3 is synonymous. 均 jūn 1 is a shumianyu synonym. Slightly differently, 都 also occurs in compound sentences headed by markers such as 由于 yóuyú 1 to mark that all the nouns in Y are involved in the events articulated in the sentence (expl c).

D

a. 无论现在还是将来，我们都要弘扬延安精神。
Wúlùn xiànzài háishì jiānglái, wǒmen dōu yào hóngyáng Yán'ān jīngshén.
Whether now or in the future, we will all aggrandize the spirit of Yen'an.

b. 不管下雨不下雨，梅先生都按时上班。
Bùguǎn xiàyǔ bù xiàyǔ, Méi xiānsheng dōu ànshí shàngbān.
Regardless whether it rains or not, Mr. Mei always gets to work on time.

c. 由于没有肋骨支撑，任何外力挤压和冲撞都会威胁她的生命。
Yóuyú méiyou lèigǔ zhīcheng, rènhé wàilì jǐyā hé chōngzhuàng dōu huì wēixié tā de shēngmìng.
Because she had no supporting ribs (after surgery), all pressures and blows from any outside force could threaten her life.

3. Indefinite Interrogative 都 Vp = Nothing/Whoever/ However all verb (Av) When 都 is used with interrogatives such as 谁 shéi 'who,' 哪儿 nǎr 'where,' 怎么 zěnma how,' etc. the structure changes them from a question to a statement meaning 'whoever,' 'wherever,' 'however,' etc. 也 yě 3 is a synonym.

a. 今天太累了，我哪儿都不想去。
Jīntiān tài lèi le, wō nǎr dōu bù xiǎng qù.
I'm exhausted. I don't want to go anywhere.

4. Subject 都 Verb = Even subject does verb action (Av) 都 is often used in a 连 lián X 都 Vp structure to mark emphasis on the noun phrase placed between 连 and 都 (expl a). Sometimes 连 is not used, but the sense of an emphasizing 'even' remains present in the structure (expl b). This usage can be subtle, so you will have to analyze the context to be sure it is present. 都 is not pronounced with stress when it marks 'even.' 也 yě 4 is a synonym.

When 都 is used in the structure 一Measure 都 Negative Verb, it means 'not even one measure' (exp c). 也 yě 3 is a synonym.

a. 连这么重要的事你都不告诉我一声。
Lián zhènme zhòngyào de shì ni dōu bù gàosu wǒ yīshēng.
This is such an important matter, and you won't even say a word to me.

b. 他昨天忙得中饭都没有吃。

Tā zuótiān máng de zhōngfàn dōu méiyou chī.
He was so busy yesterday he didn't even eat lunch.

c. 林渊源说他一点都不担心党纪处分问题，他认为他做了「最好的决定」……
Lín Yuānyuán shuō tā yī diǎn dōu bù dānxīn Dǎngjì chǔfèn wèntí, tā rènwei tā zuòle "zuì hǎo de juédìng"...
Lin Yuanyuan said that he was not in the least bit worried about Party disciplinary action. He feels that he made "the best decision"...

D

5. 都 X 了 = Already X (Av) This use of 都 marks a sense that a condition has already been reached. It also conveys a feeling of urgency and unexpectedness. X may be a time noun (expl a), Stative verb or a verb phrase (expl b). There will usually be a 了 at the end of the 都 X structure. See 已经 yǐjīng 1.

a. 都十二点了，还不睡！
Dōu shíèr diǎn le, hái bù shuì!
It's already midnight, and you're still not asleep!

b. 都快到站了，我们准备下车吧！
Dōu kuài dào zhàn le, wǒmen zhǔnbèi xià chē ba!
We're already just about to the stop. Get ready to get off!

6. 都是 X, Y = Clarifies that X is the reason for Y (Av) When X is headed with 都是, the structure marks that X is clearly the reason behind a Y statement. X may be either a noun (expl a), a verb phrase or a clause (expl b).

a. 都是你，一个人耽误了大伙儿！
Dōu shì nǐ, yī ge rén dànwū le dàhuǒr!
It's you--one person held up the whole group!

b. 都是她不对，难道你就没有不对的地方？
Dōu shì tā bù duì. Nándào nǐ jiù méiyǒu bù duì de dìfang?
It's always that she is wrong. Could it be that you are never wrong?

对 duì (對) "impact on" Coverb; 'to, towards' Coverb

1. 对 X Vp = Verb impacts X (Cv) 对 marks the following X as the thing or event affected by the verb action. X will most often be a noun phrase (expls a & b), but it may be a verb phrase (expl c) or a clause (expl d). The noun phrase may have an interpersonal relationship with the subject of the sentence (expl a), or it may be much broader in scope (expl b). The synonymous 对于 duìyú 1 may be substituted for some but not all uses the usages 对 duì 1 has; see 对于 duìyú 1 for further discussion. As you think about 对, also bear in mind the discussion below of 对 duì 2 'towards' which is used to mark the target of the verb action rather than the thing or event which the verb action affects.

Keep also in mind that the very busy 对 is also used as a verb with meanings centering on 'face towards; answer; treat, handle.' 对 is also used as a Stative verb for 'correct, right' and as a measure for 'pairs (of people, animals and things which have complementary qualities but which are usually not physically attached to each other)'; e.g, 一对鸳鸯 yī duì yuānyāng 'a pair of Mandarin Ducks.' (双 shuāng 'pair' is a measure for two symmetrical things usually having something to do with internal organs, limbs, or things worn on the limbs; e.g., 两双手套 liǎng shuāng shǒutào 'two pairs of gloves.' Neither 对 nor 双 is used with things made of attached symmetrical parts; e.g., 一把剪刀 yī bǎ jiǎndāo ' a pair of scissors').

D

a. 我们对翟老师都很尊敬。
Wǒmen duì Zhái lǎoshī dōu hěn zūnjìng.
We are all respectful of Professor Zhai.

b. 吸烟对人体有害无益。
Xīyān duì réntǐ yǒuhài wúyì.
Smoking is harmful to your health and without benefit.

c. 这种药对治疗癌症比较有效。
Zhèi zhǒng yào duì zhìliáo áizhèng bǐjiào yǒuxiào.
This medicine is relatively effective at curing cancer.

d. 住在美国的爱国侨胞对帮助祖国提高金属科技水平都很关心。
Zhùzài Měiguó de àiguó qiáobāo duì bāngzhù zǔguó tígāo jīnshǔ kējì shuǐpíng dōu hěn guānxīn.
Patriotic Overseas Chinese in America are concerned about helping their ancestral land raise the level of metallurgy.

2. 对 Np Vp = Verb towards the noun (Cv) 对 is also a member of one of one of the two sets of words which mark the location involved in a verb action. In this usage 对 specifically marks a noun phrase as the target of a verb action; this clarifies why 老师对大家说要考试 Lǎoshī duì dàjiā shuō yào kǎoshì 'The teacher told the class that there would be a test' is felt to be a one-way communication rather than a discussion. 对 may be followed by 着 zhe 1 in this usage.

对 duì 2 shares with its synonyms 朝 cháo 1 and 向 xiàng 1 a value of stationary facing the noun without actual movement towards it; e.g., 小黄对/朝/向我眨了眨眼 Xiǎo Huáng duì/cháo/xiàng wǒ zhǎle zhǎyǎn 'Huang winked at me.' However, 对 differs from 朝/向 in not being used with the names of points of the compass (西 xī 'west,' 北 běi north, '东南 dōngnán 'southeast,' etc.).

The second set of "towards" markers is 往 wàng 1 and its synonyms which mark physical movement towards something. 给 gěi 2 is a synonym in which the noun phrase is both the target and beneficiary of the verb action; consider also 跟 gēn 4, 和 hé 4 and 同 tóng 4. See 朝 cháo 1 and 往 wàng 1 for a comparative discussion of these two sets of markers.

a. 小余对你说了什么？他对我说念国语非常有意思。
Xiǎo Yú duì nǐ shuōle shénme? Tā duì wǒ shuō niàn Guóyǔ fēicháng yǒu yìsi.

What did Yu say to you? He said (to me) that studying Chinese is fascinating.

b. 留学生班昨天晚上在送别宴会上对金老师表示深切的感谢。

Liúxuésheng bān zuótiān wǎnshang zài sòngbié yànhuì shang duì Jīn lǎoshī biǎoshì shēnqiè de gǎnxiè.

The foreign students expressed heartfelt thanks to Professor Jin at the farewell banquet last night.

对于 duìyú (對於) "impact on" Coverb

1. 对于 X Vp = Verb towards X (Cv) 对于 is one of the set of words which mark the thing or event affected by a verb action. 对于 specifically marks that the subject of the sentence impacts X through a verb action. X will most often be a noun phrase (expl a), but it may be that a verb phrase is affected by the verb action (expl b). When 对于 X comes before the subject of the sentence, the 对于 X structure is usually end-marked with a comma (expl b). The synonymous 对 duì 1 can replace all usages of 对于, though the reverse is not true; e.g., 对于 is not used after auxiliary verbs (e.g., 会 huì 1、要 yào 1, etc.) or adverbs (e.g., 也 yě 1、都 dōu 1, etc.), nor is 对于 used with relationships between humans. 关于 guānyú 1 is a synonym which marks a matter related to or involved in the verb situation rather than the one impacted by it, see that discussion for further comparative comments. Also see 至于 zhìyú 1 which marks an additional target of a verb act.

a. 汉语语法对于英语为母语的学生不非常困难。

Hànyǔ yǔfǎ duìyú Yīngyǔ wéi mǔyǔ de xuésheng bù fēicháng kùnnan.

Chinese grammar is not all that hard for students who have English as a mother tongue.

b. 对于增进我们两国之间的文化交流，高级领导人的互访有很大的帮助。

Duìyú zēngjìn wǒmen liǎngguó zhījiān de wénhuà jiāoliú, gāojí lǐngdǎo rén de hùfǎng yǒu hěn dà de bāngzhù.

Visits between high ranking leaders are helpful for increasing cultural exchanges between our two nations.

而 ér (—) 'however' Conjunction; 'moreover, and' Conjunction; 'for' Conjunction

E

1. X 而 Y = X, but Y (Cj) The shumianyu word 而 always occurs between two noun phrases, two verb phrases or two clauses, but just as doufu depends for its flavor on its environment, 而 depends on the meaning of what precedes and follows it to determine whether it should be understood as marking a change of conditions 'but' (discussed here) or as marking a supplementary 'and' (discussed in 2 below). There are two circumstances in which 而 is a member of the set of conjunctions which mark Y as a change in the flow of information and should be equated to 'however, but': 1) The first is when X and Y are opposites (expl a). Note this use of 而 in the more shumianyu 不是 búshì 1 structures. 2) The second is when either X or Y is positive and the other is a negative verb phrase, 而 marks either a comparison (expl b) or two aspects of some situation (expl c). See the synonymous 但是 dànshì 1 for further discussion of this set of concession words. Consider also 却 què 1 and its synonyms.

a. 发展轻工业，投资少而收益大。
Fāzhǎn qīnggōngyè, tóuzī shǎo ér shōuyì dà.
When developing light industry, the investment is small but the return is great.

b. 茉莉花的香浓而不烈，清而不淡。
Mòlìhuā de xiāng nóng ér búliè, qīng ér bùdàn.
The fragrance of jasmine is strong but not over powering, clear but not weak.

c. 华北合适于种小麦，而不合适于种水稻。
Huáběi héshì yú zhòng xiǎomài, ér bù héshì yú zhòng shuǐdào.
Northern China is suitable for planting wheat, but it is not good for rice.

2. X 而 Y = X and Y (Cj) When 而 is placed between two conceptually similar verb phrases (expl a), it marks that the second further develops the information given by the first. When placed between two parallel clauses or verb phrases (expl b), 而 marks that Y furthers the situation articulated in X. In these supplementary environments, 而 should be equated to 'and' rather than the 'but' discussed above. In this usage 而 is a shumianyu synonym of 而且 érqiě 1, 并且 bìngqiě 1, 且 qiě 1 and 并 bìng 1. See 和 hé 1 for a discussion of a different set of "and" connectors. Note that when 而 follows 由 yóu 3 or 从 cóng 1 in a structure, it marks a progression from one verbal stage in X to another in Y; see 由 yóu 3 for examples.

a. 那个职员对工作的态度严肃而认真。
Nèige zhíyuán duì gōngzuò de tàidù yánsù ér rènzhēn.
That office worker has a serious and conscientious attitude towards work.

b. 各班都取得了良好的成绩，而以五班的成绩最为突出。
Gè bān dōu qǔdéle liánghǎo de chéngjī, ér yǐ wǔbān de chéngjī zuì wéi tèchū.
Each section had fine accomplishments, and section five's is the best.

3. 为了 X 而 Y = Do Y in order to do X (Cj) In this shumianyu pattern 而 marks the relationship between a verb phrase and the goal, style, basis, or attitude for the verb action. See 为了 wèile 2 for further comments. Markers such as 以 yǐ 1.d, 因 yīn 1.b, 由于 yóuyú 1, 对 duì 2, etc. may be used with 而 instead of 为了 for their specific values.

而且 érqiě (——) 'and, moreover' Conjunction

E

1. X, 而且 Y = X, furthermore Y (Cj) When placed between two verbs phrases (expl a) or two clauses (expl b), 而且 marks that Y is a further development of the situation introduced in X. X and Y will be structured as two roughly parallel grammatical and conceptual structures. When X is marked with 不但 bùdàn 1, 不僅 bùjǐn 1, etc., Y will be an even stronger development of X. The verb phrase in Y will generally include 也 yě 1, 又 yòu 1, 还 hái 1, etc. Note that 而且 can also appear at the head of a sentence to mark an inter-connection with the previous sentence in the text.

并且 bìngqiě 1 is a very close synonym; 况且 kuàngqiě 1 is a synonym which links two or more reasons for a situation. 而 ér 2 and 且 qiě 1 are shumianyu synonyms. The oral synonym 再說 zàishuō 'and, furthermore' differs in only marking what follows as an further reason for a situation. Consider also 且 qiě 1 and 加以 jiāyǐ 2.

a. 我們能夠而且必須完成今年人口調查工作。
Wǒmen nénggòu érqiě bìxū wánchéng jīnnián rénkǒu diàochá gōngzuò.
We can and moreover must complete this year's census.

b. 這次座談會上有不少是我的老同學，而且有的還是好朋友。
Zhèi cì zuòtánhuì shang yǒu bùshǎo shì wǒ de lǎo tóngxué, érqiě yǒude háishì hǎo péngyou.
Not a few participants in this symposium are my old classmates, and some of them are still good friends.

反 fān (一) 'to the contrary' Adverb

1. (不但) X，反 Y = (Not only) X, to the contrary it is Y (Av) The shumianyu 反 marks that Y is strongly contrary to X. The contrary sense of the sentence may be strengthened by the use of 不但 bùdàn 1 or a synonym in X. 反而 fǎn'ér 1 is a less shumianyu synonym of this usage. 反 is also used in many words to represent a core value of 'contrary, opposed.'

F

a. 此计不成，反被他人耻笑。
Cǐ jì bù chéng, fǎn bèi tārén chǐxiào.
This plan won't do; to the contrary, it is ridiculed by others.

反而 fǎn'ér (一一) 'to the contrary' Adverb

1. (不但 Negative) X, 反而 X = (Not only not) X, to the contrary it is Y (Av) 反而 strongly marks that the situation which follows it in Y is either unexpected (expl a) or is contrary to the logic of the situation given earlier in X (expl b). 反而 can be used as an adverb without a preceding 不但 (negative) verb structure, but it is more frequently found in two part sentences headed by 不但 bùdàn 1 or its shumianyu synonym 不仅 bùjǐn 1 plus a negative adverb. 反 fǎn 1 is a shumianyu synonym used in the same structural way; 反倒 fǎndào is an oral synonym. Consider also 却 què 1.

a. 同学们不仅不觉得烦恼，反而十分高兴有那次补考机会。
Tóngxuémen bùjǐn bù juéde fánnǎo, fǎn'ér shífēn gāoxìng yǒu nèi cì bǔkǎo jīhuì.
Not only did the students not feel put out, they actually were quite happy to have a make-up exam.

b. 那位羽毛球运动员在艰苦的环境中，信心不但没动摇，反而锻炼得更坚强了。
Nèiwèi yǔmáoqiú yùndòngyuán zài jiānkǔ de huánjìng zhōng, xìnxīn bùdàn méi dòngyáo, fǎn'ér duànliàn de gèng jiānqiáng le
The confidence of that badminton player not only did not waver in difficult circumstances. To the contrary, he trained even more rigorously.

仿佛 fǎngfú (彷彿) 'seems like' Adverb

1. X 仿佛 Y (似的) = Seems as if X resembles Y (Av) 仿佛 is a shumianyu member of the set of words which mark a feeling of resemblance in a sentence. X will be a noun phrase and Y will most often be a verb phrase (though see the example sentence at 一样 yīyàng 3.b). This sense of resemblance is even stronger when 一样 yīyàng 3 or a synonym appears at sentence end (expl b). 好象 hǎoxiàng 1, 象 xiàng 1, and 似乎 sìhu are colloquial while 如 rú 1, 若 ruò 2 and 如同 rútóng 1 are shumianyu synonyms. The oral 一样 yīyàng 3 and the shumianyu 一般 yībān 1 are interchangeable with 似的 shìde 1 in this structure. Note that as a shumianyu verb 仿佛 represents the concept 'about the same.'

a. 那两位教授他们仿佛是以前认识的。
Nèi liǎng wèi jiàoshòu tāmen fǎngfú shì yǐqián rènshi de.
It seems like those two professors knew each other before.

b. 看起《水浒传》时，仿佛进入了过去的时代似的。
Kànqǐ "Shuǐhǔ Zhuàn" shí, fǎngfú jìnrùle guòqù de shídài shìde.
When I started reading "All Men Are Brothers," it were as if I had entered a bygone world.

F

反正 fǎnzhèng (— —) 'in any case, anyway' Adverb; 'since' Adverb

1. X, 反正 Y = X, but in any case Y (Av) 反正 marks emphasis that Y is unaffected by whatever situation is articulated in X. 反正 often comes before the subject in Y (expl a). X will often be headed with 无论 wúlùn 1 or a synonym (expl b).

a. 他的孙女来不来还没定，反正你一定要来。
Tā de sūnnǚ lái bu lái hái méi dìng, fǎnzhèng nǐ yīdìng yào lái.
It is still uncertain whether granddaughter is coming or not, but at any rate you definitely must come.

b. 无论你将来要学中国文学还是中国历史，反正目前最重要的是得先把汉语学好。
Wúlùn nǐ jiānglái yào xué Zhōngguó wénxué háishi Zhōngguó lìshǐ, fǎnzhèng mùqián zuì zhòngyào de shì děi xiān bǎ Hànyǔ xué hǎo.
Whether you want to study Chinese literature or Chinese history in the future, (in any case) the most important thing at present is to learn Chinese.

2. 反正 Verb = Since verb (Av) In this usage 反正 marks strong affirmation about a situation. This 反正 may come in either X or Y, and it often comes before the subject. 既然 jìrán 1 is a somewhat weaker synonym.

a. 我反正要路过南京，可以顺便替你办这件事。
Wǒ fǎnzhèng yào lùguò Nánjīng, kěyǐ shùnbiàn tì nǐ bàn zhèi jiàn shì.
Since I will be going through Nanjing, I can easily take care of this matter for you.

非 fēi (—) 'has to be' Adverb

1. 非 X 不 Verb = It won't do if it is not X (Av) This structure marks that X is the only permissible possibility. X may be a verb phrase or a clause (expl a), or it may refer to a person (expl b). 得 de sometimes follows 非 with no change in meaning. 可 kě is the verbal element most commonly used after 不 bù 1 in this structure, but 行 xíng, 成 chéng or 能 néng are also used (see also the use of 才 discussed in 2 below). 非 X is an oral synonym used in oral discourses for the same meaning. Keep in mind that you will also sometimes see 非 used as a shumianyu verb that means 'is not.' Also consider the frequently seen word 非常 fēicháng 'extraordinary.'

a. 上汉语口语课的时候，非多说不可。
Shàng Hànyǔ kǒuyǔkè de shíhou, fēi duō shuō bù kě.
When in Chinese conversation class, you have to talk a lot.

F

b. 修那个新式的激光机非郭师傅不行。
Xiū nèige xīn shì de jīguāngjī fēi Guō shīfu bù xíng.
It won't do unless Mr. Guo is the one who fixes that new style laser.

2. 非 X 才 Y = It must be X, then Y (can happen) (Av) This structure goes a step further than 1 above and not only points out the situation that must exist, it describes the Y situation that will then (才) result. X and Y will both be verb phrases. 只有 X, 才 Y zhǐyǒu 1 and 除非 X, 才 Y chúfēi 1 are synonymous patterns.

a. 医生说："你这个肺炎非用抗菌药才能治好。
Yīshēng shuō: "Nǐ zhèige fèiyán fēi yòng kàngjūnyào cái néng zhìhǎo."
The doctor said, "We must use antibiotics to (then) be able to cure your pneumonia."

b. 美国人民从1776年就一直都认识到：非走资本主义道路才能发展国家经济基础。
Měiguó rénmín cóng 1776 nián jiù yīzhí dōu rènshi dào: fēi zǒu zīběn zhǔyì dàolù cái néng fāzhǎn guójiā jīngji jīchǔ.
The American people have known since 1776 that only if they took the capitalist path could they (then) develop the nation's economic base.

否则 fǒuzé (一则) 'otherwise' Conjunction

1. X, 否则 Y = X, otherwise Y (Cj) The somewhat shumianyu conjunction 否则 appears at the head of a second clause to mark that without the situation expressed in the first clause, the second clause situation could result (expls a & b). It is often used in a sentence having 除非 in the first clause; see 除非 chúfēi 1 expl c. You will also see the structure 否则的话 used for the same values. (要)不然 (yào) bùrán 1 is a synonym.

a. 他一定有要紧事找你，否则不会接连打三次电话来。
Tā yīdìng yǒu yàojǐn shì zhǎo nǐ, fǒuzé bù huì jiēlián dǎ sān cì diànhuà lái.
He certainly had something important going on. Otherwise he wouldn't make three phone calls in a row to you.

b. 世行对实施贷款项目的科技保证措施、新成果应用等方面都作了硬性规定，否则不准上马。

Shì Háng duì shíshī dàikuǎn xiàngmù de kējì bǎozhèng cuòshī, xīn chéngguǒ yìngyòng děng fāngmiàn dōu zuòle yìngxìng guīdìng, fǒuzé bùzhǔn shàngmǎ.

The World Bank has made inflexible regulations about implementing technical protective measures for loans and utilizing new results. Otherwise they would not be allowed to start a project.

给 gěi (給) '(do) for' Coverb; '(verb) towards' Coverb; "passive marker" Coverb; "cause" Verb

1. (Np1) 给 Np2 Vp = (Np1 does) verb on behalf of/for Np2 (Cv) 给 marks the second noun phrase as the beneficiary of a verb action which the first noun phrase does. Note that verbs used with "beneficiary 给" must involve an abstract transaction concept; e.g., 买 mǎi 'buy,' 教 jiāo 'teach,' 租 zū 'rent,' 拿 ná 'take,' etc. The second noun must be a sentient being (expl a) or a societal organization (expl b). The oral synonym 替 tì 1 and the shumianyu synonym 为 wèi 1 are not restricted to transaction verbs, so they have a wider range than 给 1 does.

G

You can distinguish this 给 usage from the commonly seen verb 给 gěi 'give' by what comes after 给. If you see 给 followed first by a noun and then by a verb, 给 probably marks a verb action done on behalf of someone; if there is just a noun phrase after it, 给 represents the concept 'give.' Consider also the discussions of the structurally similar passive Np1 给 (Np2) Vp at 4 and causal (Np1) 给 (Np2) Vp at 5 below; analysis of the context in which they appear is needed to determine which usage of 给 is before you.

a. 你到书店去的时候，请给我买一枝毛笔。
Nǐ dào shūdiàn qù de shíhou, qǐng gěi wǒ mǎi yī zhī máobǐ.
When you go to the bookstore, please buy a writing brush for me.

b. 那个车间的工人给东方红公社修理拖拉机。
Nèige chējiān de gōngrén gěi Dōngfānghóng Gōngshè xiūlǐ tuōlājī.
That workshop's workers repair tractors for The East is Red Commune.

2. (Np1) V 给 Np2 (Object) *OR* (Np1) V O 给 Np2 = (Np1) verbs (the O) towards Np2 (Cv) This use of 给 marks that the first noun does a verb action both in the direction of as well as to the benefit of the second noun. Usually, if the first noun knows the second, the noun phrase 2 comes before the object in the structure as in Np1 V 给 Np2 O (expl a); if the first noun is not familiar with the second, the object is placed between the verb and 给 and noun phrase 2 comes at the end of the structure as in Np1 V O 给 Np2. As an example of the distinction between a known and an unknown Np2, compare the known 'China Petroleum' in 泛美石油公司前年卖给中国石油公司一套石油探测设备 Fànměi Shíyóu Gōngsī qiánnián mài gěi Zhōngguó Shíyóu Gōngsī yī tào shíyóu tàncè shèbèi 'The Pan-American Oil Company sold a set of oil exploration equipment to the China Petroleum Company the year before last' with the unknown 'some foreign petroleum companies' second noun phrase in expl b below.

The 'towards' which 给 marks in this usage is a stationary facing towards rather than actual physical movement, and in this sense 给 gěi 2 is a synonym of 朝 cháo1, 向 xiàng 1 and 对 duì 1.

a. 燕京大学已经寄给那些学生录取通知书。
Yānjīng Dàxué yǐjīng jìgěi nèxiē xuésheng lùqǔ tōngzhīshū.

Yanjing University has already mailed acceptance letters to those students.

b. 泛美石油公司前年卖一套石油探测设备给一些外国石油公司。

Fànměi Shíyóu Gōngsī qiánnián mài yī tào shíyóu tàncè shèbèi gěi yīxiē wàiguó shíyóu gōngsī.

The Pan-American Oil Company sold a set of oil exploration equipment to some foreign petroleum corporations the year before last.

3. Np1 叫/让 Np2 给 Vp = Np1 is verbed by Np2 (Cv) This pattern marks the first noun phrase as the recipient of a verb action done by the second. In this structure 给 functions to add emphasis and structural clarity to 叫 jiào 2 and 让 ràng 2 passive patterns. See 被 bèi 1 for a general discussion of Chinese passive structures. Also note the discussion in 4 below about the passive marking function 给 has when used alone.

G

a. 我衣服总是让妈妈给洗干净了。

Wǒ yīfu zǒngshì ràng māma gěi xǐ gānjìng le.

My clothing is always washed by my mother.

b. 剩下的饭菜叫老鼠给吃掉了。

Shèngxià de fàncài jiào lǎoshǔ gěi chīdiào le.

The leftovers were eaten by the rats.

4. Np1 给 (Np2) Vp = Np1 is verbed (by Np2) (Cv) 给 marks the first noun phrase as the recipient of the verb action in this less frequently seen oral passive structure. The first noun phrase must appear in this structure, which is one way for you to distinguish this usage from 给 1 and 2 above and 5 below. The second noun phrase may (expl a) or may not (expl b) be given. In this usage 给 is a synonym of 叫 jiào 2, 让 ràng 2 and 被 bèi 1; see 被 for general comments on passive forms.

a. 帽子和夹克都给小偷偷走了。

Màozi hé jiákè dōu gěi xiǎotōu tōuzǒu le.

The hat and jacket were taken by the thief.

b. 图书馆的参考书都给收拾好了。

Túshūguǎn de cānkǎoshū dōu gěi shōushi hǎo le.

The reference books in the library have been all straightened up.

5. (Np1) 给 (Np2) Vp = (Np1) causes/allows Np2 to Vp (Vb) In this usage 给 marks that the first noun causes or allows the second noun to do a verb action. Either the first or second noun phrase may be omitted, but at least one (expl a), and sometimes both (expl b), will be present in this causal structure. In this infrequent usage 给 is a synonym of 让 ràng 1 and 叫 jiào 1.

a. 白天黑天都在备课，给我累死了。

Báitiān hēitiān dōu zài bèikè, gěi wǒ lèisǐ le.

I'm preparing classes day and night, and it's made me exhausted.

b. 情况没有那么紧要，公司要给技术人员多休息一两天。

Qíngkuàng méiyǒu nàme jǐnyào, gōngsī yào gěi jìshù rényuán duō xiūxi yī liǎng tiān.

The situation is not that critical, the company will <u>let</u> the technicians rest for another day or two.

跟 <u>gēn</u> (一) 'and, with' Conjunction; 'along with, and' Coverb; 'towards' Coverb

1. <u>Np 1 跟 Np2</u> = <u>(Both) Np1 and Np2</u> (Cj) The oral conjunction <u>跟</u> marks the co-existence of two or more conceptually equal and grammatically parallel noun phrases. The linked nouns may be either the subjects (expl a) or the objects (expl b) of the sentence. When there are more than two noun phrases, the linking comma 、 (see the entry 、 in Punctuation) marks the linkage of the earlier nouns and <u>跟</u> marks linkage of the last two items in the series. A reinforcing <u>都</u> dōu 1 is frequently placed before the verb when the nouns are the subject (expl a). The synonymous <u>和</u> <u>hé</u> 1 tends to be used more frequently than <u>跟</u> in this usage. See also the more shumianyu synonyms <u>同</u> <u>tóng</u> 1, <u>及</u> <u>jí</u> 1, <u>以及</u> <u>yǐjí</u> 1 and <u>与</u> <u>yǔ</u>1, all of which also emphasize the co-existence of multiple elements in a structure. Note that 跟 is also used as a verb to represent the concepts 'accompany, go along with' and as a noun for 'heel (of a foot).'

While English almost always has a connecter between two noun phrases, Chinese uses <u>跟</u> or a synonym only when the focus is on making clear the co-importance of both nouns to the meaning of the sentence. Compare a conjunction-less Chinese structure such as 我买书笔 Wǒ mǎi shū bǐ which does not specifically focus on purchase of two things and thus equates to the non-specific English 'n in the oral expression 'I bought books <u>'n</u> pens' with a sentence such as 我买书<u>跟</u>笔 Wǒ mǎi shū gēn bǐ which marks attention on the purchase of two items: 'I bought books <u>and</u> pens.'

a. 小杨<u>跟</u>小谢都是无锡人。
Xiǎo Yáng <u>gēn</u> Xiǎo Xiè dōu shì Wúxī rén.
Little Yang <u>and</u> Little Xie are both from Wuxi.

b. 我的导师是冯老师<u>跟</u>任老师。
Wǒ de dǎoshī shì Féng lǎoshī <u>gēn</u> Rén lǎoshī.
My advisors are Professors Feng <u>and</u> Professor Ren.

2. <u>Np1 跟 Np2 Vp</u> = <u>Np1 verbs with Np2</u> (Cv) In this usage <u>跟</u> usually marks that the first and second noun phrases are both involved in the same verb action (expls a, b, c, & d). This is reminiscent of how it is used in 1 above to focus equal attention on the linkage of two noun phrases. In a less seen function, this use of <u>跟</u> also marks the connection of Np1 to an abstract Np2 (expl e).

Note that the position of a negative adverb <u>不</u> <u>bù</u> 1 used with <u>跟</u> makes a subtle difference in meaning: when placed before <u>跟</u>, <u>不</u> marks a subjective desire (expl c); when placed after <u>跟</u> the negative marks an objective fact (expl d). <u>和</u> <u>hé</u> 2 is synonymous, as are the more shumianyu <u>同</u> <u>tóng</u> 2, and <u>与</u> <u>yǔ</u> 2.

a. 我以前经常<u>跟</u>林教授谈这些问题。
Wǒ yǐqián jīngcháng <u>gēn</u> Lín jiàoshòu tán zhèxiē wèntí.
I often used to discuss these problems <u>with</u> Professor Lin.

b. 妹妹不想<u>跟</u>我一起去学校。
Mèimei bù xiǎng <u>gēn</u> wǒ yīqǐ qù xuéxiào.
My little sister doesn't want to go to school <u>with</u> me.

c. 我不<u>跟</u>这个人见面。
Wǒ bù <u>gēn</u> zhèige rén jiànmiàn.
I don't intend to meet <u>with</u> this guy.

d. 我<u>跟</u>这个人不相识。
Wǒ <u>gēn</u> zhèige rén bù xiāngshí.
I am not acquainted <u>with</u> this person.

e. 谢经理<u>跟</u>这事没关系。
Xiè jīnglǐ <u>gēn</u> zhè shì méi guānxi.
Manager Xie has no connection <u>with</u> this matter.

G

3. <u>X 跟 Y 一样 (Vp/Sv)</u> = <u>X (verb/Stative verb) the same as Y</u> (Cv) <u>跟</u> marks that <u>X</u> and <u>Y</u> are the two items which are equal in a general way (expl a) or in terms of a verb situation (expls b & c). <u>X</u> and <u>Y</u> will be parallel noun (expl a) or verb (expl b) structures. <u>跟</u> also brings attention to the equality of both <u>X</u> and <u>Y</u> in the manner of how a verb is done; this is structured as either <u>X 跟 Y (V) (O) V 得 (Vp/Sv)</u> or <u>X (V) (O) V 跟 Y 一样 (Vp/Sv)</u> (expl c). <u>和</u> <u>hé</u> 3 and the shumianyu <u>同</u> <u>tóng</u> 3 are synonyms of this <u>跟</u> usage.

a. 许多美国人想中文<u>跟</u>日文一样。
Xǔduō Měiguórén xiǎng Zhōngwén <u>gēn</u> Rìwén yīyàng.
Many Americans think the Chinese language is the same <u>as</u> Japanese.

b. 做中国菜<u>跟</u>做法国菜一样费时间。
Zuò Zhōngguócài <u>gēn</u> zuò Fǎguócài yīyàng fèi shíjiān.
You use as much time to make Chinese dishes <u>as</u> you do French cuisine.

c. 林小姐写毛笔字写得<u>跟</u>他一样漂亮。
Lín xiǎojiě xiě máobǐ zì xiě de <u>gēn</u> tā yīyàng piàoliang.
Miss Lin writes calligraphy as attractively <u>as</u> he does.

4. <u>Np1 跟 Np2 Vp</u> = <u>Np1 verbs towards/from Np2</u> (Cv) <u>跟</u> also marks the location of a verb action. The location may be either the source for the verb action (expl a) or a stationary facing toward (expl b). In this latter usage it is a synonym of the <u>朝</u> <u>cháo</u> 1 set of markers, though it has a more restricted usage range.

a. 小马，你那个钱是<u>跟</u>谁借的？
Xiǎo Mǎ, nǐ nàge qián shì <u>gēn</u> shéi jiè de?
Little Ma, who'd you borrow that money <u>from</u>?

b. 你这个方法真好，是<u>跟</u>谁学来的？
Nǐ zheìge fāngfǎ zhēn hǎo, shì <u>gēn</u> shéi xuélái de?

This method of yours is great, where'd you learn it?

更 gèng (一) 'even more so' Adverb

1. 更 X = Even more X (Av) A member of the set of adverbs used to mark comparative conditions, 更 marks that there is a greater degree of X than before; the X condition will generally have already existed to a significant degree, though not always. X will most often be a Stative verb (expl a), but it can also be a verb phrase (expl b). Note that 更 gēng (first tone) is often used as a noun or a verb representing 'change; replace.'

G

更加 gèngjiā 1 is a more strongly toned shumianyu synonym generally used with a disyllabic X. 越发 yuèfā 1 is a synonym which differs in only being used to mark a greater degree of one particular situation; when two different types of matters are involved, 更 or 更加 must be used. For example, in 小刘下乡以后，身体更～更加～越发结实了 Xiǎo Liú xiàxiāng yǐhòu, shēntǐ gèng ~ gèngjiā ~ yuèfā jiēshí le 'After Xiao Liu was sent to the countryside, his health was much stronger' all three can be used since the focus is on one specific person's health; however, 越发 cannot be used in 小刘身体很结实，小张身体更～更加结实 Xiǎo Liú shēntǐ hěn jiēshí, Xiǎo Zhāng shēntǐ gèng ~ gèngjiā jiēshí 'Xiao Liu is healthy; Xiao Zhang is healthier' since two different people are involved. 再 zài 3 can be a synonym of 更.

When thinking of comparative structures, keep in mind that when Stative verbs are used as the verb of a sentence without a modifying adverb such as 很 hěn, 真 zhēn, 非常 fēicháng, etc., the structure itself tends to imply a slight comparison; e.g., 这个学生用功，那个学生不用功 Zhèige xuésheng yònggōng, nèige xuésheng bù yònggōng 'This student is diligent, that student is not diligent.' Consider the other main member of the other comparative adverb set, 最 zuì 1, which marks that an X condition exists in the highest degree. See 比 bǐ 1 for comments on other comparative structures.

a. 马老师告诉，他他研究这类题目的时候应该更详细一些。
Mǎ lǎoshī gàosu tā, tā yánjiū zhèi lèi tímù de shíhou yīnggāi gèng xiángxì yīxiē.
Professor Ma told him that he should be even more thorough when researching this kind of thing .

b. 那个青年到牧区去了两年以后，更懂得马克斯列宁主义了。
Nàge qīngnián dào mùqū qùle liǎng nián yǐhòu, gèng dǒngde Mǎkèsī-Lièníng zhǔyì le.
After that youth had been in the herding areas for two years, he understood Marxism-Leninism even better.

更加 gèngjiā (——) 'even more so' Adverb

1. 更加 X = Even more so X (Adv) A member of one of the sets of adverbs used to mark comparative conditions, the shumianyu 更加 marks that the X situation exists to a greater degree than before. X may be either a Stative verb (expl a) or a verb phrase (expl b). It differs from the synonymous 更 gèng 1 in having a stronger tone of voice and in usually being followed by a disyllabic X. The synonymous 越发 yuèfā 1 is a shumianyu synonym limited to marking further development of one situation; 更 and 更加 are used to refer to both the further development of one situation (expl b) and to different situations (expl a). See 更 gèng 1 for further comparative comments.

a. 经过无产阶级文化大革命，我国的无产阶级专政更加巩固，我们的党更加强大。
Jīngguò Wúchǎnjiējí Wénhuà Dàgémìng, wǒ guó de wúchǎnjiējí zhuānzhèng gèngjiā gǒnggù, wǒmen de dǎng gèngjiā qiángdà.
As a result of the Great Proletarian Cultural Revolution, our proletarian dictatorship has been further consolidated and our Party is even bigger and stronger.

b. 本来视力就不好，这么小的字就更加看不清楚了。
Běnlái shìlì jiù bù hǎo, zhème xiǎo de zì jiù gèngjiā kàn bu qīngchu le.
My eyesight is really bad. I can see such small writing even less clearly.

G

根据 gēnjù (—據) 'according to, based on' Coverb

1. 根据 X, Y= Y occurs based on X (Cv) 根据 is member of one of the six sets of words that mark the basis on which the main verb action of a sentence is done. 根据 specifically marks X as the source of information (expl a) or the premise (expl b) which forms the basis for Y. X may be a noun phrase (expl a), or it may be a verb which has no object and functions as a noun phrase (expl b). Y will be a clause or a verb phrase. 根据 X comes before the subject of the sentence most of the time and is usually end marked with a comma, which makes it easy to identify the parameters of the 根据 structure.

据 jù 1 is a more shumianyu synonym of 根据 which has only minor usage differences: e.g., 据 is used with monosyllabic nouns while 根据 is not; verbs such as 说 shuō 'speak,' 报 bào 'report,' 传 chuán 'pass on to,' 看 kàn 'look at,' etc. are used with 据, but they become nouns such as 说法 shuōfǎ 'way of speaking,' 看法 kànfǎ 'view point' when used with 根据. Note that 根据 is also a noun and a verb having to do with 'based on; foundation.'

It is important to be aware that while all six sets of these "basis for verb action markers" can be translated with 'based on; according to,' or some other English synonym, they mark different if sometimes slightly overlapping types of bases for action. These sets of synonymous 'basis' markers are: 1. 根据, 2. 按 àn 1 and 按照 ànzhào 1 which mark the standards or criteria to be followed in a verb action; 3. 照 zhào 1 which marks the model for a verb act; 4. 本着 běnzhe 1 which marks the abstract principles on which verb actions are based; 5. 凭 píng 1 which marks the thing which the subject relies upon to do a verb act; and 6. 随着 suízhe 1 which marks a background for related verb actions. Also consider the related function of 以 yǐ 1.

a. 根据最近的人口调查，证实了上海已经成为世界人口最多的城市之一。

Gēnjù zuìjìn de rénkǒu diàochá, zhèngshíle Shànghǎi yǐjīng chéngwéi shìjiè rénkǒu zuì duō de chéngshì zhīyī.

According to the recent census, it is certain that Shanghai has become one of the largest cities in the world.

b. 根据美国海军军官透露，美军炮击了一座油田附近的伊军地面雷达站。

Gēnjù Měiguó Hǎijūn jūnguān tòulù, Měijūn pàojīle yī zuò yóutián fùjìn de Yījūn dìmiàn léidázhàn.

According to what an American naval officer revealed, the American forces shelled an Iraqi ground radar station in the neighborhood of the oil field.

G

管 guǎn (一) 'regardless of (alternate possibilities)' Conjunction

1. 管 X, Y = No matter whatever X is, Y is unaffected (Cj) 管 is an oral member of one of the three sets of conjunctions which mark that no matter what the situation in X might be, Y is unaffected. Specifically, 管 marks that X is irrelevant to Y by using rhetorical force to achieve a greater emotional feeling and a stronger tone of voice than its synonym 不管 bùguǎn 1. It differs structurally from 不管 in requiring the pronoun 你 or 他 to follow it and in not allowing a Sv 不 Sv interrogative form in X; the two are structurally similar in taking an indefinite interrogative or a X 还是 Y 'or' interrogative structure in X. Shumianyu synonyms are 不论 bùlùn 1 and 无论 wúlùn 1. See 即使 jíshǐ 1 for comparative comments on the three sets of alternate/indefinite, fact and hypothesis concessive conjunctions. See also 尽管 jǐnguǎn 1. 管 is also used as a noun and as a measure having to do with 'pipes,' and it also extends to other words having to do with 'control.'

a. 管它下不下雪，咱们学生都还得上体育课。

Guǎn tā xià bu xià xuě, zánmen xuésheng dōu hái děi shàng tǐyùkè.

No matter whether it is snowing or not, we students must go P.E. class.

b. 管她是什么地位，不按规矩办事就该批评。

Guǎn tā shì shénme dìwèi, bù àn guīju bànshì jiù gāi pīpíng.

Who cares what position she has, if she doesn't do things according to the book, she should be criticized.

关于 guānyú (關於) 'concerning, about' Coverb

1. 关于 X = Concerning X (Cv) 关于 marks X as a matter related to or involved in a verb situation, but X is not the specific target of the main verb act. Whether X comes after the verb as part of the structure modifying the object (expl a) or at sentence head as an adverbial structure (expl b), X may be either a noun phrase (expl a) or a verb phrase (expl b). When used in an adverbial structure, 关于 X must come before the subject and be end marked with a comma (expl b).

对于 duìyú 1 is a synonym which differs in marking X as the target or recipient of the main verb action. When X can be understood as both the matter related to the verb action and as the matter directly affected by the verb, either 关于 or 对于 may be used; e.g., 关于/对于节约用汽油的问题，大家都很感兴趣 Guānyú/duìyú jiéyuē yòng qìyóu de wèntí, dàjiā dōu hěn gǎn xìngqù 'Everybody is interested in conserving gasoline.' In isolated sentences it can be hard to see why 关于 is used instead of 对于 and vice versa, but the presence of one or the other tells you whether the writer focused on a matter related to the main verb action of the sentence or a matter directly affected by it. Analysis of the context will provide information about which value was intended. Note that 关于 may be used a part of the title of a written work while 对于 may not. Consider also the synonymous 至于 zhìyú 1 which marks X as an additional matter affected by the verb act. Consider also the discussion at 就 jiù 3 .

a. 宋老师最近买了一些关于留学生中文发音问题的书。
Sòng lǎoshī zuìjìn mǎile yīxiē guānyú liúxuéshēng Zhōngwén fāyīn wèntí de shū.
Professor Song recently bought some books concerning the problems foreign students have with Chinese pronunciation.

b. 关于保护自然资源，国务院正在全面规划。
Guānyú bǎohù zìrán zīyuán, Guówùyuàn zhèngzài quánmiàn guīhuà.
The State Council is presently making comprehensive plans about protecting our natural resources.

G

过 guò (過) "verb in a direction" Verb Complement

1. V/Sv 过 (Np) = Verb (the noun phrase) in a direction (Vc) As a directional verb complement, 过 gives a verb phrase either a literal or figurative meaning of 'verb at (expl a), over (expl b), or through' the noun phrase that follows the 过. This 过 is also used with "competition verbs" such as 比 bǐ 'compare,' 赛 sài 'compete,' 跑 pǎo 'run,' etc. and 得 de 1 or 不 bù 3 to form verb-potential structures; e.g., 我比不过他 Wǒ bǐ bu guò ta 'I can't surpass him'; however, 过 is rarely used to form other types of verb-potentials. 过 is used after monosyllabic Stative verbs such as 长 cháng 'long,' 高 gāo 'tall,' 好 hǎo 'good,' 强 qiáng 'strong,' etc. which have positive meanings to mark "a surpassing Sv condition"; e.g., 强过几倍 qiángguò jǐ bèi 'several times stronger.' When

过 is used with verbs such as 走 zǒu 'go,' 转 zhuǎn 'turn,' 翻 fān 'translate,' etc., to mark movement from one place to another or a change of direction, 过 guo can be toneless and perhaps hard to distinguish from the more common Verb 过 guo 1 pattern. Finally, note that as a verb itself 过 guò is used for values such as 'cross (over); go (through); spend (time); after (length of time); undergo a process; exceed'; 过 guò is also used to represent the noun 'mistake.'

Be careful to analyze the context and distinguish this verb complement usage from the use of 过 as the Structural marker guo 1 to mark that a verb action did happen at least once in the past.

G

a. 我大声叫了三四次，他才回过头来看我。
Wǒ dà shēng jiàole sān sì cì, tā cái huíguò tóu lái kàn wǒ.
I yelled at him 3 or 4 times, and he finally turned back and looked at me.

b. 经理看见他公司的货车开过金门大桥。
Jīnglǐ kànjiàn tā gōngsī de huòchē kāiguò Jīnmén Dàqiáo.
The manager saw his company's truck drive across the Golden Gate Bridge.

过 guȯ (過) "verb did happen" Structural marker; "finished verbing" Structural marker

1. (T) V/Sv 过 Np = Verb did happen (to the object) (at a specific time) (Sm) The marker 过 is most frequently used to make it clear that a verb action did indeed occur, at least once, in the past. If a specific time for the verb action is given, the focus is on affirming that the verb action did occur at that time (expls a & b). If no specific time frame is given, V 过 may refer to either the near past (expl c), the relatively distant past (expl d), or a point in the intermediate past (expl e). A V 过 structure is often reinforced with a preceding 曾(经) céng(jing) 1. V/Sv 过 is of course negated with the non-occurrence marker 没(有) méi(yǒu) 1, never with the neutral negative 不 bù 1. Note that 过 is not used with non-action verbs such as 想 xiǎng 'think,' 知道 zhīdao 'know,' 在 zài 'be at,' 属于 shǔyú 'belong to,' etc. When 过 is used with a Stative verb, a specific time is generally given and there is a comparison implied with a present condition (expl d). Be sure to distinguish between this use of 过 to mark that a verb did happen, its occasional use to mark verb completion described in 2 below, and its use as the verb complement 过 guò 1 to mark the direction of a verb act.

a. 宋老师，您吃过汉堡包没有？我在波士顿的时候吃过一两次。
Sòng lǎoshī, nín chīguo hànbǎobāo méiyou? Wǒ zài Bōshìdùn de shíhou chīguo yī liǎng cì.
Professor Song, have you ever eaten a hamburger? I did once or twice when I was in Boston.

b. 抗战时期老阮不但打过仗，还负过两次伤。

Kàngzhàn shíqī Lǎo Ruǎn bùdàn dǎguo zhàng, hái fùguo liǎng cì shāng.
Not only did Lao Ruan fight in the War of Resistance, he was wounded twice.

c. 你吃过饭没有？
Nǐ chīguo fàn méiyou?
Have you eaten?

d. 中心诊所治好过那种传染性肝炎。
Zhōngxīn Zhěnsuǒ zhìhǎoguo nèi zhǒng chuánrǎnxìng gānyán.
The Central Clinic has cured that type infectious hepatitis.

e. 民委的干部以前没有看见何副主任这么高兴过。
Mínwěi de gànbù yǐqián méiyǒu kànjiàn Hé Fùzhǔrèn zhème gāoxìngguo.
The cadre in the State Nationalities Commission had never seen Vice-Director He being so happy.

G

Compare occurrence 过 and the verb completion marker 了 le 1: 过 is used to mark that a verb action did indeed occur at a time in the past; 了 simply marks completion of a verb action, whether in past, present or future situations; e.g., compare 去年我去过中国 Qùnián wǒ qùguo Zhōngguó 'I went to China last year' with 明年去了中国再去日本 Míngnián qùle Zhōngguó zài qù Rìběn 'Next year after I go to China I will then go to Japan' where 过 marks that the verb did occur at a specific point in the past and 了 marks a completion which will be in the future. Further comparison shows that 过 always marks a past verb action as done and over with while 了 marked past verb completions can reach across to the present; e.g., compare 他父亲当过消防口 Tā fùqin dāngguo xiāofángkǒu 'His father was a firefighter' which says his dad is no longer a firefighter with 他父亲当了消防口了 'His father has been a firefighter' which leaves open the possibility that he still fights fires. In addition, verb 了 marks a definite result to the verb action as in 他学了日语 Tā xuéle Rìyǔ 'He studied Japanese' which suggests that he learned it. This is something which may or may not be the case with verb 过 as is shown in 他学过日语 'He has studied Japanese' which does not comment on whether or not he learned the language. Finally, compare the focus of verb 过 on the verb action at a relatively distant time with the synonymous oral structure Sentence 来(着~的) lái (zhe~de) 1 which marks attention to the overall message about a situation that occurred, usually in the recent past.

2. V 过 Np = Finished verbing (the Np) (Sm) 过 guo can also mark verb completion. In this usage, it may be followed by 了 (expl b), which never happens with the occurrence 过 guo described above. It can be difficult to distinguish between these two usages, but the presence of a future time reference (expl a) or 了 (expl b) is a definite sign that the nearby 过 marks verb completion rather than occurrence. Note also that there is no negative form of this structure, so if you see 没 méi before a verb followed by 过, the 过 will not mark completion. Nor does 过 guo 2 combine with 得 de 2 or 不 bù 1 to form verb-potentiality structures.

a. 小丁希望我们吃过晚饭再去。

Xiǎo Dīng xīwang wǒmen chīguo wǎnfàn zài qù.
Little Ding hopes that we can leave when we have finished eating dinner.

b. 我们班真想去郑州，但是牡丹花已经开过了。
Wǒmen bān zhēn xiǎng qù Zhèngzhōu, dànshi mǔdanhuā yǐjīng kāiguo le.
Our class really wanted to go to Zhengzhou, but the peonies have already blossomed.

固然 gùrán (——) 'it is true, no doubt' Conjunction; 'of course' Conjunction

G

1. 固然 X, 但是 Y = No doubt X, but Y (Cj) 固然 marks confirmation of the factual nature of X. When Y contains 但是 dànshì 1 or a synonym, the information Y gives will usually contradict the factual situation X articulates (expls a & b). 固然 will usually come after the subject of the sentence, rarely before it, so X and Y will tend to be verb phrases. You may find 固然 between two Stative verbs where it is used in the same way to mark a contradicted factualness (expl b). Consider the functionally synonymous 虽然 suīrán 1 which differs in marking more attention on the concessive rather than the factual value of X.

a. 药固然可以治病，但是服用过量也会产生相反的作用。
Yào gùrán kěyǐ zhìbìng, dànshì fúyòng guòliàng yě huì chǎnshēng xiāngfǎn de zuòyòng.
There is no doubt that drugs can cure illnesses, but if one takes too much it can produce the opposite result.

b. 这样做，好固然好，可就是太费时间了。
Zhèiyàng zuò, hǎo gùrán hǎo, kě jiùshì tài fèi shíjiān le.
It's true that doing things this way is ok, but it really wastes time.

2. 固然 X, Y = Admittedly X, Y (Cj) In this usage 固然 also marks acknowledgment of a fact in X, but that fact is not rebutted by the contents of Y. This usage will generally occur followed by 也 yě 1 or a synonym in Y rather than 但是 dànshì 1 or its synonyms, which helps distinguish this the two usages.

a.考上了固然好，考不上也不必灰心。
Kǎoshàngle gùrán hǎo, kǎo bù shàng yě bùbì huīxīn.
Admittedly, passing the entrance exam is good, but if you can't pass it you don't need to be discouraged.

还 hái (還) 'still, yet' Adverb; "enlarged verb scope" Adverb; "lessened verb scope" Adverb; "emotion marked" Adverb

1. 还 Vp = Still verbs (Av) In a structure with one verb, this usage of 还 marks that the verb act goes on unchanged (expl a). Distinguishing this from the other uses with single verb described in 2, 3 and 4 below can be difficult, though it is easier when 着 zhe 1 follows the verb (expl b). It is also easier to distinguish this usage of 还 when it is in the second half of compound sentences; for example, when a compound sentence is headed with 虽然 suīrán 1 or other concessive conjunctions, 还 marks that Y is unaffected by the situation in X (expl c). Compare this with its other usages described in the sections below. Analysis of the wider discourse context can also be helpful in identifying which 还 is before you. 还是 háishi 3 is an oral synonym while 仍然 réngrán 1 and 尚 shàng 1 are shumianyu synonyms of 还 hái 1. See the comment in entry 4 below about the emotional nuances 还 brings to a text.

H

a. 柳老师五点三刻还在讲课。
Liŭ lăoshī wŭdiăn sān kè hái zài jiăng kè.
At 5:45 Prof. Liu was still lecturing.

b. 爸爸还睡着呢，别叫醒他。
Bàba hái shuìzhe ne, bié jiàoxĭng tā.
Dad is still sleeping. Don't wake him up.

c. 尽管这件事情很棘手，但我想我一个人还能对付得了。
Jĭnguăn zhèi jiàn shìqing hĕn jíshŏu, dàn wŏ xiăng wŏ yī ge rén hái néng duìfù de liăo.
Although this affair is quite bothersome, I think I can still handle it myself.

2. 还 Vp = Even more Vp (Av) In this usage 还 marks an enlargement of the verb scope. In addition to marking an expansion of the intensity the verb has in a single verb sentence (expl a), 还 frequently appears before the verb in comparison structures to focus particular attention on the verb condition (expl b). It is also used in the second clause in 除了 chúle 1 and 不但 bùdàn 1 structures for this value (expl c).

When used in a sentence dealing with the projected repetition of a verb action by the same subject, 还 is a synonym of the '(projected) again' marker 再 zài 1 (expl d); when used with a different verb action done by the same subject in one sentence, 还 is the equivalent of 'and, as well as, also' (expl e).

a. 像这类事情还有很多。
Xiàng zhèi lèi shìqing hái yŏu hĕn duō.
There even more things of this type.

b. 中美两国人民的友谊比海还深。
Zhōng-Mĕi liăng guó rénmín de yŏuyì bĭ hăi hái shēn.
The friendship of the Chinese and American peoples is (even) deeper than the ocean.

c. 核动力除了发电之外，<u>还</u>有什么作用？
Hédònglì chúle fādiàn zhīwài, <u>hái</u> yǒu shénme zuòyòng?
What <u>further</u> use does nuclear power have besides producing electricity?

d. 杭副部长上星期去黑龙江视察边防部队，他下个星期<u>还</u>要去吗？
Háng fùbùzhǎng shàng xīngqī qù Hēilóngjiāng shìchá biānfáng bùduì, tā xià ge xīngqī <u>hái</u> yào qù ma?
Vice-minister Hang went to Heilongjiang last week to inspect the border guards. Will he go <u>again</u> next week?

e. 中文系的同学参加联欢，<u>还</u>要唱中国民歌。
Zhōngwénxì de tóngxué cānjiā liánhuān, <u>hái</u> yào chàng Zhōngguó míngē.
The students in the Chinese Department will participate in the get-together, and they will <u>also</u> sing Chinese folk songs.

H

3. <u>还 Vp</u> = <u>Lessened verb</u> (Av) In this usage <u>还</u> marks a diminution or lightening of the verb condition. It may mark barely coming up to standards (expl a); it may mark that an specific time frame or a quantity is barely met (expl b); or <u>还</u> can mark that the verb is not doable under certain conditions (expl c).

a. 那个加拿大留学生汉语文章写得<u>还</u>可以。
Nèige Jiānádà liúxuésheng Hànyǔ wénzhāng xiě de <u>hái</u> kěyǐ.
That Canadian foreign student's Chinese compositions are <u>fairly</u> good.

b. 抗日战争爆发的时候，我<u>还</u>不到五岁。
KàngRì Zhànzhēng bàofā de shíhou, wǒ <u>hái</u> bù dào wǔ suì.
When the War of Resistance exploded, I was <u>just</u> short of 5 years old.

c. 那本书一、两年<u>还</u>写不完，别说五、六个月了。
Nèi běn shū yī liǎng nián <u>hái</u> xiě bù wán, bié shuō wǔ liù ge yuè le.
That book can't be written in just one year--don't even think of doing it in five or six months.

4. <u>还 Vp</u> = <u>"Emotional" view of the verb action</u> (Av) <u>还</u> is also used to mark an emotional value to a structure. It can mark surprised admiration (expl a), reproach (expl b), or rhetorical questioning (expl c). Note that although the verb situation remains the focus of the sentence, in all four usages of <u>还</u> discussed in this entry, <u>还</u> also brings an emotional tone to the text.

a. 这么大的暴风雨，没想到你<u>还</u>准时到了!
Zhème dà de bàofēngyǔ, méi xiǎngdào nǐ <u>hái</u> zhǔnshí dào le!
It's such a huge storm. I never thought you would <u>still</u> get here on time!

b. 你<u>还</u>学过三年中文呢，怎么连`小'字也不认识!
Nǐ <u>hái</u> xuéguo sān nián Zhōngwén ne, zěnme lián 'xiǎo' zì yě bù rènshi!
You studied <u>three years</u> of Chinese; how can you not even recognize the simple character representing the idea 'to be small'?!

c. 这<u>还</u>用说！
Zhè <u>hái</u> yòng shuō!

Is there <u>any</u> point in saying this?!

还是 <u>**háishi**</u> (還—) '(which) or' Conjunction; '(either) or' Conjunction; 'still is' Adverb

1. <u>X 还是 Y</u> = <u>Is it X, or is it Y</u> (Cj) One of the set of words which mark a structure as being interrogative, <u>还是</u> marks a question about which of two (or more) options is the answer to the question (expls a & b); this sometimes implies comparison (expl b). A reinforcing 是 or an additional <u>还是</u> may come at the head of <u>X</u> (expl b). Both <u>X</u> and <u>Y</u> will be either verb phrases (expl a) or clauses (expl b); note that in sentences such as 她是老师<u>还是</u>学生 Tā shì lǎoshī <u>háishi</u> xuésheng 'Is she a teacher or a student?' the deletion of a redundant 是 after <u>还是</u> makes <u>Y</u> appear to be a noun phrase.

H

A question mark at the end of the sentence helps distinguish between this "(question) or" from the "(choice) or" <u>还是</u> discussed below; though before you rely on this you need to be careful to see if there is another question word present. Be sure to notice that <u>或者</u> <u>huòzhě</u> 1 is never used to mark this '(question) or,' although it is a near synonym of <u>还是</u> <u>háishi</u> 2 '(choice) or.'

a. 你打棒球<u>还是</u>打排球？
   Nǐ dǎ bāngqiú <u>háishi</u> dǎ páiqiú?
   Do you play baseball <u>or</u> volleyball?

b. 是个人的事情重要，<u>还是</u>国家的事情重要？
   Shì gèrén de shìqing zhòngyào <u>háishi</u> guójiā de shìqing zhòngyào?
   Which are more important, individual concerns <u>or</u> state matters?

2. <u>X 还是 Y</u> = <u>(Either) X or Y</u> (Cj) This <u>还是</u> marks a choice between two (or more) items, it does not mark an interrogative structure. <u>X</u> and <u>Y</u> will be conceptually and grammatically parallel (expls a & b). You will often find this '(choice) or' in the <u>X</u> part of a <u>无论</u> <u>wúlùn</u> 1 structure (expl b). The absence of a question mark at the end of the sentence is the quickest way to distinguish between this usage and the '(question) or' <u>还是</u> discussed above. <u>或者</u> <u>huòzhě</u> 1 is a close synonym of this '(choice) or,' but be careful not to think of <u>或者</u> as a '(question) or' marker; Chinese makes a distinction that English does not. See also <u>和</u> <u>hé</u> 5 and the more shumianyu <u>或</u> <u>huò</u> 1.

a. 进<u>还是</u>退，上马<u>还是</u>下马，都必须慎重考虑。
   Jìn <u>háishi</u> tuì, shàngmǎ <u>háishi</u> xiàmǎ, dōu bìxū shènzhòng kǎolǜ.
   Whether to advance <u>or</u> retreat, whether to start <u>or</u> stop a project must be most carefully considered.

b. 不论是发展轻工业<u>还是</u>发展重工业，邻国及该国相邻地区都是极大的市场。
   Bùlùn shi fāzhǎn qīnggōngyè <u>háishi</u> fāzhǎn zhònggōngyè, línguó jí gāiguó xiānglín dìqū dōu shi jídà de shìchǎng.

Whether we are developing light or heavy industry, neighboring countries and their neighbors are all huge markets.

3. 还是 Verb = Still is verb (Av) As an adverb, 还是 marks that the verb situation following it is unchanged despite a previously given situation (expl a) or comparative thought (expl b). 仍然 réngrán 1, 仍 réng 1 and 尚 shàng 1 are shumianyu synonyms. This 还是 often appears as part of Y in 虽然 suīrán 1 and synonymous structures to mark that Y remains unaffected no matter the contents of X. 还是 may be shortened to 还 hái 1 when it comes directly before the verb, but not when it comes before the subject. You can distinguish this 还是 háishi from the use of 还 as an adverb before the verb 是 in 还是 hái shì 'It still is' by determining if there is a verb phrase following it.

a. 你跟他说一万遍，他还是不会相信的。
   Nǐ gēn tā shuō yīwànbiàn, tā háishi bù huì xiāngxìn de.
   If you told him a thousand times, he still would not believe you.

H

b. 还是这本词典好——编得又好，价格又便宜。
   Háishi zhèi běn cídiǎn hǎo--biàn de yòu hǎo, jiàgé yòu piányi.
   Nevertheless, this dictionary is best--it's both well done and cheap.

好象 hǎoxiàng (一像) 'seems like' Adverb

1. X 好象 Y(似的) = Seems like X resembles Y (Av) One of the set of words which mark a feeling of resemblance in a sentence, 好象 specifically marks that there seems to be an element of similarity between X and Y. X may be either a noun or verb phrase and Y will be a verb phrase. A reinforcing 一样 yīyàng 3 (expl b) or the more shumianyu 似的 shìde 1 (expl a) or 一般 yìbān 1 often ends a X 好象 Y structure. When 好象 is in the first half of a compound sentence and the second half contains 实际上 shíjìshàng 'in fact' or a synonym, the use of 好象 marks that things may seem to be one way, but in reality, or in the speaker's opinion, they are different (expl c). 象 xiàng 1 is an oral synonym, while 仿佛 fǎngfú 1, 如 rú 1, 若 ruò 2 and 如同 rútóng 1 are shumianyu synonyms. See 一样 yīyàng 3 for further comments on similarity structures. 好象 is also sometimes written as 好象是 hǎoxiàngshì.

a. 小黄回答得那么流利，好象受过多年训练似的。
   Xiǎo Huáng huídá de nàme liúlì, hǎoxiàng shòuguo duō nián xùnliàn shìde.
   Huang answered so fluently it seemed as if he must have had many years of training.

b. 宋老师讲得那么多智多谋，好象诸葛亮站在我们眼前一样。
   Sòng lǎoshī jiǎng de nàme duō zhì duō móu, hǎoxiàng Zhūgé Liàng zhàn zài wǒmen yǎnqián yīyàng.
   Professor Song lectured so knowledgeably. It were as if Zhuge Liang were standing there before our eyes.

c. 他看上去好象是文人，但实际上是个商人。
Tā kànshangqu hǎoxiàng shi wénrén, dàn shíjìshang shi ge shāngrén.
He looks as if he were a man of letters, but in reality he's a businessman.

和 hé (一) 'and' Conjunction; 'with' Coverb; "comparison" Coverb; 'towards' Coverb; 'or' Conjunction

1. X和 Y = Both X and Y (Cj) 和 marks an inter-relationship between two or more grammatically and conceptually similar structures. X and Y will both be either noun (expls a & first 和 in c) or verb phases (expls b and second 和 in c). A reinforcing 都 dōu 1 is often found before the main verb in these structures (expl a). Sometimes you ill see 和 used with separate sets of noun and verb phrases in one sentence (expl c). When 和 links verb phrases, they should be disyllabic verbs (expls b & c). When three or more items are listed, the earlier members are usually linked by 、, the enumerative comma (see examples under 、 in Punctuation), and the last two will be linked by 和. 与 yǔ 1 is a shumianyu synonym. The oral synonym 跟 gēn 1 and shumianyu synonyms 同 tóng 1, 及 jí 1, and 以及 yǐjí 1 are only used with lists of noun phrases. See 跟 gēn 1 for further comments on the emphasizing function of "and" structures in Chinese. Note that 和 is also used as a Stative verb to mean 'gentle, mild.'

a. 她父亲和母亲都没吃过杨州菜。
Tā fùqin hé mǔqin dōu méi chīguo Yángzhōu cài.
Her mother and father have both never eaten Yangzhou cuisine.

b. 中国总理说，美国可以传授企业管理经验和转让先进技术。
Zhōngguó zǒnglǐ shuō, Měiguó kěyǐ chuánshòu qǐyè guǎnlǐ jīngyàn hé zhuǎnràng xiānjìn jìshù.
The Chinese Premier said the United States can pass on experiences in business management and transfer advanced technology.

c. 耕地的数量和质量在不断减少和下降。
Gēngdì de shùliàng hé zhìliàng zài bùduàn jiǎnshǎo hé xiàjiàng.
The amount and quality of cultivated land is decreasing and falling.

2. Np 1 和 Np 2 Vp = Np1 verbs along with Np 2 (Cv) In this usage 和 marks that two noun phrases jointly do a verb action. 跟 gēn 2 is an oral while 同 tóng 2 and 与 yǔ 1 are shumianyu synonyms. See the discussion at 3 below for comments on how to distinguish this from other usages.

a. 我差不多每天和他在一起念书。
Wǒ chàbuduō měi tiān hé tā zài yīqǐ niànshū.
I study together with him almost everyday.

b. 关于波斯湾战争美国和一些国家打过招呼。
Guānyú Bōsīwān Zhànzhēng Měiguó hé yīxiē guójiā dǎguo zhāohu.

The US and other countries warned about the Persian Gulf War.

3. (Np1) 和 Np2 Vp1 (Vp2) = (Np1) (verbs) compared with Np2 (Cv) In this structure 和 marks the noun phrases which are compared. You can distinguish this from other 和 usages because the first verb phrase will be a comparison verb such as 比 bǐ 1 or 一样 yīyàng 1. When the second verb phrase is present, it gives further information about the specific manner in which the two nouns compare. 跟 gēn 3 is an oral while 同 tóng 3 and 与 yǔ 3 are shumianyu synonyms. The distinguishing features of the three sets of comparison structures are discussed at 比 bǐ 1.

a. 前面提的和这里提的是一致的。
Qiánmiàn tí de hé zhèli tí de shì yīzhì de.
What was brought up before is the same as what is brought up here.

b. 去年的国际形势和今年的不太一样了，我们的对外政策也要相应变动。
Qùnián de guójì xíngshì hé jīnnián de bù tài yīyàng le, wǒmen de duìwài zhèngcè yě yào xiāngyìng biàndòng.
Last year's international conditions are different from this year's. Our foreign policy should change in response.

H

4. Np1 和 Np2 Vp = Np1 verbs towards Np2 (Cv) 和 marks that the direction of the verb action is towards the second noun. It shares with its synonym 对 duì 2 a sense of static facing towards the second noun phrase. 跟 gēn 4 is an oral while 向 xiàng 1, 同 tóng 4 and 朝 cháo 1 are shumianyu synonyms for this usage of 和. See the discussion at 朝 cháo 1 and 对 duì 1. Also consider 给 gěi 2.

a. 我十分喜欢和中国人交朋友。
Wǒ shífēn xǐhuan hé Zhōngguórén jiāo péngyou.
I really like to make friends with Chinese people.

b. 总经理今天下午和日本商人签订了合同。
Zǒngjīnglǐ jīntiān xiàwǔ hé Rìběn shāngrén qiāndìngle hétong.
The general manager signed a contract with Japanese merchants this afternoon.

5. (不管) X 和 Y, Z = (Whether) X or Y, it is Z (Cj) In this usage 和 links the X and Y options given in a structure of alternate possibilities which do not directly affect Y. X and Y will both be either noun phrases (expl c) or verb phrases (expls a & b). When preceded by 不管 bùguǎn 1 or a synonym (expl b), this 和 usage is easier to distinguish from the four usages discussed above. See also 或者 huòzhě 1 and 还是 háishi 2.

a. 买和不买，都由自己决定。
Mǎi hé bù mǎi, dōu yóu zìjǐ juédìng.
Whether you buy it or not, it is entirely up to you to decide.

b. 无论在科技上和在设备上，近几年来，中国工业都有很大的进步。
Wúlùn zài kējì shang hé zài shèbèi shang, jìn jǐ nián lái, Zhōngguó gōngyè dōu yǒu hěn dà de jìnbù.

Whether in terms of technology or equipment, China's industries have made great progress over the last few years.

后 hòu (後) 'after' Time

1. X 后, Y = After X, Y (Tm) The shumianyu 后 marks that Y happens after X. 后 always appears immediately after X, and it is usually end-marked with a comma. See the synonymous 以后 yǐhòu 1 for further comments and examples. 后 is also used as a synonym of 以后 in the structure 自从 X 以后, Y which marks an X starting point for a Y situation; see 自从 zìcóng 1.

Note that 后 is also a synonym of the physical location markers 后边 hòubiān, 之后 zhīhòu and the oral 后头 hòutou which refer to a specific place. The absence of the location marker 在 zài 1 when 后 is used as a time marker along with the difference in structure and content make it easy to distinguish between its time and place usages.

H

a. 请您收到此信后和我们联系。
Qǐng nín shōudào cǐ xìn hòu hé wǒmen liánxì.
After you receive this letter, please get in touch with us.

b. 太原大厦实行有奖销售后，日营业额猛增到20多万元。
Tàiyuán Dàshà shíxíng yǒu jiǎng xiāoshòu hòu, rì yíng'é měngzēng dào 20 duō wànyuán.
After Taiyuan Building implemented a bonus sales system, daily business volume exploded to over 200,000 yuan.

会 huì (會) "likely to, sure to" Auxiliary verb; 'able to, good at' Auxiliary verb

1. 会 Vp = Verb event probable (Ax) 会 is a member of the set of Auxiliary verbs which mark likelihood, ability or intention. In this first usage, 会 specifically marks the likelihood of a verb action. In this usage 会 most often refers to a future event (expls a & d), but it can also mark past (expl b) or present likelihoods (expl c). 可能 kěnéng or 将 jiāng 2 is often placed before 会 (expl d) or 要 yào 3 after it (see the example in 要 yào 3) to mark the likelihood of the verb action. 不会不 Vp marks the great likelihood of the verb act; compare it with 不得不 Vp which marks the strong necessity of the verb event. Consider also the near synonyms 能 néng 1, 要 yào 3 and 可以 kěyǐ 1.

会 is also used to represent concepts such as 'assemble; get together; union; capital city; opportunity.' You will occasionally see 会 in words having to do with 'accounting' where it is read kuài.

a. 不久你就会听到好消息。

Bùjiǔ nǐ jiù <u>huì</u> tīngdào hǎo xiāoxi.
You <u>are going to</u> hear some good news before long.

b. 开始学写汉字的时候，没想到<u>会</u>这么有意思！
Kāishǐ xué xiě Hànzì de shíhou, méi xiǎngdào <u>huì</u> zhème yǒu yìsi!
When I first started learning to write Chinese characters, I never thought they <u>would be</u> so interesting.

c. 现在李经理不<u>会</u>在办公室里。
Xiànzài Lǐ jīnglǐ bù <u>huì</u> zài bàngōngshì li.
Manager Li is un<u>likely</u> to be in his office right now.

d. 這項蓋落普民意調查結果意味著工黨在五月一日的國会大選中可能<u>會</u>贏得一百五十個至兩百個議蓆。
Zhèi xiàng Gàiluòpǔ Mínyì Diàochá jiéguǒ yìwèizhe Gōngdǎng zài wǔ yuè yī rì de guóhuì dàxuǎn zhōng kěnéng <u>huì</u> yíngdé yībǎi wǔshí ge zhì liǎng bǎi ge yìxí.
The results of this Gallup Poll suggest that the (English) Labour Party <u>will probably</u> win 150 to 200 seats in the May first national elections,.

H

2.<u>会 Vp</u> = <u>Able to/ good at doing the verb</u> (Ax) In this usage <u>会</u> marks that the subject knows how to do a verb action (expl a) or is good at doing some verb act (expl b). <u>会</u> is also used as a transitive verb with this meaning; e.g., 我不<u>会</u>日语、就<u>会</u>汉语 Wǒ bù <u>huì</u> Rìyǔ, jiù <u>huì</u> Hànyǔ 'I can't speak Japanese, only Chinese.'

Both <u>会</u> and the synonymous <u>能</u> <u>néng</u> 3 can be used to mark initial learning of an ability or skill as well as general ability at a verb act. However, note that <u>能</u> <u>néng</u> 3 is used instead of <u>会</u> when the situation refers to either a re-learned ability (他病好了，<u>能</u>劳动了 Tā bìng hǎo le, <u>néng</u> láodòng le 'He is over his illness and can now work again') or the amount that something can be done (半个小时<u>能</u>车一千个螺丝 Bàn ge xiǎoshí <u>néng</u> chē yī qiān ge luósī 'In ½ hour (she) can mill a thousand screws').

a. 我们都<u>会</u>唱美国的国歌。
Wǒmen dōu <u>huì</u> chàng Měiguó de guógē.
We all <u>know how</u> to sing the American national anthem.

b. 张师傅<u>会</u>修各种钟表。
Zhāng shīfù <u>huì</u> xiū gèzhǒng zhōngbiǎo.
Master-worker Zhang <u>is skilled at</u> repairing all kinds of clocks and watches.

或 <u>huò</u> (—) '(either) or' Conjunction

1.<u>(或) X 或 Y</u> = <u>(Either) X or Y</u> (Cj) The shumianyu <u>或</u> marks a choice between <u>X</u> or <u>Y</u>, it does not mark a 'this <u>or</u> that' question. <u>X</u> and <u>Y</u> will be structurally and conceptually parallel noun or verb phrases. Other than being required in some set structures (expl a), <u>或</u> differs little from the synonymous <u>或者</u> <u>huòzhe</u> 1 and <u>还是</u> <u>háishi</u> 2. See <u>或者</u> for further discussion and examples.

a. 或大或小
Huò dà huò xiǎo
Either big or small

b. 人固有一死，或重于泰山，或轻于鸿毛。
Rén gù yǒu yī sǐ, huò zhòngyú Tàishān, huò qīngyú hóngmáo.
Everyone will certainly die once: it can be either heavier than Mt. Tai or lighter than a goose feather.

或者 **huòzhě** (——) **'(either) or' Conjunction**

1. (或者) X 或者 Y = (Either) X or Y (Cj) 或者 marks a choice between two or more options. The choices will be either structurally and conceptually parallel noun phrases (expl a) or verb phrases (expl b). Whether one or two 或者 are used depends on context; only one 或者 is used when there are two different objects (expl a) or if there is 的 de 1 marked description of one or more choice items. In other situations either one or two 或者 may be used (expl b). 还是 háishi 2 is a synonym and 或 huò 1 is a more shumianyu synonym. 或者 is also used as an adverb representing the idea 'perhaps.'

BE CAREFUL: The English language might lead you to confuse the different Chinese words for '(question) or' and '(choice) or.' 或者 is never used to mark a '(question) or.' In this it is different from 还是 háishi which is used for both types of 'or.'

a. 请你把这本辞典交给邱同学或者段同学。
Qǐng nǐ bǎ zhèi běn cídiǎn jiāogěi Qiū tóngxué huòzhě Duàn tóngxué.
Please give this dictionary to Qiu or Duan.

b. 或者升学或者下海，由你自己决定。
Huòzhě shēngxué huòzhě xiàhǎi, yóu nǐ zìjǐ juédìng.
Going on in school or going off on your own; it's up to you.

Indefinite Interrogative Pronouns

1.什么/谁/哪/哪儿/怎么都/也 = **Whatever~Any/Whoever~Anyone/Whichever~Any/Wherever~Anywhere/However~Anyway** Interrogative pronouns shift from representing questions to representing indefinite meanings when they are followed by either 也 yě 3 (expl a) or 都 dōu 3 (expl b) and/or there is no question mark at sentence end. They also shift to an indefinite meaning when they are doubled (expl c) or are used in connection with interrogative markers such 不 bù 2 (Verb 不 Verb) or 吗 ma 1 ~ 没有 méiyǒu 2 at sentence end (expl d). The presence of 都, 也 or the doubling of the interrogative pronouns plus the absence of a question mark at the end of the sentence (except with 吗 or 没有) are reliable indicators that the 什么/谁, etc. before you does not mark a question. See 都 dōu 3 and 也 yě 3 for further "Indefinite Interrogative" examples. 也 tends to be used with negative situations.

Note: 几 jǐ 'how many (less than 10)' and 多少 duōshao 'how many (10 or more)' both shift to the indefinite 'a few; a number of' when they do not receive the chief stress in the sentence; e.g.,我有几本书 Wǒ yǒu jǐ běn shū 'I have a few books'; the absence of a question mark is helpful in identifying this usage.

I

a. 已经十二点半了，但是谁也不想睡觉。
Yǐjīng shíèr diǎn bàn le, dànshì shéi yě bù xiǎng shuìjiào.
It is already 12:30, but nobody wants to go to sleep.

b. 为了让奶牛尽快适应新环境，尽快产奶，在半个月的时间里，钟玉彩住在牛场，清牛粪，挤奶，什么活都干。
Wèile ràng nǎiniú jìnkuài shìyìng xīn huánjìng, jìnkuài chǎn nǎi, zài bàn ge yuè de shíjiān, Zhōng Yùcǎi zhù zài niúchǎng, qīng niú fèn, jí nǎi, shénme huó dōu gān.
In order to get the milk cows accustomed to their new environment as quickly as possible, and to get them to produce milk as quickly as possible, for ½ month Zhong Yucai lived with the cattle, cleaned up their manure, milked them; he did whatever job there was to be done.

c. 哪本词典容易用，我就买哪本。
Něi běn cídiǎn róngyì yòng, wǒ jiù mǎi něi běn.
I will buy whichever dictionary is easy to use.

d. 附近最近盖了什么新房子没有？
Fùjìn zuìjìn gàile shénme xīn fángzi meiyou?
Have any new houses been built in this area recently?

及 <u>jí</u> (—) 'and, to' Conjunction

1. <u>Np1 及 Np2</u> = <u>Np1 and Np2</u> (Cj) One of the set of words which mark a list of items, the shumianyu <u>及</u> marks the co-existence of two or more structurally parallel noun phrases (expls a & b). <u>及</u> brings focus on the noun(s) before it. When there are three or more noun phrases in the series, the earlier items are usually separated by the Chinese linking comma (see the <u>、</u> Punctuation entry), while the last two are linked by <u>及</u> (expl a). <u>及</u> will usually be translated as 'and,' but its verbal meaning of 'reach, come up to' also supports translating it as 'to' in appropriate contexts. <u>跟</u> <u>gēn</u> 1 and <u>和</u> <u>hé</u> 1 are oral while <u>同</u> <u>tóng</u> 1, <u>与</u> <u>yǔ</u> 1 and <u>以及</u> <u>yǐjí</u> 1 are shumianyu synonyms. See <u>跟</u> <u>gēn</u> 1 for general comments on the emphasizing function this set of words has.

a. 学生、教员<u>及</u>行政人员均已放假。
Xuésheng 、jiàoyuán <u>jí</u> xíngzhèng rényuán jūn yǐ fàngjià.
The students, teachers <u>and</u> other personnel have already gone on vacation.

b. 一九五六年，政府对个体经济<u>及</u>资本主义经济进行了社会主义改造。
Yī jiǔ wǔ liù nián, zhèngfǔ duì gètǐ jīngji <u>jí</u> zīběn zhǔyì jīngji jìnxíngle shèhuì zhǔyì gǎizào.
In 1956 the government implemented socialistic reforms towards an entrepreneurial economy <u>and</u> a capitalistic economy.

J

即 <u>jí</u> (—) 'is indeed' Verb; 'promptly' Adverb; 'then' Adverb

1. <u>即 Np</u> = <u>Is indeed the noun</u> (Vb) The very shumianyu verb <u>即</u> marks that the noun phrase following it definitely equates to the noun phrase before it (expl a). <u>即</u> is also used to introduce explanatory parenthetical information and is used in much the fashion of 'i.e.,' in English (expl b). You will probably see <u>即</u> more frequently in texts from the ROC. <u>即是</u> <u>jíshì</u> 1 is a synonym which tends to be used when the following noun phrase has a more complicated structure; see <u>即是</u> <u>jíshì</u> 1. Rarely, <u>即</u> is a Conjunction used as a synonym of <u>即使</u> to mark a hypothetical <u>even if Vp1, Vp2</u> structure; see <u>即使</u> <u>jíshǐ</u> 1.

a. 中医<u>即</u>中国固有的传统医学。
Zhōngyī <u>jí</u> Zhōngguó gùyǒu de chuántǒng yīxué.
"Traditional Chinese Medical Science" <u>is precisely</u> China's own traditional medicine.

b. 法国总理珠配说："我们两国政府都有明确的政治意愿，<u>即</u>继续推进法中两国关系的发展。"
Fǎguó zǒnglǐ Zhūpéi shuō: "Wǒmen liǎngguó zhèngfǔ dōu yǒu míngquè de zhèngzhì yìyuàn, <u>jí</u> jìxù tuījìn Fǎ-Zhōng liǎngguó guānxi de jìnzhǎn."
The French Prime Minister Juppé said, "The governments of our two countries

both have a clear-cut aspiration; i.e., to continue to promote progress in the Franco-Sino relationship."

2. 即 Vp = Verb happens very soon (Av) The shumianyu 即 marks that a verb action occurs either within a short period of time (expl a) or under certain conditions (expl b). The synonymous adverb 就 jiù 1 & 2 can be substituted for all uses of the adverb 即, but the reverse is not true.

a. 服药两三天后即可见效。
Fúyào liǎng sān tiān hòu jí kě jiànxiào.
Two or three days after taking the medicine you will (then) see results.

b. 蘇崇任的一名大學部學弟覺得可疑，即請來鎖匠開門進入後，赫然發現蘇全身赤倮，橫躺浴室內，立刻向市警三分局報案。
Sū Chóngrèn de yī míng dàxuébù xuédì juéde kěyí, jí qǐng lái suǒjiang kāimén jìnrù hòu, hèrán fāxiàn Sū quánshēn chìluǒ, héng tǎng yùshì nèi, lìkè xiàng Shìjǐng Sānfēnjú bào'àn.
A college classmate of Su Chongren felt things were suspicious. He immediately called a locksmith, and after he had gotten in he discovered Su sprawled naked in the bathroom. He quickly reported the situation to the 3rd sub-station of the city police.

J

3. 即 Vp = Verb then happens (Av) In this usage, the shumianyu 即 marks that under specific conditions a verb action produces a particular result (expl a). 即 imparts an element of deduction to the situation. 就 jiù 2 is a synonym.

a. 法醫日前驗屍後，即表示死亡時間約在八天至十天。
Fǎyī rìqián yànshī hòu, jí biǎoshì sǐwáng shíjiān yuē zài bā tiān zhì shí tiān.
After examining the corpse a few days ago, the Medical Examiner (then) said that the time of death was about 8 to 10 days ago.

b. 法國在未實行家庭津貼制度以前，即有此項救助辦法。
Fǎguó zài wèi shíxíng jiātíng jīntiē zhìdù yǐqián, jí yǒu cǐ xiàng jiùzhù bànfǎ.
Before France had implemented a system of family subsidies, it (then) had this kind of assistance.

既 jì (一) 'both...and...' Adverb; 'since' Conjunction

1. 既 X, Y = X as well as Y (Av) 既 marks that X and Y (and sometimes Z too) are inter-related conceptually. Most of the time X and Y will be verb phrases which have the same subject (expls a & b). The specific relationship of X to Y is indicated by the marker used at the head of Y. For example, when Y is headed by 又 yòu 2 (expl a), the structure marks that there are two different qualities or conditions to a situation (expl a). When Y is headed by 也 and parallels X in structure, it marks that Y supplements rather than parallels the information given in X (expl b). Though you will not see it often, when X and Y are both monosyllabic Stative verbs and Y is headed with 且 qiě 1, the structure is a close shumianyu synonym of 既 X, 又 Y; e.g., 既深且广 jì shēn qiě guǎng 'Both deep and broad.'

Be careful, if the contents of Y and X do not closely parallel each other, it is likely that 既 is a shumianyu synonym of 既然 jìrán being used as a conjunction in a cause and effect structure; compare expl b here with expl 2.b below.

Note that when X and Y have the same verb but different subjects, 不但 bùdàn 1 rather than 既 must be used: e.g., 不但他锻炼了，我也锻炼了 Bùdàn tā duànliàn le, wǒ yě duànliàn le 'Not only did he exercise, I exercised too.'

a. 这项建设工程既缺人力，又缺资金，无法上马。
Zhèi xiàng jiànshè gōngchéng jì què rénlì, yòu què zījīn, wúfǎ shàngmǎ.
This engineering project lacks both manpower and capital. There is no way to proceed.

b. 治金工业部批准的新式鼓风炉既节约了用电，也减少了人力。
Zhìjīn Gōngyèbù pīzhǔn de xīnshì gǔfēnglú jì jiéyuēle yòngdiàn, yě jiǎnshǎole rénlì.
The new style blast furnace approved by the Ministry of Metallurgical Industry both conserves electricity and reduces personnel.

J

2. 既 X, Y = Since X, Y (Cj) In this usage as a conjunction, 既 is a more intensely shumianyu synonym of 既然 jìrán 1 which marks that a factual X situation has a subjective Y response to it. Y may be either a suggestion (expl a) or a rhetorical response (expl b). Both X and Y will be verb phrases (expls a & b). 既 cannot come before the subject of the sentence (expl b). Note the need to distinguish this usage from the 既 structure mentioned in 1 above. See 因为 yīnwei 1 for further discussion. Consider also 反正 fǎnzhèng 1.

a. 既来之，则安之。
Jì lái zhī, zé ān zhī.
Since we are here, we might as well stay and make the best of it.

b. 贺副部长既已点头，我也不便不同意。
Hè fùbùzhǎng jì yǐ diǎntóu, wǒ yě bù biàn bù tóngyì.
Since Vice-Minister He has agreed, it is inappropriate for me to disagree.

将 jiāng (將) "process the object" Coverb; "verb action will occur" Adverb

1. Np1 将 Np2 Vp = Noun 1 processes noun 2 (Cv) When followed by a noun phrase, the shumianyu 将 marks that the direct object of the sentence is brought before the verb phrase and brings attention to the to the handling, disposal or processing verb action applied to the object. The object will be a noun known through the context of the discourse.

When analyzing texts to distinguish this usage from the usage of 将 as a marker of definite future verb action as described in 2 below, remember that the noun object of 将 can be heavily modified and thus appear some distance away from the 将 marker. In such cases the noun will usually come after the noun modification marker 的 de 1, so search for a 的 if there are numerous characters after the 将 (expl b). When followed by a noun, 将 is the shumianyu synonym of 把 bǎ 1. See further discussion of this point at 把 bǎ 1.

a. 刘校长已经将这项教学任务承担下来了。
Liú xiàozhǎng yǐjīng jiāng zhèi xiàng jiàoxué rènwù chéngdān xialai le.
President Liu has already undertaken these educational responsibilities.

b. 设计人员将通信卫星的工作寿命延长了两倍以上。
Shèjì rényuán jiāng tōngxìn wèixīng de gōngzuò shòumìng yénchángle liǎng bèi yǐshàng.
The technicians more than doubled the life span of the communication satellite.

J

2. 将 Vp = The verb will occur (Av) When placed at the head of a verb phrase, the shumianyu 将 marks that the verb action will definitely take place in the near future. To distinguish this usage from 1 above, determine whether a noun or verb follows the 将.

Note: the adverb 将 used before time structures such as 十二年 shíèr nián '12 years,' 黄昏 huánghūn 'dusk,' 三点半 sāndiǎn bàn '3:30,' etc. means 'be near (that time)'; before quantity structures such as 够 gòu 'enough,' 容 róng 'contain,' etc., 将 (or 将将) marks 'just barely that amount, exactly that much.' Note the noun 将来 jiānglái 'future' is related in meaning but different in structural use.

a. 孔副教授编的那部《中国现代经济史》将于明年三四月出版。
Kǒng fùjiàoshòu biān de nèi bù "Zhōngguó Xiàndài Jīngji Shǐ" jiāng yú míngnián sān-sìyuè chūbǎn.
The book "A History of Modern Chinese Economics" written by Professor Kong will be published next March or April.

b. 国家计划委员会提出的新经济构想将会改变少数民族地区的精神面貌。
Guójiā Jìhuà Wěiyuánhuì tíchū de xīn jīngji gòuxiǎng jiāng huì gǎibiàn shǎoshù mínzú dìqū de jīngshén miànmào.
The new economic plan promoted by the State Planning Commission will change the mental outlook of the minority peoples.

叫 jiào (—) "cause (to happen)" Verb; "passive marker" Coverb

1. (Np1) 叫 Np2 Vp = (Np1) causes Np2 to verb (Vb) One of the set of five "causal" markers, 叫 specifically marks that the first noun phrase 'permits' (expl a), or, more commonly, 'orders, makes' (expl b) a second noun phrase do a verb action. "Causal" 叫 is sometimes written 教 jiào with no usage differences. See 使 shǐ 1 for a discussion of the similarities and differences in meaning among the other members of this set of synonymous causal structures: 让 ràng 1, 令 lìng 1, 给 gěi 5 and 使. Keep in mind that 叫 is also commonly used as a verb meaning 'shout; order; call out; name.'

It can be difficult to distinguish "causal" 叫 from the "passive" 叫 discussed in 2 below, but the fact that "passive" 叫 often has a following 给 gěi 3 as part of the structure makes it easier.

a. 马路中间不叫骑自行车。
Mǎlù zhōngjiān bù jiào qí zìxíngchē.
You are not allowed to ride bikes in the middle of the street.

b. 农具厂叫技术人员到西安去一趟。
Nóngjùchǎng jiào jìshù rényuán dào Xī'ān qù yī tàng.
The agricultural implement factory had the technical personnel go to Xian.

2. Np1 叫 Np2 (给) Vp = Np1 is verbed by Np2 (Cv) The oral passive marker 叫 introduces the second noun phrase as the doer of the verb; the first noun phrase is the recipient of the verb action. The verb will express result (expl a) or completion (expl b). 叫 frequently appears without 给 gěi in this passive structure (expl a), but when it is there, the presence of 给 directly before the verb will help you distinguish between the "passive" and "causal" uses of 叫. "Passive" 叫 is also sometimes written as 教 with no usage differences. Synonyms for "passive" 叫 are 让 ràng 2, 给 gěi 5, and, for more serious situations, 被; see 被 bèi 1 for further discussion about the passive voice in Chinese.

a. 饭碗叫那个小孩打翻了。
Fànwǎn jiào nèige xiǎohái dǎ fān le.
The rice bowl was overturned by the child.

b. 王上校叫司令部给派到新疆去。
Wáng shàngxiào jiào sīlìngbù gěi pàidào Xīnjiāng qù.
Colonel Wang was sent to Xinjiang by headquarters.

J

教 jiào (一) "cause (to happen)" Verb; "passive marker" Coverb

1. (Np1) 教 Np2 Vp = Np1 causes Np2 to verb (Vb) 教 is a variant way of writing "causal" 叫. See 叫 jiào 1 for discussion and examples.

2. Np1 教 Np2 (给) Vp = Np1 verbed by Np2 (Cv) "Passive" 叫 can also be written with the variant 教. See 叫 jiào 2 for discussion and examples.

假如 jiărú (——) 'if, suppose' Conjunction

1. 假如 X, Y = If X, Y (Cj) One of the set of many words which mark conditional structures, the shumianyu 假如 marks that X is a condition for the occurrence of a Y situation. X may mark a supposition (expl a), or, when Y has the adverb 那(么) nà(me) 1, it marks that Y is a conclusion drawn directly from X (expl b). X and Y will both be verb phrases. 假若 jiăruò, 假使 jiăshĭ and 假设 jiăshè are close but infrequently seen literary synonyms; 要是 yàoshi 1 is a common oral synonym. See 如果 rúguŏ 1 for further synonyms and an overall discussion about the set of conditional markers. Consider also the 只有 zhĭyŏu 1 set of conditional conjunctions which mark different values for X.

a. 假如只想下海，老实说，农民的儿子就用不着进什么学校。
Jiărú zhĭ xiăng xiàhăi, lăoshí shuō, nóngmín de érzi jiù yòngbuzháo jìn shénme xuéxiào.
If they just want to go into business, truthfully speaking, peasant boys do not need to go to school.

b. 假如让女孩子来做这样的工作，那就再合适不过了。
Jiărú ràng nǚ háizi lái zuò zhèiyàng de gōngzuò, nà jiù zài héshì bùguò le.
If we have girls do this sort of work, things could not be more fitting.

J

加以 jiāyĭ (——) 'bring to bear (the following verb)' Verb; 'additionally' Conjunction

1. X加以 V = Do the verb to X (Vb) 加以 marks that the verb following it is how X is to be handled. X may be either a noun phrase (expl a) or a verb phrase (expl b). The verb after 加以 must be disyllabic. 加 occurs without 以 when 加 follows a monosyllabic adverb; e.g., 多加注意 duō jiā zhùyì 'pay more attention.' There is no difference in meaning between 加 and 加以 in this usage.

Note: though 加以 is grammatically the main verb of the structure, 加以 itself is generally not translated into English and its object becomes the verb in the English structure (expls a & b). You will only see 加以 in relatively formal texts, but it can be confusing if you are not aware of how it is translated.

a. 这两个主张有难以捉摸的差别，必须加以分析。
Zhèi liăng ge zhŭzhāng yŏu nányĭ zhuōmō de chābié, bìxū jiāyĭ fēnxī.
These two proposals have subtle differences, so we must (--) analyze them.

b. 难道被压迫被剥削的劳动人民不应该对反动派彻底地加以消灭吗？
Nándào bèi yāpò bèi bōxuē de láodòng rénmín bù yīnggāi duì făndòngpài chèdĭ de jiāyĭ xiāomiè ma?

Can it be that the worker citizens who were oppressed and exploited should not thoroughly (--) exterminate the counter revolutionary clique!!!

2. Vp 1, 加以 Vp 2 = Vp 1, moreover Vp 2 (Cj) The less frequently seen shumianyu conjunction 加以 marks that the second verb phrase is an elaboration of the situation expressed in the first. See the oral synonym 而且 érqiě 1 for further synonyms and discussion.

a. 在北京外语学院的留学生学习很认真，加以中国同学的热情帮助，当然进步得很快。

Zài Běijīng Wàiyǔ Xuéyuàn de liúxuésheng xuéxí hěn rènzhēn, jiāyǐ Zhōngguó tóngxué de rèqíng bāngzhù, dāngrán jìnbù de hěn kuài.

The foreign students at the Beijing Foreign Languages Institute are all conscientious. Add to that the enthusiastic help of their Chinese classmates and of course they progress rapidly.

b. 困难本来就不少，加以我们缺乏先进设备，所以试验成果不很理想。

Kùnnan běnlái jiù bùshǎo, jiāyǐ wǒmen quēfá xiānjìn shèbèi, suǒyǐ shìyàn chéngguǒ bù hěn lǐxiǎng.

There were lots of problems to begin with. Moreover we didn't have advanced equipment, so the results of the experiments were not quite ideal.

J

即便 jíbiàn (——) 'even if (hypothesis)' Conjunction

1. 即便 X, adverb Y = Although X might happen, it is still Y (Cj) 即便 is a shumianyu member of one of the three different sets of conjunctions which mark that no matter what information X may convey, the situation in Y is unaffected. 即便 specifically marks that whatever the hypothetical situation articulated in X may be, it does not influence Y. X and Y may be either verb phrases or clauses. 即使 jíshǐ 1 and 便 biàn 5 are synonyms. See 即使 jíshǐ 1 for comparative comments and examples of the three sets of concessive conjunctions.

a. 他即便不能立刻来，也还是会来的。

Tā jíbiàn bù néng lìkè lái, yě háishi huì lái de.

Although he may not be able to come right away, he will come.

b. 你即便再有钱，那个姑娘也不一定会看上你。

Nǐ jíbiàn zài yǒu qián, nèige gūniang yě bù yīdìng huì kànshang ni.

Even if you had more money, that girl would not necessarily fall for you.

进而 jìn'ér (進—) 'proceed to the next step' Conjunction

1. X, 进而 Y = X, thus Y (Cj) 进而 is placed in Y to mark that Y is a development which has its foundation in the completed situation in X. 从而 cóngér 1 is a synonym which additionally involves a cause and effect relationship between X and Y. Also consider the usages of the set of markers discussed at 所以 suǒyǐ 1.

a. 我们在农村进行了土改，并进而开展了农业合作化运动。

Wǒmen zài nóngcūn jìnxíngle tǔgǎi, bìng jìn'ér kāizhǎnle nóngyè hézuòhuà yùndòng.

We carried out land reform in the villages and proceeded to the next step and developed the movement for organization into agricultural cooperatives.

竟 jìng (—) 'surprisingly, actually' Adverb

J

1. 竟 Vp/Sv = A verb action unexpectedly occurs/a Stative verb condition surprisingly exists (Av) 竟 marks that a verb act (expl a) or a Stative verb situation (expl b) is surprising in that it is beyond what would normally be expected. 竟然 jìngrán 1 is an exact synonym. 竟 also represents the ideas of 'finish; throughout; eventually.'

The adverb 竟 does not carry a sense of contrariness, reproach or correction, and in this it is quite different from markers such as 却 què 1, 并 bìng 2, etc. which may be given a similar English translation. See the discussion at 却 què 1.

a. 弟弟吃得忘乎所以，竟将焖在锅里给父亲的饭，铲了一小半要吃。

Dìdi chī de wànghū suǒyǐ, jìng jiāng mèn zài guō lǐ gěi fùqīn de fàn, chǎnle yī xiǎo bàn yào chī.

Forgetting what he was doing, my younger brother actually shoveled out a big chunk of dad's rice that was slowly cooking in the wok and was going to eat it.

b. 那个五岁的孩子心算的速度竟快得惊人，连计算机都赶不上了。

Nèige wǔ suì de háizi xīnsuàn de sùdù jìng kuài de jīngrén, lián jìsuànjī dōu gǎn bù shàng le.

The speed with which that 5 year old can do arithmetic in his head is so unexpectedly fast that it is alarming. Even a computer can't catch up.

竟然 jìngrán (——) 'surprisingly, actually' Adverb

1. 竟然 Vp/Sv = A verb action actually occurs/a Stative verb condition surprisingly exists (Av) 竟然 marks that a verb act or a Stative verb situation surprises in that it is not what would normally be expected. 竟 jìng 1 is an exact synonym.

竟然 does not carry a sense of contrariness, reproach or correction, and in this it is quite different from markers such as 却 què 1, 并 bìng 2, etc. which may be given the same English translation. See the discussion at 却 què 1.

a. 我们学院的新留学生宿舍竟然在几个月内完成了。
Wǒmen xuéyuàn de xīn liúxuéshēng sùshè jìngrán zài jǐ ge yuè nèi wánchéngle.
Somehow our school's new foreign student dormitory was finished in just a few months.

尽管 jǐnguǎn (儘—) 'although (fact)' Conjunction

1. 尽管 X, Y = In spite of the existence of X, it is Y (Cj) 尽管 is a shumianyu member of one of the three different sets of conjunctions which mark that no matter what the situation in X is, Y is unaffected. 尽管 specifically marks that even though the situation articulated in X is a fact, Y is unchanged (expls a & b). The close synonym 虽然 suīrán 1 gives a weaker tone of voice. X and Y may be either verb phrases or clauses. Y will usually be marked with a contrastive adverb such as 却 què 1, 还是 háishi 3, 然而 rán'ér 1, 也 yě 1, etc. As an adverb, 尽管 means 'feel free to go right ahead and verb.' J

Compare this factual situation marker 尽管 with the hypothetical situation marker 即使 jíshǐ 1 which points out that Y would not change even if the X situation should came about; for example, if expl a below were marked with 即使 instead of 尽管, it would mean 'Even if we had gained great accomplishments in economic growth, we should not be arrogantly self-satisfied.' See 即使 jíshǐ 1 for further comparative comments and examples.

a. 尽管在经济建设上取得了很大的成就，我们也不应该骄傲自满。
Jǐnguǎn zài jīngji jiànshè shang qǔdéle hěn dà de chéngjiù, wǒmen yě bù yīnggāi jiāo'ào zìmǎn.
Although we have gained great accomplishments in economic growth, we should not be arrogantly self-satisfied.

b. 尽管武汉的饮水污染率去年没上涨，省政府却还在兴建废水处理厂。
Jǐnguǎn Wǔhàn de yǐnshuǐ wūránlǜ qùnián méi shàngzhǎng, shěng zhèngfǔ què hái zài xīngjiàn fèishuǐ chǔlǐ chǎng.
Even though the rate of drinking water pollution in Wuhan did not rise last year, the provincial government is still building a waste water treatment plant.

2. X, 尽管 Y = X even though Y (Cj) When used in Y rather than X, 尽管 has the same usage values described above, but it has a greater shumianyu texture to it.

a. 这种句子并不难翻译，尽管句中有一些不认识的词儿。
Zhèi zhǒng jùzi bìng bù nán fānyì, jǐnguǎn jù zhōng yǒu yīxiē bù rènshi de cír.
This sort of sentence is not hard to translate, even if it has some unknown words.

b. 解放军战士们都坚守战场，尽管敌我力量悬殊。
Jiěfàngjūn zhànshìmen dōu jiānshǒu zhànchǎng, jǐnguǎn díwǒ lìliang xuánshū.
Despite the fact that there was a great disparity in strength between us and the enemy, the PLA soldiers resolutely held the field.

既然 jìrán (——) 'since' Conjunction

1. 既然 X, Y = Since it is X, Y (Cj) 既然 is a member of the set of markers used with cause and effect structures. Specifically, 既然 marks that a factual X situation elicits a subjective Y response. The center of gravity in the sentence is Y which may be either a suggestion (expl a) or a rhetorical question (expl b). If X and Y have different subjects, 既然 will come at the head of the sentence (expl a); if they have the same subject, 既然 will come after the subject in X (expl b). Y is usually headed by an adverb such as 就 jiù 2, 也 yě 2, or 还 hái 1 which brings its own nuances to the sentence 既 jì 2 is a shumianyu synonym which must come after the subject. 因为 yīnwei 1 is also a synonym, but it is different in focusing on X as a factual cause of a logical Y effect. 反正 fǎnzhèng 2 has a similar meaning but imparts a srtronger tone.

J

a. 既然他爱人一定要买新洗衣机，他也只好同意。
Jìrán tā àiren yīdìng yào mǎi xīn xǐyījī, tā yě zhǐhǎo tóngyì.
Since his wife insisted on buying a new washing machine, he could do nothing but agree.

b. 这个通知既然已经过期了，还留着有什么用呢？
Zhèige tōngzhī jìrán yǐjing guòqī le, hái liúzhe yǒu shénme yòng ne?
(Since) this notice has already expired, what point is there in keeping it?

即使 jíshǐ (——) 'even if (hypothesis)' Conjunction

1. 即使 X, 也(还) Y = Even if X, it is Y (Cj) 即使 is a member of one of the three different sets of concessive conjunctions which mark that no matter what the situation in X may be, the situation in Y is unaffected. 即使 specifically functions to mark that X is a hypothetical situation that does not influence Y. If X and Y represent different kinds of verb situations, X is a hypothetical condition which does not influence Y (expl a), even if it is an extreme degree of X (expl b). If X and Y refer to the same verb condition, Y will be a smaller amount of X (expl c). X and Y will be either a verb phrase or a clause. Y will usually be headed by 也 yě 1, 还 hái 1 or 都 dōu 1. 即便 jíbiàn 1, 便 biàn 5 and 纵然 zòngrán 1 are shumianyu synonyms; see also the comments at 即 jí 1. 就是 jiùshì 1, and 哪怕 X, 也 Y nǎpà...yě are oral synonyms. See 也 X 也 Y yě...yě 2 for a pattern with a similar meaning.

Note that although they are close in meaning and English translation, these three sets of concessive conjunctions differ in that the set with 虽然 suīrán and its synonyms marks only factual situations; the set with 即使 jíshǐ 1 and its synonyms mark only hypothetical situations; and the third, 无论 wúlùn 1 and its synonyms, is used only in an X formed with indefinite choice (e.g., 怎么 zěnme, 多么 duōme, etc.) or Verb 不 verb clauses. See further discussion and contrastive examples of this set of markers at 虽然 suīrán 1.

a. 学习外语，即使有时候说错了也不要紧。
Xuéxí wàiyǔ, jíshǐ yǒu shíhou shuōcuò le, yě bù yàojǐn.
When studying a foreign language, even if you make mistakes sometimes, it's no big deal.

b. 即使很微妙的错误，谢老师都要清清楚楚地纠正。
Jíshǐ hěn wēimiào de cuòwù, Xiè lǎoshī dōu yào qīngqīng-chuchu de jiūzhèng.
Even if they are very subtle errors, Professor Xie very meticulously corrects them.

c. 今年的产量即使不能达到人均一百斤，也还能达到九十斤。
Jīnnián de chǎnliàng jíshǐ bù néng dádào rénjūn yībǎi jīn, yě hái néng dádào jiǔshi jīn.
Even if this year's production can not reach 100 catties per capita, it can still get to 90.

即是 jíshì (——) 'is indeed' Verb

1. 即是 X = Is indeed X (Vb) The shumianyu 即是 marks that whatever follows it is precisely what is the topic of the discussion. 即 jí 1 is a shumianyu synonym which tends to be used when the following noun phrase is less complicated. 就是 jiùshì 1 is a commonly used synonym. You will mostly find 即是 in texts produced in the ROC.

a. 其中最重要的觀念性轉變即是：涉及兩岸事務的基本政策雖未改變，但……
Qízhōng zuì zhòngyào de guānniànxìng zhuǎnbiàn jíshì: shèjí liǎng'àn shìwù de jīběn zhèngcè suī wèi gǎibiàn, dàn...
The most important conceptual change among them was: although the basic policy involving matters between the two shores has not changed, however...

就 jiù (—) 'then' Adverb; "time frame" 'regarding, about' Coverb; 'only' Adverb; "affirmation" Adverb; 'even if' Conjunction

1. Vp1就 Vp 2/Sv = Verb phrase 1, then verb phrase 2 /Stative verb condition (Av) 就 marks that a second verb closely follows a first verb. The second element may be either a verb phrase (expls a & c) or a Stative verb (expl b). Frequently the sequencing will be further highlighted by having first verb phrase headed with 刚 gāng 'very recently' or 一 yī 1 (expl c). This and the usages described in 2 below may both be translated as 'then,' but they differ subtly. You will need to analyze the contexts to be certain of which 就 is before you. 便 biàn 1 is a shumianyu synonym only when the second element is a verb phrase.

a. 送他上了火车，我就回来了。
   Sòng tā shàngle huǒchē, wǒ jiù huílái le.
   Having seen him to the train I (then) returned.

b. 见了你我就高兴。
   Jiànle nǐ wǒ jiù gāoxing.
   Seeing you I am (then) happy.

c. 我们明天天一黑就走吧。
   Wǒmen míngtiān tiān yī hēi, jiù zǒu ba.
   Let's (then) leave as soon as it is dark out tomorrow.

J

2. 要是/为了/既然/因为/只要 X, 就 Y = If/For/Since/ Because/If only X, then Y

(Av) 就 is frequently used in compound sentences to mark that Y is both a continuation and the conclusion of the X situation. The particular coverb or conjunction found at the head of X marks whether the sentence is a hypothetical, choice, cause-result, goal, etc. structure; 就 marks that Y continues and then ends whatever the situation is in X. 便 biàn 2 is a close synonym also used with these markers. 就是 jiùshì 2 is a synonym used when X does not have one of these markers.

a. 上海警方希望民众不要惊慌，只要晚上外出时注意避开阴暗的地方，并确定旁边有人，就不会有什么事。
   Shànghǎi jǐngfāng xīwàng mínzhòng bù yào jīnghuāng, zhǐyào wǎnshang wàichū shí zhùyì bìkāi yīn'àn de dìfang, bìng quèdìng pángbiān yǒu rén, jiù bù huì yǒu shénme shì.
   The Shanghai police hope that people will not be panic-stricken. If only they will avoid dark places when they go out in the evening and be sure to be with somebody, then nothing will happen.

b. 为此，很多外地大学生本科尚未毕业，即全身心投入考研，因为拥有硕士学位，就能免受进京户口指标限制，从容寻找就业机会。
   Wèicǐ, hěn duō wàidì dàxuésheng běnkē shàng wèi bìyè, jí quán shēnxīn tóurù kǎoyán, yīnwei yōngyǒu shuòshì xuéwèi, jiù néng miǎnshòu jìn Jīng hùkǒu zhǐbiāo xiànzhì, cóngróng xúnzhǎo jiùyè jīhuì.
   For this reason, many non-Beijing students who have still not completed their undergraduate course devote themselves to research. This is because when they get an MA degree, they can (then) escape the stipulated restrictions on getting a Bejing residence card and look for employment opportunities.

c. 若是手枪、毒品之类违禁品失窃，所涉的就不只是民事赔偿问题，而是是否有人借保险箱犯罪的问题。

Ruòshì shǒuqiāng, dúpǐn zhīlèi wéijìnpǐn shīqiè, suǒ shè de jiù bùzhǐ shi mínshì péicháng wèntí, érshì shìfǒu yǒu rén jiè bǎoxiǎnxiāng fànzuì de wèntí.

If it is something contraband like guns or drugs that is stolen, what is involved is not only a question of compensation. It is also (then) a question whether or not people are making use of safety deposit boxes to commit crimes.

3. Time frame 就 Vp/Sv = Verb action/Stative verb condition at a point in time (Av) 就 may also mark either that a verb action will soon happen or that it happened long ago. When marking that a verb action (expl a) or Stative verb condition (expl b) is about to come about, a future context to the sentence is the clearest indicator of this usage (expls a & b). It can help you identify this 就 if you keep in mind that it can be part of an imminent occurrence structure with either a preceding 快 kuài 'soon' or a directly following 要 yào 3 and the change marker 了 le 3 at sentence end as reinforcement of the imminence of the verb action (expls a & b). However, be careful to remember that 了 might mark completion rather than change (expl c).

When there is a specific time reference right before 就, 就 marks that a verb act or Stative verb condition existed relatively long ago. The time reference may be an exact point in time (expl c) or a period of time (expl d). 便 biàn 3 is a shumianyu synonym of this long ago 就 marker only when a verb act occurs in the sentence.

a. 商店就关门了，现在去来不及了。
Shāngdiàn jiù guānmén le, xiànzài qù lái bù jí le.
The store is about to close (its doors). If you go now you won't be able to get there in time.

b. 鸡叫已经三遍了，天很快就亮了。
Jī jiào yǐjing sān biàn le, tiān hěn kuài jiù liàng le.
The rooster had already crowed three times, it's about to get light out.

c. 京剧七点开始，小冯六点一刻就来了。
Jīngjù qī diǎn kāishǐ, Xiǎo Féng liù diǎn yī kè jiù lái le.
The Peking Opera starts at 7:00. At 6:15 Xiao Feng had already arrived.

d. 抢救大熊猫的行动，早在60年代就开始了。
Qiǎngjiù dà xióngmāo de xíngdòng, zǎo zài liùshi niándài jiù kāishǐ le.
Efforts to save the Giant Panda (already) started in the 60's.

4. 就 Np = Concerning the noun (Cv) In this usage 就 marks that the noun following it is the target or scope of the verb action. The verb is often one which expresses a viewpoint; e.g., 说 shuō 'say,' 看 kàn 'think,' etc. When placed in front of the subject, 就 Np is usually end-marked with a comma. To distinguish this use of 就 from the 就 verb structures described above, determine whether a noun or verb phrase follows the 就. Keep in mind that the noun may be heavily modified and thus be some distance from the 就 (expl c). Consider the discussion at 关于 guānyú 1.

J

In a less frequently seen usage reminiscent of its classical meaning 'move towards,' 就 can also represent 1) the idea of 'nearby, close to'; e.g., 就进入学 jiùjìn rùxué 'go to school nearby,' 2) 'take advantage of'; e.g., 就着机会 jiù zhe jīhuì 'use the chance,' or 3) the source of a comment 就我来说 jiù wǒ lái shuō 'from my viewpoint...'

a. 这篇文章，就风格来说，不象胡适的。
Zhèi piān wénzhāng, jiù fēnggé lái shuō, bù xiàng Hú Shì de.
Judging from its style, this article doesn't seem like Hu Shih's.

b. 钱其琛首先就此次访日发表了谈话。
Qián Qíchēn shǒuxiān jiù cǐ cì fǎng Rì fābiǎole tánhuà.
First of all Qian Qizhen made a statement about this visit to Japan.

c. 会议期间，来自中日两国的120多位代表就政治、经济、技术和教育文化等共同关心的问题进行了分组讨论……
Huìyì qījiān, lái zì Zhōng-Rì liǎng guó de yī bǎi èrshí duō wèi dàibiǎo jiù zhèngzhì, jīngji, jìshù hé jiàoyù wénhuà děng gòngtóng guānxīn de wèntí jìnxíngle fēnzǔ tǎolùn...
During the conference, over 120 delegates from China and Japan held group discussions about politics, economics, technology, education and other matters of mutual concern...

J

5. 就 X = Only X (Av) In this usage, 就 marks a limitation in scope. X may be a verb phrase or a clause; X may appear to be a noun when the verb 有 yǒu 'have' is omitted (expl a). When 就 is followed by a verb phrase, 就 restricts the object of the verb phrase (expl a with 有); when 就 is followed by a clause, it is the subject that 就 restricts (expls b & c). 就 is pronounced with no stress in both cases. 只 zhǐ 1 and 仅 jǐn 'only' are synonyms.

a. 真奇怪，章老师书架上就(有)那么几本书。
Zhēn qíguài. Zhāng lǎoshī shūjià shang jiù (yǒu) nàme jǐ běn shū!
How odd! There is only that handful of books on Professor Zhang's bookshelf.

b. 这件事就我一个人知道。
Zhèi jiàn shì jiù wǒ yī ge rén zhīdao.
I am the only person who knows about this matter.

c. 就他们几个人会唱美国国歌。
Jiù tāmen jǐ ge rén huì chàng Měiguó guógē.
Only that handful of people know how to sing the American national anthem.

6. 就 Vp/Sv = Indeed the verb phrase/Stative verb (Av) When 就 is pronounced with stress in this usage, it marks that the verb situation will not easily change (expl a). When the subject is given the stress, 就 marks that it is specifically the subject that fits the criteria given in the sentence (expls b & c). It is of course impossible to "hear" the stress when reading, so analysis of the greater context of the sentence is necessary to recognize this usage of 就. 就是 jiùshì 2 and 即 jí 1 are synonyms. When the verb following 就 is 是, 便 biàn 4 is a shumianyu synonym (expl c). See 7 below in which 就 marks emphasis on numerical amounts

a. 不买，不买，就不买。
Bù mǎi, bù mǎi, jiù bù mǎi.
No, no, I will not buy it.

b. 那位工程师要的材料，我手头就有。
Nèi wèi gōngchéngshī yào de cáiliào, wō shǒutóu jiù yǒu.
I have at hand the materials that engineer requested.

c. 我们今天的汉字，就是从甲骨文发展来的。
Wǒmen jīntiān de Hànzì, jiù shì cóng jiǎgǔwén fāzhǎn lái de.
Our contemporary Chinese characters are evolved from oracle bone script.

7. 就 Amount = Emphasis on an amount (Av) When 就 is stressed in context with an amount, it marks that the following amount is thought to be small (expl a); when it is the subject of the sentence that is stressed, 就 marks that the amount given is thought to be a lot (expl b). As is the case with 6 above, it is necessary to use the context to "hear" whether the subject or the 就 is stressed.

a. 老高就讲了一个半小时，下边就讨论了。
Lǎo Gāo jiù jiǎng le yī ge bàn xiǎoshí, xiàbiān jiù tǎolùn le.
Gao talked for just 1 ½ hours. The rest of the time was for discussion.

b. 老高就讲了一个半小时，别人都没时间谈了。
Lǎo Gāo jiù jiǎng le yī ge bàn xiǎoshí, bié rén dōu méi shíjiān tán le.
Gao talked for an hour and a half! No one else had time to talk.

8. 就 Vp1/Sv,Vp2 = Even if there might be the first verb/Stative verb situation, verb 2 still occurs (Cj) In this usage 就 marks that even if the first verb were to happen, the second verb would be unchanged. You can distinguish this '(hypothetical) if' 就 8 from 就 1 and 2 by its placement in the first part of the compound sentence along with the appearance of 也 yě 2 or a synonym in the second half. The oral 就是 jiùshì 1 and the shumianyu 即使 jíshǐ 1 are two major synonyms in this usage. See 即使 for further discussion and examples.

a. 五点三刻了，你就赶到车站也来不及了。
Wǔ diǎn sān kè le, nǐ jiù gǎn dào chēzhàn yě lái bù jí le.
It's 5:45! Even if you hurry, you can't get to the station on time

b. 礼物，我绝不能收，你就再送来，我也不要。
Lǐwù, wǒ jué bù néng shōu, nǐ jiù zài sònglái, wǒ yě bù yào.
I absolutely can't accept any presents. Even if you send them again, I don't want them.

就是 jiùshì (——) 'even if (hypothesis), even' Conjunction; 'precisely, only' Adverb; "affirmation" Adverb; 'but, however'

J

Adverb

1. 就是 X, 也 Y = Even if X, it is Y (Cj) 就是 is an oral element of one of the three distinct sets of conjunctions which mark that no matter what X may say, Y is unaffected. When both X and Y are clauses or verb phrases, 就是 specifically marks that the hypothetical possibility mentioned in X does not influence Y (expl a), even if it is X to an extreme degree (expl b). When X is a noun, 就是 focuses attention on the noun much the way 连 lián 1 does (expl c). Y usually includes 也 yě 1. 就 jiù 8 and 哪怕 nǎpà are oral synonyms while 即使 jíshǐ 1 and 纵使 zòngshǐ 1 are shumianyu synonyms. See 虽然 suīrán 1 for comparative comments and examples of these three sets of concessive conjunctions.

a. 你就是写错了，也没有什么关系。
Nǐ jiùshì xiěcuò le, yě méiyǒu shénme guānxi.
Even if you wrote it incorrectly, it doesn't matter.

b. 教室里装好了空调，就是天气非常热，里边也很凉快。
Jiàoshì li zhuānghǎole kōngtiáo, jiùshì tiānqì fēicháng rè, lǐbiān yě hěn liángkuài.
When they have installed air conditioning in the classrooms, even if the weather is hotter than blazes, it will be cool inside.

c. 就是三岁小孩也不会干这蠢事。
Jiùshì sān suì xiǎohái yě bù huì gān zhè chǔnshì.
Even a three year old child would not do such a foolish thing.

2. 就是 X = Exactly X (Av) 就是 brings attention to X as the core idea in the sentence and eliminates consideration of other factors. X may upon occasion be a noun phrase, but the vast majority of the time X will be a verb phrase or a clause (expl a & b). 就 jiù 6 is an oral synonym of this adverbial use of 就是.

a. 别的学生都错了，就是他的回答对。
Biéde xuésheng dōu cuò le, jiùshì tā de huídá duì.
All the other students were wrong. His is the only correct answer.

b. 就是因为工厂领导没认真听取工人们的意见，才出现了这些困难。
Jiùshì yīnwei gōngchǎng lǐngdǎo méi rènzhēn tīngqǔ gōngrénmen de yìjiàn, cái chūxiànle zhèxiē kùnnan.
It is only because the factory leadership didn't seriously pay attention to the workers' suggestions that these problems have come up.

3. 就是 Vp = Definitely is Vp/Sv (Av) Whether used in a first or second verb phrase, this adverbial usage of 就是 marks various kinds of affirmation: it marks that a following quantity such as 半天 bàntiān 'half a day,' 好几个人 hǎo jǐ ge rén 'a good number of people,' 三个小时 sān ge xiǎoshí 'three hours,' etc. is felt to be large (expl a); it also affirms a verb situation and, when used in the second verb phrase, sometimes suggests criticism (expl b); it resolutely affirms a Stative verb or verb condition and implies refutation of a differing viewpoint (expl c). Consider also the shumianyu synonyms 即 jí

1, 即是 jíshì 1 and 便 biàn 4.

a. 弟弟一病就是半个月。
Dìdi yī bìng jiùshì bàn ge yuè.
Whenever my little brother gets sick, it lasts forever.

b. 黄道中汉语说得十分流利，就是汉字写得乱。
Huáng Dàozhōng Hànyǔ shuō de shífēn liúlì, jiùshì Hànzì xiě de luàn.
Huang Daozhong speaks Chinese quite well; it's just that his characters are sloppy.

c. 资本主义就是好。
Zīběn zhǔyì jiùshì hǎo.
Capitalism is wonderful.

4. X, 就是 Y = X, but Y (Av) In this less frequently seen usage 就是 is a member of the set of words which mark Y as a change in the direction of events started in X. Specifically, 就是 marks that the information in Y supplements or corrects that given in X. X is the focal point of the sentence, not Y. X and Y will be verb phrases or clauses. 只是 zhǐshì 1 is a close synonym. See 但是 dànshì 1 for further discussion of this set of corrective markers.

a. 这件衬衫样子很好看，就是颜色浅了点。
Zhèi jiàn chènshān yàngzi hěn hǎokàn, jiùshì yánsè qiǎn le diǎn.
This shirt is very nice, but the color is a bit light.

J

继续 jìxù (繼續) 'continue, go on' Verb

1. 继续 X = Continue X (Vb) 继续 marks that whatever follows it occurs continually and is prolonged without interruption. You will most often see a verb phrase following 继续 (expl a), but X can be a noun (expl b). 不断 bùduàn 1 is a close synonym. The synonyms 连续 liánxù and 陆续 lùxù mark events continuing on one after the other. Also consider 仍然 réngrán 1 and 还 hái 1. 继续 also represents the noun 'continuation,' and it occasionally occurs as a verb with no object following it; e.g., 塞尔维亚战争还在继续着 Sàiěrwéiyà Zhànzhēng hái zài jìxù zhe 'The Serbian War continues on.'

a. 对此，辽宁省长闻世震说，辽宁与台湾之间的经济技术合作前景应该是十分广阔的，辽宁将继续长期执行鼓励台商投资的政策；
Duìcǐ, Liáoníng shěngzhǎng Wén Shìzhèn shuō, Liáoníng yǔ Táiwān zhījiān de jīngji jìshù hézuò qiánjǐng yīnggāi shì shífēn guǎngkuò de, Liáoníng jiāng jìxù chángqī zhíxíng gǔlì Táishāng tóuzī de zhèngcè;...
Regarding this, the Governor of Liaoning Province, Wen Shizhen, said that the prospects for economic technological cooperation between Liaoning and Taiwan should be truly vast, and that Liaoning will continue for a long period to carry out a policy encouraging Taiwanese business investments;...

b. 下个星期一还要继续我们的试验。

Xiàge xīngqīyī hái yào jìxù wǒmen de shìyàn.
We will continue our experiment next Monday.

据 jù (據) 'according to' Coverb

1. 据 X, Y = Y happens based on X (Cv) 据 is a shumianyu member of one of the six sets of words which mark the basis on which the verb phrase is done. 据 specifically marks X as the foundation or source of information for what follows in the sentence. Y will be either a clause or a verb phrase. 据 differs from its close synonym 根据 gēnjù 1 in being used with an X that is structured as either monosyllabic or very short noun phrases and verb phrases (expl a). When it precedes the subject of the sentence, 据 X will often be end marked with a comma (expl a). See its oral synonym 根据 gēnjù 1 for further comparative comments. 据 often appears in the set phrases 据悉 jùxī 'it is reported,' and 据说 jùshuō 'allegedly.'

a. 据报所说，中美关系现在很紧张。
Jù bào suǒ shuō, Zhōng-Měi guānxi xiànzài hěn jǐnzhāng.
According to what the newspaper says, Sino-American relationships are tense now.

J

决 jué (决) "negative intensifier" Adverb

1.决 Negative Vp = Definitely negative verb (Av) When 决 comes directly before a negative adverb, it marks a neutral intensification of the negative nature of a verb situation. 决 is neutral in that it does not impart a sense of correcting or refuting earlier information, it simply strengthens the negative nature of the sentence. Compare this with the other negative intensifier 并 bìng 2 which simultaneously emphasizes the negative and conveys a sense of setting the record straight. 绝 is sometimes written instead of 决 for exactly the same values. The adverb 万万 wànwàn is an oral synonym. Much less frequently, 决 is also used with affirmative structures to mark intensification: see 无论 wúlùn 1.b for an example.

Grammatically either 决 or 并 could be used interchangeably in most sentences; however, the two connote different information. If expl a below were written with 并 instead of 决, it would suggest that it is wrong to believe that Xiao Meng would come even if the hour were late. Written as it is with 决, there is no suggestion that someone thought Xiao Meng would come no matter the time. Using 并 rather than 决 in expl b would mark that believing a second year student could read this novel in the original is wrong headed; 决 is more likely here since it takes four or five years of dedicated study to be able to read this classic.

a. 已经十二点三刻了，小孟决不会来了。
Yǐjīng shíèr diǎn sān kè le, Xiǎo Mèng jué bù huì lái le.

It's already twelve forty-five. Little Meng won't be coming <u>for sure</u>.

b. 翻译《红楼梦》这本古典小说，<u>决</u>不是学过一两年中文的人所能作得到的。

Fānyì "Hónglóu Mèng" zhèi běn gǔdiǎn xiǎoshuō, <u>jué</u> bù shì xuéguo yī liǎng nián Zhōngwén de rén suǒ néng zuò de dào de.

Translating the classic novel "The Dream of the Red Chamber" is <u>definitely</u> not something someone who has studied one or two years of Chinese can do.

绝 <u>jué</u> (绝) "negative intensifier" Adverb

1. <u>绝 Negative Vp</u> = <u>Definitely negative verb</u> (Av) <u>绝</u> is a variant way of writing the neutral negative intensifier <u>决</u>. There is no difference in meaning or usage between the two when they are used before a negative adverb. See <u>就 jiù</u> 8.b for an example. See the more commonly used <u>决 jué</u> 1 for further comment and examples.

Keep in mind however, that 绝 is also used for a wide number of meanings and in a number of words. Always look for a following negative adverb when you think that <u>绝</u> might be a variant way of writing <u>决</u>.

均 <u>jūn</u> (—) 'all' Adverb

1. <u>Nouns 均 Vp</u> = <u>Nouns all verb</u> (Av) The highly shumianyu <u>均</u> marks that all of a set of nouns are involved in a verb act. The nouns must come before <u>均</u>. <u>都</u> <u>dōu</u> 1 & 2 are synonymous. 均 is used in a number of words extending from the idea of 'all; each and every' and 'equal; even.'

a. 3人奋力将伤者从树下救出，欲送医院。他们连拦2辆的士，<u>均</u>被拒载。

Sān rén fènlì jiāng shāngzhě cóng shù xià jiùchū, yù sòng yīyuàn. Tāmen lián lán liǎng liàng díshì, <u>jūn</u> bèi jùzài.

Three people made strenuous efforts to pull the wounded from under the tree. Wanting to send them to the hospital, they tried to stop two taxis but were refused rides <u>both</u> times.

b. 随着今年香港社会及经济环境的变迁，移民海外人数不断增加，各公私组织或机构<u>均</u>受影响……

Suízhe jīnnián Xiānggǎng shèhuì jí jīngji huánjìng de biànqiān, yímín hǎiwài rénshù bùduàn zēngjiā, gè gōng sī zǔzhī huò jīgòu <u>jūn</u> shòu yǐngxiǎng...

Along with the vicissitudes of Hong Kong's social and economic environment this year, the number of people emigrating abroad has continually increased. <u>All</u> public and private organizations and structures have been affected...

可 kě (一) "emphasis" Adverb; 'however, but' Adverb; "permission to verb, verb possible" Auxiliary verb

1. 可 Verb = Really verb (Av) The oral 可 is used with verb phrases to mark an emphasis ranging from the emphatic (expl a) to the imperative (expl b). There will often be a 了 le 2 at sentence end (expl a), but not always (expl b). You can easily distinguish this usage from its other use described in 2 below since "emphasis" 可 rarely if ever comes at the head of a second verb phrase while 'however' 可 normally does. 可 is also used with some monosyllabic verbs to mark a psychological attitude; e.g., 可乐 kělè 'pleasurable,' and with some monosyllabic nouns to mark suitability; e.g., 可口 kěkǒu 'tasty.'

a. 老师这一问可把小柳问住了。
Lǎoshī zhè yī wèn kě bǎ Xiǎo Liǔ wènzhù le.
The teacher really stumped Liu with this question.

b. 通知晚上开复习班的事，你可记着点儿！
Tōngzhī wǎnshang kāi fùxíbān de shì, nǐ kě jìzháo diǎr!
There is a notice about tonight's review section. Don't you forget!

K

2. X, 可 Y = X, however Y (Av) In this usage 可 is a member of the set of words which mark Y as a change from the course of events given in X. 可是 kěshì 1 is a close synonym. See 但是 dànshì 1 for further discussion of this set of change markers.

a. 今天阴天，可并不太冷。
Jīntiān yīntiān, kě bìng bù tài lěng.
Today's cloudy, but it's still actually not too cold.

3. 可 Vp = Permission to verb/verb act possible (Ax) As a synonym of 可以 kěyǐ 2, the shumianyu Auxiliary verb 可 marks that doing a verb action is permissible (first 可 in expl a). As a synonym of 可以 kěyǐ 1, 可 marks that a verb action is possible or probable (second 可 in expl a). Occasionally, 可 marks worthiness (expl b); see 可以 kěyǐ 2.

Note, 不可不 Verb is a shumianyu expression which marks that a verb action must be done; 不能不 Verb and 不得不 Verb are oral synonyms which also mark necessity for a verb act. 不会不 Verb marks the extreme likelihood of a verb action occurring.

a. ……，其保险金属于职工个人所有，在职工办理退休手续后，可一次或多次领取，职工死亡的，可作为遗产处理。
..., qí bǎoxiǎnjīn shǔyú zhígōng gèrén suǒyǒu, zài zhígōng bànlǐ tuìxiū shǒuxù hòu, kě yī cì huò duō cì lǐngqǔ, zhígōng sǐwáng de, kě zuòwéi yíchǎn chǔlǐ.
..., the insurance money belongs to the individual staff and workers. After they have taken care of retirement procedures, they are allowed to withdraw it at once or in installments. Upon death, it can be handled as part of the estate.

b. 江南可游览的故址不少。
Jiāngnán kě yóulǎn de gùzhǐ bù shǎo.
There are not a few ancient sites worth visiting in the southern part of China.

可是 kěshì (——) 'but, however, still' Conjunction

1. X, 可是 Y = X, but Y (Cj) 可是 is an oral member of the set of conjunctions which mark Y as a change in the flow of information coming from X. The focus of the sentence is on a Y which either contrasts with (expl a) or supplements (expl b) the situation stated in X. X and Y will both be either a verb phrase or clause. Sometimes you will find 可是 used alone in Y, but you will also often find 虽然 suīrán 1 and its synonyms used in X (expl b). The oral 可 kě 2 is one of many synonyms; see the stronger toned 但是 dànshì 1 for further discussion of this set of conjunctions.

a. 我们餐厅做的菜看上去不怎么样，可是吃起来挺不错的。
Wǒmen cāntīng zuò de cài kàn shangqu bù zěnme yàng, kěshì chī qilai tíng bùcuò de.
Our cafeteria's dishes aren't much to look at, but they aren't bad at all.

b. 潮州我虽然住过，可是时间不长。
Cháozhōu wǒ suīrán zhùguo, kěshì shíjiān bù cháng.
Although I lived in Chaozhou, (however) it wasn't for very long.

K

可以 kěyǐ (——) "verb act possible, verb may happen" Auxiliary verb; "permission to verb" Auxiliary verb

1. 可以 Vp = Verb act is possible (Ax) 可以 is a member of the set of Auxiliary verbs which mark that a verb action is possible, permissible, or likely. In this first usage, 可以 usually marks that a verb situation is possible or probable (expls a, b, c & d). When the subject is an inanimate noun, 可以 marks that the noun can perform a certain function (expl e). Further, 可以 can mark that the subject has a certain capacity for doing a verb act (expl f), though it differs from 能 néng 3 in not also being used to mark that the subject is skilled at doing a verb. Note that the negative form of this "possible" usage is 不能 bù néng, not 不可以 (expl b); 不可以 is used to deny the permission discussed below in 2.

可 kě 3 is a shumianyu synonym which can mark either possibility or permission. 能 néng 1 is a synonym which differs in 1) tending to convey a sense that a verb action is physically possible and/or that the conditions are right for it, 2) lending an objectivity about the possibility of the verb act. 会 huì 1 is a synonym which marks that a verb action is likely to happen, and 要 yào 3 marks probability of a verb occurrence. As a

Stative verb, 可以 means 'not bad, acceptable' and a '(undesirably) high degree of.'

a. 这个教室可以坐30个人。
Zhèige jiàoshì kěyǐ zuò 30 ge rén.
This classroom can seat 30.

b. 你明天可以再来吗？我明天有事不能来了。
Nǐ míngtiān kěyǐ zài lái ma? Wǒ míngtiān yǒu shì bù néng lái le.
Is it possible for you to come again tomorrow? I have something to do tomorrow, I can't come.

c. 叶菜类是最快的，大概一个月就可以采收了。
Yè cài lèi shi zuì kuài de, dàgài yī ge yuè jiù kěyǐ cǎishōu le.
The leafy vegetables are the fastest. You can probably pick them in one month.

d. 杨日松表示，他可以确定白晓燕确实死亡时间为八至十天左右，目前他正在整理白晓燕验尸报告，……
Yáng Rìsōng biǎoshì, tā kěyǐ quèdìng Bái Xiǎoyān quèshí sǐwáng shíjiān wéi bā zhì shí tiān zuǒyòu, mùqián tā zhèngzài zhěnglǐ Bái Xiǎoyān yànshī bàogào,...
Yan Risong indicated that he could determine that time of death for Bai Xiaoyan to be 8 to 10 days or so. At present he is preparing her autopsy report...

e. 棉花可以织布，棉籽还可以榨油。
Miánhuā kěyǐ zhībù, miánzǐ hái kěyǐ zhàyóu.
Cotton can make cotton cloth, and cotton seeds can produce oil.

K

f. 二弟很能吃，一顿可以吃四大碗饭。
Èr dì hěn néng chī, yī dùn kěyǐ chī sì dà wǎn fàn.
My younger brother is a big eater, he can down four big bowls of rice at a meal.

2. 可以 Vp = Permission to do the verb (Ax) 可以 in this usage marks that permission is given to do a verb act. The negative form will be either 不可以 or 不能 (expl a). Contextual analysis is often needed to see the difference between 可以 1 and 2; they are often hard to distinguish from each other in isolated sentences. 能 néng 2 is a synonym used to mark an act permissible under specific conditions. 可以 is also occasionally used to mark that a verb action is worth doing (expl c).

a. 请问，这儿可以吸烟吗？不可以，美国差一点儿哪儿都不可以吸烟了。
Qǐngwèn, zhèr kěyǐ xīyān ma? Bù kěyǐ, Měiguó chà yīdiǎnr nǎr dōu bù kěyǐ xīyān le.
Excuse me, is it ok to smoke here? You may not smoke here. Nowadays, there is almost no place in America where one can smoke.

b. 据德国一八七一年四月十六日颁布的新帝国宪法，首相得皇帝的信任，可以永居发号施令之位。
Jù Déguó yī bā qī yī nián sì yuè shíliù rì bānbù de Xīn Déguó Xiànfǎ, shǒuxiàng dé huángdì de xìnrèn, kěyǐ yǒng jū fāhào shīlìng zhī wèi.
According to the New Imperial Constitution Germany promulgated on April 16,

1871, if the Prime Minister gained the trust of the Emperor, he could perpetually be in a position to give orders to others.

c. 故宫博物馆这次美术展览倒可以看看。
Gùgōng Bówùguǎn zhèi cì měishù zhǎnlǎn dào kěyǐ kàn kàn.
The art exhibition at the Palace Museum now is worth taking in.

况且 kuàngqiě (——) 'moreover, in addition' Conjunction

1. X,况且 Y = X, and besides Y (Cj) The relatively infrequently used 况且 is placed at the head of Y to mark that the reason given in Y either supports the reason given in X (expl a) or gives a new reason (expl b). You may find 况且 used for the same value at the start of a sentence to link the reasons given in two sentences.. 并且 bìngqiě 1 and 而且 érqiě are synonyms which do not focus on linking the reasons for the development of a situation. Also consider 且 qiě 1.

a. 这里附近有河，况且还有水井，用水一定不成问题。
Zhèli fùjìn yǒu hé, kuàngqiě hái yǒu shuǐjǐng, yòng shuǐ yīdìng bù chéng wèntí.
There are rivers in the area, and moreover there are wells. Water will certainly not be a problem.

b. 香港地方这么大，况且你又不知道他的电话号码，一下子怎么能找到他呢？
Xiānggǎng dìfang zhème dà, kuàngqiě nǐ yòu bù zhīdào tā de diànhuà hàomǎ, yī xiàzi zěnme néng zhǎodào tā ne?
Hong Kong is so large, and in addition you don't have his phone number. How can you quickly find him?

来 lái (來) 'in order to (do second verb)' Verb; 'since (time), over (time)' Auxiliary verb; 'approximately' Auxiliary verb

1. Vp1 来 Vp2 = Do Vp1 in order to do Vp2 (Vb) When 来 comes between two verb phrases, it marks that the first verb is done in order to accomplish the second. In this usage 来 lái 1 is an oral synonym of the shumianyu 以 yǐ 2. See also 以便 yǐbiàn 1. 去 qù can be used instead of 来 when the verb action is perceived as moving away from the subject of the sentence.

来 appears both by itself and in conjunction with 去 in single verb phrases to mark suggestion or intention to do a verb action: e.g., 你去买蔬菜，我来做晚饭 Nǐ qù mǎi shūcài, wǒ lái zuò wǎnfàn 'You go get some fresh vegetables, I'll make dinner.' Further, 来 is used in the structure verb 来 verb 去 to mark repeated repetitions of the verb act; e.g., 走来走去 zǒu lái zǒu qù 'walk back and forth.' Finally, 来 is also used for the very commonly seen verb 'come' as well as in words which extend from that meaning; e.g., 'cause to come; come up; do again; future.'

a. 我们星期五要开一个晚会来欢迎新来的同学。
Wǒmen xīngqīwǔ yào kāi yī ge wǎnhuì lái huānyíng xīn lái de tóngxué.
We will have a party on Friday to welcome new students.

L

b. 心里学系想通过座谈会来交流经验。
Xīnlǐxuéxì xiǎng tōngguo zuòtánhuì lái jiāoliú jīngyàn.
The Psychology Department is planning to have a symposium in order to exchange ideas.

2. Time 来, Y = Over the time period, Y (Ax) A member of one of the four sets of structures which focus attention on a time frame for a Y situation, 来 marks that a Y situation has been going on for the specified period of time and continues going on right up to the present moment. Y will be a verb phrase or a clause. 来 differs from its close synonym 以来 yǐlái 1 in being only used with lengths of time and not with specific points in time. See 以来 yǐlái 1 and 的时候 de shíhou 1 for discussions and examples of the other members of these sets of time frame markers.

a. 这几个月来，我认识了不少新的中国朋友。
Zhèi jǐ ge yuè lái, wǒ rènshile bùshǎo xīn de Zhōngguó péngyou.
Over the last few months I have made quite a few new Chinese friends.

b. 五年来，很多新型污水处理厂已经建成投产。
Wǔ nián lái, hěn duō xīnxíng wūshuǐ chǔlǐ chǎng yǐjīng jiànchéng tóuchǎn.
Many new style waste water treatment plants have been built and brought into operation over the last five years.

3. Number 来 = About that number (Ax) When placed after multiples of ten or before a measure, 来 means 'slightly more or less of that amount' (expl a). When placed right after the simple numbers 一 yī '1,' 二 èr '2,' 三 sān '3,' etc. 来 marks members of a list of reasons for a verb act (expl b).

a. 大礼堂能坐一千五百来人。
Dàlǐtáng néng zuò yī qiān wǔ bǎi lái rén.
The auditorium can seat around 1500 people.

b. 我这次去福建，一来是探亲，二来是搞社会调查。
Wǒ zhèi cì qù Fújiàn, yīlái shì tànqīn, èrlái shì gǎo shèhuì diàochá.
This time I'm going to Fukien first of all to visit relatives and secondly to do a social survey.

来着 láizhė (來—) "event did recently happen" Auxiliary verb

1. X 来着 = X did indeed happen (Ax) The oral marker 来着 is placed after X to mark affirmation that X did happen. The time frame is generally the recent past. X will be either a sentence (expl a), a verb phrase or a clause (expl b). 来的 láide is an interchangeable synonym.

Compare 来着 with the synonymous 过 guo 1 which also affirms the occurrence of a verb event, usually further in the past; for example, compare 部长去贵州来着 'The Minister did go to Guizhou ((recently))' with 部长去过贵州 'The Minister has been to Guizhou ((at least once sometime in the past)).'

a. 刚才老彭找你来着。
Gāngcái Lǎo Péng zhǎo nǐ láizhe.
Old Peng was just looking for you.

b. 原来我有一本汉泰辞典来着，最近送给那个四年级的学生了。
Yuánlái wǒ yǒu yī běn Hàn-Tài cídiǎn láizhe, zuìjìn sònggěi nèige sìniánjí de xuésheng le.
I used to have a Chinese-Thai dictionary, but I recently gave it to that senior.

L

了 lė (—) "verb completion" Structural marker; "sentence completion or/and change of condition" Structural marker

1. Verb 了 object ~complement = Verb act completed (on the object) (Sm) The character 了 represents three major grammatical functions in modern Chinese prose. 1) A 了 placed inside a sentence directly after a verb marks emphasis on past or future completion of that verb action. This use of "verb 了" is discussed in this first section. 2) A 了 placed at the end of a sentence may mark that the event or condition presented in the sentence has already occurred. Alternatively, "sentence 了" may mark a change of conditions. In addition, you will also find many examples in which a single "sentence 了" simultaneously marks both completion and change; this is frequently the case when "sentence 了" follows a Stative verb. "Sentence 了" is described in section two below.

You will also find sentences in which both a "verb 了" and a "sentence 了" occur. This is primarily discussed in the third section of this entry. 3) When 了 is pronounced liǎo, 了 marks potential for a verb action to occur. This distinctly different third grammatical usage of 了 is examined separately at 了 liǎo 1. 了 is also used as part of vocabulary such as 了解 liǎojiě 'comprehend,' 除了 chúle 1 'besides; except for,' 极了jíle 'extremely,' etc. The negatives of "verb 了," 没verb méi 1 or 没有 verb méiyou 1, mark that a verb action did not occur, not that a verb action started and was not completed.

When you see a 了 placed **within** a sentence either between the verb and its object or the verb and its complement, the 了 is being used to focus attention on the completion of the verb action. There will be an object after the 了 most of the time (expls a, b & c), but complements also occur (expl d). The object will almost always have a number-measure and/or a descriptive structure accompanying it (expls a & b); though when preceded by a complex adverbial structure, the object may be a simple noun (expl c). There may or may not be an object following the "verb 了" when used in the first clause in a compound sentences (expl e, r & s).

a. 小宋终于写完了那篇文章。
Xiǎo Sòng zhōngyú xiě wánle nèi piān wénzhāng.
Little Song finally finished that essay

L

b. 乔石还应对方要求，介绍了中国人大制度的有关情况。
Qiáo Shí hái yìng duìfāng yāoqiú, jièshaole Zhōngguó Réndà zhìdù de yǒuguān qíngkuàng.
Qiao Shi also responded to the guests's request and introduced relevant aspects of the structure of China's N.P.C.

c. 胡锦涛在听取海南省委工作汇报后讲了话
Hú Jǐntāo zài tīngqǔ Hǎinán Shěngwěi gōngzuò huìbào hòu jiǎngle huà.
Hu Jintao spoke after he heard the report from the Hainan Provincial Committee.

d. 鲜血从伤口流了出来。
Xiānxuè cóng shāngkǒu liúle chūlái.
Fresh blood flowed from the wound.

e. 你看见了该多高兴。
Nǐ kànjiànle gāi duō gāoxìng.
When you see it, you should be so happy.

When a single subject is involved in two verb acts, calculated emphasis is shown by the placing "verb 了" after one verb instead of the other to mark its completion (expls b & f). Alternatively the 了 may be placed after each of a series of verbs in a sentence (expl g) or after just the last verb (expl h) to mark sequencing or co-occurrence of verb actions. You will also find "Verb 了" placed between the syllables of a reduplicated verb to mark that a brief verb act is completed (expl I); see 一 yī 2 for a related verb structure.

f. 这样的指控，无疑敲下了「新闻自由」的警钟，也让身为新闻从业的我们，深感震撼与不安。

Zhèi yàng de zhǐkòng, wúyí qiāo xiàle “xīnwén zìyóu” de jǐngzhōng, yě ràng wèi xīnwén cóngyè de wǒmen, shēngǎn zhènhàn yǔ bù’ān.

This kind of accusation doubtlessly sounded the alarm about “Freedom of the Press,” and it causes we who are engaged in journalism to deeply feel shock and disquiet.

g. 广西建立了自然科学基金、青年科学基金、留学回国人员科学基金，支持了大批应用基础性、高科技科研项目。

Guǎngxī jiànlìle zìrán kēxué jījīn, qīngnián kēxué jījīn, liúxué huíguó rényuán kēxué jījīn, zhīchíle dàpī yìngyòng jīchuxìng, gāo kējì kēyán xiàngmù.

Guangxi established funds for natural sciences, funds for young scientists, and funds for scientists returned from abroad, and it also supported numerous items of applied basic and advanced scientific research.

h. 会议讨论并通过了这项提案。

Huìyì tǎolùn bìng tōngguòle zhèi xiàng tí’àn.

The meeting discussed and passed this proposal.

i. 他尝了尝茅台酒。

Tā chángle cháng Máotáijiǔ.

He took a taste of Maotai.

L

When there is a number-measure (object) structure after the “verb了” in a sentence, the 了 marks that the verb action is completely finished to the degree given in the N-M (O) structure. The number-measure may be a time phrase (expl j), a number of occurrences phrase (expl k), an amount (expl l), or it may include an object (expl m). This structure may also occur as the first part of a compound sentence (section 3 expl j). Note that when there is also a “sentence 了” at end of a number-measure (object) sentence, it marks that the verb action is completed but allows for the possibility that it may continue. Compare 第四十课的生词我复习了三遍 Dì sìshi kè de shēngcí wǒ fùxí le sān biàn “I reviewed the vocabulary for Lesson 40 three times” (reviewing is completed) and 第四十课的生词我复习了三遍了“I have reviewed the vocabulary for Lesson 40 three times” (may continue reviewing). Refer to section three below for further discussion on the use of both “verb 了” and “sentence 了” in one sentence.

j. 他睡了一个钟头。

Tā shuìle yī ge zhōngtóu.

He slept for one hour.

k. 国内油价今年已经涨了两次。

Guónèi yóu jià jīnnián yǐjing zhǎngle liǎng cì.

Domestic oil prices already went up twice this year.

l. ……围观的人聚集了100多号，10多分钟过去，竟无一人伸出援手。

...wéiguān de rén jùjíle yī bǎi duō hào, shí duō fēn zhōng guòqù, jìng wú yī rén shēnchū yuánshǒu.

...over 100 observers gathered, yet after ten plus minutes had gone by there was not one person offering aid.

m. 我哥哥一共念了两年大学。
Wǒ gēge yīgòng niànle liǎng nián dàxué.
My older brother studied two years of college in all.

A Stative verb 了 number-measure structure may either mark the degree of a completed change (expl n) or the amount of deviance from a standard (expl o). See the discussion at section two expls n, o p, q & r for further discussion of "sentence 了" used to mark change of a Stative verb condition.

n. 这个星期只晴了一天。
Zhèi ge xīngqī zhǐ qíngle yī tiān.
It was only clear outside one day this week.

o. 这双皮鞋大了一号。
Zhèi shuāng píxié dàle yī hào.
This pair of shoes is one size too large.

L

Occasionally, "verb了"can be understood to mark result, though this also seems to involve some element of completion (expls p & q). This usage is found in both simple (expl p) and compound sentences (expl q).

p. 这一页我涂了两行。
Zhèi yī yè wǒ túle liǎng háng.
I crossed out two lines on this page.

q. 你不爱听可以关了收音机。
Nǐ bù ài tīng kěyǐ guānle shōuyīnjī.
If you do not want to listen, you may turn off the radio.

You will also see a "verb 了" structure used as the first part of a compound sentence. When there is no "sentence 了" at the end of the sentence, the structure means that upon completion of the first verb structure, the second will happen. This is a good place to remind ourselves that 了 marks aspect, not tense. This means that while "verb 了" will most commonly be translated with the English past tense, especially in the simple sentences discussed so far, the values "verb 了" represents can also be accurately rendered with the future or present tenses. When the second half of compound sentences have 就 jiù 1 & 2, 要 yào 1 & 2, 还 hái 1 & 2, 才 cái 1 & 2, etc. in the second clause, they are solid indicators that the sentence should not be understood as referring to the past, but rather to the future (expl r) or the present (expl s). See section three for comments on the use of both "verb 了" and "sentence 了" in a compound sentence to refer to finished sequential events.

r. 我作完了功课，还得写信呢。
Wǒ zuò wánle gōngkè, hái děi xiěxìn ne.
After I have finished my homework, I still have to write some letters.

s. 一天的镜泊之行结束了，新加坡客人仍感余兴未尽。
Yī tiān de Jìngpō zhī xíng jiéshù le, Xīnjiāpō kèrén réng gǎn yúxìng wèi jìn.
After a day of travel on Mirror Lake concluded, the Singapore guests still felt the desire to continue.

Keep in mind that "verb 了" is not used in simple statements of a past or habitual event where there is no need to highlight its occurrence; 了 is used to bring attention to the completion of a specific verb action. Regard the presence of a 了 **within** a sentence as a handy guide which you can rely on to help you find the location of the core verb when reading modern Chinese prose.

2. Sentence 了 = Sentence involves completion~sentence involves a change~ sentence involves both completion and change (Sm) A 了 is placed at the end of a sentence to mark 1) that the event or condition presented in the sentence is finished, or 2) that the sentence represents a change of some sort, or 3) that there is a combination of completion and change in a situation. "Sentence 了" is used after both verb phrases and Stative verbs, and it may refer to the past, present, or future. When it refers to the past, "sentence 了" usually marks a combination of change & completion. "Sentence 了" is primarily a feature of spoken Chinese, so you will not see it as frequently as "verb 了" in written passages. Nonetheless, it is important to be aware of the values which "sentence 了" represents.

L

A 了 can be placed after a V O structure at sentence end to mark that an event involves a change of conditions; be careful to distinguish this "change" structure from the "completion" structure V 了 O discussed at expls a, b & c in section one above. The change will most often be in the present (expl a, b, c & d) or the future (expls j & r); occasionally verb object 了 refers to past change (expl e); note the discussion of V 了 O 了 in section three below.

a. 刮风了。
Guā fēng le.
The wind has started to blow.

b. 我昨天没有空儿，今天有空儿了。
Wǒ zuótiān méiyǒu kòngr, jīntiān yǒu kòngr le.
I didn't have any free time yesterday, but I do today.

c. 现在是秋天了，树上的叶子都红了。
Xiànzài shì qiūtiān le, shù shàng de yèzi dōu hóng le.

It's autumn now and the leaves on the trees have turned red.

d. 在横县，今年还出现这样的新现象：茶农入股，合伙办茶厂，蚕农入股办丝厂——企业和农户更紧密地"捆"成一体了。

Zài Héngxiàn, jīnnián hái chūxiàn zhèi yàng de xīn xiànxiàng: chánóng rùgǔ, héhuǒ bàn cháchǎng, cánnóng rùgǔ bàn sīchǎng--qǐyè hé nónghù gèng jǐnmì de "kǔn" chéng yītǐ le.

In Heng County this year there has also appeared a new phenomenon: tea growers have become shareholders and joined together to run tea processing plants, and silk growers have become shareholders and joined together to run silk plants--business and peasant households are "tieing" themselves more tightly into one entity.

e. 这几年，村里村外的姑娘已开始注意他了。

Zhèi jǐ nián, cūn lǐ cūn wài de gūniang yǐ kāishǐ zhùyì tā le.

The last few years, the girls from the village and beyond began to notice him.

A 了 structure which comes directly after the verb (with no object) at the end of a sentence or a comma end-marked structure definitely marks change when the time for the sentence is either the present (first clause in expls c, f, g & i) or the future (expls h & j). Change can involve a capability (expl f), an event (expls g, h & j) or perceptions (expl i). Note that when the 了 in a sentence ending verb 了 structure specifically refers to the past, the change will be completed and the 了 marks the combined "completion" and "change" discussed at expls k, l & m . Unless a direct reference to the past is given, it can be quite difficult to determine whether the 了 before you marks "completion," "change," or a combination of the two, so examination of the context is required (consider the possibilities at expl d above). However, when the verb is preceded by 就 jiù 3, 要 yào 1 & 2, or one of their synonyms, the structure clearly marks that a change will happen in the near future (expl j).

L

f. 这道题我会作了。

Zhèi dào tí wǒ huì zuò le.

I can handle this topic now.

g. 她一说，小姑娘就不哭了。

Tā yī shuō, xiǎo gūniang jiù bù kū le.

As soon as she spoke, the young girl stopped crying.

h. 我明天不去学校了。

Wǒ míngtiān bù qù xuéxiào le.

I am not going to go to school tomorrow (for a change).

i. 北京某机关王女士看完《大峡谷》后说："这部电影太值得看了，它有一种震撼灵魂的力量。"

Běijīng mǒu jīguān Wáng nǚshì kàn wán "Da Xiágǔ" hòu shuō: "Zhèi bù diànyǐng tài zhíde kàn le, tā yǒu yī zhǒng zhènhàn línghún de lìliàng."

After viewing "The Grand Canyon," a Ms. Wang from an agency in Bejing said, "I think this movie is definitely worth seeing, it has a type of power to stir the soul."

j. 辛晓琪十年的梦想终于要实现了。
Xīn Xiǎoqí shí nián de mèngxiǎng zhōngyú yào shíxiàn le.
Xin Xiaoqi's dream of ten years is about to be realized.

A single 了 following a verb at sentence end or before a comma can have the dual function of marking both completion and change of condition (the first expl in k, and expls l & m). You may find 已经 yǐjing 1 before the verb in this usage (expl k), which helps distinguish this 了 from the completion marking "verb 了" discussed directly above in section one (expls e, r & s). Unless there is a clear reference to the past, it can be difficult to distinguish the 了 which marks just completion from its use to mark both completion and change; consider expl g.

k. 我已经吃了，别给我做饭了。
Wǒ yǐjing chī le, bié gěi wǒ zuòfàn le.
I have already eaten. Please don't cook anything for me.

l. 他把他朋友的新自行车骑走了。
Tā bǎ tā péngyou de xīn zìxíngchē qí zǒu le.
He rode off on his friend's new bicycle.

L

m. 中国人民站起来了。
Zhōngguó rénmín zhàn qǐlái le.
The Chinese people have stood up.

A 了 following a Stative verb at sentence end will usually have the dual function of marking both completion and change of condition (expls n, o & p). But in Stative verb ending sentences which refer to the present (expl q) or the future (expl r), the 了 marks change alone. As is the case with Verb 了 structures, future Stative verb change structures containing a 就 jiù 3, 要 yào 1 & 2, etc. give a sense of imminence (expl r), and they are easier to identify as only involving change.

n. 小洪好了。
Xiǎo Hóng hǎo le.
Hong is ok now.

o. 电灯亮了。
Diàndēng liàng le.
The lights are on.

p. 孩子大了，这就好了。
Háizi dà le, zhè jiù hǎo le.
The child is older, and this is good.

q. 最近大夫不太忙了。

Zuìjìn dàifu bù tài máng le.
The doctor hasn't been too busy recently.

r. 天就要黑了。
Tiān jiù yào hēi le.
It's about to get dark.

You will occasionally find a short sentence composed of a noun ended with a 了 which marks change (expl s). Sometimes a number-measure 了 structure similarly suggests that an amount of change that has been achieved (expl t).

s. 春天了。
Chūntiān le.
It's spring.

t. 五十七岁了。
Wǔshiqī suì le.
I'm 57 now.

"Sentence 了" is also used in conjunction with the imperative 别 bié 'don't.' Examine the context to determine if the "sentence 了" marks change (2nd 了 in expl k & expl u) or completion (expl v).

L

u. 你喝了不少了，别喝了。
Nǐ hēle bù shǎo le, bié hē le.
You have drunk quite a bit--don't drink anymore.

v. 这是给老白的，你别吃了。
Zhèi shì gěi Lǎo Bái de, nǐ bié chī le.
This is to be given to Mr. White. Don't you eat it up.

Upon occasion you will see a 了 at the end of a sentence or clause to mark emotion or emphasis (expl w).

w. 他女儿长得可爱极了。
Tā nǚ'ér zhǎng de kě'ài jí le.
His daughter is so adorable.

3. V了 (Number-measure) (O) 了 or V1 了 (O), V2 (O) 了 = Both completion and change of verb actions marked (Sm) A "verb 了" along with a "sentence 了" can be in the same sentence to mark that the overall situation is completed and that a change of conditions is also involved. You will find co-occurrences of "verb 了" and "sentence 了" in both simple and compound sentences. Simple sentences will have an object after (expls a & c) or before (expl b) the verb.

a. 我已经写了回信了。
Wǒ yǐjing xiěle huí xìn le.

I have already written a return letter.

b. 这件事情我托了我们组长了。
Zhèi jiàn shìqing wǒ tuōle wǒmen zǔzhǎng le.
I have turned this matter over to the section chief.

c. 我两个弟弟都进了大学了。
Wǒ liǎng ge dìdi dōu jìnle dàxué le.
My two younger brothers have entered college.

When a simple sentence has a number-measure (object) (expl d) or a quantity (expl e) structure bracketed by the two 了, it marks that that degree of the verb action has occurred and allows for the possibility that it might continue. Examination of the larger context is necessary to determine whether the situation will continue or not. The object will usually come after the verb, but it may be transposed to the head of the sentence (expls e & j). See section one expls i, j, k, l, m & n for discussion of the use of just "verb 了" with number-measure structures to mark completion only.

d. 我学了三年中文了。
Wǒ xuéle sān nián Zhōngwén le.
I have been studying Chinese for three years now.

e. 这本小说我已经看了一半了。
Zhèi běn xiǎoshuō wǒ yǐjing kànle yībàn le.
I have read half of this novel.

L

The two 了 have the same values when used with a Stative verb (expls f & g).

f. 老师已经晚了十分钟了，我们走吧。
Lǎoshī yǐjing wǎnle shí fēn zhōng le, wǒmen zǒu ba.
The teacher is already ten minutes late. Let's leave.

g. 头发白了许多了。
Tóufa báile xǔduō le.
(My) hair has gotten quite a bit whiter.

When a compound sentence has a "verb 了" in the first clause and a "sentence 了" at the end of the second clause, it will mark that both verb acts are completed and that the second clause involves a change of condition. The first clause will often be end-marked with a comma, though this may not happen in shorter sentences. See section one expls e, f, g & h for comments on the value of "verb 了".

h. 他两点一刻下了汉语口语课就回宿舍了。
Tā liǎng diǎn yīkè xiàle Hànyǔ kǒuyǔkè juì huí sùshè le.
At 2:15 he got out of Chinese class and then returned to the dorm.

i. 他休息了两个月才上班了。
Tā xiūxile liǎng ge yuè cái shàngbān le.

He rested up for two months and then went to work.

j. 这个戏我刚看了一半就让人叫走了。

Zhèi ge xì wǒ gāng kànle yībàn jiù ràng rén jiào zǒu le.

I saw just half of the play and was called away by someone.

离 lí (離) 'away from' Coverb

1. 离 X (distance) = Distance from X (Cv) As a coverb 离 marks that X is separate, apart, or lacking. X can be a time (expl a), place (expl b), or thing (expl c). When X is a place or a time, 离 is frequently used in the structure Place/time 1 离 Place/time 2 Distance (expls a & b). Distance can be structured as either a Stative verb or a specific amount of time (expl a) or space (expl b). 离 also represents the verb 'leave, depart.'

a. 今天离新年只有两个星期了。

Jīntiān lí xīnnián zhǐyǒu liǎng ge xīngqī le.

New Year's is only two weeks from today.

b. 北京离天津有二百四十华里。

Běijīng lí Tiānjìn yǒu èrbǎi sìshi huálǐ.

Beijing is 240 (Chinese) miles from Tianjin.

L

c. 我离了辞典，差一点儿就看不懂中国报纸。

Wǒ líle cídiǎn, chà yīdiǎnr jiù kàn bu dǒng Zhōngguó bàozhǐ.

If I don't have a dictionary, I almost can't read a Chinese newspaper.

连 lián (連) 'even' Coverb

1. 连 X 都/也 Vp = Even X verbs (Cv) 连 marks emphasis on X, which may be structured as either a noun phrase (expls a & b) or a verb phrase (expl c). When X is a noun it can be either the subject (expl a) or object (expl b) of the structure, it depends on which element is being emphasized. In positive sentences, 连 tends to mark situations beyond the expected (expl a), and in negative sentences, it marks unusual events (expls b & c). 就是 jiùshì 1 is a partial synonym.

If there is no subject before the 连, the structure can sometimes be ambiguous; e.g., 连我也不认识 lián wǒ yě bù rènshi could mean either 'Even I do not know (him)' or '(He) does not know even me.' Analysis of the overall context is necessary to clarify this sort of problem. When X is a number-measure-noun structure, the number is always 'one' and the verb phrase will be negative: 他连一分钱都不给 Tā lián yī fēn qián dōu bù gěi 'He doesn't give even one cent.' There will always be an adverb before the verb, usually 也 yě 4 or 都 dōu 4. 也 tends to be used instead of 都 when the sentence is negative (expl c), but 都 is also used with negative situations (expl b).

Note: 连 is often omitted from this pattern. To understand the "even" nature of such sentences, you need to notice the presence of 都/也 and analyze the context to identify the "even" pattern. Sometimes the pattern will not be terribly obvious, and you will have to analyze the context to be sure.

连 noun means 'including the noun' when there is no 都 or 也 before the verb: e.g., 连今天是七天 Lián jīntiān shì qī tiān 'Including today it is seven days.' 连 is also used as a noun, a verb and an adverb with meanings extending from 'link, connect.'

a. 在扫盲运动中，连六十多岁的老农民都学习文化了。
Zài sǎománg yùndòng zhōng, lián liùshi duō suì de lǎo nóngmín dōu xuéxí wénhuà le.
In the campaign to wipe out illiteracy, even peasants over sixty years old learned to read.

b. 她连晚饭都没吃，就回去宿舍复习课文。
Tā lián wǎnfàn dōu méi chī, jiù huíqù sùshè fùxí kèwén.
She didn't even eat dinner. She just went back to the dorm to review.

c. 小宫学习太用功，连看电影也没兴趣。
Xiǎo Gōng xuéxí tài yònggōng, lián kàn diànyǐng yě méi xìngqu.
Little Gong works too hard. He isn't even interested in seeing a movie.

2. 连 X 带 Y = X along with Y (Cv) 连 X 带 Y marks that two monosyllabic verbs occur in very tight sequence. This generally occurs as an adverbial structure (expl a). In this use 连 gives a stronger tone of voice than the synonymous 又 X 又 Y yòu 1. When used with two thematically related noun phrases or disyllabic verb phrases (expl b), 连 gives a stronger tone of voice than the synonymous 和 hé 1. **L**

a. 三个演员连跳带唱地表演了一整个晚上。
Sān ge yǎnyuán lián tiào dài chàng de biǎoyǎnle yī zhěngge wǎnshang.
Dancing and singing, the three actors performed an entire evening.

b. 我爱人那次得流行性感冒，连打针带吃药一共用了三百块。
Wǒ àiren nèi cì dé liúxíngxìng gǎnmào, lián dǎzhēn dài chīyào yīgòng yòngle sān bǎi kuài.
When my spouse got the flu that time, we used up about $300 for shots and medicine.

了 liǎo (一) "verb able/unable to happen" Verb complement

1. Verb/Stative verb得～不了 = Verb/Stative verb condition can/cannot occur (Vc)
When you see 了 placed immediately after either 得 de 3 or 不 bù 3, 了 is pronounced liǎo and is used to mark that the verb action can or cannot be done (expl a). When used with a Stative verb, the structure tends to be in the negative form (expl b), although you might also see liǎo used in affirmative Stative verb questions.

Since liǎo 了 occurs only after 得 or 不, it is easy to distinguish liǎo 了 from the more commonly used 了 le 1 which marks verb completion and 了 le 2 that marks change of condition. 了 liǎo also represents the verb 'finish, conclude,' and it is used in words such as 了不起 liǎobuqǐ 'amazing' and 了解 liǎojiě 'comprehend.'

a. 明天我們去北戴河游泳，你去得了去不了？
Míngtiān wǒmen qù Běidàihé yóuyǒng, nǐ qù de liǎo qù bu liǎo?
We are going to go swimming at Beidaihe tomorrow. Can you go?

b. 汉语节目表演三点半开始，现在去晚不了。
Hànyǔ jiémù biǎoyǎn sāndiǎn bàn kāishǐ, xiànzài qù wǎn bu liǎo.
The Chinese class performance starts at 3:30. If we leave now, we can't be late.

历来 lìlái (歷來) 'always, constantly' Adverb

1. 历来 Vp = Has always verbed (Av) 历来 marks that the following verb action started in the past and has continued right up to the present. 历来 is used only with positive situations. It is a weaker shumianyu synonym of 从来 cónglái 1, a marker used with both negative and positive situations. See also 从 cóng 2 and 向来 xiànglái 1.

L

a. 历来如此。
Lìlái rúcǐ.
It has always been like this.

b. 中国人民历来就有勤劳勇敢的优良传统。
Zhōngguó rénmín lìlái jiù yǒu qínláo yǒnggǎn de yōuliáng chuántǒng.
The Chinese people have constantly had a fine tradition of hard work and bravery.

令 lìng (一) "cause (an emotional state)" Verb

1. Np1 令 Np2 Vp = Np1 causes Np2 to verb (Vb) 令 is a member of the set of words used to mark "cause to happen." The relatively seldom seen shumianyu 令 marks that a first noun phrase causes the second to feel an emotion; the second noun phrase must be a human being. 使 shǐ 1, 让 ràng 1 & 2, and 叫 jiào 1 & 2 are synonyms, each having its own distinct range of values; see 使 for comparative comments and examples. Originally 令 meant 'order; command,' and it is still used for that value in some vocabulary items.

a. 他们子女的成绩令父母很高兴。
Tāmen zǐnǚ de chéngjī lìng fùmǔ hěn gāoxìng.
Their children's achievements make parents very happy.

b. 中国的国际地位令人民极为满意。
Zhōngguó de guójì dìwèi lìng rénmín jí wéi mǎnyì.
China's international status makes the people extremely satisfied.

么 må (麽) "yes or no question marker" Auxiliary; "rhetorical question marker" Auxiliary

1. **Sentence 么 = Interrogative sentence** (Ax) The character 么 is sometimes used instead of 吗 må 1 at sentence-end in prose from the Republic of China to mark a question to which a yes or no answer is anticipated (expl a). See 吗 må 1 for further comments and examples. 么 is also used in the same way 吗 må 2 is to mark rhetorical questions (expl b). Both examples are from the play "Thunderstorm" written in the 1930's.

a. 我不在的时候，你常来问母亲的病么？
Wǒ bù zài de shíhou, nǐ cháng lái wèn mǔqīn de bìng ma?
When I wasn't here, did you often come to visit mom when she was sick?

b. 你不怕父亲不满意你么？
Nǐ bù pà fùqīn bù mǎnyì nǐ ma?
Aren't you afraid Father is dissatisfied with you?

吗 må (嗎) "yes or no question marker" Auxiliary; "rhetorical question marker" Auxiliary

M

1. **Sentence 吗 = Interrogative sentence** (Ax) A major member of the set of markers used with question structures, 吗 is placed at sentence end to mark a question to which either an affirmative or negative answer is expected. 吗 is more frequently used in affirmative style questions (expl a), but it can also be used in negatively structured questions (expl b). When you find 吗 used with negative questions, examination of the context is necessary to distinguish this neutral use of 吗 from its use in the reproachful negative rhetorical question structure described below in 吗 ma 2. 不 bù 2 and 没有 méiyǒu 2 are frequently seen synonyms. Also consider 还是 háishi 1. 麽 ma 1 is sometimes used synonymously in place of 吗 in Republican prose texts, but it is most commonly used as part of the word 什麽 shénma 'what.'

a. 老师讲的例子你听懂了吗？
Lǎoshī jiǎng de lìzi nǐ tīng dǒng le ma?
Did you understand the examples the teacher gave?

b. 美国农业部的代表团明天不来了吗？
Měiguó Nóngyèbù de dàibiǎotuán míngtiān bù lái le ma?
Is the delegation from the American Department of Agriculture not coming tomorrow?

2. **Sentence 吗 = Rhetorical question (implying the opposite)** (Ax) In this usage, 吗 marks a rhetorical tone of reproach and a calling to account. When the sentence is in the affirmative, this structure implies the negative is the correct answer (expl a); when the

sentence is in the negative, the affirmative is seen as correct (expl b). Though it is easier to do so when the sentence is negative, the rhetorical tone can be hard to differentiate from the "yes or no" 吗 questions discussed above, so analysis of the context is necessary. When the rhetorical question adverb 难道 nándào 'Do you mean to say' is added to the sentence, the rhetorical tone is clearer and stronger (expl b). 没有X吗 is a synonymous structure which marks surprise or suspicion about past non-events; see 没有 méiyǒu 2.

a. 你这样办能成功吗？
Nĭ zhèi yàng bàn néng chénggōng ma?
If you do it this way can you succeed?

b. 这些美丽的神话故事难道不是反映了古代劳动人民的良好愿望吗？
Zhèixiē mĕilì de shénhuà gùshì nándào bùshì fănyìngle gŭdài láodòng rénmín de liánghăo yuànwàng ma?
Don't these beautiful mythological stories reflect the good aspirations of the working people of antiquity?

没 méi (一) "non-occurrence" Adverb; "question marker" Adverb; "comparison" Verb

M

1. 没 Verb = Verb action not done/Stative verb condition not experienced (Av) One of the small set of adverbs that mark verb and Sv negation, 没 marks the non- occurrence of a verb action. While non-occurrence is by its very nature something that normally refers to the past and can generally be translated with the English past tense (expl a), it is important for you to keep in mind that 没 can also mark the non-occurrence of future verb situations as well; in future situations it often appears after 还 hái 1 (expl b). In other words, you should not automatically translate 没 into the past tense. You need to check the context for the time frame involved to determine the correct tense of the English equivalent. Furthermore, when thinking of 没 as the negative counterpart of the completion marker 了 le 1, keep in mind that 没 signals that the verb situation did not occur, it does not mark that the verb act was started and then not completed. Note: 没 is not used with verbs which do not involve an action; e.g., *没是 or *没知道 do not occur. 未 wèi 1 is a shumianyu synonym which can be used for the values of both 没 and 不 bù 1.

Compare the use of 没 with those of 不 bù 1, the other frequently seen negative adverb. 没 verb marks the non-occurrence of the verb action, while 不 verb marks the non-existence of the verb action; e.g., in 没去 the verb action "go" is itself negated, while in 不去 it is the idea of "going" rather than the verb action that is negated. 没 usually brings an objective value to a structure while 不 tends to connote a subjectiveness. When used with Stative verbs, 没 Stative verb marks a Sv condition not experienced, while 不 Stative verb marks the absence of the Sv condition; e.g., 没红 'wasn't red' marks that "redness" did not happen while 不红 'is not red' marks that a condition of "redness" does not exist. 没 Auxiliary verb is used with a limited number of Auxiliary verbs such as 要 yào 1, 能 néng 1, 敢 gǎn 'dare to,' 肯 kěn 'be willing to,' etc. to mark an objective negation of an Auxiliary verb situation. Compare this with 不 which can be used with all Auxiliary verbs to mark subjective negation of an event; e.g., compare 没能买 'not able to buy' where 没 marks an objective narration of none ability to buy with 不能买 'not able to buy' where 不 marks a subjective (from the viewpoint of the subject of the structure) inability to buy something.

Note that the adverb 没有 méiyǒu 1 is a very close synonym of this use of 没 and is used in the same ways for the same values. With this in mind, you need to remember that the adverb 没 can also negate the verb 有 'to have.' If you remember that the negative adverb-verb structure 没有 méi yǒu will be followed by a noun (except when given as a brief answer to a question) while the adverb 没有 méiyǒu 1 will have a verb after it, the two will not be too hard to differentiate. Note also that sometimes the adverb-verb 没有 structure can be shortened to just 没; i.e., 我没有钱 can also be rendered as 我没钱.

a. 我昨天忙得要死，从早到晚都没吃饭。
Wǒ zuótiān máng de yàosǐ, cóng zǎo dào wǎn dōu méi chīfàn.
I was so busy yesterday I nearly died. I did not eat all day long.

b. 如果你下个星期五还没找到工作，我就要跟你离婚。
Rúguǒ nǐ xià ge xīngqīwǔ hái méi zhǎodào gōngzuò, wǒ jiù yào gēn nǐ líhūn.
If you still have not found a job by next Friday, I am going to divorce you.

M

2. Verb phrase 没 = Has the verb phrase occurred (Av) When 没 is used at the end of a sentence to mark a neutral question, it is a synonym of 没有 méiyǒu 2. See 没有 méiyǒu 2 for comments and examples. Consider 吗 ma 1.

3. X 没 Y (这/那么) Sv = X is not as Stative verb as Y (Vb) 没 is used as a synonym of 没有 méiyǒu 3 in inferiority comparison structures to mark that X does not possess the degree of the Stative verb condition that Y does. See 没有 méiyǒu 3 for comments and examples.

没有 méiyǒu (——) "non-occurrence" Adverb; "question" Adverb; "comparison > inferiority" Verb; 'does not have' Adverb-verb

1. 没有 Verb = Verb action not done or not completed (Av) One of the set of negative adverbs, 没有 specifically marks the negation of the occurrence of a verb situation. While non-occurrence by its very nature is something that usually refers to the past (expls a & b), 没有 can mark the non-occurrence of future verb situations as well (expl c). Therefore, you should not automatically translate 没有 verb into the past tense. Check the context to determine the time frame involved. Reference to a time in the past such as 昨天 zuótian 'yesterday,' 上个月 shàng ge yuè 'last month,' 去年 qùniàn 'last year,' etc. or the presence of specific markers of past verb action such as 过 guo 1 (expls a & b) are reliable indicators that a 没有 Verb structure should be translated into the English past tense. Keep in mind that 没有 can not be used with verbs which do not involve happening or completion; e.g. *没有是, *没有知道 do not occur. See the more oral synonym 没 méi 1 for a comparative discussion of this 没有 non-completion marker with the other commnly seen negative adverb 不 bù 1. Also consider the shumianyu negative adverb 未 wèi 1.

Be careful to distinguish between this adverbial use of 没有 and 没有 méi yǒu 4 below in which the adverb 没 negates the verb 有.

a. 我没有去过乌鲁木齐。
Wǒ méiyǒu qùguo Wūlǔmùqí.
I have never gone to Urümqi.

b. 中国的政治体制改革早在七十年代末就开始了，并且一直没有停止过。
Zhōngguó de zhèngzhì tǐzhì gǎigé zǎo zài qīshí niándàimò jiù kāishǐle, bìngqiě yīzhí méiyǒu tíngzhǐguò.
Reforms of China's political structure started in the late 70's, and they never stopped.

M

c. 按照学校规定，假如九月一号没有注册，不许上课。
Ànzhào xuéxiào guīdìng, jiǎrú jiǔyuè yīhào méiyǒu zhùcè, bù xǔ shàngkè.
According to school regulations, if you have not registered by September 1, you may not attend classes.

2. Vp 没有 = "Neutral question marker" (Av) When placed at sentence end, 没有 marks a neutral question; that is, the person who poses the question has no presuppositions about the answer. Note that in this usage 没有 has none of the values described in 1 above or 3 and 4 below. The more oral synonym 没 méi 2 can replace 没有 in this usage. In southern dialects, a question can be structured as 有没有 Verb phrase. 吗 ma 1 is a synonym which expects a "yes or no" answer.

Compare the neutral Vp 没有 with the rhetorical interrogative 没有 Vp 吗 which marks suspicion or surprise and implies a request for verification. For example, compare 小范看见没有？Xiǎo Fàn kànjiàn méiyǒu with 小范没有看见吗 in which the first sentence asks the neutral question 'Did Fan see it?' and the second implies a request for verification of the supposition that Fan did see it. See the discussion of Clause 了没有 at 了 le 2; also see 吗 ma 2 for discussion of rhetorical structures with 不 bù 1.

a. 那个新加坡留学生买了那部凤凰自行车没有？
Nèige Xīnjiāpō liúxuéshēng mǎile nèi bù Fènghuáng zìxíngchē méiyǒu?
Did the Singapore student buy that Phoenix bicycle?

b. 吉林贸易代表团到了没有？

Jílín Màoyì Dàibiǎotuán dàole méiyǒu?

Has the Jilin Province Trade Delegation arrived?

3. X 没有 Y (这/那么) Sv = X is not as Stative verb as Y (Vb) 没有 is a member of one of the three sets of words used to mark comparative structures. It specifically marks that X is inferior to Y in terms of the Stative verb condition. X and Y may be either noun phrases (expl a) or verb phrases (expl b). 这么 zhème is placed before the Stative verb when the sentence compares an X with a Y which is conceptually or physically near to hand (expl a), and 那么 nàme is used when the structure compares an X with a Y which is relatively further away (expl c). A Verb 得(de) structure may be placed either between X and 没有 or between Y and (那么) Sv to form a comparison structure in which X does a verb in a less Stative verb manner than Y does (expl c). You can distinguish this usage of 没有 from 1 and 2 above as well as 4 below by the presence of a Stative verb structure at the end of the sentence. The more oral synonym 没 méi 3 can replace 没有 in all the structures in this usage. 不如 bùrú 2 is a synonymous shumianyu structure. See 比 bǐ 1 for comments on superiority comparative structures and 一样 yīyàng 1 for general comments on equality comparison structures.

a. 英语字母表没有汉字这么有意思。

Yīngyǔ zìmǔbiǎo méiyǒu Hànzì zhème yǒu yìsi.

The English alphabet is not as interesting as Chinese characters.

b. 我肚子有点儿不舒服，去没有不去好。

Wǒ dùzi yǒu diǎnr bù shūfu, qù méiyǒu bù qù hǎo.

My stomach is a bit queasy. It is better not to go.

M

c. 菲律宾女排队打得没有日本女排队那么激烈。

Fēilǜbīn nǚpáiduì dǎ de méiyǒu Rìběn nǚpáiduì nàme jīliè.

The Philippine women's volleyball team does not play as intensely as the Japanese team.

4. Np 1 没有 Np 2 = The first noun does not possess noun 2 (Av-Vb) The way to tell this simple adverb-verb structure apart from the adverbial use of 没有 described in 1 above is to determine if there is a noun rather than a verb following 没有. If there is a object, it is the usage described here wherein the verb 有 is negated by the adverb 没; if there is a verb, 没有 is being used as an adverb. Note that the verb 有 can be omitted with a resulting Np 1 没 Np 2 structure with no change in meaning; e.g., 我没有笔 and 我没笔 both mean 'I do not have a pen.' See 没 méi 1 for further discussion.

a. 我没有汽车。

Wǒ méiyǒu qìchē.

I do not have a car.

b. 西方国家没有权利干涉我国内政。

Xīfāng guójiā méiyǒu quánlì gānshè wǒ guó nèizhèng.

Western nations have no right to interfere in our domestic politics.

5. 没有 Vp 吗 = Isn't it verb phrase (Av) This rhetorical negative interrogative either marks suspicion or surprise while suggesting the that answer to the question is affirmative and implying a request for verification (expl a). See comparative comments and a further example of this rhetorical question marker at 没有 méiyǒu 2 above. Compare this with the similar disbelief rhetorical question structure (X) 不是 Y 吗 at bùshì 2.

a. 我们讨论过了，你们没有讨论吗？
Wǒmen tǎolùnguo le, nǐmen méiyǒu tǎolùn ma?
We debated it? Didn't you?

能 <u>néng</u> (一) "verb act possible, verb able to happen" Auxiliary Verb; 'good at verb act' Auxialiary Verb; "permission to verb" Auxiliary verb

1. <u>能 Vp</u> = <u>Verb action is (physically) possible</u> (Ax) <u>能</u> is a member of the set of Auxiliary verbs which mark that a verb action is probable, possible, or permitted. In this basic usage <u>能</u> often marks that a verb action is possible because conditions in general are right for the verb to happen (expl a & c). Sometimes <u>能</u> marks that it is physically possible to do the verb act (expl b). <u>能够</u> <u>nénggòu</u> 1 is a more shumianyu synonym. <u>能</u> differs from the synonymous <u>可以</u> <u>kěyǐ</u> 1 in connoting a possible physical element to the verb act (expls a & b). The synonymous <u>会</u> <u>huì</u> 1 marks that a verb action is likely while <u>要</u> <u>yào</u> 3 indicates the probability of a verb act. When the subject is an inanimate noun, <u>能</u> marks that the noun can perform a certain function (expl d).

Note: <u>不能不</u>, <u>不得不</u> <u>de</u> 1, and the shumianyu <u>不可不</u> <u>kě</u> 1 all mark that a verb must be done. <u>不会不</u> <u>huì</u> 1 marks the strong likelihood of the verb action.

a. 天这么晚了，管子工<u>能</u>来吗？
Tiān zhème wǎnle, guǎnzigōng <u>néng</u> lái ma?
It's already so late--will the the plumber be <u>able</u> to come?

b. 小徐的左腿伤好多了，<u>能</u>慢慢儿走几步了。
Xiǎo Xú de zuǒ tuǐ shāng hǎo duō le, <u>néng</u> mànmānr zǒu jǐ bù le.
The wound on Xu's left leg is much better. She <u>can</u> slowly walk a few steps now.

c. 此外，我公司在上海、南京、汕头等地投资房地产，一年也<u>能</u>得到可观的经济收益。
Cǐwài, wǒ gōngsī zài Shànghǎi, Nánjīng, Shàntóu děng dì tóuzī fángdìchǎn, yī nián yě <u>néng</u> dédào kěguān de jīngjì shōuyì.
In addition, if our company invests in real estate in Shanghai, Nanjing, Shantou, and other places, in one year we <u>can</u> earn some appreciable economic gains.

d. 橘子皮还<u>能</u>作药。
Júzi pí hái <u>néng</u> zuò yào.
Orange peel <u>can</u> make a kind of medicine.

N

2. <u>能 Vp</u> = <u>Allowed to verb</u> (Ax) In this usage <u>能</u> marks that either circumstances (expl a) or reasonableness (expl b) permit the subject to do a verb act. In both cases, the structure will most often be in the negative. <u>可以</u> kěyǐ 2 is a positive synonym which marks that permission is given to do the verb (expl b). 能够 nénggòu is rarely used for this value.

a. 这条牛仔裤不<u>能</u>再瘦了，再瘦就没法穿了。
Zhèi tiáo niúzǎikù bù <u>néng</u> zài shòu le, zài shòu jiù méi fǎ chuān le.
These blue jeans <u>can't</u> be any smaller. If they're any smaller there is no way to get them on.

b. 你可以告诉商同学这道题怎么做，可是不<u>能</u>告诉他答案。

Nǐ kěyǐ gàosu Shāng tóngxué zhèi dào tí zěnme zuò, kěshì bù néng gàosu tā dá'àn.
You may tell Shang how to do this question, but you may not tell him the answer.

3. 能 Vp = Able to/ good at doing the verb (Ax) In this use 能 marks that the subject is good at doing a verb action. For comments on similarities and differences between 能 and the synonymous 会, see 会 huì 2. 能够 nénggòu 1 is a more shumianyu synonym.

a. 洪光华的中文很不错，他能翻译漫画。
Hóng Guānghuá de Zhōngwén hěn bù cuò, tā néng fānyì mànhuà.
Hong Guanghua's Chinese is not bad; he can translate Chinese cartoons.

能够 nénggòu (——) 'verb act possible' Auxiliary Verb; 'good at verb act' Auxiliary Verb

1. 能够Vp = Verb action (physically) possible (Ax) A member of the set of Auxiliary verbs which mark that a verb action is probable, possible, or permitted, the shumianyu 能够 marks the possibility for a verb act to happen because conditions are right (expl a). 能 néng 1 is a synonym.. 能够 is also used to mark that the subject of the sentence is skilled at doing the verb act (expl b). 能 néng 3 is a synonym of this usage.

a. 珠江下游能够行驶轮船。
Zhū Jiāng xiàyóu nénggòu xíngshǐ lúnchuán.
Steamships are able to navigate on the lower reaches of the Pearl River.

N

b. 白校长能够说两种外国语。
Bái xiàozhǎng nénggòu shuō liǎng zhǒng wàiguóyǔ.
President White is able to speak two foreign languages.

凭 píng (憑) "based upon" Coverb; 'regardless' Conjunction

1. Np 凭 X Vp = Noun relies on X to verb (Cv) 凭 is a less frequently used member of one of the six sets of words used to mark the basis on which a verb phrase is done. 凭 specifically marks X as the concrete (expl a) or abstract (expl b) thing the subject of the sentence relies upon to do a verb action. Rarely, X may be a verb phrase (expl c). 靠 kào is an oral synonym. See 根据 gēnjù 1 for a general discussion of the sets of words used to mark the basis for a verb activity. 凭 is also a shumianyu verb expressing the idea of 'lean against.'

a. 听京剧要凭票入场。
Tīng jīngjù yào píng piào rùchăng.
You must have a ticket to get into the Peking Opera.

b. 这个问题我只凭记忆说，并没有去查证。
Zhèige wèntí wŏ zhĭ píng jìyì shuō, bìng méiyŏu qù cházhèng.
I am relying entirely on memory to discuss this; actually I have not checked it out.

c. 光凭教练训练不够，还要自己经常练习。
Guāng píng jiàoliàn xùnliàn bù gòu, hái yào zìjĭ jīngcháng liànxí.
Just relying on the coach training you is not enough, you have to practice regularly on your own.

2. 凭 X, Y = No matter what X is, Y is unchanged (Cj) 凭 is a relatively little used oral member of one of the three sets of conjunctions which mark that no matter what X may be, the situation in Y is unaffected. 凭 specifically marks that regardless of the amount of possibilities offered by X, things remain Y. Whether Y is a verb phrase or a clause, it will include an indefinite interrogative such as 多 duō 'much,' 哪儿 năr 'where,' etc. 无论 wúlùn 1 is a shumianyu synonym. See 虽然 suīrán 1 for a discussion of the three sets of concessive conjunctions.

P

a. 最近台北西瓜这么多凭你怎么吃也吃不完。
Zuìjìn Táibĕi xīguā zhème duō píng nĭ zĕnme chī yĕ chī bù wán.
There are so many watermelons in Taipei now that no matter how you eat them you can never run out of them.

Punctuation Markers

There are three sets of punctuation markers in Chinese: 1) Those which have uniquely Chinese shapes and usages, 2) Western style markers that are used for both some of the values they have in Western texts as well as for different Chinese values, and 3) Western style markers which are used for the same values they have in Western texts. Awareness of their shapes and usages can be a highly useful tool in your work with modern Chinese prose. Below are three charts which give you an overview of Chinese punctuation. Perhaps the two markers which are most useful for reading modern Chinese prose is the uniquely shapped 、‘listing comma’ and the more familiar ，‘comma.’ A discussion and numerous examples are given for them following the specific table in which each appears.

TABLE #1 Uniquely Chinese Punctuation Markers	
《》，〈〉，「」，﹏﹏ 书名号 shūmínghào ‘literary title’	marks literary titles (﹏﹏ marks literary titles in traditional texts only)
〔〕，〖〗，【】括弧 kuòhú ‘parentheses’	marks parenthetical material
「」，『』引号 yǐnhào ‘quotation’	marks direct speech
……省略号 shěnglüèhào ‘ellipsis’	marks omitted material
・・・，﹏﹏着重号 zhuózhònghào ‘emphasis’	marks emphasis (﹏﹏ is used to mark emphasis in PRC texts only)
。句号 jùhào ‘period’	marks the end of a sentence
々 前同号 qiántónghào ‘ditto’	marks a character immediately repeated
、顿号 dùnhào ‘listing comma’	marks lists of Noun or Verb phrases

NOTE a: ・・・ and ﹏﹏ go directly below the characters being emphasized.

NOTE b: ⋯ always appears in sets of two which occupy two character spaces …….

NOTE c: 。 is used for the same uses as is the Western period. It differs in being written with a hollow circle rather than a solid one; distinguish 。 from the solid ellipsis marker ⋯.

NOTE d: 々 is not exactly a punctuation marker, but you need to recognize the shape and be aware that it functions as a ditto mark.

NOTE e: The ‘listing comma’ 、 (also called the ‘enumerative comma’) has a unique shape and clearly defined functions, so it is very helpful when you are reading. 、 has the specific function of linking members of conceptually similar and grammatically parallel series of noun phrases or verb phrases. The noun phrases can be the subject (expl a), the object (expl b), or the place structure (expl c) of the sentence. They may also be part of the description of the subject or object (expl d). The verb phrases can be either part of the verb structure itself (expl e) or part of a structure describing a noun (expl f). Keep in mind that Chinese also sometimes use the Western style comma ， to mark lists of things (see ， expl r below)

P

Examples of 、 usages are:

a. 陪同乔石访问的乔石夫人郁文、全国人大常委会秘书长曹志、外交部副部长张德广、外交部部长助理孙广相也同机到达。

Péitóng Qiáo Shí fǎngwèn de Qiáo Shí fūren Yù Wén、Quánguó Réndà Chángwěihuì mìshū Cāo Zhì、Wàijiāobù fùbùzhǎng Zhāng Déguǎng、Wàijiāobù bùzhǎng zhùlǐ Sūn Guǎngxiāng yě tóngjī dàodá.

Madame Yu Wen who is accompanying her husband Qiao Shi on the trip、

Executive Secretary of the Standing Committee of the National People's Congress Cao Zhi, Vice-Minister of the Ministry of Foreign Affairs Zhang Deguang, and Assistant Minister of the Foreign Trade Ministry Sun Guangxiang also arrived on the same plane.

b. 这家庭旧物拍卖的东西很多，有衣服、炊具、餐具、玩具、健身器材及家用小电器。

Zhèi jiātíng jiùwù pāimài de dōngxi hěn duō, yǒu yīfu, chuījù, cānjù, wánjù, jiànshēn qìcái jí jiāyòng xiǎo diànqì.

The items put out for sale at the (American) garage sale were numerous: there was clothing, cooking utensils, eating utensils, toys, physical fitness equipment and small electrical appliances.

c. 中国银行重庆九龙坡支行行长余国容对国家、对社会、对他人只讲奉献，而对自己"严"字当头，铁面无情。

Zhōngguó Yínháng Chóngqìng Jiǔlóngpō zhīháng hángzhǎng Yú Guóróng duì guójiā, duì shèhuì, duì tārén zhǐ jiǎng fèngxiàn, ér duì zìjǐ "yán" zì dāngtóu, tiě miàn wú qíng.

Yu Guorong, the branch manager of the Chongqing, Jiulongpo branch of the Bank of China, speaks only of service to the country, to society, and to others. For herself the word 'strict' is foremost, she is impartial and incorruptible.

d. 我们实行和平统一、一国两制的方针没有改变。

Wǒmen shíxíng hépíng tǒngyī, yīguó liǎngzhì de fāngzhēn méiyǒu gǎibiàn.

Our policy of 'implementing peaceful unification' (,) and 'one nation two systems' has not changed.

P

e. 两国贸易现在发展得很好，将来还可以发展得更多、更快。

Liǎng guó màoyì xiànzài fāzhǎn de hěn hǎo, jiānglái hái kěyǐ fāzhǎn de gèng duō, gèng kuài.

Trade between the two countries is developing nicely now, and in the future it can develop more (,) and faster.

f. 经过10年锻炼，一支阵容整齐，具备"公正、献身、创新、求实、协作"精神的高技术国家队已经组成。

Jīngguò 10 nián duànliàn, yīzhī zhènróng zhěngqí, jùbèi "gōngzhèng, xiànshēn, chuàngxīn, qiúshí, xiézuò" jīngshén de gāo jìshù guójiāduì yǐjīng zǔchéng.

After ten years of training, a well balanced national team has been organized which possesses a spirit of "being just, dedicating oneself, blazing new trails, being realistic, and co-operating."

TABLE #2 Graphically Identical Markers Which Have Both Similar and Different Usages	
___ 专名号 zhuānmínghào 'proper noun'	placed under (PRC) or beside (ROC) characters to mark proper nouns
X~O 隐讳 yǐnhuì 'taboos'	marks deleted taboo words
〔 〕括号 kuòhào 'brackets'	mark parenthetical materials
· 间隔 jiāngé 篇名 piānmíng 'solid dot'	marks subdivisions of foreign names, literary titles, dates, addresses, etc. Placed at mid-level in the line
，逗号 dòuhào 'comma'	marks emphasizing pauses and grammatical structures

NOTE a: ，the Chinese comma looks very much like an English comma. In printed texts it is placed in the center of the space immediately following the last word of the structure it marks. While the Chinese comma is used in some ways which are similar to those of the English comma, the Chinese comma differs significantly in being primarily used to mark emphasizing pauses. Because it is used to mark emphasis, a Chinese comma often appears in places where you are not accustomed to finding commas in English sentences. For example, it is common to find sentences such as S，VO where the subject is separated from the verb (expls h & i) and SV，O where the verb is separated from the object (expls j & l). Parts of the descriptive structures of subjects or objects are often separated by a comma (expl k). You will also come across many examples of comma usages such as ST，VO (expls j and l) or SP，VO (expl m) where the comma appears to violate grammatical integrity. You will often see what appears to be comma splices joining items that would be separate sentences in English (expls n and p). ， is also occasionally used in place of the 、 enumerative comma to mark a list of items (expl o). Don't let the training you received in your English writing classes lead you to think of these Chinese comma usages as errors. Such usages are intended, are common, and are correct in terms of Chinese standards. Regard Chinese commas as a tool to recognize, analyze, process and understand modern Chinese prose structures.

There are also some grammatical structures which must be marked with a following comma; e.g., P，SVO: when a lengthy place comes before the subject, it will be end-marked with a ， (expl p); T，SVO: when time comes before the subject, it may be given further emphasis by being end-marked with a ， (expl q). Coverbial phrases such as 随着 suízhe 1, 根据 gēnjù 1, 除了 chúle 1, 为了 wèile, etc. must be end-marked with a comma. In addition to the one example given here (expl r), see those entries for more examples of how commas are used as grammatical markers in modern Chinese prose.

P

Examples of comma usages are:

h. 正在装配线上紧张劳动的工人，面带笑容向中国运动员伸出了热情的欢迎之手。

Zhèngzài zhuāngpèixiàn shang jǐnzhāng láodòng de gōngrén, miàn dài xiàoróng xiàng Zhōngguó yùndòngyuán shēnchūle rèqíng de huānyíng zhī shǒu.

The workers who were feverishly laboring on the assembly line(,) extended their welcoming hands to the Chinese athletes with a smile.

i. 孔子家乡山东省，正健步迈向中国旅游强省新目标。

Kǒngzi jiāxiāng Shāndōng Shěng, zhèng jiànbù màixiàng Zhōngguó lǚyóu qiáng shěng xīn mùbiāo.

Confucius' home province of Shandong(,) is vigorously striding towards the new goal of being a strong part of China's tourism.

j. 国家教委批准，今天下午，中国科学技术大学的研究生院正式建院。

Guójiā Jiàowěi pīzhǔn, jīntiān xiàwǔ, Zhōngguó Kēxué Jìshù Dàxué de yánjiūshēngyuàn zhèngshì jiànyuàn.

The State Education Commission authorized(,) that the Chinese University of Science and Technology graduate school be formally established(,) this afternoon.

k. 这又一次暴露了美国政府以维护人权为借口干涉别国内政，推行强权政治的真面目。

Zhè yòu yīcì bàolùle Měiguó zhèngfǔ yǐ wéihù rénquán wéi jièkǒu gānshè bié guó nèizhèng, tuīxíng qiángquán zhèngzhì de zhēn miànmù.

This further exposes the true face of the American government which uses the excuse of upholding human rights in order to interfere in other country's domestic politics(,) and promote power politics.

l. 香港联合交易所主席郑维健说，恒生指标数在过去的十年，由1600多点增加到1万多点。

P

Xiānggǎng Liánhé Jiāoyìsuǒ zhǔxí Zhèng Wéijiàn shuō, Héngshēng Zhǐbiāoshù zài guòqù de shí nián, yóu 1600 duō diǎn zēngjiā dào 1 wàn duō diǎn.

The Chair of the Hong Kong United Stock Exchange, Mr. Zheng Weijian, said(,) that in the last ten years(,) the Hangsing Index has increased from over 1600 points to more than 10,000 points.

m. 陈树柏在谈话中，还就他回国的所见所闻，提出了一些建设性意见。

Chén Shùbǎi zài tánhuà zhong, hái jiù tā huíguó de suǒ jiàn suǒ wén, tíchūle yīxiē jiànshèxìng yìjiàn.

In the discussions, Chen Shubai also offered some constructive ideas about what he had seen and what he had heard(,) since he returned to China.

n. 风筝是我国古老而又独特的民间艺术，历史悠久，尽管延续了2000年，依然保留着朴实无华的传统特色和乡土气息。

Fēngzheng shi wǒ guó gǔlǎo ér yòu dútè de mínjiān yìshù, lìshǐ yōujiǔ, jǐnguǎn yánxùle 2000 nián, yīrán bǎoliúzhe pǔshí wúhuá de chuántǒng tèsè hé xiāngtǔ qìxī.

Kiting is an old as well as distinctive folk art in our country, it has a long history, and even though it has lasted for 2000 years, it still preserves a simple and unadorned traditional quality and a rural flavor.

o. 高级领导人的互访，经济合作关系，两国人民之间的来往，以及其他领域的交流与合作不断增加和扩大。

Gāojí lǐngdǎorén de hùfǎng, jīngji hézuò guānxi, liǎng guó rénmín zhījiān de láiwǎng, yǐjí qítā lǐngyù de jiāoliú yǔ hézuò bùduàn zēngjiā hé kuòdà.

Visits between high ranking leaders, relationships for economic cooperation, contacts between the peoples of the two countries, as well as exchanges and cooperation in other fields have continuously increased and expanded.

p.在亲切友好的交谈中，李鹏高度赞扬中毛两国业已存在的友好合作关系。

Zài qīnqiè yǒuhǎo de jiāotán zhong, Lǐ Péng gāodù zànyáng Zhōng-Máo liǎng guó yèyǐ cúnzài de yǒuhǎo hézuò guānxi.

In intimate and friendly conversations, Li Peng highly praised the friendly and cooperative relationship which already exists between China and Mauritania.

q. 今年3月6日，美国国务院再次抛出了一年一度的1995年《国别人权报告》（下称《报告》），对世界190多个国家和地区的人权状况品头论足，指手划脚。

Jīnnián 3 yuè 6 rì, Měiguó Guówùyuàn zàicì pāochūle yīnián yīdù de 1995 nián "Guóbié Rénquán Bàogào" (xià chēng "Bàogào"), duì shìjiè 190 duō ge guójiā hé dìqū de rénquán zhuàngkuàng pǐn tóu lùn zú, zhǐ shǒu huá jiǎo.

P

On March 6th of this year(,) the American State Department once again tossed out its 1995 version of the "Annual Country Reports on Human Rights" (called "Report" in the following), and excessively critically(,) made indiscreet statements about the conditions of human rights in over 190 countries and areas in the world.

r. 为加快与国际市场衔接，深圳市将建立旅游交易市场。

Wèi jiākuài yǔ guójì shìchǎng xiánjiē, Shēnzhèn Shì jiāng jiànlì lǚyóu jiāoyì shìchǎng.

In order to more rapidly link up with international markets, the City of Shenzhen will establish a tourism market.

TABLE #3 Graphically and Functionally Similar Markers	
? 问号 wènhào 'question mark'	marks questions
! 感叹号 gǎntànhào 'exclamation mark'	marks emotional exclamations
"", '' 引号 yǐnhào 'quotation marks'	marks quoted materials
( ) 括号 kuòhào 'parenthesis'	marks parenthetical materials
: 冒号 màohào 'colon'	marks that explanatory material follows
; 分号 fēnhào 'semi-colon'	marks stress or serial information
— 破折号 pòzhéhào 'dash'	marks parenthetical information
-- 连接号 liánjiēhào 'hyphen'	marks categories of items

NOTE: These markers are used for the same values and are placed in the same positions in Chinese and English. No separate examples are given for them here, but you will find examples of their uses throughout this dictionary.

P

起 <u>qǐ</u> (—) 'starting from' Verb

1. <u>从 X 起, Y</u> = <u>Y begins with X</u> (Vb) One of the structures in a set of patterns which focus attention on the time or event prior to a <u>Y</u> situation, <u>起</u> specifically marks the point at which a <u>Y</u> situation starts. <u>X</u> usually refers to a past, present or future point in time (expl a), but it can also refer to a noun (expl b). <u>从</u> is interchangeable in this pattern with <u>由</u> <u>yóu</u> 1 (expl b) and the shumianyu <u>自</u> <u>zì</u> 1. Note that the structure <u>Verb 起</u> is also used to express both literal and abstract concepts which extend from the idea of 'rise up, start.'

Compare this value of <u>起</u> with <u>X 以来, Y</u> <u>yǐlái</u> 1 which deals only with past starting times, and <u>到 X 止, Y</u> <u>zhǐ</u> 1 which marks that <u>Y</u> stops at <u>X</u>. Consider also <u>直到 X, Y</u> <u>zhídào</u> 1 which marks <u>X</u> as a time frame for the occurrence of <u>Y</u>, and also <u>不到</u> <u>bùdào</u> 1 which marks the maximum amount of time involved in a verb situation.

a. 从下个星期一<u>起</u>，我们全体要六点半起床。
Cóng xià ge xīngqīyī <u>qǐ</u>, wǒmen quántǐ yào liù diǎn bàn qǐquáng.
From next Monday <u>on</u>, all of us will get up at 6:30.

b. 由前面<u>起</u>便是南京东路。
Yóu qiánmiàn <u>qǐ</u> biànshi Nánjīng Dōnglù.
East Nanjing Road <u>starts (from)</u> right in front of us.

前 <u>qián</u> (—) 'before' Time marker

Q

1. <u>X 前, Y</u> = <u>Before X, Y</u> (Tm) <u>前</u> can be a synonym of the time referents <u>以前</u> <u>yǐqián</u> 1 and the shumianyu <u>之前</u> <u>zhīqián</u> 1 which mark that <u>Y</u> refers to an event prior to <u>X</u> (expl a). However, note that <u>前</u> is most often used as a synonym of the physical location markers <u>前边</u> <u>qiánbiān</u>, <u>之前</u> <u>zhīqián</u> and the oral 前头 qiántou; as such, 前 more often refers to specific location rather than to a point in time.

a. 白教授解放<u>前</u>没去过中国。
Bái jiàoshòu Jiěfàng qián méi qùguo Zhōngguó.
Professor White had never been to China <u>before</u> Liberation.

且 <u>qiě</u> (—) 'moreover' Conjunction

1. <u>X, 且 Y</u> = <u>X, and moreover Y</u> (Cj) When placed between two verb phrases or clauses, the shumianyu <u>且</u> marks that the second unit of information is a further development of the situation articulated in the first (expl a). There will normally be a comma immediately preceding the <u>且</u>. You will mainly find this <u>且</u> usage in texts from the Republic of China. <u>并且</u> <u>bìngqiě</u> 1 is an oral synonym while <u>而且</u> <u>érqiě</u> 1 and <u>而</u> <u>ér</u> 2 are shumianyu synonyms. See <u>而且</u> for further discussion of this set of markers.

a. 美国是台湾现有SRAM半导体最大外销国家，且销售金额直线成长。

Měiguó shi Táiwān xiànyǒu SRAM bàndǎotǐ zuì dà wàixiāo guójiā, qiě xiāoshòu jīn'é zhíxiàn chéngzhǎng.

America is Taiwan's largest foreign market at present for SRAM semi-conductors, and the sales figures are growing steadily upward.

其所以 qísuǒyǐ (———) 'reason for' Conjunction

1. 其所以Vp, 是因为 Y = That by means of which the pronoun verbs is Y (Cj) This shumianyu structure marks the first half of a result and cause structure. It is a variant form of 所以 suǒyǐ 1, which you are invited to consult for further discussion and examples.

却 què (卻) 'however, actually' Adverb

1. X, 却 Y = Contrary to what you would expect from the information in X, the situation is actually Y (Av) The shumianyu 却 is used in Y to mark that the contents of Y represent a definite change from the conclusions that the information given in X or given earlier in the discourse would lead you to expect. 却 is used in both affirmative (expl b) and negative (expl a) sentences. 却 does not convey the sense of reproach or correction found with the otherwise synonymous adverb 并 bìng 1. X and Y will be verb phrases or clauses. X 却 却 may be headed with a reinforcing 虽然 suīrán 1 or a synonym which strengthens the sense of change 却 marks in Y. Y may also be headed with a 然而 rán'ér 1 or a synonym for greater emphasis on the change it introduces.

倒 dào 1 is an oral synonym which differs slightly in marking a sense of change from what might be normally expected. 则 zé 1 is a weaker shumianyu synonym. The synonyms 并 bìng 2 and 决 jué 1 differ from 却 in always being used directly before a negative adverb such as 不 bù 1, 没 méi 1, etc. Also see 但是 dànshì 1 for a discussion of the set of conjunctions which mark the information in Y as a change of direction from that given in X. Also see the "pure surprise" 竟 jìng 1.

a. 现在已经十二月了，天气却不怎么冷。

Xiànzài yǐjing shíèr yuè le, tiānqiè què bù zěnme lěng.

It's already December, but actually it's still not all that cold.

b. 那篇哲学文章虽短却很有说服力。

Nèi piān zhéxué wénzhāng suī duǎn què hěn yǒu shuōfú lì.

Although that philosophic treatise is very short, nonetheless it is really persuasive.

Q

然 rán (—) 'however, nevertheless' Conjunction

1. X, 然 Y = X, nonetheless Y (Cj) 然 is a shumianyu member of the set of conjunctions which mark that Y is a change from X. X and Y may be either verb phrases or clauses. The synonymous 然而 rán'ér 1 imparts a stronger tone of change. See the synonym 但是 dànshì 1 for further discussion of this set of conjunctions. 然 is also used as a word centered on the concepts of 'correct; like that' and as a suffix to adverbs and stative verbs.

a. 此事虽小，然亦不可忽视。
Cǐ shì suī xiǎo, rán yì bù kě hūshì.
Although this is a minor point, nevertheless it must not be overlooked either.

然而 rán'ér (— —) 'however, but' Conjunction

1. X, 然而 Y = X, however Y (Cj) 然而 is a somewhat shumianyu member of the set of conjunctions which mark Y as a change from the situation that the information given in X leads you to expect. The change may be either something unexpected (expl a) or something which is the opposite of X (expl b). The focus of the sentence is on Y. 然而 may also be used between two verbs phrases that form a descriptive structure (expl b). 然而 imparts a stronger tone of voice than its synonym 然 rán 1, but 然 is more shumianyu. See the synonymous 但是 dànshì 1 for further discussion of this set of words.

a. 试验虽然多次失败了，然而他们并不灰心。
Shìyàn suīrán duōcì shībài, rán'ér tāmen bìng bù huīxīn.
Although the experiments failed many times, they are not discouraged, nonetheless.

R

b. 邹同学是一个性格古怪然而十分正直的人。
Zōu tóngxué shì yī ge xìnggé gǔguài rán'ér shífēn zhèngzhí de rén.
Classmate Zou is a person who is very odd yet completely upright.

让 ràng (讓) "cause (to happen)" Verb; "passive marker" Coverb

1. (Np1) 让 Np2 Vp = (Np1) allows/causes Np2 to Verb (Vb) One of the set of "causal" markers, 让 marks that a first noun phrase allows or makes a second noun do a verb action (expls a & b) or be in an emotional state (expl c). In written texts "causal 让" often connotes a desire on the part of the first noun phrase for the situation to exist (expl a). 叫 jiào 1, 给 gěi 5, 令 lìng 1 and 使 shǐ 1 are synonymous causal markers; see 使 for overall comments on the similarities and differences among this set of five causal markers. Structural similarities between this and the "passive 让" discussed below make it necessary to analyze the context to determine which value 让 represents in any one text; note however, the presence of 给 gěi 3 as discussed in 2 below marks a clear passive use. Note that 让 is also frequently used as a verb meaning 'yield, allow.'

a. 章老师常让汉语三年级学生到他家听古典音乐。
Zhāng lǎoshī cháng ràng Hànyǔ sānniánjí xuésheng dào tā jiā tīng gǔdiǎn yīnyuè.
Professor Zhang often has third year Chinese students to his house to listen to classical music.

b. 我们决不能让国家财产受损失。
Wǒmen jué bù néng ràng guójiā cáichǎn shòu sǔnshī.
We absolutely cannot allow state property to suffer damage.

c. 每个星期考试会让学生很紧张。
Měi ge xīngqī kǎoshì huì ràng xuésheng hěn jǐnzhāng.
Having tests every week can make students very nervous.

2. Np1 让 Np2 (给) Vp = Np1 is verbed by Np2 (Cv) In this usage 让 marks the first noun phrase as the recipient of a verb action done by the second noun phrase. The verb phrase will usually involve a sense of result (expl a) or completion (expl b). When 给 gěi 4 occurs in the verb phrase there is no difference in meaning, but its presence makes it easier to see that 让 is being used in a passive structure (expl b). 给 clarifies the structural ambiguity between this and "causal 让"discussed above. 叫 jiào 2 and 给 gěi 4 are close oral synonyms for passive 让. See the shumianyu synonym 被 bèi 1 for general comments on the passive voice in Chinese.

a. 这个谜语真让你妹妹猜着了。
Zhèige míyǔ zhēn ràng nǐ mèimei cāizháo le.
The riddle was figured out by your little sister!

b. 商朝让周朝给推翻了。
Shāng Cháo ràng Zhōu Cháo gěi tuīfān le.
The Shang Dynasty was overthrown by the Zhou Dynasty.

R

然后 ránhòu (—後) 'afterwards, then, after that' Conjunction

1. X, 然后 Y = X is done first and after that Y is done (Cj) 然后 marks that after a first verb act a different second verb action occurs in quick succession. X and Y will both be either future (expl a) or past (expl b) events. When in the past, the events will be definite and consecutive. X will frequently include the adverbs 先 xiān 1or 首先 shǒuxiān 'first, first of all.' Y often has a reinforcing 又 yòu 1, 还 hái 1, etc.

Though they may seem to be the same from their English translations, 然后 and 以后 yǐhòu 1 differ from each other in three basic ways: 1. 然后 is only used as a conjunction marking sequence at the head of Y while 以后 appears at the end of X as a time frame marker, 2.然后 marks a tight sequence of actions while 以后 focuses attention on the relative time frame of events whether they are tightly sequenced or not, and 3. 以后 can also appear with in either X or Y as a time noun. See further discussion at 以后 yǐhòu 1.

a. 在北大，你得先念硕士，然后才能念博士。
Zài Běidà, nǐ děi xiān niàn shuòshì, ránhòu niàn bóshì.
At Peking University, you have to first study for a M.A., then you may study for a Ph.D.

b. 法国代表团到了轧钢厂，首先去参观电脑室，然后又去参观了工人宿舍。
Făguó dàibiăotuán dàole zhágāngchăng, shŏuxiān qù cānguān diànnăoshì, ránhòu yòu qù cānguānle gōngrén sùshè.
The French delegation arrived at the steel rolling mill. They first of all visited the computer room, and afterwards they went to visit the worker's living quarters.

仍 réng (—) 'still, yet' Adverb

1. 仍 Vp = Still verb (Av) 仍 is used with monosyllabic verbs to mark an ongoing verb situation (expl a). 仍 is even more shumianyu than its shumianyu synonym 仍然 réngrán 1. 还 hái 1 and 还是 háishi 3 are oral synonyms while 尚 shàng 1 is a very shumianyu partial synonym that shares only the idea of unchanged continuation. See also 继续 jìxù 1 which marks uninterrupted continuation.

a. 西湖仍象三十年前一样。
Xīhú réng xiàng sānshí nián qián yīyàng.
West Lake still looks like it did 30 years ago.

R

仍然 **réngrán (——) 'still, yet' Adverb**

1.仍然 Vp = Still verb (Av) The shumianyu 仍然 is most frequently used to mark that a verb situation goes on unchanged from an earlier point in time (expls a & b). When 仍然 is used in compound sentences, the Y situation is generally different from that given in X (expls a & b), X is often headed with 虽然 suīrán 1 or a synonym, and a 可是 kěshì 1, 却 què 1, etc. is used in Y (expl b). Sometimes 仍然 marks a return to an original condition (expl c). 仍 réng 1 is an even more shumianyu synonym most frequently used with monosyllabic verbs. 还是 háishi 3 is an oral synonym. 仍旧 réngjiù is a less frequently used synonym. 尚 shàng 1 is an even more shumianyu partial synonym which shares only the idea of unchanged continuation. Also consider the marker for prolonged or uninterrupted continuation, 继续 jìxù 1.

a. 下班以后，工人仍然在考虑班长提的那些工作中的问题。

Xiàbān yǐhòu, gōngrén réngrán zài kǎolǜ bānzhǎng tí de nèixiē gōngzuò zhōng de wèntí.
After they had finished their shift, the workers were still thinking about the work problems which the team leader had brought up.

b. 杨局长尽管身体不好，可是仍然坚持上班。
Yáng júzhǎng jǐnguǎn shēntǐ bù hǎo, kěshì réngrán jiānchí shàngbān.
Although his health is not good, Office Chief Yang still insists on coming to work.

c. 服务台旁边的指示牌说，“报纸看完，仍然放回原处。”
Fúwùtái pángbiān de zhǐshìpái shuō, “Bàozhǐ kàn wán, réngrán fànghuí yuánchù.”
The directions next to the desk says, “When finished with the newspapers, re-shelve them.”

如 rú (一) “similarity” Verb; ‘if’ Conjunction

1. X 如 Y 一般 (Sv) = X is like Y (Vb) 如 is a member of the set of words which mark similarity. In this structure, 如 marks that Y is a simile used to describe X (expl a) or is an activity similar to X (expl b). Stative verbs may also occur at the end of the pattern to specify the nature of the similarity (expl c). 如 is also sometimes used without 一般 yībān 1 in some set expressions to mark similarity; e.g., 我们革命意志坚如钢 Wǒmen gémìng yìzhì jiān rú gāng ‘Our revolutionary will is as strong as steel.’ See 一般 for further comments.

如 extends from its basic meaning of ‘similarity’ to function as a shumianyu marker of examples of things; e.g., 宋朝有很多大文人如欧阳修、朱熹、苏东坡、李清照等 Sòng Cháo yǒu hěn duō dà wénrén rú Ōuyáng Xiū, Zhū Xī, Sū Dōngpō, Lǐ Qīngzhào děng ‘The Song Dynasty had many great literary figures such as Ōuyáng Xiū, Zhū Xī, Sū Dōngpō, Lǐ Qīngzhào, etc.’ Synonyms of 如 are the oral 象 xiàng 1, 好像 hǎoxiàng 1 along with the shumianyu 如同 rútóng 1, 若 ruò 2 and 仿佛 fǎngfú 1. 一样 yīyàng 3, 般 bān 1 or 那样 nàyàng may be used with 如 instead of 一般 in this structure.

R

a. 湖面如镜子一般。
Húmiàn rú jìngzi yībān.
The surface of the lake is like a mirror.

b. 正如以上所说的那样，我党应该进行深入的改革。
Zhèng rú yǐshàng suǒshuō de nàyàng, wǒdǎng yīnggāi jìnxíng shēnrù de gǎigé.
Exactly as was discussed above, our party should implement deeply penetrating reforms.

c. 情况不如职员估计的那么严重。
Qíngkuàng bù rú zhíyuán gūjì de nàme yánzhòng.
The situation is not as serious as the office workers thought.

2. 如 X, 则 Y = If X, then Y (Cj) 如 is a shumianyu member of the set of words which mark conditional structures. In this usage 如 marks X as a supposition upon which the occurrence of Y depends. Y is usually marked with the shumianyu adverb 则 zé 1 or a synonym. You can distinguish between this "conditional" and the "similarity" use of 如 discussed in 1 above because 1) a "similarity" 如 structure is usually found along with 一样 or its synonym in one clause, while 2) a "conditional" 如 pattern stretches over two or more clauses with 则 or a synonym preceding the verb in the later clause. See the synonymous 如果 rúguǒ 1 for a discussion of the overall set of "conditional markers."

a. 以上各点，如有不妥之处，请批评指出。
Yǐshàng gè diǎn, rú yǒu bùtuō zhīchù, qǐng pīpíng zhǐchū.
If any of the above are inappropriate, please point them out.

b. 如采用该项新技术，则可提高两倍以上污染治理率。
Rú cǎiyòng gāi xiàng xīn jìshù, zé kě tígāo liǎngbèi yǐshàng wūrán zhìlǐlǜ.
If we utilize that new technology, we can enhance our pollution control effectiveness by over 200%.

如果 rúguǒ (— —) 'if' Conjunction

1. 如果 X, Y = If X, Y (Cj) 如果 is a member of the set of words which mark that X defines the conditional parameters needed for a Y situation. X will be a verb phrase or a clause. Y will generally be a verb phrase marked by an adverb such as 就 jiù 1, 则 zé 1, 便 biàn 1, 那么 nàme, etc. which bring their specific flavorings to the compound sentence. 的话 dehuà 1 can be added to the end of X to intensify the conditional nature of the situation (expl c); at the other extreme, 如果 can be omitted if the context is clear. When there is no overt conditional marker such as 如果, the sentence becomes an unmarked conditional (see unmarked conditional 1). 要是 yàoshi 1 and 要 yào 1 are oral synonyms while 如 rú 2 and 假如 jiǎrú 1 are more shumianyu conditional markers; 若 ruò 1 and 倘若 tǎngruò 1 are more intensely shumianyu synonyms which give a stronger sense of a conditional situation. 要不是 yàobushi 1 and 不是X, 就是 Y bùshì 1 are negative conditional markers.

R

a. 如果你不去，我实在也没办法去。
Rúguǒ nǐ bù qù, wǒ shízài yě méi bànfǎ qù.
If you do not go, there is absolutely no way I can.

b. 如果思想有了错误，一定要改正，这就叫向人民负责。
Rúguǒ sīxiǎng yǒule cuòwù, yīdìng yào gǎizhèng, zhè jiù jiào xiàng rénmín fùzé.
If your thinking is wrong, you definitely must make corrections; this is called being responsible to the people.

c. 听说这本微型小说很好，如果你星期天有空的话，可以看看。
Tīngshuō zhèi běn wēixíng xiǎoshuō hěn hǎo, rúguǒ nǐ xīngqītiān yǒu kòng dehuà,

kěyǐ kànkàn.

This micro-fiction is great. If you happen to have some time on Sunday, you can read it.

2. X, 如果 Y = X, if Y (Cj) When 如果 occurs at the head of Y, it still marks a conditional structure and the sentence has a stronger shumianyu flavor.

a. 那些外商今天该到了，如果昨天准时出发的话。

Nàxiē wàishāng jīntiān gāi dào le, rúguǒ zuótiān zhǔnshí chūfā dehuà.

If those foreign business people departed on time yesterday, they should arrive today.

若 ruò (一) 'if' Conjunction; 'seems like' Adverb

1. 若 X, Y = If X, Y (Cj) 若 is a shumianyu member of the set of conjunctions which mark that X defines the conditional parameters needed for Y. X and Y will be a verb phrases or clauses. Y will usually be marked with a connecting adverb such as 就 jiù 1 or the shumianyu 便 biàn 1, 则 zé 1, etc. (expl b). You will more frequently see 若 used in texts from the ROC than in those from the PRC. Read 如果 rúguǒ 1 for a comparative discussion and examples of the various members of this set of markers.

a. 您若坐在紧急出口的位置，并且不懂英语，请告知本航机服务员。

Nín ruò zuò zài jǐnjí chūkǒu de wèizhi, bìngqiě bù dǒng Yīngyǔ, qǐng gàozhī běn hángjī fúwùyuán.

If you are sitting in an emergency exit row and not understand English, please notify a crew member.

b. 若台灣鐵路管理局可以順利民營化，則高鐵和台灣將合併爲一個單位；……

Ruò Táiwān Tiělù Guǎnlǐjú kěyǐ shùnlì mínyínghuà, zé Gāotiě hé Táiwān jiāng hébìng wéi yī ge dānwèi;...

If Taiwan Railway Management can be smoothly privatized, Gaoxiong and Taiwan Railway will merge into one unit;...

R

2. X 若 Y = X seems like Y (Av) In this shumianyu usage as a member of the set of words that mark likeness, 若 marks that there is a similarity between X and Y. X may be either a noun or verb phrase (expl a), while Y will be a verb phrase (expl a) or a clause. See 好像 hǎoxiàng 1 for a discussion of the several members of this set of markers.

a. 綿陽工人在難以生存的情況下，爆發大規模反貪官求生存的游行示威活動，但當局對工人的現狀視若無睹，一方面……

Miányáng gōngrén zài nányǐ shēngcún de qíngkuàng xià, bàofā dà guīmó fǎn tānguān qiú shēngcún de yóuxíng shìwēi huódòng, dàn dāngjú duì gōngrén de xiànzhuàng shì ruò wú dǔ, yī fāngmiàn...

Under conditions that are hard to survive, the Mianyang workers burst forth in large scale protests against corrupt officials and living conditions. However, those in charge seemed to look but not see the workers' situation. On one hand...

如同 rútóng (——) 'seems like' Conjunction

1. X 如同 Y 一般 = X seems like Y (Cj) 如同 is a less used shumianyu member of the set of words which mark resemblance in a situation. 如同 specifically marks an element of similarity between X and Y. X will more commonly be a noun phrase, while Y will be either a verb phrase or a clause. 象 xiàng 1 and 好像 hǎoxiàng 1 are oral synonyms while 如 rú 1, 若 ruò 2 and 仿佛 fǎngfú 1 are shumianyu synonyms. 一般 may be replaced in this structure by the more colloquial 一样 yīyàng 3, in which case a Stative verb may follow Y. See 好像 hǎoxiàng 1 for further discussion of this set of "resemblance" markers.

a. 唐山1978年地震，如同天塌下来一般。
Tángshān yī jiǔ qī bā nián dìzhèn, rútóng tiān tā xiàlái yībān.
In the 1978 Tangshan earthquake it seemed like the sky was collapsing

R

尚 shàng (—) 'still, yet' Adverb

1.尚 Vp/Sv = Still verb/Stative verb (Av) The very shumianyu 尚 marks that the verb situation following it still exists in its original form (expls a, b & c). You will tend to find 尚 more often in texts from the Republic of China. 还 hái 1 is a close synonym; the pattern 尚未 Vp shàngwèi is a shumianyu synonym of 还没(有) Vp 'still have not verbed' (expl c). When 仍然 réngrán 1 and 仍 réng 1 share the sense of "continuing unchanged," they too are synonymous with 尚. See also 继续 jìxù 1 which marks uninterrupted, prolonged continuation.

a. 未经检验的疫苗其危险性实在可怕，因为含七种血清型的口蹄疫病毒，尚可衍生数十种亚型病毒，相当复杂……

Wèi jīng jiǎnyàn de yìmiáo qí wēixiǎnxìng shízài kěpà, yīnwei hán qī zhǒng xuèqīngxíng de kǒutíyì bìngdú, shàng kě yǎnshēng shùshí zhǒng yàxíng bìngdú, xiāngdāng fùzá...

Vaccine which has not undergone testing is really dangerous because a hoof and mouth virus that has seven strains of viral entities can still develop tens of new genetic variants; this is fairly complicated...

b. 权威人士指出，在西部地区设立经济特区尚不可能。

Quánwēi rénshì zhǐchū, zài xībù dìqū shèlì jīngji tèqū shàng bù kěnéng.

Authoratative sources point out that it is still not possible to establish special economic districts in the western area.

c. 此事尚未解决。

Cǐshì shàng wèi jiějué.

This matter is still not settled.

时 shí (時) 'when, while' Time word

S

1. X时, Y = When X, Y (Tm) A member of one of the four sets of words which mark attention to the time frame for a Y situation, 时 is a shumianyu synonym of 的时候 de shíhou 1 which marks that Y happens at the same time X does. 时 comes at the end of X and will often be end-marked with a comma (expls a & b). X and Y will be verb phrases or clauses. See 的时候 and 以来 yǐlái 1 for further comments and examples of time structures.

a. 在处理某项具体问题时，要多请示，不要擅自作主张。

Zài chǔlǐ mǒu xiàng jùtǐ wèntí shí, yào duō qǐngshì, bù yào shànzì zuò zhǔzhāng.

When handling some specific problem, one must ask for instructions. Do not undertake unauthorized positions.

b.章学诚又主张在研究历史时，不应崇拜古人而轻视当前的时代。

Zhāng Xuěchéng yòu zhǔzhāng zài yánjiū lìshǐ shí, bù yīnggāi chóngbài gǔrén ér

qīngshì dāngqián de shídài.
Zhang Xuecheng also advocated that when researching history we should not adore the ancients yet belittle the contemporary period.

使 shǐ (一) "cause, make happen" Verb

1. (Np1) 使 Np2 Vp = Np1 causes Np2 to verb (Vb) A member of the set of "causal" markers, 使 marks that a first noun phrase makes a second one do a verb action (to an object). Noun one will tend to represent a non-human entity, and the verb will be one that lasts for a length of time (expls a, b & c). While 使 occurs in the broadest range of topics of all the "causal" markers, it is not used with verbs having to do with "giving orders" or "permission." Synonyms are 让 ràng 1 which generally connotes that a noun is made to do a desired verb or be in an emotional state, 叫 jiào 1 which involves "ordering," and 令 lìng 1 which is used only with "emotional" causative structures. See also the less frequently used 给 gěi 5. Note that 使 is also used as a verb to mean 'order someone to do something; use' and in vocabulary items extending from those concepts.

a. 四个现代化使落后变为先进，使先进更加先进。
Sì ge Xiàndàihuà shǐ luòhòu biànwéi xiānjìn, shǐ xiānjìn gèngjiā xiānjìn.
The Four Modernizations make the backward become advanced and (make) the advanced even more advanced.

b. 这个理论帮助老百姓克服错误观念，使他们增强中国将有个光明前途的信心。
Zhège lǐlùn bāngzhù lǎobǎixìng kèfú cuòwù guānniàn, shǐ tāmen zēngqiáng Zhōngguó jiāng yǒu ge guāngmíng qiántú de xìnxīn.
This theory helped the people conquer their conceptual errors and made them increase their confidence in a bright future for China.

S

c. 保证质量，使合于规定标准。
Bǎozhèng zhìliàng, shǐ héyú guīdìng biāozhǔn.
Maintain quality and make it match the set standards.

似的 shìdė (一 一) 'seems like' Auxiliary

1. X (象) Y 似的 = X Seems like Y (Ax) 似的 is a member of the set of words which mark a sense of resemblance between elements in a structure. 似的 specifically marks similarity between X and Y. X and Y can be either noun phrases or verb phrases. 一样 yīyàng 3 is a synonym. A structure which has 似的 at the end often starts with 象 xiàng 1, 好象 hǎoxiàng 1 or the more shumianyu 仿佛 fǎngfú. See 一样 yīyàng 3 for further discussion of similarity structures. Note that except for this usage, 似 is pronounced sì.

a. 他上课总闭着眼，象是睡着了<u>似的</u>。
Tā shàngkè zǒng bìzhe yǎn, xiàng shì shuìzháole <u>shìde</u>.
When he's in class his eyes are always closed, <u>it's as if</u> he's fallen asleep.

b. 到司马老师家象到了自己家<u>似的</u>。
Dào Sīmǎ lǎoshī jiā xiàng dàole zìjǐ jiā <u>shìde</u>.
Going to Professor Sima's home <u>is like</u> going to my own home.

是...的 <u>shì...de</u> (——) "emphasis" Verb + Structural marker; "description" Verb + Structural marker; "emphatic" Verb + Sm; "passive" Verb + Sm

1.<u>S (是) T P V 的</u> = <u>Emphasis on the when, the where and/or the circumstances of a past verb action</u> (Vb + Sm) When the time, the place and/or the circumstance for a verb action appear between a <u>是</u>and a <u>的</u>, the structure emphasizes that a verb action happened in the past at a particular time (expl a), at a particular place (expls a & b), and/or for those specific circumstances (expl c). The focus of this pattern is thus different from that of <u>了</u> <u>le</u> 1 which simply marks the completion of a verb action, whether it be in the past, present, or future.

Unless the object is a pronoun or the verb has a directional complement, it is possible for the <u>的</u> to come before the object; e.g., 他<u>是</u>在书店买<u>的</u>这枝笔 Tā <u>shì</u> zài shūdiàn mǎi <u>de</u> zhèi zhī bǐ 'It was in the store that he bought this pen.' However, you will find the <u>的</u> after the object in most prose texts. <u>是</u> may be omitted when it is felt that the context makes the structure clear without it.

You can distinguish this <u>是...的</u> usage from those discussed in 2, 3 and 4 below, and each from each other, by determining what comes between the <u>是</u> and the <u>的</u>. If a time, place or circumstance structure is there, it is the usage discussed here; if there is a noun and a verb, it is the pattern described in number 2; if there is just a verb there, it is likely to be structure number 3.

S

a. 我们<u>是</u>三四年以前在美国开始学习中国话<u>的</u>。
Wǒmen <u>shì</u> sān sì nián yǐqián zài Měiguó kāishǐ xuéxí Zhōngguóhuà <u>de</u>.
<u>It was</u> in America three or four years ago that we start<u>ed</u> studying Chinese.

b. 外交部长<u>是</u>在美国国务卿为他举行的欢迎会上讲这番话<u>的</u>。
Wàijiāo bùzhǎng <u>shì</u> zài Měiguó Guówùqīng wèi tā jǔxíng de huānyíng huì shàng jiǎng zhèi fān huà <u>de</u>.
<u>It was</u> at the welcoming banquet which the American Secretary of State held for him that the Foreign Minister <u>gave</u> this talk.

c. 瑞典的第一个通讯卫星<u>是</u>用中国的"长征三号"运载火箭发射定点<u>的</u>。
Ruìdiǎn de dì-yīge tōngxùn wèixīng <u>shì</u> yòng Zhōngguó de "Chángzhēng Sān hào"

yùnzǎi huǒjiàn fāshè dìngdiǎn de.

Sweden's first communications satellite was launched into orbit using China's "Long March #3" Carrier Rocket.

2. Object 是 Subject Verbed 的 = The object was verbed by the subject (Vb + Sm) This structure marks that the verb act is set in the past, the voice passive, and the object definite; i.e., 'the noun' rather than 'a noun.' You can distinguish this from the other three 是...的 patterns by the presence of the object before the 是 plus the placement of the subject and verb between the 是 and the 的. See 被 bèi 1 for further comments on the passive voice in Chinese.

a. 本子是我朋友买的。

Běnzi shì wǒ péngyou mǎi de.

The notebook was purchased by my friend.

b. 这个学校的全部教学计划都是副校长制定的。

Zhèige xuéxiào de quánbù jiàoxué jìhuà dōu shì fùxiàozhǎng zhìdìng de.

The educational plans for this school were all formulated by the vice president.

3. S 是 Verb 的 = Emphasizes that the subject does the verb (Vb + Sm) This pattern focuses attention on the subject of the verb action. It gives a tone of emphasis to the situation; it is seldom structured negatively; and unlike S (是) T P V 的 it does not mark a past action. Rarely, it may formed as 是 S V 的; e.g., 是谁告诉你的 Shì shéi gàosù nǐ de 'Who is it that told you?!'

When you think it difficult to distinguish this from the other three patterns discussed above, keep in mind that usually only a verb or Stative verb, often accompanied by modification elements (expls a & b), may come between the 是 and the 的 in this pattern.

a. 三个星期的时间是远远不够的。

Sān ge xīngqī de shíjiān shì yuǎnyuǎn bù gòu de.

Three weeks is certainly not even remotely enough time.

S

b. 新闻广播报道：美国这次火箭发射的成功是特别有意义的。

Xīnwén guǎngbō bàodào: Měiguó zhèi cì huǒjiàn fāshè de chénggōng shì tèbié yǒu yìyì de.

The news broadcast reported that the successful launch of the American rocket this time is particularly meaningful.

4. Np1 是 described 的 (Np2) = "Noun is described but omitted" (Sm) Always be alert to the possibility that a 的 which ends a sentence marks modification of an noun that has been left out of the sentence. The best way to differentiate this commonly seen pattern from the other three 是...的 patterns discussed in this entry is to analyze the elements preceding the 的 to see if the S T or P described in usage 1, 2 or 3 are present. If they are not, there is a strong possibility that the object of the sentences has been deleted, partially to avoid redundancy and partially because the writer felt the context would make the sentence clear without the noun at the end. See 的 de 2 for further comments on this frequently seen usage.

a. 那个孩子！旧的玩具都不要，就是要新的。

Nèige háizi! Jiù de wánjù dōu bù yào, jiù shì yào xīn de.

That kid is spoiled rotten! He doesn't want any old toys, it's only new ones he wants.

b. 任何离开讲解备忘录的做法，都是违背两国人民根本利益的。

Rènhé líkāi jiǎngjiě bèiwànglù de zuòfǎ, dōu shì wéibèi liǎng guó rénmín gēnběn lìyì de.

Any procedure that deviates from the memorandum of understanding is one that goes against the basic interests of the peoples of the two countries.

虽 suī (雖) 'although (fact)' Conjunction

1. 虽 X, Y = Although X is a fact, the situation is Y (Cj) 虽 is a more shumianyu synonym of 虽然 suīrán 1 and as such marks that while X is a fact, it does not affect what happens in Y. The subject in X will always come before 虽. See 虽然 suīrán 1 for a discussion of how 虽 fits in the three sets of concessive conjunctions.

a. 问题虽少，影响却极大。

Wèntí suī shǎo, yǐngxiǎng què jí dà.

Although there are few problems, their influence is nonetheless huge.

2. X, 虽 Y = It is X even though there is Y (Cj) 虽 has the same values described above, but it conveys a stronger sense of formality when used in Y. See 虽然 suīrán 2.

a. 语言研究所仍未回复，虽已多次去电催问。

Yǔyán Yánjiūsuǒ réng wèi huífù, suī yǐ duō cì qù diàn cuīwèn.

Despite the fact that I have cabled them a great many times, the Linguistics Institute still has not responded.

S

虽然 suīrán (雖—) 'although (fact)' Conjunction

1. 虽然 X, Y = Even though X is a fact, the situation is still Y (Cj) 虽然 is a member of one of the three sets of conjunctions which mark that no matter what the situation in X is, Y is unaffected. 虽然 specifically marks the concession that although X is a recognized fact, Y remains unaffected by whatever the X situation is. X and Y may be verb phrases or clauses. If the subject is the same for both X and Y, it will come before 虽然 (expl a); if the subjects are different, the subject in X goes after 虽然 (expl b). Y is usually marked by a reinforcing contrastive adverb such as 可是 kěshì 1, 还是 háishi 2, 仍然 réngrán 1, 却 què 1, etc., each of which imparts its own nuances to the discourse. 虽 is more shumianyu than 虽然 but marks X for the same values. The shumianyu synonym 尽管 jǐnguǎn 1 gives a stronger tone of voice to these concessive factual situations. 虽说 suīshuō and 虽说是 suīshuōshi are oral synonyms. Consider 固然 gùrán 1 which confirms the factualness of X. (虽 may also be pronounced with the second tone suí.)

Note that there are three sets of these concessive conjunctions which though close in meaning, and close in English translation, differ in that one set marks factual situations (虽然 and its synonyms); one marks hypothetical situations (即使 jíshǐ 1 and its synonyms); and one is used only with indefinite (怎么 zěnme, 多么 duōme, etc.) or choice (Verb 不 verb) first clauses (不管 bùguǎn 1 and its synonyms). Compare their differences in the following three sentences:

Factual: 虽然天气这么热，他还是穿那么多 Suīrán tiānqì zhème rè, tā háishi chuān nàme duō 'Although it is so hot, he is still wearing so much clothing.'

Hypothetical: 即使天气热得要命，他也还要穿那么多 Jíshǐ tiānqì rè de yàomìng, tā yě hái yào chuān nàme duō 'Although it might be unbearably hot, he would still wear so much clothing.'

Alternative: 不管天气热不热，他总是穿那么多 Bùguǎn tiānqì rè bu rè, tā zǒngshì chuān nàme duō 'No matter whether it's hot or not, he always wears so much clothing.' **Indefinite**: 不管天气多么热，他总是穿那么多 Bùguǎn tiānqì duōme rè, tā zǒngshì chuān nàme duō 'No matter how warm it is, he always wears so much clothing.'

Examples of 虽然 are:

a. 他虽然是美国人，但是汉字却写得非常漂亮。
Tā suīrán shì Měiguórén, dànshi Hànzì què xiě de fēicháng piàoliàng.
Although he's an American, he still writes Chinese characters beautifully.

b. 虽然前进的道路上的困难还很多，但广大群众仍然充满了信心。
Suīrán qiánjìn de dàolù shang de kūnnán hái hěn duō, dàn guǎngdà qúnzhòng réngrán chōngmǎn le xìnxīn.
Although there are many difficulties on the road ahead, the broad masses are still brimming with confidence.

S

2. X, 虽然 Y = It is X even though Y (Cj) When used in Y, 虽然 has the values described above, but it has a stronger shumianyu feel and must come before the subject in Y. 虽 suī 2 is an even more shumianyu synonym.

a. 眼科大夫仍然主张尽快动手术，虽然算是一种试验疗法。
Yǎnkē dàifu réngrán zhǔzhāng jìnkuài dòng shǒushù, suīrán suànshì yīzhǒng shìyàn liáofǎ.
The ophthalmologist suggested doing the operation immediately, even though it is still considered an experimental procedure.

随着 suízhė (隨—) "verb act background" Coverb; "in relationship with" Adverb

1. 随着 X, (S) Vp = (Subject does) verb based on noun phrase background (Cv) One of the set of words which mark the background for a verb action, 随着 specifically marks that X is a prior situation which affects the occurrence of the verb action given in the following Y. X will be a noun phrase, Y will be a verb phrase or clause. See 根据 gēnjù 1 for comparative comments on the this set of six words which mark the various types of bases for verb actions.

a. 随着认识的深化，在理论上也取得了重大成果。
Suízhe rènshi de shēnhuà, zài lǐlùn shang yě qǔdéle zhòngdà chéngguǒ.
In the wake of a deepening of knowledge, they gained important theoretical results.

b. 近几年来随着我国市场的开放，国外一些大的制药公司纷纷进中国，基因工程药物也随之进入我国市场，并在我国药品市场中占有相当的份额。
Jìn jǐ nián lái suízhe wǒguó shìchǎng de kāifàng, guówài yīxiē dà de zhìyào gōngsī fēnfēn jìnrù Zhōngguó, jīyīn gōngchéng yàowù yě suízhī jìnrù wǒ guó shìchǎng, bìng zài wǒguó yàopǐn shìchǎng zhong zhànyǒu xiāngdāng de fèn'é.
Following the opening up of our country recently, a number of large foreign pharmaceutical companies have followed each other into China. Genetically engineered medicines have entered our markets along with them, and they have moreover gained a sizable share of our pharmaceutical market.

2. X, 随着 Y = Y happens in connection with X (Av) The adverb 随着 marks that Y happens in close sequence with X and is influenced by X. X and Y will be verb phrases or clauses. 随之 suízhī is a more shumianyu variant (see its use in expl b above). Whether used as an co-verb at the head of the sentence as described in 1 above or as the adverb discussed here, both uses of 随着 show the background for a following verb action.

a. 雪飘下来了，树枝随着挂满了雪花。
Xuě piāo xiàlái le, shùzhī suízhe guàmǎnle xuěhuā.
The snow drifted down, and (thus) the branches of the trees blossomed with snow flakes.

b. 由于经济建设高潮的到来，工人的生活随着也有了很大的提高。
Yóuyú jīngji jiànshè gāocháo de dàolái, gōngrén de shēnghuó suízhe yě yǒu le hěn dà de tígāo.
Due to the arrival of a high tide of economic development, the lives of the workers were (accordingly) greatly enhanced.

所 suǒ (—) "emphasizes description structure" Adverb

1. 所 Verb (的) (Noun) = The noun that was verbed (Av) The very shumianyu 所 is placed before a transitive verb that is modifying a noun to bring attention to the description the verb brings to the structure. A special feature of this structure is that the noun this structure describes will also be the recipient of the modifying verb action; e.g., in expl a the tv sets are produced, and in expl b those (results) are expected. The noun is often deleted, leaving a 所 Verbed 的 structure (expl b); the 的 can also omitted after certain verbs with no change in meaning; for example 据我所知 jù wǒ suǒ zhī 'From what I know' and 有所增加 yǒu suǒ zēngjiā 'There is an increase.' It is difficult to translate into written English the sense of certainty about the features of a noun this descriptive 所 imparts, but it can be rendered as '(the noun) that is verbed,' or 'the verbed (noun),' etc.

See 被 bèi 1 for description of the totally different use of 所 in passive structures. You will also frequently encounter 所 as part of the conjunction 所以 suǒyǐ 1. Additionally, keep in mind that when preceded by a number or a specifier, 所 is a measure for buildings.

a. 深圳工厂所生产的电视机在国际市场上非常受欢迎。
Shēnzhèn gōngchăng suǒ shēngchăn de diànshìjī zài guójì shìchăng shang fēicháng shòu huānyíng.
The television sets that the Shenzhen factories produce are extremely well received in the international market place.

b. 物理实验结果同吴副教授所预料的完全一致。
Wùlǐ shíyàn jiéguǒ tóng Wú fùjiàoshòu suǒ yùliào de wánquán yīzhì.
The results of the physics experiments are completely consistent with those Associate Professor Wu expected.

S

所以 suǒyǐ (— —) 'therefore' Conjunction; 'reason for' Conjunction

1. X, 所以 Y = X, therefore Y (Cj) 所以 is the most frequently seen member of the set of words which mark that Y is a result of X. 所以 specifically marks Y as the logical result of the events, whether real (expl a) or abstract (expl b), given in X. Keep in mind here that 所以 marks only result, not deduction. X is most frequently headed by 因为 yīnwei 1 (expl a) or the shumianyu 由于 yóuyú 1 (expl b), though a 所以 marked Y sometimes occurs without either one of these markers in X. 所以 is generally not expressed overtly in the English translation (expls a & b), but it is almost always present in the Chinese.

The different members of this set of markers can all be translated as 'therefore, thus' but they each have some connotative differences. For example, the shumianyu 因此 yīncǐ 1 may mark deduction as well as result in Y, and the shumianyu 因而 yīn'ér 1 marks an even stronger element of deduction in Y. On the other hand, the synonymous 于是 yúshì 1 simply marks a sequential relationship between actual events in X and Y, never an abstract connection. The very shumianyu conjunction 则 zé 1 is a quasi-synonym which is sometimes also used to mark a cause and result relationship between X and Y. Also consider 以至 yǐzhì 1 and 以致 yǐzhì 1. Also see 从而 cóngér 1 (and 进而 jìn'ér 1).

a. 因为自行车在半路漏了气，所以我今天迟到了，真是抱歉！
Yīnwei zìxíngchē zài bànlù lòule qì, suǒyǐ wǒ jīntiān chídàole, zhēnshi bàoqiàn!
Because my bike had a flat tire on the way here (thus) I am late. Really sorry!

b. 由于黄山风景优美，所以每年前来观光的游览者很多。
Yóuyú Huáng Shān fēngjǐng yōuměi, suǒyǐ měinián qiánlái guānguāng de yóulǎnzhě hěn duō.
Because the scenery at Mt. Huang is so beautiful, (therefore) lots of tourists visit it every year.

2. Np (之) 所以 Vp, 是因为 Y = That by means of which the noun verbs is Y (Cj) 之所以 is a classical prose expression which literally means 之 'that' 所 'which' 以 'is used.' The very shumianyu (之)所以 zhī suǒ yǐ (not suǒyǐ) comes between the subject and verb in the first part of a result and cause structure where it marks the connection between the X result and the Y cause. When there is no identifying noun phrase preceding 所以, 其 qí 'it' replaces 之. Y will usually be marked with 是因为 shì yīnwèi or 就在于 jiù zàiyú. It is difficult to translate 之所以 Verb into English, but the structure in which it occurs can be represented by 'the reason' (expls a & b).

a. 爷爷耳朵之所以有点儿聋，是因为年纪大了。
Yéye ěrduo zhī suǒ yǐ yǒu diǎnr lóng, shì yīnwei niánjí dà le.
The reason grandfather is a little deaf is that he's gotten older.

b. 最高检察长之所以有信心，就在于检察机关始终秉公执法。
Zuìgāo jiǎncházhǎng zhī suǒ yǐ yǒu xìnxīn, jiù zàiyú jiǎnchá jīguān shǐzhōng bǐnggōng zhìfǎ.
The reason the Chief Procuratorate is confident is that the investigative officers always carry out the law impartially.

S

所有(的) suǒyǒu(de) (———) 'all (nouns)' Adjective

1. 所有(的) Nouns = All the nouns (Aj) 所有 is used to mark that the total number of individual nouns within a particular category of nouns is included in a verb situation. The nouns may either be the subject or the object of the sentence. A 的 is commonly placed between 所有 and the noun (expl a), but not always (expl b). A reinforcing 都 dōu 1 often appears before the verb (expls a & b).

The more shumianyu 一切 yīqiè 1 is a synonym which has the same English translation but somewhat different usages: 所有 refers to all the nouns within a category, whether or not the noun category can be sliced into smaller units; e.g., 所有流体 suǒyǒu liútǐ 'all fluids' and 所有开水 suǒyǒu kāishuǐ 'all boiled water' are both correct Chinese usages. On the other hand, 一切 is used only with broad categories of things which can be divided into smaller sub-categories, 一切 may not be used with items which do not subdivide; e.g., 一切流体 'all fluids' is acceptable, but *一切开水 is not. Further, 一切 is never followed by 的 while 所有 frequently is. Finally, 一切 also represents the pronoun 'everything' while 所有 is only used to quantify nouns.

Keep in mind that while the English word 'all' may be used with both nouns and verbs, the Chinese 所有(的) is used only with nouns! If you want to create the equivalent of the English phrase "(nouns) all verb," you must place 都 dōu 1 right before the verb--都 never goes before a noun, and 所有(的) never goes before a verb. A sentence will often have 所有(的) Noun followed by a reinforcing 都 before the verb (both expls below), but 所有(的) and 都 are very different to the Chinese even though both can be translated as 'all.' See 都 dōu 1 for a discussion of its usage features.

a. 我听说所有的美国大学生都会使用电脑。
Wǒ tīngshuō suǒyǒude Měiguó dàxuésheng dōu huì shǐyòng diànnǎo.
I hear that all American college students can use a computer.

b. 那个实验室里的所有图书和仪器都是从日本买来的。
Nèige shíyànshì li de suǒyǒu túshū hé yíqì dōu shì cóng Rìběn mǎi lái de.
All the books and instruments in that laboratory were purchased from Japan.

S

倘若 <u>tǎngruò</u> (——) 'if' Conjunction

1. <u>倘若 X, Y</u> = <u>If X, Y</u> (Cj) <u>倘若</u> is a shumianyu member of the prolific set of words which mark that <u>X</u> is a condition which affects the occurrence of <u>Y</u>. <u>倘若</u> itself marks a greater degree of supposition and is more shumianyu than its synonymous conditional markers <u>如果</u> <u>rúguǒ</u> 1 and <u>假如</u> <u>jiǎrú</u> 1. While you will not frequently see <u>倘若</u>, it is included here as representative of a number of shumianyu conditional markers such as 倘使 tǎngshǐ, 倘或 tǎnghuò and 倘 tǎng that are not discussed in this dictionary. See <u>如果</u> <u>rúguǒ</u> 1 for a discussion of conditional structures.

a. <u>倘若</u>不去观察，不作实验，仅仅依据看书本来学习，这种知识是没有用处的。

<u>Tǎngruò</u> bù qù guānchá, bù zuò shíyàn, jǐnjǐn yījù shūběn lái xuéxí, zhèi zhǒng zhīshi shì méiyǒu yòngchù de.

<u>If</u> one does not observe or does not experiment but solely relies on books for learning, this type of knowledge has no use.

替 <u>tì</u> (—) "do for" Coverb

1. <u>Np1 替 Np2 Vp</u> = <u>Np1 does Vp on behalf of Np2</u> (Cv) <u>替</u> is one of the set of three words which mark that a first noun phrase does a verb action on behalf of a second noun. <u>替</u> is used with a full range of verbs rather than just the abstract transaction verbs to which its synonym <u>给</u> <u>gěi</u> 1 is limited; for example, expl a below has a transaction verb and expl b has a Stative verb. <u>(Np1) 为 Np2 Vp</u> is a synonymous shumianyu structure; see <u>为</u> <u>wèi</u> 1. See <u>给</u> <u>gěi</u> 1 for further discussion. As a verb 替 is also used for the idea of one person taking the place of another in doing a verb activity rather than doing it to benefit someone else (expl c).

a. 小金要去医院看病，你<u>替</u>她请一天假吧。

Xiǎo Jīn yào qù yīyuàn kànbìng, nǐ <u>tì</u> tā qǐng yī tiān jià ba.

Little Jin has to go to the hospital to see the doctor. Why don't you request a day off <u>for</u> her?

b. 《中国现代历史》考试小于考了第一名，我们都非常<u>替</u>他高兴。

"Zhōngguó Xiàndài Lìshǐ" kǎoshì Xiǎo Yú kǎole dì-yī míng, wǒmen dōu fēicháng <u>tì</u> tā gāoxìng.

Lao Yu came in first on the test in "Contemporary Chinese History," and we are all really happy for him.

c. 王太太伤风了，刘先生<u>替</u>她教今天的英语语法课。

Wáng tàitai shāngfēng le, Liú xiānsheng <u>tì</u> tā jiāo jīntiān de Yīngyǔ yǔfǎ kè.

Mrs. Wang has caught a cold. Mr. Liu is teaching today's English grammar class <u>instead of</u> her.

同 tóng (一) 'and' Conjunction; 'with' Coverb; 'towards' Coverb

1. **Np1 同 Np2 = Both Np1 and Np2** (Cj) 同 is a slightly shumianyu marker that links together two or more grammatically and conceptually similar noun phrases. The linked noun phrases may be either the subject or object of a sentence. When there is a list of more than two nouns, 同 is placed before the last one and earlier members tend to have the enumerative comma marker 、 between each one to mark their inter-relationship (see 、 in Punctuation); note that Chinese usually does not have a comma directly before 同 (or its synonyms) in this usage. A reinforcing 都 dōu 1 is often placed before the verb in this pattern.

Oral synonyms are 跟 gēn 1 and 和 hé 1, while 及 jí 1, 以及 yǐjí 1 and 与 yǔ 1 are shumianyu synonyms. See 跟 gēn 1 for overall comments about patterns of noun linkage in Chinese. Note that 同 is also used as a verb centered on the meaning 'same, identical.' (See 一样 yīyàng 1 for comments on the use of 同 in comparison structures.)

a. 汉英同汉日字典目前都买不到了。
Hàn-Yīng tóng Hàn-Rì zìdiǎn mùqián dōu mǎi bù dào le.
Both Chinese-English and Chinese-Japanese dictionaries are unavailable now.

b. 云南省技术投资公司同云南省钢铁公司是该省现代化样板机构。
Yúnnán Shěng Jìshù Tóuzī Gōngsī tóng Yúnnán Shěng Gāngtiě Gōngsī shì gāi shěng xiàndàihuà yàngbǎn jīgòu.
The Yunnan Technological Investment Corporation and The Yunnan Iron and Steel Company are models of organizational modernization in that province.

2. **Np1 同 Np2 Vp = Np 1 verbs along with Np2** (Cv) 同 is also used to mark that two noun phrases jointly do a verb action. The noun phrases will always be the subject of the sentence. Synonyms are the oral 跟 gēn 2 and 和 hé 2 as well as the shumianyu 与 yǔ 2.

a. 我前年同杜先生到昆明去了。
Wǒ qiánnián tóng Dù xiānsheng dào Kūnmíng qù le.
The year before last Mr. Du and I went to Kunming.

T

b. 翻译同外国代表团一起到福州参观访问。
Fānyi tóng wàiguó dàibiǎotuán yīqǐ dào Fúzhōu cānguān fǎngwèn.
The translator went on a visit to Fuzhou with the foreign delegation.

3. **(X) 同 Y Vp1 (Vp2) = (X) (verbs) compared with Y** (Cv) This usage of 同 marks comparison of X and Y. X and Y can be verb phrases (expl a) or noun phrases (expl b). You can distinguish this comparison usage of 同 from its three other usages through of the presence of comparison verbs such as 一样 yīyàng 1 (expls a & c), 比 bǐ 1 or a synonym (expl b) in the first verb position. When the second verb phrase is present in this structure, it tells exactly how the two noun phrases compare with each other (expl c); otherwise the structure marks a general comparative statement. See further discussion of comparative Coverbs at 跟 gēn 3. 和 hé 3 and the clearly shumianyu 与 yǔ 2 are synonyms of this usage. 同 can also appear in the first verb phrase in an equality

comparison structure; see the discussions at 一样 yīyàng 1 and 与 yǔ 2.

a. 学汉语同学别的外语一样，必须多听，多说，多写。
Xué Hànyǔ tóng xué bié de wàiyǔ yīyàng, bìxū duō tīng, duō shuō, duō xiě.
Studying Chinese and studying other foreign languages are the same; you have to listen, speak and write a lot.

b. 这个国家妇女的政治地位同资本主义国家中妇女应有的不大相称。
Zhèige guójiā fùnǚ de zhèngzhì dìwèi tóng zīběn zhǔyì guójiā zhong fùnǚ yīng yǒu de bù dà xiāngchèn.
Women's political status in this country does not quite match up with what it should be in a capitalist nation.

c. 今年的气候同往年一样暖和。
Jīnnián de qìhòu tóng wǎngnián yīyàng nuǎnhuo.
The weather this year is as warm as in the past.

4. Np1 同 Np2 Vp = Np1 verbs towards Np2 (Cv) In this usage 同 marks the direction of a verb action. As is the case with its oral synonyms 跟 gēn 4, 和 hé 4 and 对 duì 1 and shumianyu synonyms 向 xiàng 1 and 朝 cháo 1, 同 marks stationary facing towards rather than physical movement towards a place. You will need to analyze the general context in which 同 occurs to distinguish this usage from the other 同 structures discussed above.

a. 他上午已同我告别了。
Tā shàngwǔ yǐ tóng wǒ gàobié le.
He already said goodbye to me in the morning.

b. 有事要同群众商量。
Yǒushì yào tóng qúnzhòng shāngliang.
There is a matter to discuss with the masses.

T

Unmarked Conditional ‘(if)’

1. X, 就/还/也/将 Y = (If) X, then Y The term “Unmarked Conditional” refers to the frequently seen Chinese practice of creating “if” sentences without using a marker such as 如果 rúguǒ 1, 要是 yàoshi 1, 假如 jiǎrú 1, etc. in X. Actually, the word “unmarked” is somewhat misleading. While X is itself unmarked, more often than not there is a marker such as 就 jiù 1, 还 hái 1, 会 huì 1, etc. at the head of the verb phrase in Y; this is often a clue that the sentence is a conditional structure (expls a & c). Less frequently, the whole sentence is unmarked (expl b). Occasionally, an “Unmarked Conditional” structure appears as part of a larger sentence (expl c). X and Y will be either verb phrases or clauses. It is sometimes difficult to decide if you are looking at an “Unmarked Conditional” or simply two co-ordinate clauses. When this happens it is helpful to analyze the immediate and general context. Your general knowledge of the world can also help you decide whether something is representing an “if” situation.

a. 课本太贵，学生就不买。
Kèběn tài guì, xuésheng jiù bù mǎi.
If the textbooks are too expensive, the students will not buy them.

b. 我国经济不好，人民的生活水平提高不了。
Wǒ guó jīngji bù hǎo, rénmín de shēnghuó shuǐpíng tígāo bu liǎo.
If our economy is not healthy, the people’s standard of living cannot rise.

c. 在国际竞争的环境中，离开了科技进步，我国社会生产力就不可能迅速发展。
Zài guójì jìngzhēng de huánjìng zhong, líkāile kējì jìnbù, wǒ guó shèhuì shēngchǎnlì jiù bù kěnéng xùnsù fāzhǎn.
In an environment of international competition, if we deviate from making progress in science and technology, it will not be possible for our productivity to develop rapidly.

U

外 wài (—) 'besides; except for' Coverb

1. X 外, 还/也/又 Y = Besides Y, also X (Cv) 外 is a less infrequently used shumianyu synonym of 以外 yǐwài 1 & 2. You may consider 外 an abbreviation which functions in the same way 以外 does. That is, when Y contains an adverb such as 还 hái 1, 也 yě 1 or 又 yòu 1, 外 represents the idea that 'in addition to the contents of X, there is also Y.' With 都 dōu 1 in Y it means 'except for X, there is Y.' X may be either a noun phrase or a verb phrase while Y will be a verb phrase or a clause. See 除了 chúle 1, 2, & 3 for further discussion and examples. 外 is also commonly used to refer to a concept such as 'outside; beyond'; e.g., 大门外 dàmén wài 'outside the main gate,' or 三十里外 'over 30 li.'

a. 中国除汉族外，还有五十多个民族。
Zhōngguó chú Hànzú wài, hái yǒu wǔshí duō ge mínzú.
Besides the Han nationality, China also has over 50 other ethnic groups.

b. 海外华侨除投资办厂外，他们还热心于家乡的公共设施建设，如修路、架桥、兴建学校、兴办医院等。
Hǎiwài huáqiáo chú tóuzī bànchǎng wài, tāmen hái rèxīn yú jiāxiāng de gōnggòng shèshī jiànshè, rú xiūlù, jiàqiáo, xīngjiàn xuéxiào, xīngbàn yīyuàn děng.
In addition to investing and running factories, overseas Chinese are also enthusiastic about the construction of public facilities in the countryside: for example, building roads, erecting bridges, building schools, building and running hospitals, etc.

万 wàn (萬) '10,000' Number noun

1. 万 = Ten thousand (Nu) 万 is the marker for units of ten thousand. If you wish to do business in China, it is crucial for know that Chinese numbers over ten thousand are structured in terms of how many units of 'ten thousand' are involved; this differs from the Western practice of structuring large numbers in units of 'one thousand.' To arrive at the correct English equivalent for a large Chinese number, multiply the number before the 万 by 10,000. For example, in expl a below multiply 878 by 10,000 to arrive at 8,780,000; in expl b multiply 1800 by 10,000 to arrive at 18 million. In more recent texts you may also see a number rendered as a fraction of 万. In these texts multiply the 万 by the fraction; e.g., in expl c multiply 10,000 by 4.2 to get 42,000. Alternatively, it may be easier for you to memorize that 千万 qiānwàn = 'ten million,' 百万 = 'one million,' and 十万 = 'hundred thousand' and do simpler mathematical computations.

When moving from English to Chinese numbers, either mentally or literally draw a line between the fourth and fifth whole number from the right. After placing a 万 between those two numbers, translate how many tens, hundreds or thousands will come before the 万; e.g., 65,493,257.5 > 6549/3257.5 > 6,549万 = 六千五百四十九万. Next, translate the numbers after the 万 into the appropriate 'thousands,' 'hundreds,' etc. 3,257.5 > 三千两百五十七・五. Finally, place the larger number in front of the smaller to obtain 六千五百四十九万三千两百五十七・五 liùqiān wǔbǎi sìshijiǔ wàn sānqiān liǎngbǎi wǔshiqī diǎn wǔ '65,493,257.5.' See 万万 wànwàn 1 for comments on numbers larger than 100,000,000. 万 is also be used for the adverb 'absolutely.' 万 is also used in many vocabulary items for a value of 'an enormously large amount of' (see 百万富瓮 in expl b).

a. 上海市一九八九年年底的人口为八百七十八万人。
Shànghǎi Shì yī jiǔ bā jiǔ nián niándǐ de rénkǒu wéi bābǎi qīshibā wàn rén.
The population of Shanghai at the end of 1989 was 8,780,000.

b. 听说连集汇是个百万富瓮，有一千八百多万元人民币。
Tīngshuō Lián Jíhuì shì ge bǎiwàn fùwēng, yǒu yīqiān bābǎi duō wàn yuán Rénmínbì.
I hear that Lian Jihui is a millionaire. He has over 18,000,000 yuan.

c. 到目前，上海"下海"科技人员总数已达4.2万余人。
Dào mùqián, Shànghǎi "xià hǎi" kējì rényuán zǒngshù yǐ dá sì diǎn èr wàn yú rén.
At present, the number of sci-tech personnel in Shanghai who have gone into the business world is over 42,000 people.

往 wǎng (一) 'towards' Coverb

1. Verb 往 Np = Verb towards a place (Cv) 往 is used after movement verbs such as 开 kāi 'drive,' 送 sòng 'send,' 飞 fēi 'fly,' 派 pài 'send,' etc. to mark physical movent towards the following place or direction. 往 may also be pronounced in the fourth tone in this usage; note that 往 seems to be in a state of transition towards being pronounced wàng in all patterns. You might 往 wàng 1 a synonym which has a wider usage range.

往 is used orally with a very few monosyllabic verbs or Stative verbs in the structure 往 V/Sv 里 Vp to mark that the action of the verb phrase is towards the verb or Stative verb; e.g., 打蛇要往死里打 Dǎ shé yào wǎng sǐ lǐ dǎ 'When beating a snake, you must beat it to(wards) death.' As a vocabulary item 往 represents the verb 'go' and is used as part of many words having to do with movement or the past.

W

a. 本店遷往台北市中山北路四段三巷七十一號。
Běn diàn qiān wǎng Táiběi Shì Zhōngshān Běilù sìduàn sānxiàng qīshiyī hào.
This store has moved to #71, Alley #3, North Chungshan Rd., Section #4, Taipei.

b. 第三农具厂的产品运往全国各地。
Dì-sān Nóngjùchǎng de chǎnpǐn yùn wǎng quánguó gèdì.
The products of the #3 Agricultural Implements Factory are shipped to all parts of the country.

往 wàng (一) 'towards' Coverb

1. 往 Np Vp = Verb towards the noun (Cv) 往 is one of the set of words which mark the location involved in a verb action. 往 specifically marks that the verb act involves physical movement towards a noun phrase. The noun phrase will most often be the name of a direction (expl a), but you will also see 往 used with the name of a place (expl b) or an organization (expl c). If the noun phrase represents a person or animal, it must be structured to include a place locator; e.g., 往他那儿看 Wàng tā nàr kàn 'Look at him,' not *往他看.

When 往 wàng 1 is used in a 往下 verb structure, it may mean either 'verb downwards' as in 往下落 wàng xià luò 'fall downwards,' or it may mean "continue verbing" as it does in 往下写 wàng xià xiě 'write on'; similarly, when used with 后, 往 may mean either 'verb towards the rear' as in 往后退 wàng hòu tuì 'retreat to the rear' or as part of the adverb 往后 'henceforth' 往后听妈妈的话 Wànghòu tīng māma de huà 'Listen to mom from now on.' You may occasionally find older texts in which this marker is written as 望.

朝 cháo 1 and 向 xiàng 1 are synonyms which differ from 往 in specifically marking stationary facing towards something. 往, 朝 and 向 may appear to be interchangeable because in many situations there is the sense of both facing towards and physical movement towards which allows either of them to be used; e.g., in the sentence 飞机往/朝/向东南飞 Fēijī wàng/cháo/xiàng dōngnán fēi 'The airplane flies towards the southeast' all three can be used because actual movement as well as facing towards are involved. In different environments other factors come into play; e.g., in 往出版社投稿 Wàng chūbǎnshè tóugǎo 'Submit a manuscript to the publisher' 往 is used since the manuscript physically moves; 朝 would not be used since the subject does not actually face in the direction of the publisher as part of the act of mailing; yet 向 could be used since 出版社 is a human organization (expl c). See 朝 and 向 for further comparative comments and examples.

The 'towards' synonym 对 duì 2 differs from 往 in marking a noun phrase as the target of a verb action, not movement towards it. 给 gěi 2 is a synonym which marks the noun phrase as both the target and beneficiary of the verb action. When used with a place name, 到 dào 2 is an oral synonym that has a narrower usage rang. 往 wǎng 1 is a synonymous coverb with a more restricted range of usage. Consider also 跟 gēn 4, 和 hé 4, 同 tóng 4 and 于 yú 1.

W

a. 从公园往东走半里路。
Cóng gōngyuán wàng dōng zǒu bàn lǐ lù.
Go (to the) east from the park for ½ mile.

b. 小范常常从家里往学校跑来。
Xiǎo Fàn chángcháng cóng jiāli wàng xuéxiào pǎo lái.
Fan often runs to school from home.

c.涉外的经济纠纷案件还得往对外经济联络部报告。
Shèwài de jīngji jiūfēn ànjiàn hái děi wàng Duìwài Jīngji Liánluòbù bàogào.
Economic crimes which involve foreign interests must still be reported to the Ministry for Economic Relations with Foreign Countries.

望 wàng (—) 'towards' Coverb

1. 望 Np Vp = Verb towards the noun (Cv) 望 is used in some older texts to mark that a verb action involves physical movement towards a location. This function is now most commonly represented by 往 wàng 1. See 往 for comments and examples.

万万 wànwàn (萬萬) 'hundred million' Number noun

1. 万万 = Hundred million (Nu) 万万 functions in a manner structurally similar to 'ten thousand' 万 wàn 1. To arrive at the correct English equivalent for a number containing 万万, multiply the amount before 万万 by 100,000,000 and the amount between it and the following 万 wàn by '10,000.' In the first example below, multiply 万万 by 4 and 万 by 5000 to arrive at four hundred million plus fifty million > 450,000,000. In the second example, multiply 万万 by 1 and 万 by 4,966 to arrive at 149,660,000. For a discussion on how to understand numbers between '100,000,000' and '10,000,' see 万 wàn 1. 亿 yì 1 is an exact synonym of 万万. 万万 is also used with negative verb phrases for the adverb 'absolutely.'

a. 一九四九年中国的人口是四万万五千万人。
Yī jiǔ sì jiǔ nián Zhōngguó de rénkǒu shì sìwànwàn wǔqiān wàn rén.
In 1949 China's population was 450,000,000.

b. 地球离太阳有一万万四千九百六十六万公里。
Dìqiú lí tàiyáng yǒu yīwànwàn sìqiān jiǔbǎi liùshiliù wàn gōnglǐ.
The earth is 149,660,000 kilometers from the sun.

为 wéi (爲) 'be, act as' Verb; '(verb) to be, as' Verb complement; "passive marker" Coverb (also see 为 wèi)

1. Np1 为 Np2 = Np1 is/acts as Np2 (Vb) When 为 occurs between two noun phrases in written texts, it is a shumianyu synonym for 是 'to be' (expl a) or 作 'act as' (expl b); in this usage 为 is pronounced with the second tone. Note that 为 is generally not used orally for this meaning. You can distinguish this usage of 为 from its other second and fourth tone usages because it comes between two noun phrases with neither 以 yǐ 1 nor verbs preceding (see the discussion at 2 below) or following (see the discussion at 4 below) it. See 为 wèi 1 for comments on how to distinguish wéi and wèi.

a. 上海为世界大城市之一。
Shànghǎi wéi shìjiè dà chéngshì zhīyī.
Shanghai is one of the major cities of the world.

b. 国家政策将有利于变经济落后地区为经济发达的现今地区。
Guójiā zhèngcè jiāng yǒulì yú biàn jīngji luòhòu dìqū wéi jīngji fādá de xiànjīn dìqū.
The government's policies will be helpful in changing economically backward areas into economically very advanced regions.

2. Np1 Verb 为 Np2 = A first noun verbs to be/act as a second noun (Vc) When 为 follows a verb as its complement, 为 marks that a noun verbs or is verbed so as 'to be' or 'act as' some other noun (expls a & b); this usage often connotes an element of change (expl b). When the first noun phrase is a pronoun, it can come between the verb and the 为; e.g., expl b could be structured as 选她为代表⋯⋯Xuǎn tā wéi dàibiǎo... 'Select her to be a representative...' Verb 为 frequently occurs in the structure Np1把 Np2 Verb 为 Np3 = Np1 verbs Np2 so that it is Np3 (expl a); see 把 bǎ 1 for further comments on this common pattern.

a. 老姚常常把"十"字读为"千"字！。
Lǎo Yáo cháng cháng bǎ "shí" zì dúwéi "qiān" zì!
Little Yao always reads the character for 'ten' as the one for 'one thousand'!

b. 她当年选为第一届全国人民代表大会的代表。
Tā dāngnián xuǎnwéi dì yī jiè quánguó rénmín dàibiǎo dàhuì de dàibiǎo.
She was selected to be the representative to the first National People's Congress that year.

3. 以 X 为 Y = Take X to be Y (Vb) This very common shuymianyu structure marks that X is taken to be/act as Y. X and Y will usually be noun phrases (expl a), though they can be verb phrases (expl b). See 以 yǐ for further discussion and an example of this combination of 以 with 为.

a. 以雷锋同志为榜样。
Yǐ Léi Fēng wéi bǎngyàng
Have comrade Lei Feng as a model.

b. 出版社并不是说任何文章以短为好。
Chūbǎnshè bìng bùshì shuō rènhé wénzhāng yǐ duǎn wéi hǎo.
Actually, the publisher is not saying that 'short is good' for any and all writings.

4. Np1 为 Np2 (所) Vp = Np1 is verbed by Np2 (Cv) In this usage, 为 is a shumianyu member of the set of passive markers. The 所 before the verb can help you easily recognize this use of 为 wéi as a highly shumianyu synonym of the passive marker 被 bèi 1 (expl b). Even when there is no 所, you can use the presence of a noun phrase and a

W

following verb phrase after the 为 to distinguish "passive" 为 from the other usages (expl a). See 被 bèi 1 for overall comments on Chinese passive structures.

a. 旅客都为西湖之美迷住了。
Lǚkè dōu wéi Xī Hú zhī měi mízhù le.
Tourists are entranced by the beauty of West Lake.

b. 主席指出这一点已为事实所证明。
Zhǔxí zhǐchū zhèi yī diǎn yǐ wéi shìshí suǒ zhèngmíng.
The chairperson pointed out that this matter has been verified by the facts.

未 wèi (一) "verb negation" Adverb

1. 未 Vp = Verb action not done (Av) One of the small set of adverbs that mark the negation of verbs, the very shumianyu 未 is most often used as a synonym of 没 méi 1 to mark the non-occurrence of a verb act (expl a), but 未 is also used as a synonym of the neutral negative marker 不 bù 1 (expl b). 未 tends to be frequently used in ROC texts, less often in PRC writings. 未 is also used in a few shumianyu idioms; e.g., 未卜先知 wèi bǔ xiān zhī 'foresee.' It also is used in some words which tend to have meanings extending from its basic negative value. See 没 méi 1 and 不 bù 1 for further discussion and examples of this set of negative adverbs.

a. 郑女认为施工单位在施工处未设置任何警告标志，显然置公共安全於不顾，实在可恶。
Zhèng nǚ rènwéi shīgōng dānwèi zài shīgōngchù wèi shèzhì rènhé jǐnggào biāozhì, xiǎnrán zhì gōnggòng ānquán yú bù gù, shízài kěwù.
Ms. Zheng believes that the construction unit did not put up any warning signs. This clearly shows that they were not concerned about public safety, and that's truly detestable.

b. 关于将来的出路问题，未知您今后将作如何打算。
Guānyú jiānglái de chūlù wèntí, wèi zhī nín jīnhòu jiāng zuò rúhé dǎsuàn.
I do not know what plans you will make about options for the future.

W

为 wèi (爲) 'do for' Coverb; 'for the purpose of' Coverb (also see 为 wéi)

1. (Np) 为 X Vp = (Noun) does verb for (the benefit of)/on behalf of X (Cv) The formal 为 is used to mark that X is the beneficiary of a verb action. X will usually be a noun phrase (expls a & b), but occasionally it will be a verb phrase (expl c). 为 is also used in a similarly formed structure to mark "purpose"; this is discussed in 2 below. You will have to analyze the discourse context to distinguish between the two, but that task is made easier by the fact that the "benefit 为"discussed here is never followed by 了 le 1 or 着 zhe 1.

为 has two oral synonyms: 给 gěi 1, which is limited to use with abstract transaction verbs, and 替 tì 1. These two synonyms are used for less serious and less formal matters; e.g., neither would be substituted for 为 in the examples given below.

You can distinguish second tone wéi usages from fourth tone wèi by examining the structures in which they appear: wèi never appears in combination with 以 yǐ 1, with 所 in a passive structure, as the verb between two noun phrases, or as a complement after a verb; conversely, you will not find a verb object structure after wéi, nor will you find wéi used with 而 ér 3.

a. 为人民服务！
Wèi rénmín fúwù!
Serve (on behalf of) the people!

b. 香港纺织品交易所作为中介人，热心地为买卖双方服务。
Xiānggǎng fāngzhīpǐn jiāoyìsuǒ zuò wéi zhōngjièrén, rèxīn de wèi mǎimài shuāngfāng fúwù.
The Hong Kong Textile Exchange acts as an intermediary, and it enthusiastically serves (for) both buyers and sellers.

c. 人民总医院的试验为治疗艾滋病找到了新型药物。
Rénmín zǒngyīyuàn de shìyàn wèi zhìliáo àizībìng zhǎo dàole xīn xíng yàowù.
The People's General Hospital found new medicines for curing aids.

2. 为 X Vp = Do verb (in order) to/for (the purpose of) X (Cv) This structure marks X as the reason (expl a) or goal (expl b) for a verb action. X can be either a noun phrase (expl a) or a verb phrase (expl b). Y will be either a verb phrase or a clause. 了 le 1 or 着 zhe 1 often appear after this 为; in fact, 为了 is so very common it is given an entry of its own; see 为了 wèile 1 for discussion of a variant of "purpose" 为.

a. 为在座的各国朋友的健康、为我国与各国人民之间的友谊干杯！
Wèi zài zuò de gèguó péngyou de jiànkāng, wèi wǒguó yǔ gèguó rénmín zhījiān de yǒuyì gānbēi!
Let us drink to (for purpose of) the health of all of our foreign friends who are in attendance and to (for the purpose of) friendship between our nation and the peoples of all countries!

b. 人民为实现四个现代化一心一意地工作。
Rénmín wèi shíxiàn sì ge xiàndàihuà yīxīn yīyì de gōngzuò.
The people are working with one heart and one mind in order to realize the Four Modernizations.

3. Np 为 Vp1 而 Vp2 = Np1 does Vp2 in order to do Vp1 (Cv) The presence of 而 ér 1 in this variant of #2 above imparts a strong flavor of the classical literary language to this structure. It is a more erudite way to mark a value of "do something for a purpose." 了 follows 为 in this structure only when the first and second verb phrases have verbs representing opposite actions (expl b). See 为了 wèile 2.

a. 两位总理表示，双方将为促进东北亚地区的经济合作和保障本地区的和平与稳定而共同努力。

Liǎng wèi zǒnglǐ biǎoshì, shuāngfāng jiāng wèi cùjìn Dōngběi Yà dìqū de jīngji hézuò he bǎozhàng běn dìqū de hépíng yǔ wěndìng ér gòngtóng nǔlì.

The two prime ministers stated that both sides would work together in order to promote economic cooperation in Northeast Asia and protect the peace and stability of this area.

b. 解放军为了前进而后退。

Jiěfàngjūn wèile qiánjìn ér hòutuì.

The People's Liberation Army retreated in order to advance.

4. 为 Vp1 起见, (Np) Vp2 = (Np) does Vp2 for Vp1 purpose (Cv) In this variant of the 为 "do for a purpose" structure, 为 continues to mark the purpose behind the second verb phrase. The first verb phrase is generally a short verb structure such as 慎重 shènzhòng 'prudent,' 方便 fāngbiàn 'convenient,' 醒目 xǐngmù 'striking,' etc., it is never a noun phrase.

a. 为方便读者起见，书后附有两个索引。

Wèi fāngbiàn dúzhě qǐjiàn, shūhòu fù yǒu liǎng ge suǒyǐn.

There are two indices appended to the book for the convenience of the readers.

b. 为醒目起见，课文中的生词都添上星号了。

Wèi xǐngmù qǐjiàn, kèwén zhong de shēngcí dōu tiān shang xīnghào le.

In order to make them stand out clearly, the new vocabulary items in the texts are all marked with asterisks.

为了 wèile (為—) 'in order to, for the purpose of' Coverb

1. 为了 X, (Np) Vp or (Np) 为了 X Vp = (Np) verbs for the purpose of X (Cv) This structure marks X as the purpose or goal for the verb action in Y. X will usually be a verb phrase (expls a & b), but it can be a noun phrase (expl c). Y will be a clause (expls a & b) or a verb phrase (expl c). When 为了 X precedes the subject of the sentence, which it commonly does, the 为了 X structure must be end-marked by a comma (expls a & b); look for the comma, it will help you find the end of a 为了 structure, even when it is long (expl b). The 为了 structure can also be use in the second half of a sentence for the same values (expl c). 为着 wèizhe 1 can replace 为了 to indicate that X is an ongoing action. See 为 wèi 2 for a synonymous "purpose" structure.

W

a. 为了解决人口问题，中国政府只让每个家庭生一个孩子。

Wèile jiějué rénkǒu wèntí, Zhōngguó zhèngfǔ zhǐ ràng měi ge jiātíng shēng yī ge háizi.

(In order) to solve the population problem the Chinese government only allows each family to have one child.

b. 为了抢占经济、科技发展的"制高点"，许多国家都把发展高技术作为国家发展战略的重要组成部分。

Wèile qiángzhàn jīngji, kējì fāzhǎn de "zhìgāodiǎn", xǔduō guójiā dōu bǎ fāzhǎn gāo jìshù zuò wéi guójiā fāzhǎn zhànlüe de zhòngyào zǔchéng bùfen.

In order to seize the "commanding heights" of economic and technological development, many nations make the development of high technology an important formative element in their strategy for national development.

c. 我们都是来自五湖四海，为了一个共同的目的都到一起来了。

Wǒmen dōu shi láizì wǔhú sìhǎi, wèile yī ge gòngtóng de mùdì dōu dào yīqǐ lái le.

We come from all corners of the land and have joined together for a common goal.

2. Np 为了 Vp1 而 Vp2 = Np does Vp2 in order to do Vp1 (Cv) The use of the very shumianyu 而 ér 1 gives the structure a more erudite tone, though it is difficult to translate this quality into English. See 为 wèi 3 for further comments and examples of this shumianyu "purpose" structure.

a. 目前在中国，许多人为了办事方便而走后门。

Mùqián zài Zhōngguó, xǔduō rén wèile bànshì fāngbiàn ér zǒu hòumén.

At present many people in China utilize "the rear door" to facilitate transactions.

为着 wèizhė (爲—) 'for the purpose of, in order to' Coverb

1. (Np) 为着 X Vp = (Np) is doing a verb action for the purpose of X (Cv) The 着 marks the ongoing nature of the verb action in this variant of 为 wèi 2 "for the purpose of" structures. X may be either a noun or verb phrase. See 为了 wèile 1 for further comments and examples.

a. 成千上万的先烈，为着人民的利益，在我们的前头英勇牺牲了。

Chéngqiān shàngwàn de xiānliè, wèizhe rénmín de lìyì, zài wǒmen de qiántóu yīngyǒng xīshēng le.

Tens of thousands of martyrs bravely sacrificed themselves for (the purpose of) the people's interests.

W

为止 wéizhǐ (爲—) 'up until' Time word

1. 到 T 为止, Y = Y up to a point in time (Tm) 为止 is a member of one of the four sets of words which mark the time frame for the following Y situation. 为止 specifically marks that the time element before it is the end point for a following Y activity. 到 dào 1 is sometimes placed at the head of this pattern. Y will be a verb phrase or a clause. 为止 is also used without Y (expl b) See 止 zhǐ 1 for further comments.

a. 到目前为止，全市40家排油大户每年自行处理852吨含油废水。
Dào mùqián wéizhǐ, quánshì sìshí jiā páiyóu dàhù měinián zìxíng chǔlǐ bābái wǔshièr dūn hányóu fèishuǐ.
Up to the present, 40 of the city's largest oil dischargers have voluntarily processed 852 tons of oil bearing waste water annually.

b. 今天的讨论到此为止。
Jīntiān de tǎolùn dào cǐ wéizhǐ.
That is all for today's discussion.

无论 wúlùn (無論) 'regardless of (alternative/indefinite possibilities)' Conjunction

1. 无论 X, Y = No matter what X says, Y is unchanged (Cj) 无论 is a member of one of the three different sets of conjunctions which mark that no matter what the X situation may be, Y remains the same. 无论 specifically marks that regardless of the indefinite or alternative possibilities given in X, Y is unaffected. X will be either an alternate choice structure such as (是) X 还是 Y (expl a) or an indefinite structure containing an interrogative such as 多么 duōme 'how much so,' 怎么 zěnme 'how,' 哪 nǎ 'which,' etc. (expls b & c). Whether the Y verb phrase is headed with 也 yě 1 or 都 dōu 1, there is no difference in meaning.

不论 búlùn 1 is a very close synonym used both orally and in prose texts. 不管 bùguǎn 1 and 凭 píng 2 are oral synonyms. See 虽然 suīrán 1 for comparative comments and examples of these three sets of alternate/indefinite, fact and hypothesis concessive conjunctions. Consider also the comments at 尽管 jǐnguǎn 1. You will also run into the idiomatic shumianyu phrase 无论如何 wúlùn rúhé 'no matter what/how.'

a. 无论是锻炼还是学习，她都非常努力。
Wúlùn shì duànliàn háishi xuéxí, tā dōu fēicháng nǔlì.
Whether exercising or studying, she is extraordinarily hard working.

b. 无论任务多么艰巨，工作们都决必要按时完成。
Wúlùn rènwù duōma jiānjù, gōngzuòmen dōu jué bìyào ànshí wánchéng.
No matter how arduous the duties are, the workers must complete them on time.

c. 无论哪一门功课都要好好学习
Wúlùn nǎ yī mén gōngkè dōu yào hǎohāo xuéxí.
No matter what class it is, you must study diligently.

W

2. X, 无论 Y = X is unchanged regardless of Y (Cj) When 无论 is placed in Y, it continues to mark that one situation does not change the other, but it differs slightly in also conveying a shumianyu tone of voice. Y has the same structural features listed for X in the discussion above.

a. 冯部长总是那样乐观，无论发生什么事情。

Féng bùzhăng zǒngshì nèiyàng lèguān, wúlùn fāshēng shénme shìqing.
Minister Feng is always so optimistic, regardless of whatever happens.

b. 他象驴子一样顽固，他打定了主意后就不会改变，无论怎么劝他。

Tā xiàng lǘzi yīyàng wángù, tā dǎdìngle zhǔyì hòu jiù bù huì gǎibiàn, wúlùn zěnme quán tā.

He is as stubborn as a mule. Once he's decided on something, he won't change no matter what you say.

先 <u>xiān</u> (一) 'first' Adverb

1. <u>先 Vp1, 再/才/后 Vp2</u> = <u>First do verb 1, then does verb 2</u> (Av) <u>先</u> is placed at the head of a first verb phrase to mark that it will lead to a second verb phrase action. The second verb phrase will usually include an adverb such as <u>才</u> <u>cái</u> 2, <u>再</u> <u>zài</u> 2 (note that this <u>再</u> marks that a verb will happen at a point in time rather than marking that the verb will be repeated) or the adverb 后 hòu 'then' to mark the linkage.

a. 你<u>先</u>拟个提纲再写。
Nǐ <u>xiān</u> nǐ ge tígāng zài xiě.
Make an outline <u>before</u> you start to write.

向 <u>xiàng</u> (一) 'towards' Coverb

1. <u>向 Np Vp</u> = <u>Verb towards the noun</u> (Cv) <u>向</u> is a member of one of the two sets of words which mark the location involved in a verb action. <u>向</u> specifically marks the verb act involves a "stationary facing in the direction of the place." The location which <u>向</u> marks can be any type of noun phrase ranging from the name of a direction (expl a), to the name of a person, place or thing (expl b), to an abstract concept (expl c). <u>着</u> <u>zhe</u> 1 may be used after <u>向</u> (expl c), except with monosyllabic place names, to mark the ongoing nature of the verb situation. 向 also appears in some words having to do with 'direction.'

<u>朝</u> <u>cháo</u> 1 is a close oral synonym which has usage restrictions that <u>向</u> does not: for example, 1) while <u>向</u> is used with abstract verbs where the noun phrase represents human beings, <u>朝</u> may not be; e.g., <u>向</u>群众学习 xiàng qúnzhòng xuéxí 'Learn from the masses' rather than *<u>朝</u>群众学习; and 2) <u>向</u> may come after a verb as described in 2 below, <u>朝</u> does not.

Consider the two differing sets of "towards" markers by comparing "static facing towards" <u>向</u> with the "physical movement towards" <u>往</u> <u>wàng</u> 1. Since situations often allow for the possibility of both facing and moving towards something, either the <u>向</u> or the <u>往</u> set could be correctly used in many texts (as is the case in expl a but not in expls b & c below). However, there are times when only one fits; e.g., in 白宫大门<u>向</u>北开 'The main door to the White House opens to the north' <u>往</u> could not be used since the sentence does not mean that the door is physically moving. (The other major "stationary facing towards" synonym <u>对</u> <u>duì</u> 2 could not be used here since a direction can not be the target of a verb action.) See <u>朝</u> <u>cháo</u> 1 for a further comparative discussion of the members of the "stationary towards" set of markers and <u>往</u> <u>wàng</u> 1 for the "physical movement towards" markers. <u>给</u> <u>gěi</u> 2 is a synonym which marks the noun phrase as both the target and beneficiary of the verb action.

X

a. 你一直<u>向</u>北走几分钟，就可以到人民公园。

Nǐ yīzhí xiàng běi zǒu jǐ fēn zhōng, jiù kěyǐ dào Rénmín Gōngyuán.
Go straight (to the) north for a few minutes, and you'll arrive at the People's Park.

b. 我有件事向您请教。
Wǒ yǒu jiàn shì xiàng nín qǐngjiāo.
I have a matter I would like to ask your opinion on.

c. 我国的发电能力向着新的阶段发展。
Wǒ guó de fādiàn nénglì xiàngzhe xīn de jiēduàn fāzhǎn.
The ability of our country to produce electricity is moving towards a new stage.

2. Vp 向 Np = Verb towards the noun (Cv) 向 is used after a small number of monosyllabic verbs such as 杀 shā 'kill,' 推 tuī 'push,' 驶 shǐ 'drive,' etc. to mark the direction towards which the verb action occurs; 了 le 1 may occur after 向 in this usage. The noun phrase may be either the name of a direction or the name of a place, but not the name of a human. When the noun phrase has to do with human beings, 向 must come before the verb as structured in usage 1 above.

a. 长江流向东海。
Chángjiāng liú xiàng Dōnghǎi.
The Yangtze flows to the China Sea.

b. 那条新公路通向西藏拉萨。
Nèi tiáo xīn gōnglù tōng xiàng Xīzàng Lāsà.
That new highway is open to Lhasa, Tibet.

象 xiàng (像) 'resembles' Verb; 'seems like' Adverb

1. X 象 Y (一样) (Vp/Sv) = X seems like Y (Vb) 象 is a member of the set of words which mark resemblance. The verb 象 functions to mark that similarity of some sort exists between X and Y (expls a & b). X and Y will be noun phrases (expls a & b). A 象 structure may include 一般 yībān 1, 似的 shìde 1 or by 一样 yīyàng 3 and/or be ended with a verb phrase or a Stative verb structure (expl b), but it is often the case that no end marker or verb structure is used (expl a). Synonyms for 象 are 好象 hǎoxiàng 1 and the more shumianyu markers 仿佛 fǎngfú 1, 如 rú 1, 若 ruò 2 and 如同 rútóng 1. Note that 象 is also used at the head of a list of nouns with the meaning 'for example.' See 好象 hǎoxiàng 1 and 一样 yīyàng 3 for further discussion of similarity patterns.

a. 看样子，他很象个教师。
Kàn yàngzi, tā hěn xiàng ge jiàoshī.
Looking at him, he really seems like a teacher.

b. 这一次王书记没象上次那样坐飞机，而是走的水路。
Zhèi yī cì Wáng shūjì méi xiàng shàng cì nàyàng zuò fēijī, ér shì zǒu de shuǐlù.
This time Secretary Wang did not go by airplane like he did last time. He traveled by water.

2. 象 Vp (一样) = Seems like a certain verb condition (Av) 象 is also used as an adverb to mark that a verb act seems to have a certain quality to it (expls a & b). 一样 yīyàng 3 or a synonym often appears at the end of a 象 adverb structure (expl b). See 好象 hǎoxiàng 1 for further discussion and examples.

a. 我象在哪儿见过那个姑娘，但是记不清是在什么地方。
Wǒ xiàng zài nǎr jiànguo nèige gūniang, dànshì jì bù qīng shì zài shénme dìfāng.
It seems like I've seen that girl somewhere before, but I can't remember where.

b. 欧阳老师关心我象关心她自己的女儿一样。
Ōuyáng lǎoshī guānxīn wǒ xiàng guānxīn tā zìjǐ nǚ'ér yīyàng.
Professor Ouyang looks after me as if she were looking after her own daughter.

向来 xiànglái (—來) 'always/never' Adverb

1. 向来 Vp = Always verbed (Av) 向来 is an oral member of one of a set of adverbs which mark the ongoing nature of a verb situation. 向来 is most frequently used with a following affirmative verb phrase to mark that the verb situation has always been so, right up to the present (expl a). When followed by the negative adverb 不 bù 1, 向来 marks that the verb situation has not happened and probably will not happen (expl b).

The shumianyu synonym 历来 lìlái 1, used only in positive situations, has a weaker tone to it while 从 cóng 2, used only in negative situations, is a stronger toned shumianyu synonym. See 从来 cónglái 1, a stronger toned synonym mainly used with negative situations, for further discussion and examples of this set of markers.

a. 老马向来很可靠。
Lǎo Mǎ xiànglái hěn kěkào.
Mr. Ma has always been reliable.

b. 浦小姐向来不喝啤酒不吸烟。
Pǔ xiǎojiě xiànglái bù hē píjiǔ bù xīyān.
Miss Pu has never drunk beer or smoked.

X

要 yào (一) 'want to/intend to' Auxiliary verb; 'should' Auxiliary verb; "verb act possible" Auxiliary verb; 'if' Conjunction

1.**S 要 Vp = Subject wants to do the verb act** (Ax) In this usage, 要 marks that the subject is determined to do a verb act. It can be difficult to distinguish 要 1, 2 & 3 from each other, and it is often easy to make a case for either understanding in a sentence. Thus, consideration of the broader context in which you see 要 is essential.

The negative idea 'do not want to verb' is 不想 bùxiǎng or 不愿意 bù yuànyi, not 不要 which is the negative form of 要 yào 2. When 要 represents a transitive verb meaning 'want; order; request,' it will be directly followed by a noun, so it is easily distinguishable from its other uses.

a. 小男孩儿大声叫出，"我要吃热狗。"
Xiǎo nán háir dàshēng jiào chū, "Wǒ yào chī règǒu."
The little boy screamed, "I want to eat a hot dog."

b. 新华社香港分社副社长郑国雄昨天表示，中方对于港英当局表示要释放两百多名滞港越南船民一事非常关注。
Xīnhuáshè Xiānggǎng fēnshè fùshèzhǎng Zhèng Guóxióng zuótiān biǎoshì, Zhōngfāng duìyú Gǎng Yīng dāngjú biǎoshì yào shìfàng liǎng bǎi duō míng zhì Gǎng Yuènán chuánmín yīshì fēicháng guānzhù.
The head of the Hongkong branch of the New China News Agency, Zheng Guoxiong, said yesterday that the Chinese are paying close attention to the matter of the British authorities indicating that they want to release 200 some Vietnamese boat people who are detained in Hong Kong.

2. **要 Vp = Verb action has to be done** (Ax) In this usage, 要 marks that the verb act must be done (expls a & second 要 in b). The negative form is 不要, and it is generally used for the strong negative imperative 'Don't verb!'

a. 陆大夫说："他的病还没有全好，出院后还要休息一两个星期。"
Lù dàifu shuō, "Tā de bìng hái méiyou quán hǎo, chūyuàn hòu hái yào xiūxi yī liǎng ge xīngqī."
Dr. Lu said, "He is not completely over his illness. After he gets out of the hospital, he will need to rest one or two more weeks."

b. 副总理李岚清强调，要扩大机电产品出口，就要有明确的奋斗目标。
Fùzǒnglǐ Lǐ Lánqīng qiángdiào, yào kuòdà jīdiàn chǎnpǐn chūkǒu, jiù yào yǒu míngquè de fèndòu mùbiāo.
Vice Premier Li Lanqing emphasized that if we want to expand our exports of machinery and power generating equipment, we must have clear objectives.

Y

3.**要 Vp = Verb act is probable** (Ax) In this less frequently seen usage, 要 marks that a verb act is likely (expls a & b). 会 huì can be placed before the 要 to strengthen the sense of probablity of the verb action happening; e.g., 看样子会要下雪 Kàn yàngzi huì yào xiàxuě 'Looks like it will snow.' The negative form is 不会, not 不要 which is the negative for 2 above. 能 néng 1, 可以 kěyǐ 1 and 会 huì 1 are synonyms; see 可以 kěyǐ 1 for a comparative discussion.

When 要 is preceded by 快 kuài 'soon' or 就 jiù 3 with 了 le 2 at the end of the sentence, it marks that a verb action is imminent; e.g., 飞机就要起飞了 Fēijī jiù yào qǐfēi le 'The plane is just about to take off.' In a comparative structure, 要 marks an estimate about probability; e.g., 今天要比昨天冷得多 Jīntiān yào bǐ zuótiān lěng de duō 'I suspect today is a lot colder than yesterday.'

a. 我们班明天要看京剧。
Wǒmen bān míngtiān yào kàn jīngjù.
Our class will go the Peking Opera tomorrow.

b. 这次会议大概要到月底才能开。
Zhèi cì huìyì dàgài yào dào yuèdǐ cái néng kāi.
It will probably be the end of the month when this conference will start.

4. 要 X = If X, Y (Cj) In its usage as an oral member of the set of words which mark that X defines the conditional parameters for Y, 要 is thought of as an abbreviation of 要是 yàoshi 1. X will usually be a verb phrase (expl 1 & first 要 in 2.b above), though 要 noun phrase structures also occur (expl b). 的话 dehuà 1 can be placed at the end of X to intensify its conditional nature; see 的话 dehuà 1.

You can distinguish this function of 要 from its use as a transitive verb; e.g., 我要钱 Wǒ yào qián 'I want money' and its uses as an Auxiliary verb discussed above by noticing that as an conjunction 要 comes at or near the head of two or more linked clauses. See 如果 rúguǒ 1 for a comparative discussion of this set of conditional markers.

a. 明天要下雨，运动会就不举行了。
Míngtiān yào xiàyǔ, yùndònghuì jiù bù jǔxíng le.
If it rains tomorrow, the meet will not be held.

b. 那有什么用？要我就不买。
Nà yǒu shénme yòng? Yào wǒ jiù bù mǎi!
What good is that? If it were me, I would not buy it!

要不(然) yàobù(rán) (———) 'otherwise' Conjunction

Y

1. X, 要不(然) Y = X, otherwise Y (Cj) 要不(然) marks that Y is either a hypothetical conclusion to X (expl a) or that X and Y are alternatives (expl b). X and Y will be clauses or verb phrases. 要不然 gives a slightly stronger tone than 要不 does. The 不 in the fuller 要不然 yàoburán has no tone. See the weaker synonym 不然 bùrán 1 for further comments and examples.

a. 作任何工作都要依靠党，要不然工作就不能作好。
Zuò rènhé gōngzuò dōu yào yīkào dǎng, yàoburán gōngzuò jiù bù néng zuò hǎo.
In whatever you do you must rely on the Party, otherwise you won't be able to do the work.

b. 可以坐电车去，要不的话，坐地铁也行。
Kěyǐ zuò diànchē qù, yàobù dehuà, zuò dìtiě yě xíng.
We can go by trolley; or going by subway is also ok.

要不是 yàobushi (———) 'if it were not for' Conjunction

1. 要不是 X, Y = If not for X, Y (Cj) A negative member of the set of words which are conditional markers, 要不是 marks both that the X condition actually happened and that it determined what happened in Y. X is usually a verb phrase (expl a), though it can be a noun phrase (expl b). Y will generally be headed by 就 jiù 1, 也 yě 1, etc. See 如果 rúguǒ 1 for a discussion of other conditional markers.

a. 要不是你把我叫醒，我不知道要睡到什么时候呢！
Yàobushi nǐ bǎ wǒ jiàoxǐng, wǒ bù zhīdào yào shuìdào shénme shíhou ne!
If you had not awakened me, I don't know how long I would have slept!

b. 要不是党的教育，我就不会有今天的进步。
Yàobushi dǎng de jiàoyù, wǒ jiù bù huì yǒu jīntiān de jìnbù.
If were not for education by the Party, I would not have made the progress I have today.

要是 yàoshi (——) 'if' Conjunction

1. 要是 X, Y = If X, Y (Cj) 要是 is an oral member of the set of words which mark that X defines the conditions under which Y may occur. X will generally be a verb phrase (expls a, b & d), but a noun phrase is also possible (expl c). The Y verb phrase will usually be marked with an adverb such as 就 jiù 1, 也 yě 1, 还 hái 1, 便 biàn 1, etc. which brings its own values to Y. 的话 dehuà 1 can be added to the end of X to intensify the conditional nature of the situation (expl d). 要是 can be omitted from X if the context is clear; in that case the sentence becomes an unmarked conditional (see unmarked conditional 1). 要 yào 1 is an oral synonym and 要不是 yàobushi 1 'if it were not for' is a negative conditional marker; see 如果 rúguǒ 1 for comments on the many synonymous 'if' markers.

a. 明天要是刮大风，飞机就不能起飞了。
Míngtiān yàoshi guā dàfēng, fēijī jiù bù néng qǐfēi le.
If it is really windy tomorrow, the airplane will not be able to take off.

b. 要是干训班结束得快，他下星期五就回来。
Yàoshi gànxùnbān jiéshù de kuài, tā xià xīngqīwǔ jiù huílái.
If the cadre training class ends quickly, he will return next Friday.

c. 我要是个大人，我也一定出国学习有机化学。
Wǒ yàoshi ge dàrén, wǒ yě yīdìng chūguó xuéxí yǒujī huàxué.
If I were an adult, I'd sure go abroad to study organic chemistry too.

d. 要是有人来找我的话，就说我在老吴家。
Yàoshi yǒu rén lái zhǎo wǒ dehuà, jiù shuō wǒ zài Lǎo Wú jiā.
If it happens that anybody comes looking for me, tell them I'm at Wu's.

也 yě (一) 'also' Adverb; 'still (verbs)' Adverb; 'even' Adverb; "tactful tone of voice" Adverb

1. X,也 Y = X, and also Y (Av) 也 is often used to mark a connection between the verb phrases in X and Y. In these sentences, 也 comes at the head of the Y verb phrase. The similarity may be that different subjects both do the same verb (expl a); sometimes X is clear from context and is not given (expl b). The similarity may be that the subject does two, or more, different verbs (expl c). 也 is also used when the subjects and verbs are the same but the objects differ (expl d). Occasionally you will see 也 in a compound sentence where the subjects and verb phrases are different but which still has an overall similarity in content (expl e). Finally, X may contain any of a range of markers such as 假如 jiǎrú 1, 不但 bùdàn 1, etc., which bring condition, succession, etc. values to the sentence (expls c & d). 亦 yì 1 is a shumianyu synonym.

也 is used in very few words, so when you see it in a text, you may expect that 也 is being used for one of the values described in this entry.

a. 风停了，雨也住了。
Fēng tíng le, yǔ yě zhù le.
The wind stopped, and the rain also stilled.

b. 同时，城市汽车尾气污染也在加重，氮氧化物已成为广州、北京的首要污染物。
Tóngshí, chéngshì qìchē wěiqì wūrán yě zài jiāzhòng, dànyǎng huàwù yǐ chéngwéi Guǎngzhōu, Běijīng de shǒuyào wūránwù.
At the same time, automotive tailpipe pollution is increasing in the cities. Nitrates have already become the primary pollutant in Guangzhou and Beijing.

c. 欧盟深化改革和扩大成员国，不仅关系到欧洲的前途和未来欧洲的政治版图，也涉及各国的主权和民族利益。
Ōuméng shēnhuà gǎigé hé kuòdà chéngyuánguó, bùjǐn guānxi dào Ōuzhōu de qiántú hé wèilái Ōuzhōu de zhèngzhì bǎntú, yě shèjí gè guó de zhǔquán he mínzú lìyì.

Intensifying reforms and enlarging the membership of NATO not only relates to the future of Europe and the shape of future European politics, it also touches on national sovereignty and the interests of the people.

d. 华侨会馆不仅是侨胞回到国内时的家，也是全球侨胞团结的象征。

Huáqiáo Huìguǎn bùjǐn shì huáqiáo huídào guónèi shí de jiā, yě shì quánqiú qiáobāo tuánjié de xiàngzhēng.

The Overseas Chinese Meeting Hall is not only a home when compatriots are returning to China, it is also a symbol of the solidarity of Chinese throughout the world.

e. 第四十四届世乒赛冷门迭爆的同时，也出现了一个小插曲。

Dì sìshisì jiè shì bīng sài lěngmén diébào de tóngshí, yě chūxiànle yī ge xiǎo chāqǔ.

At the same time an unexpected winner burst forth in the 44th World Pingpong Competition, another drama also occurred.

2. (虽然/既/即使) X, 也 Y = (Although/Since/Even if) X, still Y (Av) In this usage 也 marks that Y is unaffected by the situation in X. Sometimes there will not be a marker in X (expls a & b), but more often X will be headed with markers such as 既然 jìrán 1, 只要 zhǐyào 1, etc. which bring their own further values to the sentence (expls c & d). You can often distinguish this from 也 1 by the differences in structure and disimilarity of meaning between X and Y.

a. 你不说我也知道。

Nǐ bù shuō wǒ yě zhīdao.

Even if you don't say it, I still know.

b. 预查显示，我国城市独生子女人格的基本状况良好，但也存在着不可忽视的严重问题。

Diàochá xiǎnshì, wǒguó chéngshì dúshēng zǐnǚ réngé de jīběn zhuàngkuàng liánghǎo, dàn yě cúnzàizhe bùkě hūshì de yánzhòng wèntí.

The survey shows that the basic moral condition of the children in one-child families in our cities is good, but there still exist important questions that cannot be overlooked.

c. 老爷即使干不了重活，也可以干点儿轻活嘛。

Lǎoye jíshǐ gān bu liǎo zhònghuó, yě kěyǐ gān diǎnr qīnghuó ma.

Even if grandpa can't do any heavy work, he still can do some light stuff.

d. 虽然已经下起大雨来了，我们也要按时到达目的地。

Suīrán yǐjing xià qǐ dà yǔ lái le, wǒmen yě yào ànshí dàodá mùdì dì.

Even though it has started raining heavily, we will still reach our destination on time.

3. Indefinite interrogative 也 Vp = Nothing/Nowhere/No matter how/Nobody verbs (Av) When combined with a preceeding interrogative pronoun (e.g., 谁 shéi 'whoever,'

怎么 zěnma 'however,' 什么 shénma 'whatever,' etc.) 也 marks a shift from a question to a statement (expls a & b). The verb phrase will most often be negative (expls a & b). A variation is Verb 也 Verb 不 result (expl c). 都 dōu 3 is synonymous. See the section on Indefinite Interrogative Pronouns for further comments and examples.

a. 考试时谁也不说话，只听见老师沙沙的脚步声。
Kǎoshì shí shéi yě bù shuōhuà, zhǐ tīngjiàn lǎoshī shāshā de jiǎobùshēng.
During exams nobody talks; there is only the soft sound of the teacher's footsteps.

b. 这个瓶子拧得太紧了，怎么拧也拧不开。
Zhèige píngzi nǐng de tài jǐn le, zěnma nǐng yě nǐng bu kāi.
This bottle is closed too tightly. No matter what I try, I still can't open it.

c. 怎么办，我这件新衬衫洗也洗不干净了。
Zěnme bàn, wǒ zhèi jiàn xīn chènshān xǐ yě xǐ bu gānjìng le.
What shall I do? No matter what I can't get my new blouse clean.

4. X 也 Vp = Even X verbs (Av) In this usage 也 marks emphasis on X, which may be a noun (expl a), a number measure (noun) structure (expl), or a verb (expl). When X is a noun, 连 lián 1 is often placed at the head of the structure and the noun may be either the subject or object of the sentence; the verb phrase tends to be negative, though not always (expl a). See 连 for further comment and examples. When 连 is not used, the even X verbs usage is subtle and you will need to examine the context to identify it. 都 dōu 4 is a synonym of this usage.

a. 现在连偏僻的农村也用上了拖拉机。
Xiànzài lián piānpì de nóngcūn yě yòngshàngle tuōlājī.
Nowadays even remote villages are (also) using tractors.

b. 两姐妹留著长长的头发，外貌有些柔弱，一点也不像角力选手。
Liǎng jiěmèi liúzhe cháng cháng de tóufa, wàimào yǒuxiē róuruò, yīdiǎn yě bù xiàng juélì xuǎnshǒu.
The two sisters have very long hair and have a rather delicate appearance. They do not look like wrestlers at all.

5. 也 vp = Tactful tone of voice (Av) In this usage 也 marks a tactful tone of voice; it has none of the values discussed in 1-4 above. Careful examination of the context is needed to identify this value because 也 comes directly before the verb as it does in other usages. This pattern can also be structured with a "maximum adverb" such as 再 zài 2, 至多/少 zhìduō/shǎo 1, etc. preceding X (expl d); alternatively an adverb such as 永远 yǒngyuǎn 'forever' may appear.

a. 你这个办法也不错。
Nǐ zhèi ge bànfǎ yě bùcuò.
This way of your doing things isn't bad at all.

b. 音量也就是这样了，不能再大了。
Yīnliàng yě jiùshì zhèi yàng le, bùnéng zài dà le.
I'm afraid that this is the way the volume is, it can't be made louder.

c. 最远也就是二十米左右。
Zuì yuǎn yě jiùshì èrshí mǐ zuǒyòu.
At the most it is still about 20 meters.

NOTE: If there is more than one 也 in a sentence, it could well be the 也 Vp 1, 也 Vp 2 structure discussed in the next entry.

也…也 yě...yě (——) 'as well, both, and' Adverb; 'whether (hypothesis)' Adverb

1. 也 Vp1 也 Vp2 = Do the first verb as well as the second verb (Av) This structure is used to mark the simultaneous existence of two (expl a) or more verb situations (expl b). It is generally used only with transitive verbs, and in this it differs slightly from the synonymous 又 Vp1 又 Vp2 yòu...yòu 1 which is used with both verbs and Stative verbs. When the structure has the same subject, 又 Vp1 又 Vp2 tends to be used; when the verbs have different subjects 也 Vp1 也 Vp2 tends to be used though it is also used when the subjects are the same. Also consider 连 lián 2.

a. 范同学也不抽烟也不喝酒，她没有这类嗜好。
Fàn tóngxué yě bù chōuyān yě bù hē jiǔ, tā méiyǒu zhèi lèi shìhào.
Our classmate Fan doesn't smoke, and he doesn't drink. He doesn't have these kinds of bad habits.

b. 少年先锋队也学政治，也学业务，也参加劳动。
Shàonián Xiānfēngduì yě xué zhèngzhì, yě xué yèwù, yě cānjiā láodòng.
The Young Pioneers study politics, a trade, and they participate in physical labor.

2. X 也 Verb, Negative X 也 Verb = Whether X or not, the verb happens (Av) This structure marks that regardless whether the hypothetical situation given in X happens or not, the verb will happen. See 即使 jíshǐ 1 for a discussion of different hypothetical markers.

a. 毛大夫说可以去我也去，他说不可以去我也去。
Máo dàifu shuō kěyǐ qù wǒ yě qù, tā shuō bù kěyǐ qù wǒ yě qù.
Whether Dr. Mao says I may go or not, I will go.

一 yī (—) 'as soon as'; Adverb; 'for a while' Adverb; "particular noun" Number

Y

1. 一 Vp 1, 就 Vp 2 = As soon as verb 1, then verb 2 (Ad) One of the set of words which shows sequencing in verb actions, 一 marks a tight sequence of verb activities; the verbs are usually monosyllabic. When in a structure with two different verbs, 一 marks that the second verb action or condition happens in very close sequence to the first (expls a & c). The two verbs may have the same (expl c) or different subjects (expl a). The second verb phrase is usually headed by 就 jiù 1 to highlight the sequence of actions (expls a & b), though 才 cái 1 can be used instead to mark that the situation has an unexpected aspect to it (expl c).

When the first and second verb phrases have the same verb, 一 denotes that whenever the verb act happens, it reaches a specific degree or result (expl b). Distinguish between this use of 一 in verb sequences and its use with single verb structures discussed in 3 below. See 以前 yǐqián 1 and 以后 yǐhòu 1 for other markers of verb sequences.

a. 朱敏同学很聪明，老师一教他怎么写一个汉字，他马上就明白了。

Zhū Mǐn tóngxué hěn cōngming, lǎoshī yī jiāo tā zěnme xiě yī ge Hànzì, tā mǎshang jiù míngbai le.

The student Zhu Min is quite bright. As soon as the teacher shows him how to write a character, he immediately understands.

b. 陈牧师很会讲道，一讲就讲了两三个小时。

Chén mùshī hěn huì jiǎngdào, yī jiǎng jiù jiǎngle liǎng sān ge xiǎoshí.

Pastor Chen can really preach. Whenever he preached, he talked for two or three hours.

c. 我把箱子打开一看，才知道里边装的全是黄金。

Wǒ bǎ xiāngzi dǎkāi yī kàn, cái zhīdao lǐbiān zhuāng de quán shì huángjīn.

As soon as I opened the chest and took a look, I realized it was filled with gold.

2. Verb 一 verb = Verb for a while (Av) When placed between the two parts of a repeated monosyllabic verb, 一 represents the idea that the verb action does not take a lot of effort (expl a) and/or does not last long (expl b). This structure is often used as a gentle imperative (expl a). The verb is usually either one that has not yet occurred (expl a) or one that happens frequently (expl b). When a specific instance of the repeated verb action has already been completed, 了 le 3 usually replaces 一.

a. 老坐着腿会麻了，动一动就会好了。

Lǎo zuòzhe tuǐ huì má le, dòng yī dòng jiù huì hǎo le.

If you have been sitting for quite a while, your legs can get numb. Move a bit and you'll be ok.

b. 遇到什么困难，书记总是先到各家各户听一听老百姓的意见。

Yùdào shénme kùnnan, shūjì zǒngshì xiān dào gè jiā gè hù tīng yī tīng lǎobǎixìng de yìjiàn.

When she ran into a problem, the Secretary would always go to all the families to listen to what the people were thinking.

3. 一 Vp = Suddenly or thoroughly verb (Av) When used in a sentence structured with a single verb rather than the multiple verb structures discussed in 1 above, 一 verb marks a strengthened quality of completeness (expl a) or suddenness (expl b) to the verb action.

The exception to this value of 一 Vp is 一 used with 是 in the structure 一是 X, 二是 Y, 三是 Z which marks a list of conditions (expl c). You can distinguish this usage from the others discussed in this entry by determining whether a measure or a verb comes after 一. When followed by a measure, which is much more frequently seen, 一 represents the concept of 'one unit of something' rather than a verb action; also consider the discussion below in #4.

a. 那本小说值得一看。
Nèi běn xiǎoshuō zhíde yī kàn .
That novel is worth a read.

b. 团长的那马猛然一惊，直立起来。
Tuánzhǎng de nèi mǎ měngrán yī jīng, zhílì qǐlái.
The regimental commander's horse suddenly startled and reared straight up.

c. 学习汉语时必需用功：一是练习口语，二是阅读课文，三是记住语法.
Xuéxí Hànyǔ shí bìxū yònggōng: yīshì liànxí kǒuyǔ, èrshì yuèdú kèwén, sānshì jìzhù yǔfǎ.
When studying Chinese you must be industrious: first, practice orally; second, read the texts; third, remember the grammar.

4. Specifier 一 noun = This/that particular noun (Nu) When 一 is preceded by either 这 zhèi 'this' or 那 nèi 'that' or a synonym and followed by an abstract noun structure which does not include a measure, 一 marks that attention is being focused on that individual noun. To distinguish this from its more common use with a following measure to simply mark a numerical amount (i.e., 'one') of a noun, look for the presence or absence of a measure after the 一.

a. 这一办法很解决问题。
Zhèi yī bànfǎ hěn jiějué wèntí.
This particular method is very effective with problems.

已 yǐ (一) 'already' Adverb

1. 已 X = Already X (Av) 已 is a shumianyu adverb which marks that X, generally a verb but sometimes a Stative verb, is either completed (expl b) or has reached a certain degree of completion in the relatively near past (expl a). 已 often connotes a possibility that the verb action could continue (expl a). Compare this with 曾 céng 1 which marks that a verb action did indeed happen at some point in time, usually in the relatively distant past, but is no longer occurring. See 已经 yǐjīng 1, a close synonym, for further comments and examples. 已 may also be used as the verb 'cease' and the adverbs 'to' or 'later on' in very shumianyu texts.

a. 经过三场比赛，胜负已成定局。

Jīngguò sān chǎng bǐsài, shèngfù yǐ chéng dìngjú.

After three matches, the outcome was <u>already</u> a foregone conclusion.

b. 教育部官员指出，教育部已完成「学校卫生法」草案，并在
法规会进行讨论。

Jiàoyùbù guānyuán zhǐchū, Jiàoyùbù yǐ wánchéng "Xuéxiào Wèishēng Fǎ" cǎo'àn, bìng zài fǎguīhuì jìnxíng tǎolùn.

Officials of the Ministry of Education pointed out that the Ministry has <u>already</u> completed a draft of "The Law About Health in Schools" and has had meetings to discuss it.

以 yǐ (一) 'use, take, base on' Coverb; 'use' Verb; 'in order to' Conjunction

1. 以 Np Vp = <u>Use the noun to do a verb</u> (Cv) The shumianyu 以 marks the noun phrase following it as either something used to do a verb action (expls a & b) or as the conceptual basis for a verb action (expl c). The noun phrase will always represent an abstract concept. 用 <u>yòng</u> 1 and the less commonly used 拿 ná 'take' are oral synonyms which differ in being used both with nouns representing concrete objects and those representing abstract concepts. 以 is also used for this value in the even more shumianyu pattern 以 Np 而 Y in which 而 <u>ér</u> 3 marks the relationship between a noun representing a goal, attitude or basis and the verb condition articulated in <u>Y</u> (expl c).

Keep in mind that 以 is also placed before some monosyllabic place or time words to create words which represent place, time, amount or scope; e.g., 以前 <u>yǐqián</u> 1, 以后 <u>yǐhòu</u> 1, 以及 <u>yǐjí</u> 1, 以上 yǐshàng 'plus,' etc. 以 can also come after a verb such as 给 gěi 'give' and 供给 gōngjǐ 'supply' to convey a meaning of 'give.' It also is used in verbs such as 予以 yǔyǐ 'bestow' or 借以 jièyǐ 'for the purpose of' to add a sense of 'in order to' to the verb structure.

a. 我们要以孙中山先生遗训的精神教育青年。

Wǒmen yào yǐ Sūn Zhōngshān xiānsheng yíxùn de jīngshén jiàoyù qīngnián.

We must <u>use</u> the teachings of Sun Yatsen to educate our youth.

b. 以高技术发展新产品，提高产品的质量，掌握市场竞争的主动权。

Yǐ gāo jìshù fāzhǎn xīn chǎnpǐn, tígāo chǎnpǐn de zhìliàng, zhǎngwò shìchǎng jìngzhēng de zhǔdòngquán.

<u>Use</u> advanced technology to develop new products, enhance the quality of products, and control initiative in the competition for markets.

c. 我们祖国以有这样古老的文化而骄傲。

Wǒmen zǔguó yǐ yǒu zhèiyàng gǔlǎo de wénhuà ér jiāo'ào.

Our country <u>takes</u> having this ancient culture as a point of pride.

2. 以 X 为 Y = Take X to be/act as Y (Vb) This shumianyu structure is very common in modern prose. It marks that X, which may be either a noun (expls a & c) or verb (expl b) phrase, is taken to be or act as Y, which may be either a noun (expl c) or verb (expls a & b) phrase. 以 X 为 Y can also form a descriptive structure (expl c). Note that 为 has the second tone in this usage; see 为 wéi 3. An equivalent oral structure is 把 O1作为 O2; see 把 bă 1.

a. 客观规律不以人们的意志为转移。
Kèguān guīlǜ bù yǐ rénmen de yìzhì wéi zhuănyí.
Objective laws do not shift based on people's desires.

b. 中国北方以面食为主，而南方则以米饭为主。
Zhōngguó běifāng yǐ miànshí wéi zhŭ, ér nánfāng zé yǐ mĭfàn wéi zhŭ.
In northern China wheat is taken as the staple food, while in the south it is rice.

c. 以总工程师刘一达为首的课题组，在采用新技术处理垃圾方面，取得了突破性研究成果。
Yǐ Zŏnggōngchéngshī Liú Yīdá wéi shŏu de kètízŭ, zài căiyòng xīn jìshù chŭlĭ lājī fāngmiàn, qŭdéle tūpòxìng yánjiū chéngguŏ.
In the area of using new technology to process trash, the task group which has Chief Engineer Liu Yida as the head has achieved some striking research results.

3. Clause 1 以 Clause 2 = Do Clause 1 in order to do clause 2 (Cj) When placed at the head of the second half of a compound sentence, the shumianyu conjunction 以 marks that the first clause is done in order to accomplish the goal expressed in the second. The second clause is the focal point of the sentence. 以便 yĭbiàn 1 is a shumianyu synonym. Vp1 来 Vp2 lái 1 is an oral synonym.

a. 该工厂又增添了一些新设备以适应国际市场竞争形势。
Gāi gōngchăng yòu zēngtiānle yīxiē xīn shèbèi yǐ shìyìng guójì shìchăng jìngzhēng xíngshì.
That factory added some more new equipment in order to respond to competitive international market conditions.

b. 牧师应该具有高度的人道主义精神以解除人们的痛苦。
Mùshi yīnggāi jùyŏu gāodù de réndào zhŭyì jīngshén yǐ jiěchú rénmen de tòngkŭ.
Ministers must have a high degree of moral understanding so that they can relieve people's suffering.

亿 yì (億) 'hundred million' Number

1. 亿 = Hundred million (Nu) 亿 is a variant way of writing 100,000,000. See the completely synonymous 万万 wànwàn 1 for comments on how Chinese structure numbers of 100,000,000 or more.

a. 美国的有关资料表明，在两亿美国人中，约有800万人患哮喘。

Měiguó de yǒuguān zīliào biǎomíng, zài liǎng yì Měiguórén zhōng, yuē yǒu bā bǎi wàn rén huàn xiàochuǎn.

Relevant American data shows that among 200,000,000 Americans there are about 8,000,000 who have asthma.

b. 主管财物的副总经理李永安说，按一九九三年五月末中国的物价水平测算，三峡工程静态投资为九百亿元人民币。

Zhǔguān cáiwù de zǒng jīnglǐ Lǐ Yǒng'ān shuō, àn yī jiǔ jiǔ sān nián wǔ yuè mò Zhōngguó de wùjià shuǐpíng cèsuàn, Sānxiá gōngchéng jìngtài tóuzī wéi jiǔ bǎi yì yuán RMB.

Executive Vice-president Li Yongan, who is in charge of finances, said that when it is calculated according to price levels in China at the end of May, 1993, the investment in the Three Gorges Engineering Project is 90,000,000,000 RMB.

亦 yì (—) 'also, too' Adverb

1. 亦 Vp = Also do the verb (Av) 亦 is a very shumianyu adverb used to mark that either the same subject is doing a different verb phrase action (expl a), or that a second subject is doing the same verb action a first subject is doing (expl b). 亦 is frequently used in texts from the ROC, you will see it less often in PRC texts. 也 yě 1 is a close synonym. 亦 is also used in the word 亦即 yìjí 'i.e.' and the idiomatic phrase 亦步亦趋 yì bù yì qū 'blindly imitate somebody's every move.'

a. 除了海上走私，亦可经由旅客夹带、从第三国以快递寄送等。

Chúle hǎishàng zǒusī, yì kě jīng yóu lǚkè jiādài, cóng dì sān guó yǐ kuàidì jìsòng děng.

Besides smuggling (Cuban cigars) by sea, they can also use tourists to smuggle them or send them by express mail from a third country, etc.

b. 台中政府观光科长刘淑媚指出，国防部目前并无暂缓裁撤后里马场的打算，而马场场长周志源亦指出，未接获任何新的指示，……

Táizhōng zhèngfǔ guānguāng kēzhǎng Liú Shūmèi zhǐchū, Guófángbù mùqián bìng wú zànhuǎn cáichè Hòulǐ Mǎchǎng de dǎsuàn, ér mǎchǎng chǎngzhǎng Zhōu Zhìyuán yì zhǐchū, wèi jiēhuò rènhé xīn de zhǐshì,....

The head of the Tourist Section of the Taizhong government pointed out that the Ministry of Defense had definitely not postponed the plan to dissolve the Houli horse ranch, and the head of the ranch, Zhou Zhiyuan, also pointed out that he had not received any new directives,...

一般 yībān (——) "similarity" Stative verb

1. X 仿佛 Y 一般 (Sv) = X is similar to Y (in a Sv condition) (Sv) 一般 is a shumianyu member of the set of words which mark similarity. X and Y are usually noun phrases. When used with a Stative verb, 一般 marks a similarity in the Sv condition of X and Y, not that they are exactly the same (expls a, b, & metaphorically c). The Sv will be monosyllabic and have a positive meaning; e.g., 大 dà 'big' appears with 一般, but 小 xiǎo 'small' does not, you will find 长 cháng 'long' in an 一般 structure but not 短 duǎn 'short,' etc. (expl a). 一样 yīyàng 3 and 似的 shìde 1 are synonymous with 一般, but they are not as shumianyu. The synonym 般 bān 1 can be used instead of 一般 in descriptive structures of two or more syllables with no change in meaning.

Instead of 仿佛 fǎngfú 1, oral synonyms such as 象 xiàng 1 (expl b) and 好象 hǎoxiàng 1 along with their shumianyu synonyms 同 tóng 3, 和 hé 3 (expl a), 如 rú 1 and 如同 rútóng 1 can appear in conjunction with 一般; which particular combination of words is used depends on the degree of shumianyu formality desired. 一般 is frequently used as part of a noun or verb descriptive structure; when it modifies a noun 一般 is immediately followed by 的 de 1 (expl c) and when describing a verb 地 de 1 follows 一般. 一般 is also used as a Stative verb meaning 'common; normal; ordinary.' See 一样 yīyàng 3 for an overall discussion of similarity patterns.

a. 她哥哥和你一般高。
Tā gēge hé nǐ yībān gāo.
Her older brother and you are pretty much the same height.

b. 昨天发射的长征四号运载火箭象流星一般。
Zuótiān fāshè de Chángzhēng Sìhào Yùnzài Huǒjiàn xiàng liúxīng yībān.
The "#4 Long March Carrier Rocket" launched yesterday flew like a meteor.

c. 那是铁一般的事实，谁也否认不了的。
Nà shì tiě yībān de shìshí, shéi yě fǒurèn bù liǎo de.
That is an iron-like fact, absolutely no one can deny it.

一边 yībiān (一邊) "simultaneous verb actions" Adverb

1. 一边 Vp1, 一边 Vp2 (一边 Vp3) = Verb 1 and verb 2 (and verb 3) occur at the same time (Av) 一边 is one of the set of words which mark that two or more verb actions occur concurrently. 一边 draws attention to the fact that two, or more, verb situations occur at the same time; generally, verb phrase 1 started before the following verb phrase(s). The focus is often on the second verb phrase. The verb phrases may or may not have the same subject, but they tend to be grammatically parallel. 一边 is only used with concrete actions, it is not used with abstract verb situations. Y

The shumianyu synonym 一面 yīmiàn 1 is used with both abstract and concrete situations. Used only with structurally simple verb phrases, the synonymous 边 biān 1 connotes a tighter inter-relatedness of verb activities. The synonymous 一方面 yīfāngmiàn 1 differs in marking either two aspects of one activity or the co-existence of two inter-related activities which occur either sequentially or simultaneously. Note that 一边 is also used as a place structure: e.g., 他在一边坐着 Tā zài yībiān zuòzhe 'He is sitting to one side.'

a. 我昨天看见你一边走路上学校，一边看书，要多小心啊。
Wǒ zuótiān kànjiàn nǐ yībiān zǒulù shàng xuéxiào, yībiān kànshū, yào duō xiǎoxīn a!
I saw you walking to school and reading at the same time yesterday. You should be more careful.

b. 商店里的服务员一边整理商品，一边聊天。
Shāngdiàn li de fúwùyuán yībiān zhěnglǐ shāngpǐn, yībiān liáotiān.
The clerks were straightening up the goods and shooting the breeze at the same time.

以便 yǐbiàn (——) 'in order to' Conjunction

1. Clause 1, 以便 Clause 2 = Do clause 1 in order to do clause 2 (Cj) The very shumianyu marker 以便 is placed at the head of the second of two clauses to mark that the first clause is helpful in doing the second. The second clause is the focal point of the sentence. A comma usually comes immediately before 以便. 以便 may also be written 以便于 yǐbiànyú. 以 yǐ 3 is a shumianyu synonym. See also 来 lái 1.

a. 他提高了声音讲话，以便使坐在后边的人也能听清楚。
Tā tígāole shēngyīn jiǎnghuà, yǐbiàn shǐ zuò zài hòubian de rén yě néng tīng qīngchu.
He raised his speaking voice in order to make the people sitting in the rear also be able to hear clearly.

b. 南非共和国总统曼德拉决定，在一九九七年底和中华民国断交，以便和中华人民共和国建交。
Nánfēi Gònghéguó Zǒngtǒng Màndélà juédìng, zài yī jiǔ jiǔ qī niándǐ hé Zhōnghuá Mínguó duànjiāo, yǐbiàn hé Zhōnghuá Rénmín Gònghéguó jiànjiāo.
The President of the Republic of South Africa, Mandela, decided to break diplomatic relations with the Republic of China at the end of 1997 in order to establish relations with the People's Republic of China.

一点儿 yīdiǎnr (一點兒) 'a little bit' Number; 'not in the least little bit' Adverb

1. Verb/Stative verb 一点儿 (Object) = Verb/Sv (the object) a bit (Nu) The number 一点儿 comes after a verb (expl a) or a Stative verb (expl b) to mark that there is a minor amount in the verb phrase situation. 一点儿 may be followed by an object in this structure (expl c). In oral usage the 一 and/or the 儿 may be dropped, and this results in a Verb点儿, Verb 一点, or Verb 点 structure with no change in meaning. When 一点儿 is preceded by 这么 zhème or 那么 nàme the structure means 'an extremely small amount or condition' and may come either before or after the verb (expl d). Consider also the very different adverbial use of 一点儿 described in 2 below.

Because both the number 一点儿 and the adverb 有一点儿 yǒu yīdiǎnr 1 can be translated as 'a little bit,' English speakers tend to regard them as being interchangeable; however, the number 一点儿 must come AFTER the verb (except when used with 这么 zhème or 那么; see expl d), and the adverb 有一点儿 must come BEFORE the verb, as do all Chinese adverbs (see the first ½ of expl c). Note that 一点儿 is a noun meaning 'a little bit,' and as such it sometimes comes after the verb 有 to mean 'have a little bit.'

a. 你叫的菜不够，再添一点儿吧。
Nǐ jiào de cài bù gòu, zài tiān yīdiǎnr ba.
You haven't ordered enough dishes, why don't you add a little more?

b. 最近几个星期伊拉克和伊朗的边境上安静一点了。
Zuìjìn jǐ ge xīngqī Yīlākè hé Yīlǎng de biānjìng shang ānjìng yīdiǎn le.
The last few weeks the border between Iraq and Iran has been a bit quieter.

c. 我有点儿口渴，请给我一点儿咖啡。
Wǒ yǒu diǎnr kǒukě, qǐng gěi wǒ yīdiǎnr kāfēi.
I am a bit thirsty, please give me a little bit of coffee.

d. 西瓜还没长好，只有这么一点儿大。
Xīguā hái méi zhǎng hǎo, zhǐyǒu zhème yīdiǎnr dà.
The watermelons are still not ready--they are still so tiny.

2. 一点儿 (Object) 都/也 negative Verb/Stative verb = Verb (the Object)/Sv not the least little bit (Av) This structure is always phrased negatively to mark that the verb situation does not exist at all (expl a); when the object is given, the verb does not affect the object in the slightest way at all (expls b & c). The object may come either between 一点儿 and 都/也 (expl b) or after the verb (expl c). Use the presence 也 or 都 and a negative adverb to distinguish this adverbial usage from the use described in 1 above.

a. 今天我一点儿也不热。
Jīntiān wǒ yīdiǎr yě bù rè.
I am not the least bit hot today.

b. 哎呀，我一点儿钱也没有！
Àiyā, wǒ yīdiǎnr qián yě méiyǒu!

Oh no, I don't have any money at all!

c. 美国国务卿一点儿都不了解中国外交部长的立场。

Měiguó Guówùqīng yīdiǎnr dōu bù liǎojiě Zhōngguó Wàijiāo bùzhǎng de lìchǎng.

The American Secretary of State does not understand the position of the Chinese Minister of Foreign Affairs at all.

一方面 yīfāngmiàn (———) "co-occurrence of verb actions" Adverb

1. 一方面 X, (另/又)一方面 Y = On the one hand X, (and) on the other hand Y

(Av) One of the set of four words which mark the co-occurrence of related verb actions, 一方面 either marks two aspects of one activity that occur at the same time (expl a), or the co-existence of two inter-related activities, which may occur either simultaneously or sequentially (expl b). X and Y will have the same subject and may be either verb phrases or clauses. Y is frequently also headed with 另 lìng 'another' (expl a) and have 又 yòu 1, 也 yě 1 or 还 hái 1 which bring their own further values to Y. The shumianyu synonym 一面 yīmiàn 1 and the oral synonym 一边 yībiān 1 differ a bit in marking the simultaneous occurrence of related verb actions.

a. 我下次到台灣去，打算一方面學國語，另一方面教英文。

Wǒ xià cì dào Táiwān qù, dǎsuàn yīfāngmiàn xué Guóyǔ, lìng yīfāngmiàn jiāo Yīngwén.

The next time I go to Taiwan, I plan to study Chinese on one hand and teach English on the other.

b. 农具工厂设计人员一方面努力提高生产，一方面尽量减少废水排放。

Nóngjù gōngchǎng shèjì rényuán yīfāngmiàn nǔlì tígāo shēngchǎn, yīfāngmiàn jǐnliàng jiǎnshǎo fèishuǐ páifàng.

The technicians at the agricultural implements factory work hard to enhance production on one hand and reduce the discharge of waste water on the other.

以后 yǐhòu (—後) 'after' Time marker

1. X 以后, Y = After X, Y (Tm) 以后 is a member of one of the four sets of words used to mark attention to the time frame of a Y situation. Specifically, 以后 marks that Y happens after X. 以后 always comes directly after X and will usually be end-marked with a comma. X will usually be a clause or verb phrase (expls a & c), but you will sometimes find that X is a noun phrase (expl b). 以后 can refer to either the past (expl a & b) or the future (expl c), but never to 'after' or 'behind' as a physical place. 后 hòu 1 and 之后 zhīhòu 1 are shumianyu synonyms which are used to focus attention on the time frame for Y but which differ in also being used to refer to a place. Keep in mind that 以后 can also be used as a time noun with the meaning of 'hereafter, afterwards.'

以前 yǐqián 1, 的时候 de shíhou 1 and their synonyms are the other members of this set of time frame markers. See 以来 yǐlái 1 for an overview of the four different sets of time frame markers. See 自从 zìcóng 1 for other comments and examples.

a. 小黎说完以后，学生们就笑了起来。
Xiǎo Lí shuōwán yǐhòu, xuéshengmen jiù xiàole qilai.
After Li finished speaking, the students started laughing.

b. 春秋战国以后，秦始皇统一了中国。
Chūnqiū Zhànguó yǐhòu, Qínshǐhuáng tǒngyīle Zhōngguó.
After the Spring and Autumn and the Warring States periods, The First Emperor of Qin unified China.

c. 孙铭文担任厂长以后，各方面的工作都会很有起色。
Sūn Míngwén dānrèn chǎngzhǎng yǐhòu, gè fāngmiàn de gōngzuò dōu huì hěn yǒu qǐsè.
After Sun Mingwen takes over as factory head, everything will begin looking up.

以及 yǐjí (——) 'and' Conjunction

1. X 以及 Y = X plus Y (Cj) The somewhat shumianyu 以及 is a member of the set of conjunctions which mark a list of two (expl b) or more (expl a) grammatically and conceptually parallel noun or verb phrases; the list will be composed of either all noun (expl a) or all verb (expl b) phrases, they are never intermingled. The order in which the phrases appear may suggest a ranking for importance, time sequence or category; the focus of the structure tends to be on the items before 以及. Synonyms are the oral 跟 gēn 1 and 和 hé 1 as well as the more shumianyu 及 jí 1, 同 tóng 1, and 与 yǔ 1. Note that unlike the traditional English language practice, a comma is not usually placed directly before any of these listing conjunctions.

a. 小沉、小何以及另外两个同学都在课上作了报告。
Xiǎo Chén, Xiǎo Hé yǐjí lìngwài liǎng ge tóngxué dōu zài kè shang zuòle bàogào.
Little Chen, Little He plus two other classmates gave a report in class.

b. 总理会见代表团时提出了两个问题：怎么推动两国之间的民间交往以及怎么增进科技交流。
Zǒnglǐ huìjiàn dàibiǎotuán shí tíchūle liǎng ge wèntí: zěnme tuīdòng liǎng guó zhījiān de mínjiān jiāowǎng yǐjí zěnme zēngjìn kējì jiāoliú.
When the Premier received the delegation he raised two questions: how to stimulate contacts among the peoples of the two countries as well as how to increase scientific-technological exchange.

已经 yǐjīng (—經) 'already' Adverb

1. 已经 X = Already X (Av) 已经 marks that X is completed or has reached a certain degree. While X will usually be a verb phrase (expl a), it will sometimes be a Stative verb (expl b), and upon occasion an amount (expl c). When X is a verb, 已经 marks that the verb action happened in the relatively near past and suggests the possibility that the verb action could continue occurring (expl a). Compare this with 曾经 céngjīng 1 which marks that a verb action indeed happened at some point in time, usually in the relatively distant past, but is now completely finished. 已 yǐ 1 is a very close shumianyu synonym. Note that some dictionaries give yǐjīng as the pronunciation for 已经 and some have yǐjing.

When used with a single monosyllabic verb, the 已经 headed verb structure must have a 了 le 2; e.g., 风已经停了 Fēng yǐjīng tíng le 'The wind has stopped.' 已经 before a quantity (expl c) or a Stative verb (expl b) marks that an amount or condition has been achieved. The quantity structure must be followed by 了; the Stative verb must be one that takes a 了 or a verb complement such as 起来 qǐlái 'start verbing.' Note that when 已经 occurs before adverbs such as 快 kuài 'soon' or 差不多 chàbuduō 'almost,' etc., the structure means 'the verb action is on the brink of happening'; e.g., 火车已经快开了 Huǒchē yǐjīng kuài kāi le 'The train is leaving very soon.'

a. 一些西方国家已经开始采取促进对外推销香烟的手段。
Yīxiē Xīfāng guójiā yǐjīng kāishǐ cǎiqǔ cùjìn duìwài tuīxiāo xiāngyān de shǒuduàn.
Some Western nations have already begun adopting some measures to promote the sale of cigarettes abroad.

b. 天已经黑了，咱们回宿舍吧。
Tiān yǐjīng hēi le, zámen huí sùshè ba.
It's already dark. Let's go back to the dorm.

c. 我学习汉语已经两年半了。
Wǒ xuéxí Hànyǔ yǐjīng liǎng nián bàn le.
I have already been studying Chinese for 2 ½ years.

以来 yǐlái (—來) 'since' Auxiliary

Y

1. X 以来, Y = Starting from X and continuing right up to the present, Y (Ax) A member of one of the four sets of structures which articulate the time frame for a Y situation, 以来 marks that Y started at X and continues right up to the present moment. X will be either a specific point or length of time in the past (expl a) or a previous event (expl b). Y will be a verb phrase or a clause. X 以来 can also be headed by either 自 zì 1, 从 cóng 1, or 自从 zìcóng 1 with no change in meaning. 来 lái 2 is a synonym which differs from 以来 by being used only when X refers to a length of time.: e.g., 两个月来

liǎng ge yuè lái 'for two months.' Neither 自从 nor 自 appears with 来 lái 2.

The other three sets of these time structures are 1) 以前 yǐqián 1, 以后 yǐhòu 1, 的时候 de shíhou 1 and their synonyms which mark the time frame for a Y event; 2) 从X起 qǐ 1 and its synonyms which mark X as the past, present or future starting point for an on going Y; and 3) 到 X(为)止 zhǐ 1 and its synonyms which mark X as the point of time at which Y stopped. Consider also 直到 X, 才 Y zhídào 1 which marks X as the time frame at which a Y situation finally started; also refer to 不到T bùdào 1 which marks the maximum length of time for a verb occurrence.

a. 九月十五号以来我们学校已经考了三次试了。
Jiǔyuè shíwǔhào yǐlái wǒmen xuéxiào yǐjīng kǎole sān cì shì le.
Since the fifteenth of September, we have already had three tests at school.

b. 中美建交以来，双边关系取得了显著的进展。
Zhōng-Měi jiànjiāo yǐlái, shuāngbiān guānxi qǔdéle xiǎnzhù de jìnzhǎn.
Ever since China and the United States established diplomatic relations, the relationship between the two sides has made striking progress.

一面 yīmiàn (——) "simultaneous verb actions" Adverb

1. (一面) Vp1, 一面 Vp2, (一面 Vp3) = Verb 1, verb 2 (and verb 3, 4, etc.) occur simultaneously (Av) 一面 is a somewhat shumianyu adverb which comes directly at the head of verb phrases to mark the simultaneous occurrence of two (expl a) or more (expl b) verb activities. The activities which 一面 marks may be either abstract (expl a) or concrete (expl b). When only one 一面 is used, it comes before the last verb. 一边 yībiān 1 is an oral synonym, though it differs in not being usable with abstract concepts. The synonymous 一方面 yīfāngmiàn 1 differs somewhat in marking two aspects of one verb action or the co-existence of two inter-related, perhaps sequential verb activities.

a. 美国有许许多多青年都是一面工作，一面学习。
Měiguó yǒu xǔxǔ-duōduō qīngnián dōu shì yīmiàn gōngzuò, yīmiàn xuéxí.
America has many, many young people who work and study at the same time.

b. 那位太极拳专家一面讲解，一面示范，一面纠正功作。
Nèi wèi tàijíquán zhuānjiā yīmiàn jiǎngjiě, yīmiàn shìfàn, yīmiàn jiūzhèng gōngzuò.
The expert at Taijiquan simultaneously gave explanations, demonstrated the moves, and made corrections in the moves.

因 yīn (—) 'because' Conjunction

1. 因 X, Y = Because X, Y (Cj) A shumianyu synonym of 因为 yīnwei 1, 因 marks X as the factual cause of a Y situation (expls a & b). 而 ér 1 or 2 may be added to Y to intensify the shumianyu tone of the structure (expl b). See 因为 yīnwei 1 for a broader discussion.

a. 因病请假。
Yīn bìng qǐng jià.
Take leave because of illness.

b. 因发生意外情况而放弃了聘请顾问的计划。
Yīn fāshēng yìwài qíngkuàng ér fàngqìle pìnqǐng gùwèn de jìhuà.
They abandoned their plans to hire consultants due to unexpected conditions.

因此 yīncǐ (——) 'therefore' Conjunction

1. X, 因此 Y = X , for this reason Y (Cj) A member of the set of words which mark that a Y situation results from X, the shumianyu 因此 specifically marks that Y is either a conclusion based on an X event (expl a) or a result of X (expl b). An element of deduction may also be part of Y. X and Y will be verb phrases or clauses. You will often find 因此 Y used after an X headed by 由于 yóuyú 1 to form a very shumianyu cause and result structure; however, 因此 is generally not used when 因为 yīnwei 1 occurs in X.

The synonymous 所以 suǒyǐ 1 focuses on Y as a logical result of X, though 所以 differs in never bringing a trace of deduction to Y. 因而 yīn'ér 1 is a shumianyu synonym which brings a stronger sense of deduction to Y. 因此 can also appear at the start of a sentence to connect it with previous discourse, a usage which 因而 does not have. See also 于是 yúshì 1.

a. 他事先作了充分准备，因此得到了圆满的结果。
Tā shìxiān zuòle chōngfèn zhǔnbeì, yīncǐ dédàole yuánmǎn de jiéguǒ.
He made complete preparations beforehand and consequently got perfect results.

b. 由于全体技术社员的努力，因此这项科研任务提前完成了。
Yóuyú quántǐ jìshù shèyuán de nǔlì, yīncǐ zhèi xiàng kēyán rènwù tíqián wánchéng le.
Because of the hard work of all of the technicians, (therefore) that research project was completed ahead of schedule.

Y

因而 yīn'ér (——) 'thus, therefore' Conjunction

1. X, 因而 Y = X, thus a Y result (Cj) 因而 is a less frequently seen shumianyu member of the set of words which marks that the Y situation results from X. 因而 specifically marks that Y is a result or a deduction based on X. 因而 is frequently used with the shumianyu 由于 yóuyú 1 at the head of X, but 因而 never occurs with 因为 yīnwei 1 in X. 因而 is synonymous with the less deductive 因此 yīncǐ 1, but 因而 is not used at the head of a sentence to connect it to previous discourse. 所以 suǒyǐ 1 is a synonym which strongly marks a logical cause and effect rather than deductive relationship of X to Y. See also 于是 yúshì 1, 以至 yǐzhì 1, and 以致 yǐzhì 1

a. "五四"运动高举了反帝反封建的旗帜，因而使中国革命进入了一个新的阶段。
"Wǔsì" yùndòng gāojǔle fǎn dì fǎn fēngjiàn de qízhì, yīn'ér shǐ Zhōngguó gémìng jìnrùle yī ge xīn de jièduàn.
The "May 4th Movement" highly raised the banner of anti-imperialism and anti-feudalism, thus causing the Chinese revolution to enter a new stage.

因为 yīnwei (—爲) 'because' Conjunction

1. 因为 X, 所以 Y = Because X, (therefore) Y (Cj) A frequently seen member of the set of markers for cause and effect relationships, 因为 marks focus on X as a fact which leads to a Y result. When X and Y have different subjects, 因为 must come before X; when X and Y have the same subject, the subject may come either before 因为 or in Y. X and Y will be clauses or verb phrases. Y is usually headed by 所以 suǒyǐ 1 or a synonym. Either 因为 or 所以 is commonly deleted when the context is sufficiently clear without one of them. 由于 yóuyú 1 is a shumianyu synonym with slightly different usages. 因 yīn 1 is a more strongly shumianyu synonym. 既然 jìrán 1 is a synonym which marks emphasis on a subjective Y response to X.

Note that 因为 is also used as a coverb to mark the cause of a verb act; e.g. 他们兄弟因为一件小事吵了半天 Tāmen xiōngdì yīnwei yī jiàn xiǎo shì chǎole bàn tiān 'Those brothers quarreled for a long time over nothing.'

a. 因为天黑了，所以不能打篮球了。
Yīnwei tiān hēi le, suǒyǐ bù néng dǎ lánqiú le.
Because it has gotten dark out, (therefore) we can't play basketball anymore.

b. 因为治疗及时，所以杨上尉不久就回到前线去了。
Yīnwei zhìliáo jíshí, suǒyǐ Yáng shàngwèi bùjiǔ jiù huídào qiánxiàn qù le.
Because his treatment was prompt, (so) Lt. Yang soon returned to the front lines.

2. X, 因为 Y = X, because Y (Cj) When 因为 is used in Y rather than X, it emphasizes that Y is the cause or conclusion of the sentence. (之)所以 often appears in X to strengthen the connection of the X result to Y; see 所以 suǒ yǐ 2.

a. 上星期六没有去看他，因为我要复习功课。
Shàng xīngqīliù méiyǒu qù kàn tā, yīnwei wǒ yào fùxí gōngkè.
I didn't go visit him last Saturday because I had to do some reviewing.

b. 八十年代社会秩序不稳定，因为食品价格上涨幅度太快。

Bāshí niándài shèhuì zhìxù bù wěndìng, yīnwei shípǐn jiàgé shàngzhǎng fúdù tài kuài.

Social order was unstable in the 80's because the rate of food price increases was too rapid.

以前 yǐqián (— —) 'before, prior to' Time marker

1. X 以前, Y = Before X, Y (Tm) 以前 is a member of one of the four sets of words which mark attention on the time frame for a Y situation. 以前 specifically marks that Y happens before X. 以前 always comes directly at the end of X and is usually end-marked with a comma. X can be either a verb phrase (expl a & b) or a noun phrase (expl c), while Y will be a verb phrase or a clause. As a marker of time, 以前 can refer to the future (expl a), but more often it will refer to the past (expls b & c). 以前 never refers to 'before' as a physical place. Its shumianyu synonyms 前 qián 1 and 之前 zhīqián 1 differ in that they can refer to either a point in time or to a physical place. Finally, as a noun 以前 also represents the concept of 'before, in the past' and is placed before the verb.

以后 yǐhòu 1, 的时候 de shíhou 1 and their synonyms are the other members of this set of time frame markers. See 以来 yǐlái 1 for an overview of all four sets of markers.

a. 我还没学会汉语以前，当然不能去联合国找翻译工作。

Wǒ hái méi xuéhuì Hànyǔ yǐqián, dāngrán bù néng qù Liánhéguó zhǎo fānyì gōngzuò.

Of course I won't be able to go to the United Nations to look for a translator's position before I have mastered Chinese.

b. 一九七九年中美建交以前，两国人民没有友好往来。

Yī jiǔ qī jiǔ nián Zhōng-Měi jiànjiāo yǐqián, liǎng guó rénmín méiyǒu yǒuhǎo wǎnglái.

Before China and the United States established diplomatic relations in 1979, there were no friendly contacts between the peoples of the two countries.

c. 去年国庆节以前，那位中国社会科学院的研究员还在泉州研究方言。

Qùnián guóqìngjié yǐqián, nèi wèi Zhōngguó Shèhuì Kēxuéyuàn de yánjiūyuán hái zài Quánzhōu yánjiū fāngyán.

Prior to National Day last year, that researcher from the Chinese Academy of Social Sciences was still in Quanzhou researching dialects.

一切 **yīqiè (——) 'all' Specifier**

1. 一切 Noun = All the nouns (Sp) 一切 marks that all items within a general category of nouns are included in a verb situation. The 一切 marked nouns may be either the subject or the object of a sentence. 一切 is used only with things which can be divided into sub-categories; e.g., 一切流体 yīqiè liútǐ 'all liquids.' 一切 is not used with things which cannot be further divided into sub-categories; e.g., *一切开水 yīqiè kāishuǐ 'all boiled water' is wrong. In this way 一切 differs somewhat from its synonym 所有(的) suǒyǒu(de) 1 which is used with all nouns, whether they can be sub-divided or not. See 所有 for further comparative discussion and examples. Note that 的 de 1 is never used after 一切, though a reinforcing 都 dōu 1 or a shumianyu 均 jūn 1 'all' will often appear before the verb. 一切 is also used as a pronoun to represent the concept of 'all; everything.'

a. 回国的一切手续都办好了。
Huíguó de yīqiè shǒuxù dōu bàn hǎo le.
All the paperwork for going back home has been taken care of.

b. 帝国主义和一切反动派都是纸老虎。
Dìguó zhǔyì hé yīqiè fǎndòngpài dōu shì zhǐ lǎohǔ.
Imperialism and all reactionaries are paper tigers.

以外 **yǐwài (——) 'besides; except for' Coverb**

1. X 以外, Y = Besides/except for X, Y (Cv) 以外 is usually found as part of the structure 除(了)X 以外, Y which marks that Y contains additional information about an X situation (expl a). The key to deciding whether X is to be understood as 'besides, in addition to' or as 'except for' lies in the adverb used in Y. When 还 hái 1, 也 yě 1, or 就 jiù 1 occur in Y, the structure is the inclusive 'besides' (expl a). When Y has 都 dōu 1 or a negative adverb, it is an exclusive 'except for' sentence (expl b). Rarely, you will find 以外 at the end of X without 除了 at the head to impart a terse tone, though there is no change in meaning.

外 wài 1 and 之外 zhīwài 1 are synonyms which may or may not be preceded by 除了 or the more shumianyu 除; see 除 chú 1 for discussion and examples. 以外 is also used to represent the place concept 'outside; beyond'; e.g., 长城以外 Chángchéng yǐwài 'beyond the Great Wall.'

a. 这种稻种除了产量高以外，抗旱能力也比较强。
Zhèi zhǒng dàozhǒng chúle chǎnliàng gāo yǐwài, kànghàn nénglì yě bǐjiào qiáng.
In addition to the yield of this type of rice seedlings being high, its drought resistance abilities are also relatively strong.

b. 除了這間以外，所有的屋子都打掃了。

Chúle zhèi jiān yǐwài, suǒyǒu de wūzi dōu dǎsǎo le.
Except for this room, all of the rooms have been cleaned.

一样 yīyàng (一樣) "comparison > equality" Stative verb; "similarity" Stative verb

1. X 跟 Y 一样 (Sv/Vp) = X is the same as Y (in the Stative verb/verb situation) (Sv) As a member of one of the three sets of structures which mark comparison, 一样 specifically marks that X and Y are equal. When a verb phrase (expls a & c) or a Stative verb (expl b) is given at the end of the structure, X and Y are equal in that verbal sense; when there is no Stative verb or verb phrase, the structure marks that X and Y are the same without saying exactly how. X and Y may be either noun phrases (expls a & c) or verb phrases (expl b). X 有 Y (这/那么) Sv is a less frequently used oral synonym. X 与 Y 同/相同 X yǔ Y tóng/xiāngtóng is a synonymous shumianyu structure; see 与 yǔ 2.

When you keep in mind that this "equality" usage of 一样 is marked by a preceding 跟 or a synonym, it will help you distinguish it from its "similarity" usage discussed in 3 below. 跟 gēn 3 is interchangeable with 和 hé 3 or the more shumianyu 同 tóng 3 in this structure. Also, note that 一般 yībān 1 is different from 一样 yīyàng 1; it marks similarity rather than equality, and so is a synonym of 一样 yīyàng 3 only as it is described in section 3 below.

The second set of comparison markers involves "superiority" and is structured using 比 bǐ 1 and its synonyms; the third set focuses on "inferiority" using 沒有 méiyǒu 3 and its synonyms. See 比 bǐ 1 for further discussion and examples.

a. 昨天古诗课小毛跟小谷一样都迟到了。
Zuótiān gǔshīkè Xiǎo Máo gēn Xiǎo Gǔ yīyàng dōu chídào le.
Mao and Gu were equally late for the classical poetry class yesterday.

b. 学习写中国字跟学习说中国话一样有意思。
Xuéxí xiě Zhōngguózì gēn xuéxí shuō Zhōngguóhuà yīyàng yǒu yìsi.
Learning to write Chinese characters is as interesting as learning to speak Chinese.

c. 封建思想和帝国主义一样对群众有害。
Fēngjiàn sīxiǎng hé dìguó zhǔyì yīyàng duì qúnzhòng yǒuhài.
Feudal ideology and imperialism are equally harmful to the masses.

2. Np1 跟 Np2 (V) (O) V 得一样 (Sv) = The first and second nouns verb (an object) in the same (Stative verb) manner (Sv) In this equality pattern, 一样 marks an equality in the way two nouns verb an object. The verb phrase structure may have just the verb (expl a), or it may have the object and the verb (expl b), or it can be structured with the verb given before and repeated after the object (expl c). Placement of the (Vp) V 得 element is flexible. It may come either before the second noun phrase (expl b), after it (expls a & c), and sometimes it straddles the second noun phrase in the structure Np1 V O 跟 Np2 V 得一样 (Sv). 跟 gēn 3 is interchangeable with 和 hé 3 and the more shumianyu 同 tóng 3 in this structure.

a. 我哥哥跟我妹妹吃得一样多。
Wǒ gēge gēn wǒ mèimei chī de yīyàng duō.
My older brother eats as much as my younger sister.

b. 史同学《经济日报》看得跟老师一样快！
Shǐ tóngxué "Jīngji Rìbào" kàn de gēn lǎoshī yīyàng kuài!
Our classmate Shi reads the "Financial Daily" as quickly as the teacher!

c. 中国男篮队跟美国的芝加哥公牛队打篮球打得一样好。
Zhōngguó nánlánduì gēn Měiguó de Zhījiāgē Gōngniúduì dǎ lánqiú dǎ de yīyàng hǎo.
The Chinese men's basketball team plays basketball as well as the Chicago Bulls.

3. (X) 好象 Y 一样 = (X) seems like Y (Sv) In this usage 一样 is part of a structure which marks an element of similarity. You can distinguish this value from the "equality" value discussed above because "similarity" 一样 must be used in conjunction with 好象 hǎoxiàng 1 or a synonym. X and Y may be either a noun phrase or a verb phrase. 似的 shìde 1 and 一般 yībān 1 are more shumianyu synonyms for 一样 in this usage, but are not used in the "equality" structures discussed in 1 and 2 above. 象 xiàng 1 and 似乎 sìhu are oral synonyms for 好象 hǎoxiàng 1 while 仿佛 fǎngfú 1, 如 rú 1, and 如同 rútóng 1 are shumianyu synonyms. The choice of one over the other reflects the degree of formality intended in the text.

Note: unless it is used in conjunction with 好象 or its synonyms, 一样 marks "equality" as is discussed in 1 and 2 above.

a. 你好象发烧一样。
Nǐ hǎoxiàng fāshāo yīyàng.
You look like you're running a fever.

b. "象雷锋一样地生活、工作、战斗" 是中国七十年代的口号。
"Xiàng Léi Fēng yīyàng de shēnghuó, gōngzuò, zhàndòu" shì Zhōngguó qīshí niándài de kǒuhào.
"Live, work, and struggle like Lei Feng" was a Chinese slogan of the 70's.

以至 **yǐzhì (——) 'so...that...' Conjunction; 'up to, down to' Conjunction**

1. X, 以至 Y = X develops to the extent of Y (Cj) When 以至 comes at the head of Y, it marks that a Y result extends and intensifies the situation given in X and simultaneously marks that the condition given in X is itself quite intense. The Y situation may be either positive (expl b) or negative (expl a) in nature. 以至 will often be followed by 都 dōu 1, 也 yě 1, etc. You may find this marker phrased as 以至于 with no difference in meaning. The synonymous 以致 yǐzhì 1 differs in generally being used with negative and/or undesirable situations.

a. 小章看书非常专心，以至我走到他身边，他都没有发觉。

Xiǎo Zhāng kàn shū fēicháng zhuānxīn, yǐzhì wǒ zǒu dào tā shēn biān, tā dōu méi fājué.

Little Zhang studies so very intently that when I came up to him he didn't notice at all.

b. 她的琴声婉转悠扬，动听极了，以至连树上的鸟儿听了之后都羞愧得不好意思再鸣叫了。

Tā de qínshēng wǎnzhuǎn yōuyáng, dòngtīng jíle, yǐzhì lián shù shang de niǎor tīngle zhīhòu dōu xiūkuì de bù hǎo yìsi zài mǐngjiào le.

Her qin playing is sweet and melodious to the extent that even the birds in the trees are embarrassed to sing after hearing it.

2. Np/Vp 以至 following Np/Vp = First noun/verb phrase and also as much as the following noun/verb (Cj) 以至 is placed between two (expl a), or more (expl b), noun (expl a) or verb (expl b) phrases to mark progression from the first to the following. The progression marked is usually from the smaller to the greater (expl a), though you will find exceptions (expl b). When there are three or more noun or verb phrases, 以至 is placed before the last one (expl b). This usage is to mark progression rather than result, so it is easily distinguishable from the "intensity" usage described above.

a.那个科技人员的科研成果，在今天以至今后都会产生重要影响。

Nèi ge kējì rényuán de kēyán chéngguǒ, zài jīntiān yǐzhì jīnhòu dōu huì chǎnshēng zhòngyào yǐngxiǎng.

The research achievements of that technician will have an important influence right away as well as in the future.

b. 我们到了西湖参观的时候，了解了种茶、采茶以至加工茶叶的全过程。

Wǒmen dàole Xī Hú cānguān de shíhou, liǎojiěle zhòng chá, cǎi chá yǐzhì jiāgōng cháyè de quán guòchéng.

When we arrived at West Lake for a visit, we learned about the whole process of planting, picking as well as processing tea.

以致 yǐzhì (——) 'as as result, consequently' Conjunction)

Y

1. X, 以致 Y = X with the result that Y (Cj) 以致 is a member of the set of words which mark that Y is the result of an X cause. An 以致 marked Y result is usually bad and/or undesirable (expls a & b). X and Y will be either clauses or verb phrases. X will often be headed with 因为 yīnwei 1, 由于 yóuyú 1, etc (expl b). The synonymous 以至 yǐzhì 1 differs in 1) Y being an extension and result of the X situation, and 2) being used with both positive and negative Y situations. Also consider 因而 yīn'ér 1 and 所以 suǒyǐ 1.

a. 为了学好普通话，她从早到晚不断地练习，以致嗓子都沙哑了
Wèile xué hǎo pǔtōnghuà, tā cóng zǎo dào wǎn bùduàn de liànxí, yǐzhì sǎngzi shāyǎ le.
In order to master putonghua she continuously practiced from morning to night. As a result she got hoarse.

b. 由于他在工作中的疏忽，以致发生事故。
Yóuyú tā zài gōngzuò zhōng de shūhu, yǐzhì fāshēng shìgù.
Because of his carelessness on the job (consequently) an accident occurred.

用 yòng (一) 'use, utilize' Verb

1. 用 X Vp = Use X to verb (Vb) 用 marks that X is used to do a verb action. The vast majority of the time X will a noun representing either a real thing (expl a), or an abstract concept (expl b). But you will also occasionally find 用 followed by 以 yǐ 3, 来 lái 1 or a complement such as 作 zuò 'act as' to mark that the noun or verb phrase preceding 用 is used to do a verb act (expl c). 以 yǐ 1, a very shumianyu synonym of 用, is used only with abstract nouns. 用 is also used as a transitive verb centered on the concept of 'use, employ.' Additionally, 用 is used in some polite phrases to mean 'please eat/drink/smoke, etc.' For example, 请用饭吧 Qǐng yòng fàn ba 'Please have something to eat.'

a. 美国人不用毛笔写信。
Měiguó rén bù yòng máobǐ xiěxìn.
Americans do not use a writing brush to write letters.

b. 爱国华侨用忘我的精神为公民服务。
Àiguó huáqiáo yòng wàngwǒ de jīngshén wèi rénmín fúwù.
Patriotic overseas Chinese serve the people with a spirit of selflessness.

c. 在中国药里，黄连常用作清热解毒剂。
Zài Zhōngguó yào li, huánglián cháng yòngzuò qīngrè jiědú jì.
In Chinese medical usage, the rhizome of Chinese goldthread is often used as a dosage for reducing fever and detoxification.

由 yóu (一) "agent marker" Coverb; 'from, by means of, through' Coverb

1. 由 X Vp = Verb done by X (Cv) 由 marks focus on Y as the person (expl a & b) or event (expl c) that does a verb action. The focal point of the sentence is on the Y noun after 由. When it is given, the noun phrase which is the recipient of the verb action usually comes before the 由 (expl a & c), but it may came after the verb (expl b). Verb phrases in this structure generally have a neutral to positive meaning.

Though technically not a passive structure, a 由 X Vp structure is usually translated with the English passive marker 'by' (particularly consider expl b). For further comments and examples of Chinese passive structures see 被 bèi 1. See the comments in 2 below about how to distinguish this 由 from its use to mark 'from.' Note that 由 is also used in nouns having to do with 'reason; cause,' and as a verb meaning 'allow.'

a. 工厂冒黑烟的污染问题将由该市的环保局解决。
Gōngchǎng mào hēiyān de wūrán wèntí jiāng yóu gāi shì de huánbǎojú jiějué.
Factory smoke pollution problems will be solved by the EPA in that city.

b. 今天由全国妇女联合会副主席主持记者招待会。
Jīntiān yóu quánguó fùnǚ liánhéhuì fùzhǔxí zhǔchí jìzhě zhāodàihuì.
The press conference will be presided over today by the Vice-chair of the National Association of Women.

c. 大哥的肺炎是由掉进冰水受寒引起的。
Dàgē de fèiyán shì yóu diàojìn bīngshuǐ shòuhán yǐnqǐ de.
My brother's pneumonia was caused by falling in icy water and getting a chill.

2. 由 X = Verb from/by means of X (Cv) In this usage 由 marks the starting place (expls a & b), the starting time (expl c), or the condition (expl d) for a verb action. X will most frequently be a place (expls a & b) or time structure (expl c), but it can also be a verb phrase (expl d). Its use with place names, time nouns, or verb phrases makes this 'from 由' easier to distinguish from the 'by 由' discussed above. 从 cóng 1 is an oral and 自 zì 1 a shumianyu synonym. See the discussion in 3 below of the synonymous shumianyu 由 structure.

a. 由武汉到乌鲁木齐，坐火车慢，坐飞机快。
Yóu Wǔhàn dào Wūlǔmùqí, zuò huǒchē màn, zuò fēijī kuài.
Going by train from Wuhan to Urumqi is slow, and going by plane is fast.

b. 若有火警，请由楼梯步行逃出。勿用电梯。
Ruò yǒu huǒjǐng, qǐng yóu lóutī bùxíng táochū. Wù yòng diàntī.
In case of fire, exit by the stairs. Do not use the elevator.

c. 大学图书馆开放时间上午由八点到十一点半，下午由两点到六点。
Dàxué túshūguǎn kāifàng shíjiān shàngwǔ yóu bā diǎn dào shíyī diǎn bàn, xiàwǔ yóu liǎng diǎn dào liù diǎn.
The University Library is open from 8:00 to 11:30 AM and from 2:00 to 6:00 PM.

d. 东北枫叶经霜，由绿变红。
Dōngběi fēngyè jīng shuāng, yóu lǜ biàn hóng.
When the maple leaves in Manchuria are touched by frost, they change from green to red.

3. 由 X 而 Y = From X to Y (Cv) In this more shumianyu structure, 由 also marks X as the starting point (expl a) or cause (expl b) of a situation. 而 ér 2 marks further progression of the situation to Y (expls a & b). X and/or Y may be either a noun phrase (expl a) or a verb phrase (expl b). The shumianyu structure 由 X 及 Y jí 1 is synonymous.

a. 这条灌渠是由南而北走的。
Zhèi tiáo guànqú shì yóu nán ér běi zǒu de.
This irrigation canal goes from the south to the north.

b. 这个公路由附近三个农村共同出力而顺利竣工。
Zhèige gōnglù yóu fùjìn sān ge nóngcūn gòngtóng chūlì ér shùnlì jùngōng.
This highway was smoothly completed through the collective efforts of three neighboring villages.

又 yòu (一) 'again, also, and' Adverb

1. 又 Verb = Verb again (Av) 又 is a main member of the set of markers for repeated verb actions. When used with a specific point in time, 又 almost always marks either 1) repetition of a factual (expls a & first 又 in c) or habitual (second 又 in expl c) verb situation 'again,' or 2) the second in a sequence of two or more different factual verb actions 'also' (expl b). The time reference may be explicitly marked with a time word (expls a & c), and/or it may implicitly marked by a 过 guo 1, 要 yào 1, etc. (expl b). The vast majority of the time, the time referent will be to the past, as you might expect since the verb situation is accepted as fact, so the English equivalent will be past tense (expls a & b); but 又 can also mark something experience says will definitely happen again in the future (both 又 in expl c), so do not automatically think that 又 refers to the past.

When the same verb is used more than once in a sentence, 又 marks the repetition of that particular verb action (expl a). When there are two different verb actions involved, 又 generally marks the occurrence of a second, different verb after the first (expl b); a variant of this second value is V1 又 V2, V2 又 V1 in which 又 marks that the verbs alternate with each other; e.g., 谈又打，打又谈 Tán yòu dǎ, dǎ yòu tán 'Talk and fight, fight and talk.' 又 can also be used with measures to mark numerous repetitions of the measures; e.g., 一天又一天 yītiān yòu yītiān 'day after day.' 又 also marks tones of voice such as 'change in expectations,' 'denial,' or 'rhetorical questions'; e.g., 下雪又有什么关系！ Xià xuě yòu yǒu shénme guānxi 'And what does it matter if it is snowing!' At the end of letters, 又 marks a postscript. See also 又 Vp1 又 Vp2 yòu...yòu 1.

再 zài 1 is a synonym which marks the projected repetition or continuation of a verb action, usually in the future; 还 hái 2 can be a synonym used to mark the projected repetition or continuation of a verb action by the same subject; e.g., 他昨天写过，明天还写 Tā zuótiān xiěguo, míngtiān hái xiě 'He wrote yesterday and will write again tomorrow.' 重 chóng 1 is a synonym used with monosyllabic verbs to mark a complete re-doing of the verb activity; e.g., 叫他重写 Jiào tā chóng xiě 'Have him to write it all over again.' See also 重新 chóngxīn 1.

a. 真奇怪，小高上个月犯过流行性感冒，这个星期又犯过一次。
Zhēn qíguài, Xiǎo Gāo shàng ge yuè fànguo liúxíngxìng gǎnmào, zhèige xīngqī yòu fànguo yī cì.
How odd, Gao had the flu last month, and he got it again this week.

b. 丁云让帕兰卡坐下以后，又给她端来一杯花茶。
Dīng Yún ràng Pàlánkǎ zuòxià yǐhòu, yòu gěi tā duānlái yī bēi huāchá.
After Ding Yun had Palanka sit down, she (also) served her a cup of jasmine tea.

c. 明天又是星期一，汉语课又要考生词。
Míngtiān yòu shi xīngqīyī. Hànyǔ kè yòu yào kǎo shēngcí.
Tomorrow is another Monday. We will have a vocabulary test in Chinese again.

又...又 yòu...yòu (—...—) 'also, as well as, both' Adverb

1. 又 Vp1 又 Vp2 = Verb1 as well as verb2 (Av) 又 Vp1 又 Vp2 marks the simultaneous existence of two or more verb actions or Stative verb conditions which are usually supportive of each other. This pattern is most frequently used with co-occurrences of two or more verbs (expl a) or Stative verbs (expl b), though a single 又 can occur with just the second verb (expl c). 又 is usually used only when the verbs and Stative verbs have the same subject; the synonymous structure 也 V1 也 V2 yě...yě 1 is used only with verbs and appears both when the subject is the same and when the verbs and Stative verbs have different subjects; see 也 Vp1 也 Vp2 yě...yě 1. Consider 连 lián 2.

a. 他又会写律诗又会写微型小说，本事大着呢。
Tā yòu huì xiě lǜshī yòu huì xiě wēixíng xiǎoshuō, běnshì dà zhe ne.
He can write regulated poetry as well as ultra-short short stories. His talent is huge!

b. 七十年代末、八十年代初的口号是又红又专。
Qīshi niándài mò bāshi niándài chū de kǒuhào shì yòu hóng yòu zhuān.
The slogan at the end of the 70's was "Be red as well as expert."

c. 陈师傅是一个模范工程师，又是人民代表。
Chén shīfu shì yī ge mófàn gōngchéngshī, yòu shì rénmín dàibiǎo.
Mr. Chen is a model engineer, and he is also a people's representative.

有一点儿 yǒu yīdiǎnr (——點兒) 'a little bit, somewhat' Adverb

1. 有(一)点(儿) Vp = Verb a little bit (Av) 有一点儿 is used with both verbs (expl a) and Stative verbs (expl b) to mark a slight degree of a verb situation. It is generally used with undesirable situations (expls a & b), and when it precedes a Stative verb 有一点儿 marks a degree of criticism or dissatisfaction (expl b). The 一 and/or 儿 may be omitted to create 有一点, 有点儿, or 有点 structures which have no differences in meaning or usage from 有一点儿.

Because the adverb 有一点儿 and the noun 一点儿 yīdiǎnr 1 may both be translated as 'a little bit,' English speakers tend to confuse their different usage patterns. See 一点儿 yīdiǎnr 1 for a discussion on how to distinguish them.

a. 副校长发言长而空，我听得有点儿不耐烦了。
Fùxiàozhǎng fāyán cháng ér kōng, wǒ tīngde yǒu diǎnr bù nàifán le.
The Vice-principal's talk was long and dull. Listening to it I felt somewhat impatient.

b. 那个服务员今天已经工作了十个半小时了，大概有点儿累。
Nèige fúwùyuán jīntiān yǐjīng gōngzuòle shí ge bàn xiǎoshí le, dàgài yǒu diǎnr lèi.
That clerk has already worked 10 ½ hours today, she is probably a bit tired.

由于 yóuyú (—於) 'because' Conjunction; 'due to' Coverb

1. 由于 X, Y = Because X, Y (Cj) The shumianyu 由于 focuses attention on X as the factual cause behind a Y result. X and Y may be either verb phrases or clauses. Y will usually be headed by 所以 suǒyǐ 1 (expl a) or the more shumianyu 因此 yīncǐ 1, 因而 yīn'ér 1 (expl b) or 从而 cóngér. 因为 yīnwèi 1 is a close synonym which differs in not being used with these last three markers; 由于 is never used in Y, which also differs from 因为 usage. The synonymous 既然 jìrán 1 marks emphasis on the Y result of a subjective X. See 2 below for comments about how distinguish between conjunction and coverbial uses of 由于.

a. 由于胡老师辅导正确，所以这一班的写作成绩提高得相当快。
Yóuyú Hú lǎoshī fǔdǎo zhèngquè, suǒyǐ zhèi yī bān de xiězuò chéngjī tígāo de xiāngdāng kuài.
Because Professor Hu teaches so accurately, this class's composition scores improved quite rapidly.

b. 由于轻工业发展较好，因而为重工业的发展提供了大量的资金。
Yóuyú qīnggōngyè fāzhǎn jiào hǎo, yīn'ér wèi zhōnggōngyè de fāzhǎn tígōngle dàliàng de zījīn.
Because the development of light industry was relatively good, it provided a large amount of funds for the development of heavy industry.

2. 由于 Np = Because of the noun phrase (Cv) As a coverb, 由于 marks the noun phrase that is the reason behind the events discussed in the sentence. 由于 may appear either before the subject (expl a) or object (expl b) of a sentence. It often appears after 是 when used with the object of the sentence (expl b). While their English translations are very similar, conjunction 由于, discussed in 1 above, can be distinguished from this coverbial 由于 because conjunction 由于 comes only at the head of the sentence with 所以 suǒyǐ 1, 因此 yīncǐ 1, etc. usually appearing in Y; this does not happen when 由于 is used as a coverb.

a. 由于各种各样的原因，那次肝脏移植手术失败了。
Yóuyú gè zhǒng gè yàng de yuányīn, nèi cì gānzàng yízhí shǒushù shībài le.
Due to all kinds of reasons, that liver transplant operation failed.

b. 第三生产大队创造出出色的成绩是由于他们同心协力刻苦钻研。
Dì-sān Shēngchǎn Dàduì chuàngzào chū chūsè de chéngjī shì yóuyú tāmen tóngxīn xiélì kèkǔ zuānyán.
That the Third Production Brigade achieved a striking record is a result of their own concerted and assiduous study.

于 yú (於) "location marker" Coverb

1. Verb 于 X = Verb in/at/from/towards X (Cv) The shumianyu place marker 于 usually comes after the verb, a contemporary reminder that place came after the verb in classical prose. In this usage 于 marks X as the place (expl a), time (expl b), target, or scope (expl c) of the verb action. X will usually be a noun phrase (expls a & b), though when it is a target or goal of a verb, X can also be a verb phrase (expl c). 在 zài 1, 2, & 4 is an oral synonym with difference usage patterns. 当 dāng 1 is a shumianyu synonym used before the verb phrase to mark time or place. Verb 于 structures can also be translated as a passive (expl d) or a comparison structure (expl e), though they are not grammatically so.

a. 黄河发源于青海。
Huánghé fāyuán yú Qīnghǎi.
The Yellow River has its origins in Qinghai Province.

b. 他生于一八八三年，死于一九四八年，一生都为教育而努力。
Tā shēng yú yī bā bā sān nián, sǐ yú yī jiǔ sì bā nián, yīshēng dōu wèi jiàoyù ér nǔlì.
He was born in 1883 and died in 1948. His whole life was spent working for education.

c. 全厂机械师致力于教徒弟搞技术革新。
Quán chǎng jīxièshī zhìlì yú jiāo túdì gǎo jìshù géxīn.
All of the master machinists in the factory put their efforts into teaching the apprentices to work at technological innovation.

Y

d. 这次比赛张三负于李四。
Zhèi cì bǐsài Zhāng sān fù yú Lǐ Sì.
Zhang San was defeated by Li Si in this match.

e. 为人民而死重于泰山。
Wèi rénmín ér sǐ zhòng yú Tàishān.
To die for the people is greater than Mt. Tai.

2. 于 Np Vp = Verb at/towards the noun (Cv) When 于 comes before the verb, it is a shumianyu way of marking either the time (expl a), the scope (expl b) or the object (expl c) of a verb action. 于 is particularly common in front of time structures in texts from the ROC (expl d). When marking time or scope, 于 is a synonym of 在 zài 3; when marking the thing impacted by the verb act, 于 is a synonym of 对 duì 1.

a. 您的来信于今日收到。
Nín de láixìn yú jīnrì shōudào.
Your letter was received (at) today.

b. 于数学之外，他还特别喜欢音乐。
Yú shùxué zhīwài, tā hái tèbié xǐhuan yīnyuè.
Besides mathematics, he especially likes music.

c. 按时锻炼于身体有益。
Ànshí duànliàn yú shēntǐ yǒuyì.
Regular exercise is beneficial to your health.

d. 南韩红十字会于四月卅日正式以该会总裁姜英勋的名义，致电北韩，接受北韩所提，于三日在北京召开“南北韩红十字会会谈”的提议。
Nánhán Hóngshízìhuì yú sì yuè sà rì zhèngshì yǐ gāi huì zǒngcái Jiāng Yīngxūn de míngyì, zhìdiàn Běihán, jiēshòu Běihán suǒ tí, yú sān rì zài Běijīng zhāokāi “Nán-Běihán Hóngshízìhuì Huìtán” de tíyì.
On the 30th of April the South Korean Red Cross sent a cable to North Korea in the name of its Director General, Jiang Yingxun, accepting the suggestion North Korea made that the “South and North Korean Red Cross Conference” be held in Beijing on the 3rd.

与 yǔ (與) ‘and’ Conjunction; ‘together with’ Coverb

1. X 与 Y = X and Y (Cv) The very shumianyu 与 is one of the set of words which mark the co-existence of two conceptually equal and grammatically parallel items. X and Y may be two noun phrases (expls a & b) or two verb phrases (expl c). In addition to frequent use in shumianyu toned texts (expls b & c), 与 tends to be the conjunction of choice in literary titles (expl a). Less strongly shumianyu synonyms are 和 hé 1, 同 tóng 1, 及 jí 1 and 以及 yǐjí 1. See the oral synonym 跟 gēn 1 for general comments on conjunctions which connect noun phrases. Note that as a verb 与 means ‘give; get along with’ and fourth tone 与 yù represents the idea ‘participate in.’

Y

a. 《语言教学与研究》

"Yǔyán Jiàoxué Yǔ Yánjiū"
"Language Teaching and Research"

b. 试验成功与失败，全在此一举。
Shìyàn chénggōng yǔ shībài, quán zài cǐ yī jǔ.
The success or failure of the experiment hangs on this move.

c. 劳动群众是何等兴奋与激动。
Láodòng qúnzhòng shì héděng xīngfèn yǔ jīdòng.
How excited and agitated the laboring masses are.

2. Np1 与 Np2 Vp = Np1 and Np2 verb (CV) 与 marks that two noun phrases are jointly involved in doing a verb action. 跟 gēn 2 and 和 hé 2 are oral synonyms and 同 tóng 2 is a shumianyu synonym of this usage. Note the use of 与 in the equality comparison structure X 与 Y (不) 同/相同 = X is (not) the same as Y (expl b); this pattern is a shumianyu synonym of X 跟 Y (不) 一样 gēn 1. See 比 bǐ 3 for a discussion of comparison structures.

a. 为争取抗战的胜利，中国人民与日本帝国主义作了艰苦卓绝的斗争。
Wèi zhēngqǔ Kàngzhàn de shènglì, Zhōngguó rénmín yǔ Rìběn dìguó zhǔyì zuòle jiānkǔ zhuōjué de dòuzhēng.
In order gain victory in The War of Resistance, the Chinese people waged a struggle of extreme hardships and difficulties with Japanese imperialism.

b. 目前的生产情况与去年同期的不同。
Mùqián de shēngchǎn qíngkuàng yǔ qùnián tóngqī de bùtóng.
Present production conditions are different from last year's.

愈 yù (一) 'the more' Adverb

1. 愈 Sv1/Vp1 愈 Sv2/Vp2 = The more there is of the first verb situation, the more there is of the second (Av) The shumianyu 愈 is generally used in sets of two, sometimes three or four, to mark that as the first verb situation increases, the following verb condition(s) also increase. The verbs may be Stative verbs (expls a & b), or they may be verb phrases (second half of expl b). The two verb phrases may either have the same subject (expl a), or each may have its own subject (expl b). 是 shì 'is' may follow either the first or all 愈 markers for emphasis (expl b). See the commonly used oral synonym 越 yuè 1.

Y

a. 孙中山先生听到表扬愈多，愈谦虚谨慎。
Sūn Zhōngshān xiānsheng tīngdào biǎoyáng yù duō, yù qiānxū jǐnshèn.
The more Sun Yat-sen received praise, the humbler and more circumspect he was.

b. 风雨愈是大，雨中的竹子愈是显得挺拔。
Fēngyǔ yù shì dà, yǔ zhōng de zhúzi yù shì xiǎn de tǐngbó.

The greater the wind and rain, the more the bamboo in the rain shows itself to be tall and straight.

越 yuè (—) 'the more' Adverb

1. 越 Sv1/Vp1 越 Sv2Vp2 = The more there is of the first verb situation the more there is of the second (Av) 越 is generally used in sets of two (expls a & b), though there can be a string of three or four 越 (expl c), to mark that as the first verb situation increases, the following verb situation(s) also increase(s). There may be one subject for both verbs phrases (expl a), or each 越 marked verb phrase may have its own subject (expls b & c). The verb phrases may be verb-object structures (expl a) or Stative verbs (expl b & c). 是 shì 'is' may be added after either the first or all 越 markers for emphasis. 越来越 Vp yuèlái yuè 1 is a synonymous structure which focuses attention on an increase in the verb phrase condition over time. 愈 yù 1 is a more shumianyu synonym of 越, but it is used less often. 越 is also used in words having to do with 'exceed; go over,' which perhaps suggests why it is part of the name for the country on the far southern edge of China, 越南 Yuènán 'Vietnam.' Also consider the adverb 越发 yuèfā 1.

a. 学生越听助教的演讲，越觉得一点儿意思都没有。
Xuésheng yuè tīng zhùjiào de yǎnjiǎng, yuè juéde yīdiǎr yìsi dōu méiyǒu.
The more the students listened to the T.A.'s lecture, the more they felt that it was not at all interesting.

b. 不知怎么回事，局长的声音越大，工作人员反而越不想听。
Bù zhī zěnme huí shì, júzhǎng de shēngyīn yuè dà, gōngzuò rényuán fǎn'ér yuè bù xiǎng tīng.
I don't know how to explain it. The louder the section chief is, the more the workers tune out.

c. 吸烟量越大，持续的时间越长，开始吸烟的年龄越早，患冠心病的可能性也就越大。
Xīyānliàng yuè dà, chíxù de shíjiān yuè cháng, kāishǐ xīyān de niánlíng yuè zǎo, huàn guānxīnbìng de kěnéngxìng yě jiù yuè dà.
The more one smokes, the longer the length of time one smokes, and the younger one starts, the greater the possibility of getting coronary diseases.

越发 yuèfā (—發) 'even more so' Adverb

Y

1. 越发 X = Even more so X (Av) A member of one set of adverbs used to mark comparative conditions, 越发 marks that there is an even greater degree of some previously mentioned X present in a situation. X may be either a Stative verb or a verb phrase (expl a). 越发 is a shumianyu synonym of 更 gèng 1 and 更加 gèngjiā 1, but 越发 differs from them in being only used to mark the further development of one specific situation (expl a). See 更 gèng 1 for further comments. Consider also the usages of 越 yuè 1.

a.假若情况真是这样，那就越发值得我们注意了。
Jiǎruò qíngkuàng zhēn shì zhèi yàng, nà jiù yuèfā zhíde wǒmen zhùyì le.
If matters are indeed like this, they deserve our attention even more so.

越来越 yuèlái yuè (—來—) 'more and more' Adverb

1. Np 越来越 Sv/Vp = The noun is progressively more and more in a Stative verb/ verb condition (Av) 越来越 marks that with the passage of time, which is not necessarily overtly given in the structure, the noun phrase is in the Stative verb or verb phrase condition to a greater and greater degree. A Stative verb will usually come after 越来越 (expls a & b), but it may occasionally be followed by a verb (expl c). Unlike the synonymous 越 yuè 1, a 越来越 structure has only one subject, which must come directly before it. The very shumianyu structure 愈来愈 yùlái yù 1 is a near synonym.

a.世界上的人口越来越多。
Shìjiè shang de rénkǒu yuèlái yuè duō.
The population of the world is getting larger and larger.

b. 八十年代美国的国际贸易逆差越来越惊人。
Bāshi niándài Měiguó de guójì màoyì nìchā yuèlái yuè jīngrén.
America's Deficit of Payments became more and more startling in the 80's.

c. 冬天的黑乌乌的云彩，越来越堆得厚了。
Dōngtiān de hēiwūwū de yúncǎi, yuèlái yuè duī de hòu le.
The black winter clouds piled up thicker and thicker.

愈来愈 yùlái yù (—來—) 'more and more' Adverb

1. Np 愈来愈 Sv = The noun phrase is progressively getting more and more in a Stative verb condition (Av) The shumianyu structure 愈来愈 marks that with the passage of time, which may not be overtly given in the sentence, the noun gets in the verb phrase condition to a greater and greater degree. The verb phrase will usually be a Stative verb. 越来越 yuèlái yuè 1 is a close synonym.

a. 东亚经济情况愈来愈坏。
Dōngyà jīngji qíngkuàng yùlái yù huài.
The economic situation in East Asia is getting worse and worse.

于是 yúshì (於—) 'thereupon, consequently' Conjunction

1. X, 于是 Y = X, consequently Y (Cj) 于是 is a member of the set of words which mark that Y is a result of X. 于是 specifically marks that Y is the consequence of the situation in X, though the causal relationship may not be terribly direct. Both X and Y will be actual events, never abstractions. Both may be either verb phrases or clauses. 于是 may also come at the head of a sentence in order to mark its link to the preceding sentence in the discourse. The synonymous 所以 suǒyǐ 1 differs slightly in marking either a factual or abstract situation. See 所以 for a discussion of the conjunctions which mark cause and effect relationships between X and Y.

a. 同学们这么一鼓励，于是我又恢复了信心。
Tóngxuémen zhème yī gǔlì, yúshì wǒ yòu huīfùle xìnxīn.
With my classmates encouraging me so, I (consequently) regained confidence.

b. 几个问题都讨论完了，于是就提前散会了。
Jǐ ge wèntí dōu tǎolùn wán le, yúshì jiù tíqián sànhuì le.
The questions had all been discussed, so the meeting broke up early.

在 zài (一) "location" Coverb; "ongoing verb action" Adverb

1. 在 P Vp = Where the verb takes place (Cv) 在 is the most frequently seen member of the small set of words that mark where a verb action takes place. 在 is placed at the head of a location structure to mark the actual (expls a & b) or abstract (expl c) place for a verb action. The location structure is usually end marked with 上 shàng 'above,' 下 xià 'below,' 里 lǐ 'inside,' 中 zhōng 'amongst,' 外 wài 'outside,' 内 nèi 'in,' etc. (expls a & c); however, end-markers are not used when 1) the location is the official name of a place, or 2) when the location is an organization, institution or a familiar building (expl b). You can use the fact that 在 comes at the head and the end-markers come at the end of a location structure to determine its length, even when it is long (expl c). 在 is frequently omitted when the location structure is the very first element in a sentence. A location structure will nearly always be end marked with a comma when it precedes the subject of a sentence, which is additional handy information for finding the end of a long place structure (expl c).

The shumianyu synonym 当 dāng 1 is never used with these end markers, and although the shumianyu synonym 于 yú 1 usually comes after the verb, it also marks the place of a verb action; see 于 yú 1. Note that 在 also comes after a verb to mark the location of the result of a verb action; see 2 below. Keep in mind that 在 is also used as a verb to represent 'exist; be (located) at'; e.g., 我家在银行左边 Wǒ jiā zài yínháng zuǒbian 'My home is to the left of the bank.'

a. 小刘在阅览室后边找新来的英文杂志。
Xiǎo Liú zài yuèlǎnshì hòubian zhǎo xīn lái de Yīngwén zázhì.
Liu is in the back of the reading room looking for the new English magazines.

b. 张小姐说她想今年在国语中心学中文。
Zhāng xiǎojie shuō tā xiǎng jīnnián zài Guóyǔ Zhōngxīn xué Zhōngwén.
Miss Johnson said she wants to study Chinese at The Mandarin Center this year.

c. 在党中央的关心帮助下，深圳经济特区很快就训练出了一群极有能力的科技人员。
Zài dǎng zhōngyāng de guānxīn bāngzhù xià, Shěnzhēn Jīngji Tèqū hěn kuài jiù xùnliàn chū yī qún jí yǒu nénglì de kējì rényuán.
Under the caring help of the Party's Central Committee, the Shenzhen special Economic Zone quickly trained a highly capable group of technicians.

2. V 在 P = Result of a verb action is at a place (Cv) 在 Place comes directly after the verb rather than before it to mark that what follows 在 is the place where the result of the verb action remains. For example, in expl a below the message is that the bicycle is at the friend's place, in expl b it is that the characters are in the notebook regardless of where the writing takes place, and in expl c the funds are in the bank no matter where the loans were negotiated; compare this with the description above of 在 placement before the verb to mark where the verb action itself occurs.

Z

For all except the "verbs of localized action" described in the next paragraph, the difference between 在 Place Verb and Verb 在 Place is one of either simply articulating that a verb event happens somewhere; e.g., 他在床上睡 Tā zài chuáng shang shuì 'He is in bed sleeping,' or focusing on the location of the result of the verb action; e.g., 他睡在床上 'He is sleeping on the bed.' The focal points of the two constructions differ. However, there are a few verbs such as 住 zhù 'live,' 产 chǎn 'produce,' and 生长 shēngzhǎng 'grow up' with which the place of result may come either before or after the verb with no change of meaning or focus; e.g., 他住在天津~他在天津住 Tā zài Tiānjīn zhù 'He lives in Tianjin.' Note however, when the verb has a verb complement, the place of result must go before the verb; e.g., 在上面写清楚 Zài shàngmian xiě qīngchu 'Write it clearly on it.'

Verb 在 Place differs in meaning from 在 Place Verb with verbs of localized action; that is, verbs such as 写 xiě 'write,' 跳 tiào 'jump,' 掉 diào 'fall,' 打 dǎ 'hit,' 扔 rēng 'throw,' etc. For example, compare the Verb 在 place sentence 那个男孩儿把球扔在床上 Nèige nán hár bǎ qiú rēng zài chuáng shang 'That boy throws a ball onto the bed' and the 在 Place Verb sentence 那个男孩儿在床上扔球 Nèige nán hár zài chuáng shang rēng qiú 'That boy is on the bed throwing a ball.'

Note that although the shumianyu 于 yú 1 comes after the verb to mark location, it is a synonym of 在 zài 1, not of this usage.

a. 我的自行车放在我的朋友家里。
Wǒ de zìxíngchē fàng zài wǒ péngyou jiā li.
I left my bicycle at my friend's house.

b. 第十四课的生词都要写在本子里。
Dì shísì kè de shēngcí dōu yào xiě zài běnzi li.
The vocabulary for Lesson 13 must be written in the notebook.

c. 跟世界银行借的运输基础修改的资金已经放在中国银行了。
Gēn Shìjiè Yínháng jiè de yùnshū jīchǔ xiūgǎi de zījīn yǐjīng fàng zài Zhōngguó Yínháng le.
The funds borrowed from the World Bank for improving our transportation infrastructure have been placed in the Bank of China.

3. 在 T Vp = Verb at a point in time (Cv) 在 may be placed at the head of time structures with most verbs to direct attention to the point in time at which the verb action takes place. These time structures will come before the verb phrase (expls a & b). See 4 below for the less common structure Vp 在 time which is restricted to certain verbs. 于 yú 2 is a shumianyu synonym commonly used in ROC texts instead of 在.

a. 校车在下午四点差一刻到达，在四点零五分离开。
Xiàochē zài xiàwǔ sì diǎn chà yī kè dàodá, zài sì diǎn líng wǔ fēn líkāi.
The school bus arrives at a quarter of four in the afternoon and leaves at 4:05.

b. 吕先生在到了辛辛拿提以后才学会了英语。
Lǚ xiānsheng zài dàole Xīnxīnnátí yǐhòu cái xuéhuìle Yīngyǔ.

It was only after Mr. Lü arrived in Cincinnati that he mastered English.

4. Vp 在 T = Verb at a time (Cv) 在 is used after a limited number of verbs to highlight the time of the the verb action. The verbs will be ones representing concepts of 'birth,' 'death,' 'placement' (expl a), 'occurrence' (expl b), etc. Compare this with #3 above. 于 yú 1 is shumianyu synonym when used with time structures.

a. 高校长十分忙，这件事情放在以后再谈，好吧？
Gāo xiàozhǎng shífēn máng, zhèi jiàn shìqing fàng zài yǐhòu zài tán, hǎo ba?
President Gao is very busy, let's talk about this later, ok?

b. 芦沟桥事变发生在一九三七年七月七号。
Lúgōuqiáo Shìbiàn fāshēng zài yī jiǔ sān qī nián qī yuè qī hào.
The "Marco Polo Bridge Incident" occurred on July 7, 1937.

5. Np 在 Vp = The noun is verbing (Av) 在 is placed before activity verbs such as 打 dǎ 'hit,' 看 kàn 'look,' 前进 qiánjìn 'advance,' 跑 pǎo 'run,' etc. to mark focus on the ongoing aspect of a verb condition (expls a & b). 在 verb is usually translated with the English 'verb-ing.' 在 Vp is often used as part of the structure 正在 verb zhèngzài 1 in which 正 zhèng 1 marks focus on the time frame for a progressive verb action and 在 signals attention to the progressive nature of the verb action itself (expl c). 在 Vp differs from 正 Vp in also being used with verbs which are ongoing for a long time rather than at a particular time frame; e.g., 等 děng 'wait,' or with verbs which are done repeatedly; e.g., 考虑 kǎolǜ 'think over.' See 正在 zhèngzài 1 for further discussion.

The synonymous 着 zhe 1 may be added after the verb which has a 在 or 正在 before it to intensify focus on the progressive nature of the verb action. 呢 ne can also be added to the end of 在 Vp in some dialect areas to strengthen the progressive aspect of the verb activity.

a. 孩子们在哭，可能是想多吃点儿糖。
Háizimen zài kū, kěnéng shì xiǎng duō chī diǎr táng.
The children are crying, perhaps they want some more candy.

b. 经济在开放，科学在发展，时代在前进。
Jīngji zài kāifàng, kēxué zài fāzhǎn, shídài zài qiánjìn.
The economy is opening up, science is expanding, and the era is advancing.

c. 中国人民正在一心一意地为建设具有中国特色的社会主义现代化国家而努力。
Zhōngguó rénmín zhèngzài yīxīn yīyì de wèi jiànshè jùyǒu Zhōngguó tèsè de shèhuì zhǔyì xiàndàihuà guójiā ér nǔlì.
The Chinese people are working whole heartedly to build a modernized socialist state which has definite Chinese characteristics.

Z

再 zài (一) 'again' Adverb; 'then' Adverb; "intensified Stative verb" Adverb

1. 再 Verb = Verb again (Av) A major member of the set of words which mark repetition of a verb action, 再 specifically marks a projected repetition (expls a & c) or projected continuation (expl b) of a verb action. This explains why 'goodbye' is 再见 rather than *又见. Since 再 deals with expected rather than realized repetitions, it almost always refers to future events (expls a & b). But 再 can also mark situations in the past where repetition of a verb action was expected (expl c), so do not automatically translate 再 in the future tense. Note that a 再也不 Verb structure has the meaning of 'Never verb again!'; e.g. 那我再也不吃了！Nà wǒ zài yě bù chī le 'I will never ever eat that again!' When used in a 再一个 Noun or a 再一次 verb structure, 再 marks an additional noun or an additional time.

Other members of the set of verb repetition markers are 又 yòu 1 which marks factual or habitual verb repetition; 还 hái 2 which deals with projected verb repetition by the same subject; and 重 chóng 1 and 重新 chóngxīn 1 which mark a complete re-doing of a verb act.

a. 请你再说一遍。
Qǐng nǐ zài shuō yī biàn.
Please say it again.

b. 还很早啊，再坐一会儿，好吗？
Hái hěn zǎo a, zài zuò yīhuìr, hǎo ma?
It's still early, huh. Why don't you stay for a while longer?

c. 他说系主任昨天上午要再来我们班演讲。不知道怎么的，她没来。
Tā shuō xì zhǔrèn zuótiān shàngwǔ yào zài lái wǒmen bān yǎnjiǎng. Bù zhīdào zěnme de, tā méi lái.
He said that the department chair was going to come to our class to lecture again yesterday morning. I don't know why, she didn't come.

2. Time reference 再 Vp = Verb will happen at a time (Av) 再 is also occasionally used to mark that a verb act will take place at a particular point in time (expl a). It is also marks that a second verb will happen after a first verb takes place; in this it is similar to 然后 ránhòu 1 (expl b). See 先 xiān 1.

a. 今天来不及了，明天再回答大家的问题吧。
Jīntiān lái bu jí le, míngtiān zài huídá dàjiā de wèntí ba.
We can't get to them today. Let's respond to everybody's questions tomorrow.

b. 我不想现在去中国，等到我会说中文的时候再去。
Wǒ bù xiǎng xiànzài qù Zhōngguó, děng dào wǒ huì shuō Zhōngwén de shíhou zài qù.
I'm not planning to go to China now. Wait until I can speak Chinese, then I'll go.

3. 再 Stative verb = Increased Stative verb condition (Av) When used with Stative verbs, 再 marks an intensified degree of the Stative verb condition and imparts an implied comparison (expls a & b). 最 zuì 1.d and 更 gèng 1 are synonyms of this particular usage.

a. 我们那次玩儿得好极了，好得不能再好了。
Wǒmen nèi cì wár de hǎo jí le, hǎo de bù néng zài hǎo le.
We had a great time then, it could not have been better.

b. "清华学报"的编辑说我这篇文章还可以写得再精练些。
"Qīnghuá Xuébào" de biānjí shuō wǒ zhèi piān wénzhāng hái kěyǐ xiě de zài jīngliàn xiē.
The editor of the "Qinghua Journal" said I could re-write my article more succinctly.

则 zé (則) 'then, thus' Conjunction; 'however' Conjunction

1. X, 则 Y = X, thus Y (Cj) 则 retains a variety of subtle values from its centuries of use in classical writings, but in modern expository prose its primary structural usages can be divided into the two values identified in this entry. As a shumianyu synonym of 就 jiù 1 or 便 biàn 1, 则 marks the chronological sequence (expl a) and/or the cause and result (expl b) relationship of two verb phrases or clauses. The synonymous 所以 suǒyǐ 1 can also be translated as 'thus,' but in marking Y as the logical result of X it differs from 则; logic is not part of 则. X and Y may be verb phrases or clauses. 则 is also used as a measure for subsections of written materials; e.g., 两则新闻 liǎng zé xīnwén 'two pieces of news.'

a. 歌声刚落，则响起了一阵热烈的掌声。
Gēshēng gāng luò, zé xiǎngqǐ le yīzhèn rèliè de zhǎngshēng.
The song barely ended, and then there resounded a round of ardent applause.

b. 物理的基本原理之一是"物体热则涨，冷则缩。"
Wùlǐ de jīběn yuánlǐ zhīyī shì "wùtǐ rè zé zhǎng, lěng zé suō."
One of the basic principles of physics is, "When materials are hot they (thus) expand, when cold they (thus) contract."

2. X, 则 Y = X, however Y (Cj) 则 also marks comparison (expl a) and, sometimes, a change from what would expected from the events articulated in X (expl b). As such it is a weaker synonym of 却 què 1. X and Y will be either verb phrases or clauses.

It can be difficult to decide which of these two values is before you, so you will need to analyze the overall context of a 则 structure to be sure. See 但是 dànshì 1 for a discussion of the set of conjunctions which mark a change in Y.

Z

a. 今年南方是大雪纷飞，北方则春暖花开。
Jīnnián nánfāng shì dàxuě fēnfēi, běifāng zé chūnnuǎn huākāi.

This year snowflakes were falling wildly in the South; however, the North was spring-like and flowers were blooming.

b. 这篇小说虽没名，内容则很丰富。
Zhèi piān xiǎoshuō suī méimíng, nèiróng zé hěn fēngfù.
Although that novel is not well known, nevertheless its contents are rich.

照 zhào (一) 'according to' Coverb

1. 照 X Vp = Verb based on X (Cv) 照 is a member of one of the six sets of words which mark X as the basis on which a Y verb action is done. 照 specifically marks X as the model on which the following verb action is based. X will be a noun (expl a), or, sometimes, a verb phrase (expl b). Note that although they appear to be similar, this model/information marker 照 differs from 按照 anzhào 1 which generally marks X as the principles, rules or goals for a verb action; also consider the related but different function of 按 àn 1. See 根据 gēnjù 1 for comparative comments on these and other members of this set of words.

Note that 照 is also used as a verb representing the idea of 'reflect, illuminate.' It is also infrequently used as a synonym of 朝 cháo 1 '(face) towards'; e.g., 照这个方向前进 Zhào zhèige fāngxiàng qiánjìn 'Proceed in this direction.'

a. 我们书法课是照着字帖一笔一笔地写。
Wǒmen shūfǎ kè shì zhàozhe zìtiē yī bǐ yī bǐ de xiě.
Our calligraphy class writes the characters stroke by stroke according to what is in the copy book.

b. 对外经济联络部照每年增产百分之17.3计算。
Duìwài Jīngji Liánluòbù zhào měi nián zēngchǎn bǎi fēn zhī shíqī diǎn sān jìsuàn.
The Ministry for Economic Relations with Foreign Countries makes plans based on an annual production increase of 17.3%.

2. 照 X Vp = Verb in accordance with understood standards (Ad) As an adverb 照 marks that a verb action is done according to certain criteria, criteria which need not be overtly stated in the sentence. This conceptually related adverbial usage can be distinguished from its use as a coverb usage described above by its position immediately before the verb.

a. 明天中午有电影，不去看的班级课照上。
Míngtiān zhōngwǔ yǒu diànyǐng, bù qù kàn de bānjíkè zhào shàng.
There is a movie at noon tomorrow. Those classes and grades not attending it should go to class according (to the regular schedule).

着 zhė (—) "verb action ongoing" Auxiliary verb

1. **V/Sv 着 = Verb/Stative verb (condition) is going on** (Ax) When placed directly after a verb or Stative verb, the aspect marker 着 specifically marks the progressive nature of the verb action or condition. Verb 着 is most commonly translated into English by "verb-ing" (expl b); however, when used with "existential situations" (expl a) or with Stative verbs (expl c) there are other ways to render the ongoing nature of the verb situation. 着 may also be used in conjunction with combinations of 正 zhèng 1, 在 zài 1, or 正在 zhèngzài 1 (expl b) placed before the verb and 呢 ne (expl c) placed at sentence end to mark varying degrees of the ongoing nature in a verb situation. Stative verb 着 marks a "high degree of the Stative verb condition" with a bit of exaggeration involved (expl c).

着 is often written as 著 zhe 1 in texts from the Republic of China. Note that 着 is also used to represent the noun zhāo 'move (in a game)'; and the verbs zháo 'touch, feel, burn'; and zhuó 'wear, touch.''

a. 墙上写着"严禁吸烟"这四个大字。
Qiáng shang xiězhe "YÁN JÌN XĪ YĀN" zhèi sì ge dà zì.
Written on the wall are the four big characters "It is Strictly Forbidden to Smoke."

b. 国家民族事务委员会正在开着一次重要的座谈会。
Guójiā Mínzú Shìwù Wěiyuánhuì zhèngzài kāizhe yīcì zhòngyào de zuòtánhuì.
The State Nationalities Commission is holding an important symposium.

c. 多着呢!
Duōzhe ne!
That's an awful lot!

2. **V1 着 (O) Vp2 = Do verb 2 while doing verb 1 (to object 2)** (Ax) This structure marks that the first verb activity provides an ongoing background for the second. The focus of the structure is on the second verb phrase. The verb in the first position tends to be one whose action can last over a period of time.

a. 孩子們唱着歌奔向國父紀念館。
Háizimen chàngzhe gē bēnxiàng Guófù Jìniànguǎn.
Singing songs, the children rushed to Sun Yat-sen Memorial Hall.

b. 国庆节的时候活泼的中学生弹着吉他跳迪斯科。
Guóqìngjié de shíhou huópō de zhōngxuésheng tánzhe jítā tiào dísīkē.
On National Day the buoyant middle school students danced disco dances while playing the guitar.

著 zhė (—) "ongoing verb action" Auxiliary verb

1. **V/Sv 著 = Verb/Stative verb (condition) is going on** (Ax) 著 is a variant way of writing 着 zhe 1 & 2 that is commonly used in texts from the ROC (expl a). There is no difference in meaning or usage between 着 and 著, both mark the ongoing aspect of a

Z

verb act; see 着 zhe 1 for discussion and more examples. Note that 著 is also represents the verb zhù representing concepts such as 'write; famous,' the verb zhuó 'wear clothing; start; move (game pieces),' as well as zhāo 'hit the bull's eye,' and zháo 'take, bear.'

a. 許多人在山明水秀的郊區購置新屋，却發現窗外美麗的青山間遍佈著癩痢頭般的墓地；……

Xǔduō rén zài shān míng shuǐ xiù de jiāoqū gòuzhì xīn wū, què fāxiàn chuāng wài měilì de qīng shān jiān biànbùzhe làilì tóu bān de mùdì;...

Many people buy new homes in green and neat areas of the suburbs only to find tombs laying like scabby heads everywhere in the beautiful mountains outside their windows;...

正 zhèng (一) "ongoing verb situation" Adverb; "serendipity verb situation" Adverb

1. (T) 正 V/Sv = verb action/Stative verb situation is ongoing at a point in time (Av)

正 marks that a Stative verb situation (expl a) or a verb action (expls b & c) is ongoing at a specific point in time. The progressive nature of the situation is sometimes reinforced with a 着 zhe 1 after the verb (expl a) and/or 呢 ne at the end (expl a & b); this is especially the case with monosyllabic verbs and Stative verbs. 正 is often combined with 在 zài 5, the adverb which focuses attention on the ongoing nature of the verb activity itself, to create the structure 正在 which focuses attention on both the time and action aspects of an ongoing verb; see 正在 zhèngzài 1. Contextual analysis is necessary to distinguish 正 V/Sv from the structurally similar item #2 below. As you work with this very common character, remember it also represents a verb and a Stative verb having to do with 'correctness.'

a. 小季正忙着备课呢，没有时间陪我去看电影。

Xiǎo Jì zhèng mángzhe bèikè ne, méiyǒu shíjiān péi wǒ qù kàn diànyǐng.

Little Ji is being busy preparing for class, she doesn't have time to go to a movie with me.

b. 经理正发言呢，等一会儿他会见你。

Jīnglǐ zhèng fāyán ne, děng yīhuìr tā huì jiàn nǐ.

The manager is giving a talk at the moment. Wait a while and he can see you.

c. 目前养猪农民正面临空前未有的紧急危难，作为负责任的执政党自须立刻……

Mùqián yǎngzhū nóngmín zhèng miànlín kōngqián wèiyǒu de jǐnjí wēinàn, zuò wéi fù zérèn de zhízhèng dǎng, zì xū lìkè...

At present the hog farmers are facing an unprecedented pressing disaster. The responsible party in power must itself immediately...

2. 正 Vp/Sv = Serendipity verb/Stative verb (Av) This use of 正 marks that the verb/Stative verb situation is coincidentally fortuitous, not that it is ongoing. Note that 正 Vp can also mark an air of affirmation; e.g., 正如上文所述 Zhèng rú shàng wén suǒ shù 'Precisely as stated above.'

a. 你来的真巧，我正要找你。
Nǐ lái de zhēn qiǎo, wǒ zhèng yào zhǎo ni.
You came at precisely the right time, I was just going to look for you.

b. 我们到了人民大会堂的时候，里边正演少数民族节目呢。
Wǒmen dàole Rénmín Dàhuìtáng de shíhou, lǐbiān zhèng yǎn shǎoshù mínzú jiémù ne.
We arrived at the Great Hall of the People just at the moment there was a program about minority peoples going on.

正在 zhèngzài (— —) "ongoing verb action" Adverb

1. 正在 Vp/Sv = Verb/Stative verb situation ongoing at a point in time (Av) As is discussed in their separate entries, 正 focuses on the time aspect involved in an ongoing verb condition while 在 focuses on the progressive nature of the verb or Stative verb itself. Used together, 正在 calls attention to the overall ongoing nature of a verb action (expls a & c) or Stative verb condition (expl b). 在 differs from 正在 and 正 by its additional use with verbs actions which can be ongoing for a very long time; e.g., 等 děng 'wait,' or ones which are repeatedly done; e.g., 考虑 kǎolǜ 'consider.' A 正 structure can only be negated with 不是, never with 不 or 没有. The synonymous 着 zhe I can also be placed after the verb to enhance the ongoing aspect of the verb action. See 正 zhèng 1 and 在 zài 2 for comments and examples of their individual usages.

a. 我们昨天晚上去尹教授家的时候，他正在准备明天的考试。
Wǒmen zuótiān wǎnshang qù Yǐn jiàoshòu jiā de shíhou, tā zhèngzài zhǔnbèi míngtiān de kǎoshì.
When we went to his home last night, Professor Yin was writing tomorrow's test.

b. 小白正在不高兴，她姐姐进来把她朋友带走了。
Xiǎo Bái zhèngzài bù gāoxìng, tā jiějie jìnlái bǎ tā péngyou dài zǒu le.
Miss White is (being) unhappy. Her sister came in and took off with her friend.

c. 吴部长指出，中美人民的友好往来正在增加。
Wú bùzhǎng zhǐchū, Zhōng-Měi rénmín de yǒuhǎo wǎnglái zhèngzài zēngjiā.
Foreign Minister Wu pointed out that friendly contacts between the Chinese and American peoples are increasing.

之 zhī (—) "description marker" Structural Marker

1. **Description 之 Noun = Noun that is described** (Sm) 之 is the shumianyu synonym for the noun modification marker 的 de 1, and as such 之 imparts a strong flavor of formality to a text. The primary function of 之 in modern prose is to mark that the words before 之 modify the noun which follows it (expls a & b). Sometimes a word that would normally function as a verb becomes a noun after 之 (expl b). As is the case with 的 de 1, you will find it highly useful to focus on 之 when looking for the core noun of a noun phrase. 之 is also used to represent the third person pronoun 'he; she; it' when it is the object of a sentence in shumianyu prose texts (expl c). Rarely, 之 also represents the shumianyu verb 'go.'

之 and 的 do have some usage differences: 1) 之 is not used to mark omitted nouns in the way that 的 de 2 is. 2) 之 is not used to mark relationships between nouns; e.g., *我之书 is wrong. 3) 之 is not used with single syllable modification; e.g., *红之苹果 is wrong. 4) 之 is used in certain place, scope and time phrases where 的 does not occur; e.g., 之间、之外、之后 could not be rendered *的间、*的外、*的后, etc. And 5) 之 is used with some set phrases where 的 does not occur. For example, in fractions 四分之一 sì fēn zhī yī '1/4,' percentages 百分之九十九·九 bǎi fēn zhī jiǔshi jiǔ diǎn jiǔ '99.9%,' idioms 一孔之见 yī kǒng zhī jiàn 'a limited view' and in words such as 之所以 suǒyǐ 1, 的 does not occur.

a. 公民有言论自由和信仰自由之权利。
Gōngmín yǒu yánlùn zìyóu hé xìnyáng zìyóu zhī quánlì.
Citizens have the right of freedom of speech and freedom of belief.

b. 少数民族有发展先后之不同。
Shǎoshù mínzǔ yǒu fāzhǎn xiānhòu zhī bùtóng.
Minority groups have differences in developmental sequence.

c. 设法改装收割机，使之适合山区农事。
Shèfǎ gǎizhuāng shōugējī, shǐ zhī shìhé shānqū nóngshì.
Determine a way to retrofit the harvester, and make it suitable for mountain agriculture.

止 zhǐ (—) 'up until' Time word

1. **X 止 Y = Y ends at an X point** (Tm) A member of one of the four sets of structures which focus attention on the time frame for Y events, 止 specifically marks that the Y event ended with the X time frame given before 止. X will be a time structure, and Y will be a verb phrase or a clause. This pattern may be headed with 到 dào 1 (expl a) and/or end with the synonymous 为止 wéizhǐ 1 with no change in meaning. 止 is also used as a verb for meaning extending from 'stop, cease.'

The other three sets of time structures are 自从X以来，Y yǐlái 1 which marks that a presently on going Y situation started at a particular point in time, 从X起 qǐ 1 which marks the past, present or future starting point for Y, and 以后 yǐhòu 1 and its synonyms which mark a time frame related to a Y situation. Consider also 直到X，才Y zhídào 1 which marks that Y did not happen at all until X, and 不到 búdào 1 which marks the maximum amount of time involved in a verb action.

a. 到六月止已有一百多个美国学生在这儿学习过书法。
Dào liù yuè zhǐ yǐ yǒu yībǎi duō ge Měiguó xuésheng zài zhèr xuéxíguo shūfǎ.
By June, over one hundred American students had studied calligraphy here.

b. 从本月十号到十六号止，首都国际机场有了三十多班机飞往美国。
Cóng běn yuè shí hào dào shíliù hào zhǐ, Shǒudū guójì jīchǎng yǒu le sānshí duō bānjī fēiwǎng Měiguó.
From the 10th to the 16th of this month, the Capital International Airport (in Beijing) had over 30 flights to America.

只 zhǐ (一) 'only' Adverb

1. 只X = Only X (Av) You will most frequently see 只 followed by a verb phrase where it marks that the verb activity is limited in scope (expls a & b), but it can mark that a following noun is limited in amount (expl c). When there is a second verb phrase in the sentence, it tends to contain a negative adverb such as 不 bù 1 or 没 méi 1 (expls a & b). In the infrequent cases when 只 comes directly before a noun phrase to mark a limitation to the amount of the noun, there must be a Number Measure structure associated with that noun phrase (expl c). 就 jiù 1 is a synonymn of 只 in its use at the head of a verb phrase.

祇 and 衹 are variant ways of writing 只 that you will most often see in texts from the ROC. Also keep in mind the specific, different values of 只 in the patterns 只有 zhǐyǒu 1 and 只要 zhǐyào 1.

a. 今天要考的历史课我只翻了翻，还没有仔细准备。
Jīntiān yào kǎo de lìshǐ kè wǒ zhǐ fānle fān, hái méiyǒu zǐxì zhǔnbèi.
I've only glanced at the history lessons we're going to have a test on today, I haven't thoroughly prepared.

b. 那位工程师只会讲英语，不会讲汉语！
Nèiwèi gōngchéngshī zhǐ huì jiǎng Yīngyǔ, bù huì jiǎng Hànyǔ!
That engineer can only speak English, she doesn't know Chinese

c. 他们去年提高产量，只玉米就收了三十五万斤。
Tāmen qùnián tígāo chǎnliàng, zhǐ yùmǐ jiù shōule sānshiwǔ wàn jīn.
They increased production last year. They got 350,000 catties of corn alone.

祇 zhǐ (—) 'only' Adverb

1.祇 X = only X (Av) 祇 is a variant form of 只 zhǐ 1 that you will frequently see in texts from the ROC. It too marks that a verb activity is limited in scope or amount (expl a). You will find this marker written in two ways, both 祇 and 衹. See 只 zhǐ 1 for further comments and example sentences.

a. 我們祇能證實兩樁事常連接在一起，一在前，一在後。
Wǒmen zhǐ néng zhèngshí liǎng zhuāng shì cháng liánjiē zài yīqǐ, yī zài qián, yī zài hòu.
We can only prove that two events are often joined together, one before, one after.

至 zhì (—) 'to, until' Coverb

1. 至 X = to X (Cv) 至 is a shumianyu word which marks the end point of an X situation. X may be a time (expl a), a place or an abstract condition (expl b). 自 X 至 Y is a shumianyu synonym of the pattern 从 X 到 Y (expl a). 到 dào 2 is a synonym with a greater range of usages.

a. 自冬至夏
Zì dōng zhì xià
From winter to summer

b. 继续斗争，直至取得彻底胜利。
Jìxù dòuzhēng, zhízhì qǔdé chèdǐ shènglì.
Continue to fight until complete victory is won

直到 zhídào (— —) 'not until, only when' Conjunction

1. 直到 X, Y = Only when X, Y (Cj) 直到 marks X as an event which gives a time frame for a Y situation. X can be either a time noun (expl a) or a verb phrase (expl b). When the verb in Y is preceded by 才 cái 1, it marks that the Y situation did not happen until X (expl a); when Y has 还 hái 1, it marks that the Y situation continuously happened until X (expl b).

Note that when used in the structure 从 X 直到 Y, 直到 marks Y as part of the scope of a verb action rather than its time frame; see 从 cóng 1.

See 以来 yǐlái 1 for a discussion of four related sets of time frame markers; see also 不到 bùdào 1 which marks the maximum length of time involved in a verb situation.

a. 昨天我们学生团体去八达岭游览，直到天黑才回来。
Zuótiān wǒmen liúxuéshēng tuántǐ qù Bādálǐng yóulǎn, zhídào tiānhēi cái huílái.
Yesterday our foreign student group went to Badaling, and only when it got dark

did we finally return.

b. 直到他的影子望不见了，他的未婚妻还站在那儿。
Zhídào tā de yǐngzi wàng bu jiàn le, tā de wèihūnqī hái zhàn zài nàr.
His fiancee went on standing there until his shadow could no longer be made out at all.

至多 zhìduō (——) 'at the most' Adverb

1. 至多 X = At the most X (Av) 至多 marks that X is the maximum degree involved in the discussion. X will usually be a verb phrase (expl a), but it can also be an amount (b). When used with either 多 duō or 少 shǎo, 至 is a synonym of 最 zuì1, but not elsewhere. See also the example sentence given for 至少 zhìshǎo 1.

a. 前面就是太魯閣，至多還有兩三里路就到了。
Qiánmiàn jiùshì Tàilǔgé, zhìduō hái yǒu liǎng sān lǐ lù jiù dào le.
Toroko Gorge is right ahead. At the most it's two or three more miles and we'll be there.

b. 这次旅游在济南住不久，至多一天半。
Zhèi cì lǚyóu zài Jìnán zhù bù jiǔ, zhìduō yī tiān bàn.
On this tour we will not stay in Jinan very long, at most a day and a half.

之后 zhīhòu (—後) 'after' Time marker

1. X 之后, Y = After X, Y (Tm) A member of one of the four sets of words which mark attention to the time frame for a Y event, the shumianyu 之后 specifically marks that Y happens after X. X may be either a time noun (expl a) or a verb phrase (expl b). 之后 is a shumianyu synonym of 以后 yǐhòu 1, but it is not used as a synonym of the time noun 以后 'hence forward.' 之后 is also used in the structure 自从 X 之后, which marks the starting point for a following event; see 自从 zìcóng 1 for comments and examples. As a shumianyu synonym of the place words 后边 hòubiān and 后头 hòutou, 之后 can also refer to a physical location. See 以来 yǐlái 1 for discussion of the parameters of the four sets of time frame markers.

a. 一小时之后，请你来我办公室一趟，有事跟你商量。
Yī xiǎoshí zhīhòu, qǐng nǐ lái wǒ bàngōngshì yī tàng, yǒushì gēn nǐ shāngliang.
Please come to my office in an hour, I have something to discuss with you.

b. 今天下班之后，就要到新的工作岗位去了。
Jīntiān xiàbān zhīhòu, jiù yào dào xīn de gōngzuò gǎngwèi qù le.
After we finish work today, we will be going to a new work station.

之前 **zhīqián** **(——) 'before' Time marker**

1. X之前, Y = Before X, Y (Tm) 之前 is a shumianyu member of one of the four sets of words which mark attention on the time frame for a Y event. 之前 specifically marks that Y happens before X. It is a shumianyu synonym of the time markers 前 qián 1 and 以前 yǐqián 1, though it differs in not sharing the meaning 'previously.' X may be either a time noun (expl a) or a verb phrase (expl b). See 以前 yǐqián 1, 以后 yǐhòu 1 and 以来 yǐlái 1 for further comments and examples of these sets if time reference markers.

As a shumianyu synonym of the location markers 前边 qiánbiān, 前头 qiántou, and 前 qián, 之前 can also refer to a physical place. You will need to examine the context to determine whether 之前 represents time or simply a place.

a. 两个礼拜之前，他在杭州遇到过我。
Liǎng ge lǐbài zhīqián, tā zài Hángzhōu yùdàoguo wǒ.
Two weeks ago, he ran into me in Hangzhou.

b. 陆大夫开刀之前，手术室要作彻底消毒。
Lù dàifū kāi dāo zhīqián, shǒushùshì yào zuò chèdǐ xiāodú.
Before Dr. Lu operates, the operating room must be thoroughly disinfected.

至少 **zhìshǎo** **(——) 'at the least' Adverb**

1. 至少 X = X at the least (Av) 至少 marks that X is the smallest degree involved in a situation. X will generally be a verb phrase (expl a), but it can also be an amount (expl b). See 至多 zhìduō 1 for the other side of the coin.

a. 荆老师已经说过，这个学期的作文至少要一万字。
Jīng lǎoshī yǐjing shuōguo, zhèi ge xuéqī de zuòwén zhìshǎo yào yīwàn zì.
Professor Jing has said that this semester's composition will require at least 10,000 characters.

b. 高先生今年至少六十五岁。
Gāo xiānsheng jīnnián zhìshǎo liùshiwǔ suì.
Mr. Gao is at least 65 years old now.

只是 **zhǐshì** **(——) 'but, however' Conjunction**

1. X, 只是 Y = X, but Y (Cj) 只是 is an oral member of the set of conjunctions which mark Y as a change in the direction of events stated in X. 只是 specifically gives a light, tactful tone of voice to the supplementary or corrective information Y provides. X is the focal point of the sentence, not Y. X and Y will be verb phrases or clauses. 就是 jiùshì

4 is a close synonym. 不过 bùguò 1 is an oral synonym which imparts a slightly stronger tone to Y. See the even stronger toned synonym 但是 dànshì 1 for further discussion of this set of corrective conjunctions. Note that 只是 also functions as an adverb which imparts a sense of 'merely; simply.'

a. 这套家具好是好，只是贵了些。
Zhèi tào jiājù hǎo shi hǎo, zhǐshì guì le xiē.
This set of furniture is certainly good, it's just that it's a bit expensive.

之所以 zhī suǒ yǐ (— — —) 'reason for' Conjunction

1. Np 之所以 Vp, 是因为 Y = That by means of which the noun verbs is Y (Cj) This shumianyu structure marks the first section of a result and cause structure. It is a variant form of 所以 suǒyǐ 2, which you should consult for further discussion and examples.

之外 zhīwài (—) 'besides' Coverb; 'except for' Coverb

1.除 X之外, Y = Besides/Except for X, Y (Cv) An X ended with the more shumianyu 之外 will usually be headed with 除 chú 1 or a synonym. Use of 都 dōu 1 in Y marks that the structure has a meaning of 'except' (expl a). When Y has a 还 hái 1 or a synonym, it should be translated as 'besides, in addition to' (expl b). See 除了 chúle 1 for further discussion and examples. You will occasionally see 之外 used in the idiomatic shumianyu expression 除此之外 chú cǐ zhīwài 'besides; except for.'

a. 除了这块地之外，别的地都种暴玉米。
Chúle zhèi kuài dì zhīwài, biéde dì dōu zhòng bàoyùmǐ.
Except for this piece of ground, other places all grow popcorn.

b. 除了已经缴清的之外，他还欠人民币七十一万元。
Chúle yǐjing jiǎoqīng de zhīwài, tā hái qiàn rénmínbì qīshiyī wàn yuán.
In addition to what has already been handed over, he still owes 710,000 RMB.

只要 zhǐyào (— —) 'as long as, if only' Conjunction

1. 只要 X, Y = Provided that X takes place, Y can happen (Cj) One of the set of four markers which flag X as one condition that is necessary for Y to take place, 只要 specifically marks that X is one condition among others that if fulfilled will allow Y to occur. X may be a clause or a verb phrase, depending on the scope of the subject. Y will usually be a verb phrase head-marked by 就 jiù 1 or its shumianyu synonym 便 biàn 1 (expls a & b), though 就/便 is not used when Y is either a rhetorical question or a S是V

的 structure. 只要 can be used in Y with the same values it has in X (expl c).

Compare 只要 with 只有 zhǐyǒu 1 which marks that X is the one and only condition that will allow Y to happen. See the discussion of the three synonymous yet differing members of this set of markers at 只有 zhǐyǒu 1.

Note that 只 is sometimes used as the adverb 'only' with the verb 要 'want'; e.g., 我只要一本辞典。 Wǒ zhǐ yào yī běn cídiǎn 'I only want one dictionary.'

a. 只要我们有愚公移山的精神，就没有什么不能克服的障碍。
Zhǐyào wǒmen yǒu Yú Gōng Yí Shān de jīngshén, jiù méiyǒu shénme bù néng kèfú de zhǎng'ài.
As long as we have the spirit of the "Foolish Old Man Who Moved the Mountain," then there are no obstacles we can not overcome.

b. 同学们只要刻苦钻研，便能登上科学的高峰。
Tóngxuémen zhǐyào kèkǔ zuānyán, biàn néng dēngshàng kēxué de gāofēng.
Providing you study very assiduously, you can mount to the heights of science.

c. 整理这些材料并不难，只要有时间。
Zhěnglǐ zhèixiē cáiliào bìng bù nán, zhǐyào yǒu shíjiān.
It really isn't hard to arrange these materials, if you have the time.

之一 zhīyī (— —) 'one of' Pronoun

1. Noun 之一 = One of the nouns (Pn) 之一 is a shumianyu word used at the end of a structure to focus attention on a noun which is one member of a particular set of nouns. You will also find 之一 used in fractional numbers such as 三分之一 sān fēn zhī yī '1/3.' See the discussion at 之 zhī 1.

a. 空气是一切生物生存的必要条件之一。
Kōngqì shì yīqiè shēngwù shēngcún de bìyào tiáojiàn zhīyī.
Air is one of the prerequisites for the existence of all living beings.

只有 zhǐyǒu (— —) 'Only if' Conjunction

1. 只有 X, 才 Y = Only if X happens, can Y then occur (Cj) One of the set of four markers which mark X as a necessary condition for Y, 只有 specifically marks that X is the only condition under which Y could possibly take place; all other possibilities are excluded. X can be a noun phrase (expl c), a verb phrase or a clause (expls a & b). Y will be a verb phrase which will usually be marked by 才 cái 1 (expls a & b), though 还 hái 1 also occurs. 只有 can also be placed at the head of Y for added emphasis on the necessity of the Y situation (expl c).

The other members of this set of markers are: 除非 chúfēi 1 which makes the same point negatively (literally 除 'get rid of' the 非 'not') and with a stronger tone of voice; and 只要 zhǐyào 1 which marks that X is one possible condition among others which allows the occurrence of a Y event. Consider also 非 fēi 1.

Note: be alert for the possibility that 只 is an adverb being used with 有 yǒu 'have' or 要 yào 'want,' etc.; e.g., 我只有爱，没有钱 'I only have love, no money.'

Comparative examples of these four members of the set of condition markers are:

1. 只有上中心诊所，你的病才能治好。
   Zhǐyǒu shàng Zhōngxīn Zhěnsuǒ, nǐ de bìng cái néng zhì hǎo.
   Only if you go to the Central Clinic can your illness be cured.
   (no other hospitals or course of action can be effective)
2. 只要上中心诊所，你的病就能治好。
   Zhǐyào shàng Zhōngxīn Zhěnsuǒ, nǐ de bìng jiù néng zhì hǎo.
   If only you would go to the Central Clinic, your illness could be treated.
   (other hospitals might also be effective)
3. 除非上中心诊所，你的病才能治好。
   Chúfēi shàng Zhōngxīn Zhěnsuǒ, nǐ de bìng cái néng zhì hǎo.
   Only if you go to the Central Clinic can your illness (then) be cured.
   (unless you do this you won't get well).
4. 非去中心诊所，病治不好了。
   Fēi qù Zhōngxīn Zhěnsuǒ, bìng zhì bu hǎo le.
   If you don't go to the Central Clinic, your illness can not be cured.
   (if you do not do this, negative things will result).

Following are some examples of the exclusive 只有:

a. 只有在紧急情况下，才能动用你爸爸的信用卡。
   Zhǐyǒu zài jǐnjí qíngkuàng xià, cái néng dòngyòng nǐ bàba de xìnyòngkǎ.
   Only under the most pressing conditions may you then (and only then) use your father's credit card.
b. 我国只有依靠科学技术进步，才能大幅度地提高经济效益和增加生产。
   Wǒ guó zhǐyǒu yīkào kēxué jìshù jìnbù, cái néng dà fúdù de tígāo jīngji xiàoyì hé zēngjiā shēngchǎn.
   Only if we rely on progress in scientific technology can we then greatly raise economic benefits and increase production.
c. 如果下大雨，比赛只有延期。
   Rúguǒ xià dàyǔ, bǐsài zhǐyǒu yánqī.
   If it rains a lot, there must be a postponement of the game.

Z

至于 zhìyú (—於) 'as for, concerning' Coverb

1. 至于 X = About X (Cv) 至于 marks that X is an additional, relevant matter which is being brought into the discourse. A 至于 X structure usually comes at the head of a second or third phrase, but it sometimes comes at the head of a sentence to link it to the previous dicussion. X may be a noun phrase (expl a) or a verb phrase (expl b). A 至于 structure is usually end-marked with a comma. 关于 guānyú 1 is a synonym which marks X as a matter directly related to or involved in a verb action;对于 duìyú 1 is a synonym which marks X as the matter which the verb act impacts. Unlike 对于, 至于 is not used in the titles of literary works. See 关于 for further comparative comments on this set of words. When it is immediately followed by another verb 至于 is also used to represent to concept of 'go so far as' (see 纵使 zòngshǐ 1.b for an example).

a. 我们先讨论这几个问题，至于其他的问题，以后再讨论。
Wǒmen xiān tǎolùn zhèi jǐ ge wèntí, zhìyú qítā de wèntí, yǐhòu zài tǎolùn.
Let's first discuss these problems; as for other questions, we can discuss things some more later.

b. 我只知道这个人是著名的科学家，至于他有什么著作，我就不太清楚了。
Wǒ zhǐ zhīdao zhèige rén shi zhùmíng de kēxuéjiā, zhìyú tā yǒu shénme zhùzuò, wǒ jiù bù tài qīngchu le.
I only know that that person is a famous scientist. As far as what works he has written, I am not too clear.

自 zì (一) 'from' Coverb

1. 自 X Vp = Verb (starting) from X (Cv) A shumianyu synonym of 从 cóng 1 and 由 yóu 2, 自 marks X as the place or time from which a verb action originates. When X is a place, 自 marks X as the location from which the verb action started (expl a).

When X is a point in time rather than a place (expls b & c), 自 is a member of one of the four sets of words which mark a starting time prior to a Y action. In this usage, 自 may mark either a past (expl c) or future (expl b) starting time for a Y situation; the synonymous 自从 zìcóng 1 is only used with past events. 自 is occasionally also structured with a 起 qǐ 1 following X to mark the starting time frame for Y (expl b); however, note that when 自 is structured with 以来 yǐlái 1, the time frame must refer to a starting point that is in the past (expl c). In this last usage 自 is synonymous with 自从 X 以来 zìcóng 1. See 以来 yǐlái 1 for comparative comments and examples on this sets of markers. 自 is also used in words having to do with 'self.'

a. 中国民航每日有三次自广州飞往三藩市的航班。
Zhōngguó Mínháng měi rì yǒu sān cì zì Guǎngzhōu fēiwǎng Sānfánshì de hángbān.
CAAC has three flights daily from Canton to San Francisco.

b. 自即日（起）生效。

Zì jírì (qǐ) shēngxiào.
It takes effect (starting) from that date.

c. 自入夏以来，这个地区连下了几场暴雨了。
Zì rù xià yǐlái, zhèige dìqū lián xiàle jǐ chǎng bàoyǔ le.
Ever since summer started, this place has had thunder storms one after the other.

2. V 自 P = Verb from a place (Cv) 自 is used after a very few verbs such as 寄 jì 'mail,' 来 lái 'come,' 引 yǐn 'draw forth,' 译 yì 'translate,' etc. to mark the place from which that verb action originates. Consider also 于 yú 1.

a. 以下原文选自《水浒传》。
Yǐxià yuánwén xuǎnzì "Shuǐhǔ Zhuàn".
The following text is selected from "Tales of the Water Margin."

b. '守株待兔'这个成语出自《韩非子》。
'Shǒu zhū dài tù' zhèi ge chéngyǔ chūzì "Hán Fēizǐ".
The idiom 'Hold on to the tree trunk and wait for a rabbit' comes from the "Han Feizi."

自从 zìcóng (—从) 'ever since' Coverb

1. 自从 X, Y = Ever since X, Y (Cv) 自从 is a member of one of the four sets of structures which mark X as a time or event prior to a Y situation. Specifically, 自从 marks X as either a past point in time (expl a) or a past event (expl b & c) that was the starting point for a Y situation which has been going on since X and continues to happen right up to the present. Y will be a verb phrase or a clause. 自从 is most frequently used in the pattern 自从 X 以来, Y (expl c); see 以来 yǐlái 1. 自 X, Y zì 1 is a synonymous structure which differs in being used to mark future as well as past X starting points for a Y situation.

The other three sets of X time structures are 从 X 起 qǐ 1 which specifically marks X as the past, present or future point at which Y starts, 以后 yǐhòu 1 which marks a time or event before another situation occurred, and 到 X 为止 zhǐ 1 which identifies X as the end point at which Y stopped. See also 直到 X, 才 Y zhídào 1 which marks X as a time referent for Y; also consider 不到 bùdào 1 which marks the maximum length of time for a verb action and 然后 ránhòu 1 which marks a sequence of two completed verb actions.

a. 自从去年十一月四号下午五点差三分到今天，我已经戒了一年多烟了。
Zìcóng qùnián shíyī yuè sì hào xiàwǔ wǔdiǎn chà sān fēn dào jīntiān, wǒ yǐjīng jièle yìnián duō yān le.
Since 3 minutes of 5:00 on November 4 of last year, I've sworn off cigarettes for over a year.

b. 自从水库建成后，每年的水稻亩产量增加了三倍。

Zìcóng shuǐkù jiànchéng hòu, měi nián de shuǐdàomù chǎnliàng zéngjiāle sān bèi.
Ever since the reservoir was completed, the annual rice production capacity per mou has tripled.

c. 自从到武汉以来，我了解了许多中国社会主义建设的情况。
Zìcóng dào Wǔhàn yǐlái, wǒ liǎojiěle xǔduō Zhōngguó shèhuì zhǔyì jiànshè de qíngkuàng.
Since I have been in Wuhan, I have come to understand a great deal about the building of socialism in China.

纵然 zòngrán (縱—) 'even if' Conjunction

1. 纵然 X, 也 Y = Even if X, Y (Cj) 纵然 is a shumianyu member of one of the three sets of concessive conjunctions which mark that a Y situation is unaffected by X. 纵然 specifically marks that X is a hypothetical condition which does not affect Y (expl a). The situation in X may sometimes appear to be factual (expl b). X and Y may be either a verb phrase or a clause, depending on placement of the subject of the sentence. The verb in Y will usually be headed by 也 yě 1, 还 hài 1, or 都 dōu 1 which bring their own nuances to the sentence. 纵然 is more shumianyu than its more frequently used synonym 即使 jíshǐ 1 and thus imparts a more formal tone to the text. 纵使 zòngshǐ is a close shumianyu synonym not covered in this work. See 即使 and 虽然 suīrán 1 for comments and comparative examples of the three sets of concessive conjunctions.

a. 纵然成功的希望不大，我们也要试试。
Zòngrán chénggōng de xīwang bù dà, wǒmen yě yào shìshì.
We will try even if there isn't much hope of success.

b. 纵然有千难万险，也挡不住英勇的探险队员。
Zòngrán yǒu qiān nán wàn xiǎn, yě dǎng bù zhù yīngyǒng de tànxiǎn duìyuán.
Even though there are myriad hardships and hazards, they can't stop the dauntless explorers.

最 zuì (—) 'most, -est' Adverb

1. 最 X = Most X, X-iest (Av) A member of the set of adverbs used to mark a comparative condition, 最 marks that the X condition exists in the greatest degree. X will most often be a Stative verb (expls a & b); when X is a verb it is limited to verbs which represent an abstract emotional, evaluative, or impressionistic situation; e.g., 愿意 yuànyì 'willing,' 讨厌 tǎoyàn 'detest,' 了解 liǎojiě 'comprehend,' etc. (expl c). X can also sometimes be a generic place name such as 左边 zuǒbian 'left (side),' 前线 qiánxiàn 'front lines,' etc. When X is a Stative verb, it can either function as the core verb of the sentence (expl a) or as part of a descriptive structure (expl b).

A 最 X descriptive structure is usually followed by the descriptive marker 的 de 1, but sometimes when X is monosyllabic there is no 的; in such cases the descriptive structure and the noun form a tightly related conceptual unit; e.g., 最快速度 zuìkuài sùdù 'highest speed,' 最高气温 zuìgāo qìwēn 'highest temperature.' When it is followed by a period of time or an amount, 最 X marks what follows it as the fullest amount of a time or quantity (expl d). 再 zài 2 is a synonym in this particular usage. 顶 dǐng is an oral synonym in all usages; it differs only in requiring a following 的 marker when part of a descriptive structure. 至 zhì 1 is a synonym only when used with the Stative verbs 多 duō 'much' or 少 shǎo 'little' for a meaning of 'at the most; at the least.'

The other overt member of this set of comparative adverbs is 更 gèng 1 which marks that X exists in a comparatively greater degree.

a. 黑龙江的冬天今年来得最早。
Hēilóngjiāng de dōngtiān jīnnián lái de zuì zǎo.
Winter came the earliest in Heilongjiang this year.

b. 珠穆朗玛峰是世界上最高的山峰。
Zhūmùlǎngmǎfēng shì shìjiè shang zuì gāo de shānfēng.
Mt. Everest is the highest mountain in the world.

c. 孙先生是我们大学最受欢迎的老师。
Sūn xiānsheng shì wǒmen dàxué zuì shòu huānyíng de lǎoshī.
Professor Sun is the best received instructor in our school.

d. 这部书最贵也要不了一百块钱。
Zhèi bù shū zuì guì yě yào bù liǎo yībǎi kuài qián.
At the most (expensive) this set of books can't be 100 yuan.

INDEX I: GRAMMATICAL MARKERS

Both full form and simplified character versions of the markers are listed in this index. All characters are listed in ascending order of their **total** number of strokes. Within a stroke count group, characters are listed alphabetically; within an entry, items are listed by ascending **total** number of strokes in the second character in the compound.

When a character in this index is followed by "see also," that signifies that in addition to being used by itself as a grammatical marker, it is also used as part of the marker(s) that follow in the entry; e.g., "并 bìng, see also 并且 bìngqiě" means that you will find the character 并 is used both as a marker itself and as part of another marker. When a character is followed by "only in," it signifies that the character occurs only as part of the marker(s) following it. It is not used by itself as a marker; e.g., "加 jiā: only in 加以,..." tells you that you will find 加 used as a grammatical marker only as part of the marker(s) which follow. When none of these comments follows the listed character, this signifies that the character is itself used as a marker but does not occur as part of a compound covered in this work; e.g., 与 yǔ.

(NOTE: 阝 and 辶 are each counted as 3 strokes in this work.)

One Stroke 一笔

一 yī, see also 之一 zhīyī, 一方面 yīfāngmiàn, 一切 yīqiè, 一边 yībiān, 有(一)点(儿) yǒu(yī)diǎn(r), 有(一)點(兒) yǒu(yī)diǎn(r), 一点儿 yīdiǎn(r), 一面 yīmiàn, 一般 yībān, 一样 yīyàng, 一樣 yīyàng, 一點兒 yīdiǎn(r), 一邊 yībiān

Two Strokes 二笔

了 le, see also 为了 wèile, 除了 chúle, 爲了 wèile

了 liǎo

又 yòu, see also 又...又 yòu...yòu

Three Strokes 三笔

才 cái

么 ma

万 wàn, see also 万万 wànwàn

也 yě, see also 也...也 yě...yě

已 yǐ, see also 已经 yǐjīng, 已經 yǐjīng

亿 yì

于 yú, see also 由于 yóuyú, 于是 yúshì, 至于 zhìyú, 关于 guānyú

与 yǔ

之 zhī, see also 之一 zhīyī, 之外 zhīwài, 之后 zhīhòu, 之所以 zhīsuǒyǐ, 之後 zhīhòu, 之前 zhīqián

Four Strokes 四笔

比 bǐ

不 bù, see also 不仅 bùjǐn, 不只 bùzhǐ, 不光 bùguāng, 不过 bùguò, 不论 bùlùn, 不如 bùrú, 不但 bùdàn, 不单 bùdān, 不到 bùdào, 不是 bùshì, 要不 yàobù, 要不是 yàobushì, 要不然 yàoburán, 不断 bùduàn, 不單 bùdān, 不過 bùguò, 不然 bùrán, 不僅 bùjǐn, 不管 bùguǎn, 不論 bùlùn, 不斷 bùduàn

从 cóng, see also 从而 cóngér, 自从 zìcóng, 从来 cónglái

反 fǎn, see also 反而 fǎn'ér

方 fāng: only in 一方面 yīfāngmiàn

及 jí, see also 以及 yǐjí
仅 jǐn: only in 不仅 bùjǐn
历 lì: only in 历来 lìlái
切 qiè: only in 一切 yīqiè
仍 réng, see also 仍然 réngrán
少 shǎo: only in 至少 zhìshǎo
为 wéi, see also 为止 wéizhǐ
为 wèi, see also 为了wèile, 为着 wèizhe, 因为 yīnwei
无 wú: only in 无论 wúlùn
止 zhǐ, see also 为止 wéizhǐ, 爲止wéizhǐ

Five Strokes 五笔

本 běn, see also 本着 běnzhe
边 biān, see also 一边 yībiān
对 duì, see also 对于 duìyú
发 fā: only in 越发 yuèfā
加 jiā: only in 加以 jiāyǐ, 更加 gèngjiā
叫 jiào
可 kě, see also 可以 kěyǐ, 可是 kěshì
令 lìng
吗 ma
且 qiě, see also 而且 érqiě, 并且 bìngqiě, 况且 kuàngqiě, 並且 bìngqiě
让 ràng
外 wài, see also 之外 zhīwài, 以外 yǐwài
未 wèi
以 yǐ, see also 之所以 zhīsuǒyǐ, 以及 yǐjí, 加以 jiāyǐ, 可以 kěyǐ, 以外 yǐwài, 以后 yǐhòu, 以至yǐzhì, 以来 yǐlái, 以來 yǐlái, 所以 suǒyǐ, 其所以 qísuǒyǐ, 以便 yǐbiàn, 以後 yǐhòu, 以前 yǐqián, 以致 yǐzhì
用 yòng
由 yóu, see also 由于 yóuyú, 由於 yóuyú
正 zhèng, see also 正在 zhèngzài
只 zhǐ, see also 不只 bùzhǐ, 只有 zhǐyǒu, 只是 zhǐshì, 只要 zhǐyào

Six Strokes 六笔

并 bìng, see also 并且 bìngqiě
此 cǐ: only in 因此 yīncǐ
地 de
当 dāng
多 duō: only in 至多 zhìduō
而 ér, see also 从而 cóngér, 反而 fǎn'ér, 因而 yīn'ér, 而且érqiě, 进而 jìn'ér, 然而 rán'ér, 進而 jìn'ér, 從而 cóngér
仿 fǎng: only in 仿佛 fǎngfú
关 guān: only in 关于 guānyú
光 guāng: only in 不光 bùguāng
过 guò, see also 不过 bùguò

过 guo
好 hǎo: only in 好象 hǎoxiàng, 好像 hǎoxiàng
后 hòu, see also 之后 zhīhòu, 以后 yǐhòu, 然后 ránhòu
会 huì
尽 jǐn: only in 尽管 jǐnguǎn
决 jué
论 lùn: only in 不论 bùlùn, 无论 wúlùn
吗 ma
如 rú, see also 不如 bùrú, 如同 rútóng, 如果 rúguǒ, 假如 jiǎrú
似 shì: only in 似的 shìde
同 tóng, see also 如同 rútóng
先 xiān
向 xiàng, see also 向来 xiànglái, 向來 xiànglái, 向着 xiàngzhe
亦 yì
因 yīn, see also 因为 yīnwei, 因此 yīncǐ, 因而 yīn'ér, 因為 yīnwei
有 yǒu: only in 有一点儿 yǒuyīdiǎnr, 有一點兒 yǒuyīdiǎnr, 只有 zhǐyǒu, 沒有 méiyǒu, 所有(的) suǒyǒu(de)
在 zài, see also 正在 zhèngzài
再 zài
则 zé: see also 否则 fǒuzé
至 zhì, see also 至于 zhìyú, 至少 zhìshǎo, 以至 yǐzhì, 至多 zhìduō, 至於 zhìyú
自 zì, see also 自从 zìcóng, 自從 zìcóng

Seven Strokes 七笔

把 bǎ
但 dàn, see also 不但 bùdàn, 但是 dànshì
彷 fǎng: only in 彷彿 fǎngfú
否 fǒu: only in 否则 fǒuzé, 否則 fǒuzé
佛 fú: only in 仿佛 fǎngfú
更 gèng, see also 更加 gèngjiā
还 hái, see also 还是 háishi
即 jí, see also 即使 jíshǐ, 即便 jíbiàn, 即是 jíshì
进 jìn: only in 进而 jìn'ér
均 jūn
決 jué
来 lái, see also 从来 cónglái, 历来 lìlái, 以来 yǐlái, 向来 xiànglái, 来着 láizhe, 越来越 yuèlái yuè, 愈来愈 yùlái yù
连 lián
沒 méi, see also 沒有 méiyou
况 kuàng: only in 况且 kuàngqiě
时 shí: only in 的时候 de shíhou
却 què
纵 zòng: only in 纵然 zòngrán

即是 jíshì, 是...的 shì...de, 於是 yúshì, 要不是 yàobushi, 要是 yàoshi, 倒是 dàoshi, 就是 jiùshì, 還是 hàishi
虽 suī, see also 虽然 suìrán
為 (see 12 strokes 爲)
要 yào, see also 要不 yàobù, 要不是 yàobushì, 只要 zhǐyào, 要是 yàoshì, 要不然 yàoburán
则 zé: see also 否则 fǒuzé
者 zhě (also see 8 strokes 者): only in 或者 huòzhě
祇 (also see 8 strokes 祇)

Ten Strokes 十笔

般 bān, see also 一般 yībān
被 bèi
除 chú, see also 除了 chúle, 除非 chúfēi
倒 dào, see also 反倒 fǎndào, 倒是 dàoshi
根 gēn: only in 根据 gēnjù, 根據 gēnjù
候 hòu: only in 的时候 de shíhou
继 jì: only in 继续 jìxù
連 lián
能 néng
起 qǐ
時 shí, see also 的時候 de shíhou
倘 tǎng: only in 倘若 tǎngruò
样 yàng: only in 一样 yīyàng
致 zhì: only in 以致 yǐzhì

Eleven Strokes 十一笔

從 cóng, see also 從而 cóngér, 自從 zìcóng, 從來 cónglái
得 de
都 dōu (also see 12 strokes 都)
既 jì, see also 既然 jìrán
假 jiǎ: only in 假如 jiǎrú
將 jiāng
教 jiào (variant of 叫 jiào)
進 jìn; only in 進而 jìn'ér
竟 jìng, see also 竟然 jìngrán
据 jù, see also 根据 gēnjù
离 lí
续 xù: only in 继续 jìxù
望 wàng (variant of 往 wàng)
着 zhe, see also 为着 wèizhe, 本着 běnzhe, 向着 xiàngzhe, 来着 láizhe, 來着 láizhe, 随着 suízhe, 隨着 suízhe, 著 zhe (variant of 着 zhe)

Twelve Strokes 十二笔

曾 céng, see also 曾经 céngjīng, 曾經 céngjīng
朝 cháo
單 dān: only in 不單 bùdān

等 děng, see also 等等 děngděng
都 dōu (see also 11 strokes 都)
發 fā: only in 越發 yuèfā
就 jiù, see also 就是 jiùshì
絕 jué (variant of 決 jué)
給 gěi
過 guò, see also 不過 bùguò
過 guo
嗎 ma (see 13 strokes 嗎)
然 rán, see also 不然 bùrán, 仍然 rèngrán, 然而 rán'ér, 然后 ránhòu, 纵然 zòngrán, 固然 gùrán, 然後 ránhòu, 要不然 yàoburán, 虽然 suīrán, 既然 jìrán, 竟然 jìngrán; 雖然 suīrán
随 suí: only in 随着 suízhe
替 tì
為 wéi, see also 為止 wéizhǐ
為 wèi, see also 為了 wèile, 因為 yīnwei, 為着 wèizhe
無 wú: only in 無論 wúlùn
象 xiàng, see also 好象 hǎoxiàng
越 yuè, see also 越发 yuèfā, 越来越 yuèlái yuè, 越來越 yuèlái yuè, 越發 yuèfā
着 zhe (also see 11 strokes 着)
著 zhe (also see 13 strokes 著)
最 zuì

Thirteen Strokes 十三笔

當 dāng
跟 gēn
話 huà: only in 的話 dehuà
會 huì
僅 jǐn: only in 不僅 bùjǐn
經 jīng: only in 已經 yǐjīng, 曾經 céngjīng
嗎 ma
萬 wàn, see also 萬萬 wànwàn
新 xīn: only in 重新 chóngxīn
與 yǔ
愈 yù, see also 愈来愈 yùlái yù, 愈來愈 yuèlái yuè
照 zhào, see also 按照 ànzhào
著 zhe (also see 12 strokes 著)

Fourteen Strokes 十四笔

對 duì, see also 對於 duìyú
管 guǎn, see also 不管 bùguǎn, 尽管 jǐnguǎn, 儘管 jǐnguǎn
麼 me
像 xiàng, see also 好像 hǎoxiàng

Fifteen Strokes 十五笔

論 lùn: only in 不論 bùlùn, 無論 wúlùn

隨 suí: only in 隨着 suízhe
樣 yàng: only in 一樣 yīyàng
億 yì
Sixteen Strokes 十六笔
還 hái, see also 還是 háishi
儘 jǐn: only in 儘管 jǐnguǎn
據 jù, see also 根據 gēnjù
歷 lì: only in 歷來 lìlái
憑 píng
Seventeen Strokes 十七笔
點 diǎn, see also (一)點(兒) (yī)diǎn(r), 有(一)點(兒) yǒu (yī)diǎn(r)
雖 suī, see also 雖然 suīrán
縱 zòng: only in 縱然 zòngrán
Eighteen Strokes 十八笔
斷 duàn: only in 不斷 bùduàn
Nineteen Strokes 十九笔
邊 biān, see also 一邊 yībiān
纔 cái (variant of 才 cái)
關 guān: only in 關於 guānyú
離 lí
Twenty Strokes 二十筆
繼 jì: only in 繼續 jìxù
Twenty-one Strokes 二十一笔
續 xù: only in 繼續 jìxù
Twenty-four Strokes 二十四笔
讓 ràng

INDEX II: ENGLISH-TO-CHINESE

English equivalents of the Chinese grammatical markers in this dictionary are given in this index. In many cases, markers are listed under two or more common equivalents; the hope is that you will find the Chinese equivalent of an English language concept one way or the other. On the other hand, do not think that because two or more Chinese markers are listed under the same English equivalent that they automatically have exactly the same meaning or usages; for example, consider the entries under "but," "according to," or "and" which have differences ranging from the minor to the major.

able to 得 de 2; 会 huì 2; 能 néng 2 & 3; 能够 nénggòu
about 对于 duìyú 1; 关于 guānyú 1; 就 jiù 4
about so much 来 lái 3
according to 按 àn 1; 按照 ànzhào 1; 本 běn 2; 本着 běnzhe 1; 根据 gēnjù 1; 据 jù 1; 凭 píng 1; 照 zhào 1, 2
act as 为 wéi 1, 2 & 3
actually 并 bìng; 竟 jìng 1; 竟然 jìngrán 1; 却 què 1
admittedly 固然 gùrán 2
adverb 地 de 1
affirmation 便 biàn 4
after 后 hòu 1; 然后 rànhòu 1; 以后 yǐhòu 1; 之后 zhīhòu 1
afterwards 然后 ránhòu 1
again 重 chóng 1; 重新 chóngxīn 1; 还 hái 2; 又 yòu 1; 再 zài 1
all 都 dōu 1, 2 & 3; 均 jūn 1; 所有(的) suǒyǒu(de) 1; 一切 yīqiè 1
allow 给 gěi 5; 可 kě 3; 可以 kěyǐ 2; 能 néng 2; 让 ràng 1
already 都 dōu 5; 已 yǐ 1; 已经 yǐjing 1
also 也 yě 1; 亦 yì 1; 又 yòu 1; 又...又 yòu...yòu 1
although 尽管 jǐnguǎn 1 & 2; 虽 suī 1 & 2; 虽然 suīrán 1 & 2
always 从来 cónglái 1; 历来 lìlái 1; 向来 xiànglái 1
and 并 bìng 1; 并且 bìngqiě 1; 而 ér 2; 而且 érqiě 1; 跟 gēn 1, 2 & 3; 和 hé 1 & 2; 及 jí 1; 既 jì 1; 同 tóng 1; 也 yě 1; 也...也 yě...yě 1; 以及 yǐjí 1; 又 yòu 1; 与 yǔ 1 & 2
and so forth 等 děng 1; 等等 děngděng
anyway 反正 fǎnzhèng 1
arrive at 到 dào 1
as a result 以致 yǐzhì 1
as if 仿佛 fǎngfú 1
as for 至于 zhìyú 1
as long as 只要 zhǐyào 1
as much as 以至 yǐzhì 1
as soon as 一 yī 1
as well as 也...也 yě...yě 1; 以至 yǐzhì 2
at 于 yú 1 & 2; 在 zài 1, 2, 3 & 4
away from 离 lí 1

based on 按 àn 1; 按照 ànzhào 1; 本 běn 2; 本着 běnzhe 1; 根据 gēnjù 1; 据 jù 1; 凭 píng 1; 以 yǐ 1 & 2; 照 zhào 1, 2
be 为 wéi 1, 2 & 3
because 因 yīn 1; 因为 yīnwei 1 & 2; 由于 yóuyú 1 & 2
before 前 qián 1; 以前 yǐqián 1; 之前 zhīqián 1
begin with 起 qǐ 1
besides 除 chú 1; 除了 chúle 1 & 3; 外 wài 1; 之外 zhīwài 1; 以外 yǐwài 1
both 都 dōu 1
both...and 既 jì 1; 也…也 yě...yě 1; 又…又 yòu...yòu 1
but 不过 bùguò 1; 但 dàn 1; 但是 dànshì 1; 倒 dào 1; 倒是 dàoshì 1; 而 ér 1; 就是 jiùshì 4; 可 kě 2; 可是 kěshì 1; 却 què 1; 然 rán 1; 然而 rán'ér 1; 只是 zhǐshì 1; 则 zé 2
by 被 bèi 1; 的 de 5; 给 gěi 3 & 4; 让 ràng 2; 是…的 shì...de 2; 为 wéi 4; 由 yóu 1
by means of 用 yòng 2

cause 给 gěi 5; 叫 jiào 1; 教 jiào 1; 令 lìng 1; 让 ràng 1; 使 shǐ 1
comparison-inferiority 不如 bùrú 1 & 2; 沒 méi 3; 沒有 méiyǒu 3
comparison-sameness 一样 yīyàng 1 & 2
comparison-superiority 比 bǐ 1 & 2
concerning 对于 duìyú 1; 关于 guānyú 1; 至于 zhìyú 1
consequently 于是 yúshì 1; 以致 yǐzhì 1
constantly 历来 lìlái 1
continue 继续 jìxù 1; 不断 bùduàn 1
contrary 反 fǎn 1; 反而 fǎn'ér 1
co-occurrence 一方面 yīfāngmiàn 1

definitely negative 并 bìng 2; 才 cái 4.c; 决 jué 1; 绝 jué 1
description 的 de 1 & 2; 是…的 4; 之 zhī 1
did indeed 曾 céng 1; 曾经 céngjīng 1
distance from 离 lí 1
do for 给 gěi 1; 来 lái 1; 替 tì 1; 为 wèi 1
down to 以至 yǐzhì 2
due to 因 yīn 1; 由于 yóuyú 1 & 2

emphasis 并 bìng 2; 才 cái 4; 纔 cái 1; 曾 céng 1; 曾经 céngjing 1; 的 de 3, 4 & 6; 就 jiù 7; 就是 jiùshì 3; 可 kě 1; 是…的 shì...de 1, 2 & 3; 所 suǒ 1; 一 yī 4; 再 zài 3
end at 为止 wéizhǐ 1; 只 zhǐ 1
-er 更 gèng 1
-est 最 zuì 1
etc. 的 de 2; 等 děng 1; 等等 děngděng 1
even 都 dōu 4; 连 lián 1; 也 yě 4
even if 便 biàn 5; 即便 jíbiàn 1; 即使 jíshǐ 1; 就 jiù 8; 就是 jiùshì 1;纵然 zǒngrán 1
even though 尽管 jǐnguǎn 1; 虽 suī 1; 虽然 suīrán 1 & 2; 纵然 zǒngrán 1
ever since 自从 zìcǒng 1

exactly 就是 jiùshì 2
except 除 chú 1; 除了 chúle 2 & 3; 外 wài 1; 以外 yǐwài 1; 之外 zhīwài 1

first 先 xiān 1
following 随着 suízhe 1 & 2
(do) for 给 gěi 1; 来 lái 1; 替 tì 1; 为 wèi 1
for 对 duìyú 1; 对于 duìyú 1
for (purpose of) 为 wèi 2, 3 & 4; 为了 wèile 1 & 2; 为着 wèizhe 1
for a while 一 yī 2
from 从 cóng 1; 离 lí 1; 由 yóu 2; 自 zì 1 & 2

go on 继续 jìxù 1; 不断 bùduàn 1
good at 会 huì 2; 能 néng 1 & 3; 能够 nénggòu 1
however 不过 bùguò 1; 但 dàn 1; 但是 dànshì 1; 倒 dào 1; 而 ér 1; 就是 jiùshì 4; 可 kě 2; 可是 kěshì 1; 却 què 1; 然 rán 1; 然而 rán'ér 1; 只是 zhǐshì 1; 则 zé 2
hundred million 万万 wànwàn 1; 亿 yì 1

if 的话 dehuà 1; 假如 jiǎrú 1; 如 rú 2; 如果 rúguǒ 1 & 2; 若 ruò 1; 倘若 tǎngruò 1; unmarked conditional 1; 要 yào 4; 要是 yàoshì 1; 只要 zhǐyào 1; 只有 zhǐyǒu 1
if not 不是 bùshì 1
if not for 要不是 yàobushì 1
if only 只要 zhǐyào 1
impact on 对 duì 1; 对于 duìyú 1
in 于 yú 1
in addition to 除 chú 1 & 3; 除了 chúle 1 & 3; 况且 kuàngqiě 1; 之外 zhīwài 1; 以外 yǐwài 1;
indeed 便 biàn 4; 即 jí 1; 即是 jíshì 1; 就 jiù 6
indefinite interrogative 都 dōu 3; indefinite interrogative; 也 yě 3
in order to 为 wèi 2, 3 & 4; 为了 wèile 1 & 2; 为着 wèizhe 1; 以 yǐ 3; 以便 yǐbiàn 1
intend to 要 yào 1
isn't it 不是 bùshì 1
instead of 替 tì 1

just happened 才 cái 3

least 至少 zhìshǎo 1
let 让 ràng 1
like 般 bān 1; 仿佛 fángfú 1; 好象 hǎoxiàng 1; 如 rú 1; 若 ruò 2; 如同 rútóng 1; 似的 shìde 1; 象 xiàng 1; 一般 yībān 1
likely to 会 huì 1
list complete 等 děng 2
listing comma 、 dùnhào 1
little bit (一)点(儿) (yī)diǎn(r) 1; 有(一)点(儿) yǒu (yī)diǎn(r)
located at 于 yú 1 & 2; 在 zài 1 & 2

make 给gěi 5; 叫jiào 1; 教jiào 1; 令lìng 1; 让ràng 1; 使shǐ 1
manner of doing verb 得de 1
modification (noun) 的 de 1 & 2; 是…的 shì...de 4; 之 zhī 1
more and more 愈 yù 1; 越 yuè 1; 越来越 yuèlái yuè 1; 愈来愈 yùlái yù 1
(even) more (than) 比bǐ 1 & 2; 更gèng 1; 更加 gèngjiā 1; 还 hái 2; 越发 yuèfā 1
moreover 并bìng 1; 并且bìngqiě 1; 而且 érqiě 1; 加以 jiāyǐ 1; 况且 kuàngqiě 1; 且 qiě 1
most 至多 zhìduō 1; 最 zuì 1
must be 非 fēi 1 & 2

negative intensifier 并 bìng 2; 决 jué 1; 绝 jué 1
negative 不 bù 1; 沒 méi 1; 沒有 méiyou 1; 未 wèi 1
never 从 cóng 2; 从来 cónglái 1; 向来 xiànglái 1
nevertheless 然 rán 1
no doubt 固然 gùrán 1
no matter what 不管 bùguǎn 1; 不论 bùlùn 1 & 2; 无论 wúlùn 1 & 2
not as 不如 bùrú 1; 沒 méi 3; 沒有 méiyou 3
not at all (一)点(儿) (yī)diǎn(r) 2
not equal to 不如 bùrú 1 & 2
no matter 不管 bùguǎn 1; 不论 bùlùn 1 & 2; 管 guǎn 1; 凭 píng; 无论 wúlùn 1 & 2
not only 不单 bùdān 1; 不但 bùdàn 1; 不光 bùguāng 1; 不仅 bùjǐn 1; 不只 bùzhǐ 1
not that much 不到 bùdào 1
not until 直到 zhídào 1

object marker 把 bǎ 1; 将jiāng 1
on 于 yú 1 & 2
one of 之一 zhīyī 1
only 就 jiù 5; 只 zhǐ 1; 衹 zhǐ 1
only if 除非 chúfēi 1; 只有 zhǐyǒu 1
only when 直到 zhídào 1
or 还是 háishi 1 & 2; 和 hé 5; 或 huò 1; 或者 huòzhě 1; 要不(然) yàobu(rán) 1
or else 不然 bùrán 1; 要不然 yàoburán 1; 否则 fǒuzé 1
otherwise 不然 bùrán 1; 要不然 yàoburán 1; 否则 fǒuzé 1
over period of time 来 lái 2

passive markers 被 bèi 1; 的 de 5; 给 gěi 3 & 4; 叫 jiào 2; 教 jiào 1; 是…的 shì...de 2; 为 wéi 4; 1. 于 yú 1.d & e
past tense 曾 céng 1; 曾经 céngjīng 1; 过 guo 1; 了 le 1, 2, 3 & 4; 是…的 shì...de 1
precisely at 当 dāng 1
probable 会huì 1
proceed 进而 jìn'ér
promptly 即 jí 2
punctuation see the section "Punctuation Markers"

unable to verb 不 bù 3
unexpectedly 竟 jìng 1; 竟然 jìngrán 1;
unless 除非 chúfēi 2
until 为止 wéizhǐ 1; 止 zhǐ 1; 至 zhì 1
up to 以至 yǐzhì 2
use 以 yǐ 1; 用 yòng 1

verb background 随着 suízhe 1 & 2
verb can happen 得 de 3; 会 huì 1; 可以 kěyǐ 1; 了 liǎo 1; 能 néng 1; 能够 nénggòu 1
verb coincidental 正 zhèng 2
verb finished 过 guo 2
continue verbing 继续 jìxù 1; 不断 bùduàn 1
do verb to 加以 jiāyǐ 1
verb happened 曾 céng 1; 曾经 céngjīng 1; 过 guo 1; 了 le 1, 3 & 4
verb in a direction 过 guò 1
verb-ing 在 zài 5; 着 zhe 1 & 2; 著 zhe 1; 正 zhèng 1; 正在 zhèngzài 1
verb lessened 还 hái 3
verb likely 会 huì 1
verb modification 地 de 1; 得 de 1 & 2
verb ongoing 在 zài 5; 着 zhe 1 & 2; 著 zhe 1; 正 zhèng 1; 正在 zhèngzài 1
verb permissible 可以 kěyǐ 1; 能 néng 2
verb possible 能 néng 1; 能够 nénggòu 1
verb probable 会 huì 1; 要 yào 3
verg sequential 一方面 yīfāngmiàn 1
verb to the point of 到 dào 3
verb will happen 将 jiāng 2; 要 yào 3

want to 要 yào 1
when 的时候 de shíhou 1; 时 shí 1; 一 yī 2
whether or not 也...也 yě...yě 2
while 的时候 de shíhou 1; 时 shí 1; 一 yī 2
with 跟 gēn 1 & 2; 和 hé 2 & 3; 连 lián 2; 同 tóng 2 & 3; 用 yòng 1; 与 yǔ 2

yet 不过 bùguò 1; 倒是 dàoshi 1; 还 hái 1; 仍 réng 1; 仍然 réngrán 1; 尚 shàng 1